The Poet's Calling in the English Ode

PAUL H. FRY

The Poet's Calling in the English Ode

Yale University Press
New Haven and London
1980

Published with assistance from the
Frederick W. Hilles Publication Fund
of Yale University.

Designed by James J. Johnson
and set in IBM Journal Roman type.
Printed in the United States of America by
Edwards Brothers, Inc., Ann Arbor, Mich.

Published in Great Britain, Europe, Africa, and
Asia (except Japan) by Yale University Press,
Ltd., London. Distributed in Australia and
New Zealand by Book & Film Services, Artarmon,
N.S.W., Australia; and in Japan by Harper & Row,
Publishers, Tokyo Office.

Library of Congress Cataloging in Publication Data

Fry, Paul H
    The poet's calling in the English ode.

    Includes index.
    1. English poetry—History and criticism. 2. Odes—
History and criticism. I. Title.
PR509.03F7   821'.04   79-20554
ISBN 0-300-02400-2

Iunoni ante omnis, cui vincla iugalia curae.

Contents

Acknowledgments

To those two who have heard me and helped me from the beginning, Harris Friedberg and Brigitte Peucker;

For encouragement I could not have done without, to Maria DiBattista, Alfred MacAdam, and especially Michael Seidel;

To those who have read this manuscript with such steady and generous care, Angus Fletcher, Geoffrey Hartman, John Hollander, and James Nohrnberg;

To Ellen Graham at Yale University Press, who has borne with me so cheerfully and helpfully;

For advice, lore, and conversation, to Nicholas Asher, Charles Berger, Peter Bloom, Leslie Brisman, Michael Cooke, Jonathan Culler, Robert Fitzgerald, John Hodgson, Jocelyne Kolb, Penelope Laurans, Edward Mendelson, Hillis Miller, Ross Murfin, Barbara Packer, Richard Selzer, Robert Shaw, Roger Swearingen, and my students, among whom I would single out Mark Pennington;

For friendship, in their absence, to John Danford, Laurie Fendrich, Stephen Henriques, and Barbara MacAdam;

To the English Department and the Trustees of Yale University for granting me a year's leave of absence under the auspices of the Morse Fellowship;

To the A. Whitney Griswold and the Frederick W. Hilles foundations for partial subsidization of the manuscript and of publication, respectively.

Only an attraction to error as powerful and resilient as my own could defeat the vigilance of all these friendly persons and institutions. None of them is responsible for my lapses.

Introduction
The Man at the Gate

Where shall I find
Bravura adequate to this great hymn?
—Wallace Stevens, "Le Monocle de Mon Oncle"

In his own opinion, Allen Tate's "Ode to the Confederate Dead" was a novelty. He assumed that in having written an *ironic* ode he had done what had not even been tried since the seventeenth century: "I suppose it is a commentary on our age that the man at the gate [i.e., the speaker of Tate's ode] never quite achieves the illusion that the leaves are heroic men, so that he may identify himself with them, as Keats and Shelley too easily and too beautifully did with nightingales and west winds."[1] In other words, Tate would imply, the ode after the seventeenth century has always remained a symptom of the blithe Romantic hope that the poet-prophet "may identify himself," in some more or less literal sense, with whatever it is that his poem invokes. Tate's own ode, he says, is about "the cut-off-ness of the modern 'intellectual man' from the world" (ibid.), whereas most odes are meant to integrate their speech with the speech of common life. Hence the turn of the screw in having written an ode: "I have been asked why I called the poem an ode. . . . I suppose in so calling it I intended an irony: the scene of the poem is not a public celebration, it is a lone man by a gate" (ibid., pp. 256–57).

I think that what Tate says here about his own ode can and should be said about all important odes. Yet further, each of the poets who had recourse to the presumptive naïveté of an ode before the coming of Modernism betrayed very grave doubts in advance about the decidedly unironic faith that compensates, in Modernism alone, for the "cut-off-ness" of *all* poetry; I mean the faith so strongly evinced by Tate's description of his poem's ending as a "fusion" (ibid., p. 261) of previously conflicting elements. Not only is the ode from its first

1

appearance a vehicle of ontological and vocational doubt, as I shall maintain, but it also raises questions more steadily than any other poetic mode about the aesthetic shibboleth of the unified whole. Not one of the odes I shall discuss is hopeful enough about the resources of artistry to suppose a "fusion" of any kind to have been brought about either by its argument or by its ending.

The "man at the gate," both in Tate's powerful ode and in his criticism, is one of our most sensitive threshold figures, shut out as he is by the cemetery wall, but his frustrated attempt to "identify himself" with the leaves beyond the wall, to be present to them, is not so acute as its counterpart in, say, "Keats and Shelley." There is a uniquely modern comfort in taking it for granted that the gate is closed. We would like to go through, it troubles our metaphysics that we cannot "cross the bar," but still, happily enough, we do have our proper bounds marked off by the neat map, or replica, that is our poem. The gate is closed, but precisely because it is closed we discover the formal consolation of a whole in which to dwell. From Ben Jonson to Keats to Tate himself (as poet, not as critic), the ode writer at the gate must live with a rather more abysmal frustration. He notices that the gate seems to be open, gapingly open; there is properly speaking no threshold at all between the self and what is unknown or other, and against this dizzying knowledge—the knowledge of being exposed, edgeless, undefined—the protection of form can only be simulated. The ode writer himself closes the gate, not to make up for what he fails to see, but to hide what he does see. His invocation of absent things is a revocation or exorcism of disturbing presences, but such presences cannot be quite shut out, and remain, not to fuse, but to confuse the formality of the poet's calling.

II

That both things and spirits are absent from words, and most obviously so from written words, seems scarcely to require comment. When we read poetry or any other writing, common sense is always at hand to remind us that as readers we need not trouble ourselves with the metaphysics of presence. Literature being a pleasant art of illusion, we admire its legerdemain without being taken in. Absence, we may feel in any case, is all for the good because it "leaves something to the imagination." Hence we may understandably wonder why so much criticism continues to be written about the "problem" of presence and absence. It is the poets themselves, however, and not a handful of critics deranged by metaphysics, who have never allowed the presentational claims of poetry to be disregarded. The history of lyric and of defenses of poetry is one long proclamation that poetry is verbal magic, an embodied Word, originary and cosmogonic. Even Mallarmé, as little credulous about such metaphors as any poet, speaks of "the Orphic explanation of the Earth, which is the poet's sole Duty" (and then, imagining the feat accomplished, he calls it "this dream, this Ode").[2] Criticism, then, is always moved to reopen the question of lyric "efficacy" in response to lyric claims.

The poetry that wants to be taken for verbal magic might well have for its motto Coleridge's famous definition of the symbol in *The Statesman's Manual*: "It always partakes of the reality which it renders intelligible; and while it enunciates the whole, abides itself as a living part in that Unity, of which it is the representative."[3] We go on heeding the synecdochic idealism of this poetics because, not just as poets but even merely as readers, we are uncomfortable without substance in our words. The ode survives in our anthologies because it is the most challenging proving ground of presentation; the ode is the Letter that most boldly and openly tests the possibility of calling in the Spirit, of *invoking* the reality in which it would "partake," despite the poet's burden of knowing that where there is no distance there is no need for a calling, and where there is no discreteness of parts there is no need for a predication that "enunciates the whole."

Having given the ode a motto, we may also supply a myth, the descent of Orpheus for Eurydice in medieval allegory, which will serve to illustrate the poetics of the symbol. In some interpretations of the Ovidian account, "Eurydice is the passional or concupiscent side" of the Orphic personality, while other readings see "the lovers as symbolizing the art of oratory and its subject matter."[4] This whole spectrum of interpretation is relevant, as we shall see, to the question of what it is that invocation calls for but in some ways fears to encounter. *Oraia-phones*, according to Fulgentius, descends to recover *Eur-dike*: voice, or music, goes in quest of thought, but when Eurydice "compares the corporeal and transitory notes to the profound theory of the art of music, she . . . flees again to her deep knowledge because she cannot appear in notes."[5]

Here Fulgentius looks forward to the modern myth of the signifier's descent for the signified, and gives us a model for an oral or incantatory poet's quest for completeness. For the *writers* of odes, however, the parable must be shifted somewhat, since their longing is directed mainly toward the vocal origins of their craft. They would have us believe what Francis Berry has taken to be true, that "most poetry is vocal sound . . . and not the sign *for* vocal sound printed on a page."[6] From this standpoint, as from the standpoint that derives thought from the Christian Logos, voice and thought are so closely intertwined (as action and agent) that they cannot be separated. In the ode, then, Orpheus becomes writing, torn from self-presence and scattered to the winds by the chirographic maenads who were meant to spread his word, and Eurydice becomes voice, the famous echo of Virgil:

> Then, when his Head, from his fair Shoulder torn,
> Wash'd by the Waters, was on *Hebrus* born;
> Ev'n then his trembling Tongue invok'd his Bride;
> With his last Voice, *Eurydice*, he cry'd,
> *Eurydice*, the Rocks and River-banks reply'd.
>
> [Dryden's *Georgics* IV. 761–65] [7]

III

The odes discussed in these chapters can all be grouped under the heading "Odes of Presentation." Most of them are poems of the type that is usually termed, with a wise vagueness, "sublime" or "great" odes. I offer a label of my own without any wish to criticize those now in use, but only to give some advance notice of my thesis about such poems. Before proceeding further with a thesis, however, it may be helpful to review the many poetic types that are all called odes.

The term "ode" has a checkered history, in part because it is derived from a Greek word for "song" and differs little in root meaning, therefore, from "sonnet," "hymn," "carmen," "cantata," "canzone," and countless other terms. Appealing to usage does not clarify matters as much as one could wish because poets have often seemed to use the word so indiscriminately that most readers pay no attention to its presence in a title. Historians of the ode[8] are more embarrassed about the problem of canonical selection than, say, historians of the elegy, because the widely differing sorts of lyric that are entitled odes cannot be said to be subspecies of a master type. The consensus definition, again wisely vague, that is sanctioned by early writers on the ode like Edmund Gosse and William Sharp[9] may be put as follows: an ode is a celebratory poem of address in elevated language written on an occasion of public importance—with the proviso, of course, that more often than not it is up to the poet to decide what is "public" and what is "important."

With this definition, as far as it goes, there can be no quarrel. It is certainly no objection that it fails to cover all the isolated types: brief "anacreontic" odes about merrymaking in defiance of old age, "Horatian" odes in short, regular stanzas on anacreontic as well as moral and political themes that take Horace's *sermo merus* for their stylistic norm, and epistolary odes addressed to friends or public persons on every subject imaginable. Although these types often do exert their various influences over what I am calling the "ode of presentation" simply because they share a label, it does not seem possible to group them together theoretically. My brief descriptions of each type will already reveal the confusion of criteria that any too exquisitely divisive labels must risk.[10] The reason why the words "elegy" and "satire" seem more usefully to rope off poetic kinds than "ode" does is that "elegy" and "satire" are *modal* terms that allow enormous flexibility of reference. They describe orientations but tend not to prescribe a set style, form, or occasion—or even, necessarily, a set theme. It is in the loose spirit of such terms that I propose the "ode of presentation" as a mode, and propose further to reduce that clumsy designation, once its province is understood, back to the single word "ode."

Odes of the sort I have in mind are closely related to the Pindaric ode, which is, in the English tradition, a magniloquent poem with abrupt transitions written either in irregular stanzas or in regular stanzaic triads. Since the Pindaric model is reinterpreted by each succeeding poet, I shall take up its implications in later chapters, as need arises. Pindar is rivaled in importance as a model for the ode by the Hebrew psalmody and, from the mid-eighteenth century onward, by Milton's minor poems and characteristic turns of voice. What is yet more important, as Kurt Schlüter has shown, is the derivation of the ode from the structure and occasion of the Greek and Latin cult hymns, largely through the intermediary channel of the "literary hymns" that flourished in Alexandria, Augustan Rome, the Italian Renaissance (both Neo-Latin and vernacular), and the French Pléiade.

The relation of the ode to its hymnic forebears is extremely complex, and warrants careful comment even in an introduction. Authoritatively for the English Renaissance, Scaliger distinguished six types of literary hymn: theurgic, valedictory, celebratory, genealogical, mythic, and inventive.[11] It is hard to imagine a hymn of one type that would not at the same time infringe on several other types; and indeed, what I mean by an "ode of presentation" involves all six types at once, in the following relation to each other: Since a *numen* is invoked, even if it is only a thing made numinous as a listening power, the ode is "theurgic." But since what is invoked cannot be revealed in itself but only in being imagined, and in being said, further, to listen and preside, the ode is "inventive" and theurgic at the same time. An inventive ode necessarily takes for its occasion the happy coming to birth, through its own presentation, of the invoked power; hence it is "celebratory." But since a celebration is weakened if it has more than a single object, every ode is, in effect, monotheistic, and part of its business is to banish all rival powers from its fane or triumphal setting; hence an ode is celebratory and "valedictory" at the same time. In heralding the coming to be of its nominated power, the ode affirms its status as an origin or its descent from an origin; hence it is "genealogical." And since its birth story is, again, necessarily invented, the ode finally is also "mythic"—or what we now call "mythopoeic." Every ode I shall consider is complicated by the need to perform all of these offices at once, even though in the process each ode comes to have an irreversibly divided identity, irresolute between hymnic offices (theurgy, celebration, genealogy) and the arrogation of divinely cosmogonic powers (invention, exorcism, mythopoeia).

Schlüter's *Englische Ode* (p. 31) outlines the normative structure of a classical hymn. The invocation is followed by a *pars epica* or *epischer Mittelteil*, which explains to the god who he is, how he came to exist, and how ubiquitous he is in nature and history. Having thus flattered the god, the poet finally turns to his own hopes, and petitions the god for some favor, often adding a vow of future service. A hymn with this structure is like a prayer, and reenacts the ritual of participation in the divine performed by the shamans of nearly all primitive cultures. These elementary facts and conclusions about the hymn uncover something very peculiar about secular *odes* that imitate the structure of prayer. Whereas their hymnic offices become formulaic and provide a ready-made context for ecstatic discourse, their cosmogonic offices in that context oblige the poet to pray to himself. The result, as Martin Price has said, is the "evocation of deep-lying powers within the poet."[12] In working out this idea it should be possible to account for the survival of what remains perhaps the most archaic, the most unblushingly "poetic" way of speaking in existence. "Invocation," as Jonathan Culler has written, "is a figure of vocation."[13] It is the poet's most widely recognized trademark.

The ode is never a hymn.[14] What it loses in ecstasy it gains in the hope of originary strength. It is, as we shall often discover, a Satanic answer to a hymn, a radically Dissenting or Nonconforming poem even where the poet wishes it to be otherwise. Though it can never exclaim, with Charles Wesley's hymn "For Christmas Day," "Veil'd in flesh, the Godhead see,/Hail th'Incarnate Deity,"[15] it does have a way of proclaiming its *own* power of incarnation. It is instructive that in the seventeenth century the Cavaliers wrote songs and light-hearted odes, while the Roundheads and other antinomians were beginning to write odes of a spiritually ambitious kind. In his "Satire on the Rebellion," the Cavalier Alexander Brome is markedly conscious of the difference:

> Yea, David's psalms do now begin to be
> Turn'd out of church, by hymns extempore.

Or again:

> Behold a glorious Phoebus tumbling down,
> While the rebellious bards usurp the crown.
>
> [Chalmers, X. 665]

Like the hymn, the ode or "hymn extempore" longs for participation in the divine, but it never participates communally, never willingly supplies a congregation with common prayer because it is bent on recovering a priestly role that is not pastoral but hermetic. The ode never says, as does Cleanthes in his "Hymn to Zeus," "it is proper that all mortals should call upon you."[16]

We are speaking here of poets as poets, not as men and women whose religious faith may be fully satisfied by a book of common prayer. Isaac Watts, who wrote both hymns and odes, knew the difference between them very well, and it is consistent both with his delightful personality and his inferiority as an ode writer that he preferred hymns:

> Now the swift transports of the mind

> Leave the fluttering Muse behind;
> A thousand loose Pindaric plumes lie scattering down the wind.
>
> [Chalmers, XIII. 41]

Similarly, Cowley, the most distinguished ode writer of his day, clearly knew the difference between his own work and the hymnody of Crashaw: "Ah wretched we, poets of Earth! But thou/Wert living the same poet which thou'rt now" ("On the Death of Mr. Crashaw," Chalmers, VII. 76).

We can reflect further on the key distinction between theurgy and the invention that imitates theurgy by considering Shelley's ironically entitled "Hymn to Intellectual Beauty." In the opening lines he pretends that his incomparably esoteric numen is an object of common prayer by singing apparently in behalf of a congregation:

> The awful shadow of some unseen Power
> Floats though unseen among us
>
> . . . .
>
> It visits with inconstant glance
> Each human heart and countenance
>
> . . . .
> Why dost thou pass away and leave our state?

Hereafter the poem lapses into the first-person singular and the language of private experience, by no means with the purpose of declaring, with collective intimacy, "A mighty fortress is my God." Shelley's hymn is an ode.

In seeming to verge here toward an absolute notion of what an ode is, I had best restate the dilemma of an ode in terms of my own dilemma in writing this book. I have had to ask myself, does the ode develop or change? Can it be periodized, dramatized as an evolution? Could it be traced, for example, from an Age of Knowledge and Statement to an Age of Doubt and Discovery? I have suspected not; in the considerable odes of every era, a burden of doubt subverts the assertion of knowledge. Only the hymn speaks from knowledge, while the ode always hopes for knowledge. As Emil Staiger succinctly expresses the difference, Hölderlin "longed for this 'Oneness and Unifying Power' . . . in his odes; he praised it in his hymns."[17] Actually, of course, Staiger is implying more than he or anyone can know about questing and knowledge or absence and presence in Hölderlin. Whether through our own ironizing influence or through some unavoidable irony in the nature of vocative discourse, we have found even such shamans as survive today to be stronger in invention than in theurgy. Perhaps there is no such thing as a hymn of participation; if so, then the difference between hymn and ode is simply the difference between common prayer and personal prayer.

By imitating hymnody, however, an ode reveals *its* conception of a hymn as a being-present to a transcendent, originary voice. The aim of the ode is to recover and usurp the voice to which hymns defer: not merely to participate in the presence of voice but to *be* the voice. The quest for voice is by no means confined to the ode;[18] it is possibly the theme of all writing, and it is certainly the theme of the quieter lyrics to which the ode is related in its sphere of concern, the Meditative Lyric and the Conversation Poem. But whereas the lyric that is not an ode seeks voice without fanfare, as if by a spontaneous course of thought, the ode denies itself the illusionism of full-throated ease and writes itself hoarse. It redoubles the difficulty of presentation as if to show that the cultivated artlessness of other modes is only an evasion of its own rhetoric.[19] Some explanation like this one is needed to show why the archaic extravagance of the ode survives. Good poets have always commanded the means of avoiding extravagance, and no literary period has been so baroque in taste as to forget the caveat of simplicity altogether. The ode persists, then, as a critique of simplicity-as-presence; its outrageous tropes call in question the possibility of presence in tropes of any kind. At the same time, of course, it aspires to a positive decorum of its own. Considered as an entertainment, the ode is not a sleight of hand but a performance on the high wire, not an illusion but an enchantment—or incantation. We shall see at length what it is that an ode attempts to spellbind.

If the irony of an ode lies in its doubtful relation to vocality, its pathos lies partly in its vacillation of confidence, in the "fluttering," as Isaac Watts perceptively put it, that may lead to a calamitous Phaeton-fall, or *sparagmos*, of the Pindaric eagle: "A thousand loose Pindaric plumes lie scattering down the wind." As a deliberately rhetorical test of originary strength, the ode must resist the danger—and the temptation—of unoriginal rhetoric. There is certainly a trace of masochism in both the irony and the pathos of the ode. To write an ode is to honor the company of fools: court hacks, windy curates, triflers with nature, versifiers upon milady's fan—laureates, in short. The very word "ode," which resonates with vocal overreach (the letter *O* looms large in our study), has been enough to call down journalistic ridicule from antiquity to the present. The more casual writings of some of the best ode writers themselves (Gray's letters, for example) are full of the self-mockery that disarms ridicule. Heavy, old-fashioned, and solemn, the ode necessarily confronts the unlikelihood of being new more candidly than any other lyric kind, and proposes unflinchingly to turn that confrontation to advantage. We may think of all the strained motives here alleged for the persistence of the ode as a loser's moral victory, as a way of overcoming the fear of failure by guaranteeing failure; or perhaps, more suggestively, we can begin to think of these motives as a psychic discipline. It was Mallarmé, again, who insisted that "official verse must be used only in the crisis moments of the soul."[20]

IV

In order to penetrate the strange logic of an ode, one needs especially to understand two figures of speech, invocation and prolepsis (or anticipation), and one figure of thought, irony—"for which," as Kenneth Burke remarks, "we could substitute dialectic."[21] Of course, none of these figures appears exclusively in the ode, but it may still be said that no other type of utterance depends on the co-presence of all three, or intermixes them in quite the same way. For example, epic invocation cannot properly be called an interpolated ode because it is not dialectical. Its aim is not to present that which is invoked but rather to unfold whatever the invoked power is requested to furnish for narrative. In epic invocation, the muse is present merely in the fruits of her memory, and no more direct immanence is required of her. (This is said only in theory, in full awareness that any substantial invocation can be detached to some extent from its context.) So too the invocation of a religious hymn is not dialectical, since neither the existence nor even the presence of an established deity depends on the mechanics of prayer. A god of that kind is within us or at least knows of our doings whether we can bespeak its presence or not. From these exclusionary examples it would appear that dialectic (or irony) obtrudes upon the invocation of an ode in order to channel the poet's uneasiness, in the first place, about having sought inspiration to describe inspiration;[22] and also, secondly, to register his doubt about the existence and willingness to listen of whatever is invoked. On this view, Faust's call to the signs in a magic book—"Antwortet mir, wenn ihr mich hört!" (I. 439)—is followed by a moment that belongs to the ode: "Welch Schauspiel! Aber ach! ein Schauspiel nur!" This sublation-by-doubling or pivot of thought around the antithetical sense of a word resembles the doubling back that results from "Thou wast not born for death, immortal bird" in Keats: "Forlorn! The very word is like a bell/To toll me back to my sole self!"

Keats's address is not, however, an invocation but an apostrophe. If dialectic in the ode is a turning back upon or against the self, according to Socrates' understanding of dialectic as an "interrupting question," apostrophe, the blanket form of *invocatio*, is defined in all the Rhetorics as a turning aside to address some absent hearer. Hence dialectic, the figure of thought (which subverts *itself*), and apostrophe, the figure of speech, subvert each other, and the poet confirms his solitude by crying out for company. In fact, though, apostrophe in general does not call for the presence of the addressee. "O tempora o mores!" "Great God! I'd rather be/A pagan suckl'd in a creed outworn." The poet speaks these asides to a pro tem audience and then re-turns to the audience that is understood to be listening, as it were, under contract. Since what is being listened to is often a narrative, Puttenham punningly calls apostrophe a "Turne Tale."

Invocation, which is the motive of an ode, we may call a stubborn apostrophe, a purposeful calling in rather than a calling out.[23] The predicative technique of invocation is derived from prayer,[24] and, as of prayer, a certain durability of effect is required of invocation, an endurance written on the heart. Prayer, says George Herbert, is "Gods breath in man returning to his birth,/The soul in paraphrase"—or, the logos approximated in the grapheme. On the lyric scale of value, presence is scarcely worth remarking if it is felt in passing or as a recollection, since evanescent joys avail little. The test of presence is permanence, indelibility. Faust's *apostrophe* to the sign of the Macrocosm, then, is followed by an *invocation* to the Earth-Spirit, the difference being that the Earth-Spirit actually appears. But then it disappears, and its contemptuous vanishing returns Faust to his sole self:

> *Geist.* Du gleichst dem Geist, den du begreifst,
> Nicht mir! (Verschwindet)

Faust. (Zusammenstürzend). Nicht dir?
Wem denn?
Ich Ebenbild der Gottheit!
Und nicht einmal dir!

[I. 512–17]

This exchange may help to clarify the meaning of the shamanistic participation that invocation strives for. The poet who can prolong presence, who can in-form or put under constraint his god or daemon, has "taken on," strictly speaking, the identity he has striven for. The longer he constrains his visitant, the more clearly his prayer becomes a prayer to himself.

The cross-purposes of invocation and dialectic, then, set the dynamics of an ode in motion. By itself, this interplay might prove to be processual, developmental, and might lead, as the phrase is, to discovery. Dialectic motivates change, and invocation in theory could motivate constancy through change. But now enters the figure that thwarts change in all discouse, namely, anticipation, or prolepsis. Prolepsis is the figure that forecloses a topic before it is fairly entered upon. The Rhetorics do not recognize the term in this broad sense, and in the long run I shall have to make my case through the force of example, but even the Rhetorics can be read in such a way that they put the case in so many words. *Prolepsis*, according to the summary of Richard Lanham, is a catalytic figure that leads to *interpretatione*, "a repetition or amplification in other words."[25] Merely to repeat or amplify a dilemma; it is in this sense that the "scene" of an ode features, as Allen Tate says, a man stranded at the gate. In the Romantic lyric of discovery, of faring forward, prolepsis is manifestly a figure to be avoided at all costs. It makes the progress of dialectic purposeless by exposing its end in its beginning, by showing, in other words, that a painstaking conclusion is really a foregone conclusion; and it subverts invocation by predicating the absence of the invoked power, firmly and finally, before the tropes of presentation—metaphor and metalepsis—have a chance to move in and cancel distance. The priority of prolepsis dooms the first movements of both dialectic (Welch *Schauspiel*) and invocation (0 *thou*) to self-defeat.

Prolepsis as I view it is the Leviathan of rhetoric; it rises up from its definition to swallow rhetoric itself. Prolepsis plus interpretation: Freud would recognize this composite figure as an emblem of compulsion neurosis. Prolepsis reveals the linkage between the repressed and the compulsion to repeat, always to repeat by displacement, always "in other words," that keeps the return of the same at bay: "When anything has not happened in the desired way," says Freud, "it is undone by being repeated in a different way."[26] The beginning of an ode is very often its prolepsis, but not necessarily; what gets repeated may be what Helen Vendler, in speaking of Keats's odes, has called an "experiential beginning,"[27] a confused but arresting passage of special intensity somewhere in the middle of the poem that has seen further than was intended and repeats itself correctively, involutes or veils itself, in both the opening and closing phases of its argument. As I shall repeatedly show, the proleptic "knowledge" of every ode is the reduction of first and last things from transcendental explanations to the moments of sex and death, moments that are often one and the same.

In Allen Tate's ode, the gate to the cemetery stands open. What the "man" in every ode sees through the gate is the prefigurativity of death as his determination and inspiring ground. He sees, in other words, a primal scene, his banishment from which he reads as death. Shamanism takes its inspiration from the dead; the Norse seers even lay in barrows to await their vision,[28] as did, in a sense, the too impatient Orpheus. The "modern man" of whom Tate speaks gives up totemism and seeks rather to take his inspiration from an uncovering of death in general, not of some one dead person, as the ground of being. The ode differs from elegy, as later we shall see at leisure, chiefly in coming upon death while meaning to talk about birth; whereas in the typical movement of an elegy it is the other way around. Every ode I consider in the chapters that follow, from Jonson to Keats, will come to acknowledge death, as if by accident, as the origin, conqueror, and end of everything except poetry, reserving the ideal of poetic form as a defense against death that saves appearances and closes the gate.

In the long run, however, the defense afforded by the ideal of form crumbles into fragments, and the ode concedes that death is not only the motive of desire but the mother of beauty. I quote from the end of the "Ode to the Confederate Dead":

> Leave now
> The shut gate and the decomposing wall:
> The gentle serpent, green in the mulberry bush

> Riots with his tongue through the hush—
> Sentinel of the grave who counts us all!

This is the most abrupt gesture of closure in Tate's ode, but it is more than usually disturbed by clairvoyance about the unenclosed; his closing figures, both gate and grave, are frayed and rotted open by the figure of the "decomposing wall." Here is the decomposition of his ode, its erosion by repetition. It is clear beyond the need for comment that these lines have opened themselves, at the last minute, to the return, the erotic return, of the repressed. Concerning the ode in general, we may allow this returning force to come into view as gradually and deductively as possible; for the moment we can call it a daemon.

However fully invocation may seem at last, in any ode, to have informed its numen, and however neatly dialectic may seem at last to have synthesized absence and presence, the single sequence of prolepsis and interpretation undoes the achievement of shape, yielding the ode to its palinodic and, I think, its most beautiful cadences, last notes that fall away from afflatus to the shapelessness of being in the atmosphere of being.[29] To document and explain this decline, this dying fall, will largely occupy the following chapters. An an interpreter, I shall merely confirm, over and over, what Allen Tate himself concedes at the heart of his ode (1. 33) in saluting those psychological and cultural prolepses (denying teleological change and the ideal of totality) that are largely repressed, or certainly "muted," in the history of celebration:

> You know who have waited by the wall
> The twilight certainty of an animal,
> Those midnight restitutions of the blood
> You know—the immitigable pines, the smoky frieze
> Of the sky, the sudden call: you know the rage,
> The cool pool left by the mounting flood,
> Of muted Zeno and Parmenides.

Against this knowledge the ode attempts to pray for a final change.

1

The Pressure of Sense of Some Odes of Jonson and Drayton

> Therefore repetition, if it is possible, makes a man happy, whereas recollection makes him unhappy—provided he gives himself time to live and does not at once, in the very moment of birth, try to find a pretext for stealing out of life, alleging, for example, that he has forgotten something.
>
> —Kierkegaard, *Repetition*

These first chapters contain a series of interpretations that give way to a pause for general comment at the end of chapter 3. Rather more than in later chapters, I hew to the texts and forms of Jonson, Drayton, Milton, and Dryden, taking seriously as I do the axiom that "there are many ways to transcend formalism, but the worst is not to study forms."[1] Indeed, I have pored over the forms of these texts in order to place in intricate relief the force of the inchoate in odes of any period. In every ode of substance, an unstructuring or deformation occurs at the moment when form is most heroically overstrained. One knows this moment intuitively, perhaps, but in order to realize it in description and to discover how the overstrain of form becomes a theme of the ode—possibly even its motivating theme—then one must assay a responsive overstrain of reading. That is the notion, in any case, that has dictated the arrangement of these first chapters, and, to a lesser extent, of the book as a whole.

I

The theme of "To the Immortall memorie, and friendship of that noble paire, Sir LUCIUS CARY, and Sir H. MORISON," is the theme of nearly everything Jonson wrote, namely, the identification and description of humane virtue.[2] The structure of this ode, being in many ways a dramatic structure as well as a dramatic interpretation of Pindaric structure, aligns the poem more closely with Jonson's plays and especially with his masques than with most of his other lyric forms. From the outset, we can expect to find a conflict in this poem between its theme of steadfastness in virtue and the variability of its Pindaric form. Jonas Barish, in defining Jonson's strain of "antitheatricality," points to his "distrust of movement, which connects with . . . an ideal of stasis in the moral and ontological realm."[3] It would follow that at the other extreme of Jonson's talent there must be an answering distrust of fixity—not of moral fixity, perhaps, but of the constriction of what poetry can say. In short, if there is an urge toward univocity in Jonson's dramatic texts, there is also a movement in certain of his lyrics toward a mixed outlook.[4] The Pindaric ode is well suited for lyric ambivalence, since the dialectic of its structure brings it closer to dialogue than to the pointed univocity of brief forms like the epigram or of linear forms like the narrative, epistle, and couplet elegy.

Jonson's satires and encomia identify humane virtue unequivocally, either by negative or positive means. These are not often truly simple poems; they are nuanced, complexly reserved and reserving, but they do remain certain about the presence, or at least the accessibility, of praiseworthy character. His anacreontic and designedly coarse pieces, on the other hand, rehearse the disadvantages of virtue, and they exert their distinct, classically inherited voices to invest the alternatives to virtue with an assured accent and decorum of their own.

In contrast with all these modes of assurance, the ode, for Jonson, is the poem of the "Counterturn," in which assurance comes to betray its function. In the ode "To Desmond," to which I shall return, Jonson praises the political prisoner Desmond, yet subtly suggests in the closing lines that he has been justly accused of treason. The ode "To Sydney" opens with the hearth at Penshurst "crown'd with smiling fire" and closes within the broader circle of a "flame/Of love," but the circular structure of the poem is forced open by the subjunctive mood and emphatic enjambment of its last cementing: "Then/The Birth-day shines, when logs not burne, but men." The enjambment makes us wonder when "Then" is. Owing to the compression of this passage, furthermore (neither space nor meter will permit saying "not only logs"), it is impossible for logs and men to burn at once, and the question arises, as a barely audible subversion, whether the flame that crowns the family circle is not burned out inside. In turning now to the Cary-Morison Ode, with its notorious "Ben/Jonson" and "twi-/Lights," it is worth noting that enjambment is a dubious emblem at once of the closed circle and the self-consciously open shape of the Pindaric strophe. Enjambment is one of the key points of interest, for the "regular" Jonson, in irregular structures that challenge closure.[5]

It is not too much to say, however strange this may sound in reference to Jonson and his period, that the Cary-Morison Ode exists in its chosen form to question the metaphysics of presence and to test the conventional figures of presentation that must be rationalized if they are to be called successful: circle and sphere, part and whole, transmission of qualities, ascent and descent, appearing and hiding. A full account of this poem's self-deformation will have to be rather intricate, but its argument is simply enough stated: a life perfectly lived, in which there is perfect harmony between behavior and essential character, is given to the world as an exemplum, and the trim perfection of this sort of life, specifically its short-poem-like quality, is what suits it to survive itself, written for posterity in a friend's memory and a poet's record. Since a prose statement like this one (with which Jonson's usual practice would suggest that he began) could readily be versed in an epigram or a couplet elegy, it remains to ask why, in this case, an experimental Pindaric is suitable.

It is not enough to allege the classicist's love of virtuoso imitation for its own sake, if only because of Jonson's oft-stated belief that imitation for its own sake belongs only to apprenticeship. For a poet like Jonson, maturity *is*, precisely, the power of the judgment to match forms and topics. Moral maturity may be given this definition as well, and the Cary-Morison Ode sums its point in just such terms:

> Life doth her great actions spell
> By what was done and wrought
> In season, and so brought
> To light: her measures are, how well
> Each syllab'e answered, and was form'd, how faire;
> These make the lines of life, and that's her ayre.

> [59–64]

We may and should certainly assume, then, that Jonson's Pindaric choice is a significant one. He has chosen a form that can be brought to strain against the very idea of form as it appears in these lines.

In Pindar there is rarely a correlation between thematic and formal turning points; indeed, the gaps between Strophe, Anti-strophe, and Epode in Pindar are often the points of his strongest enjambment of syntax and theme. Jonson saves the full enjambment of stanzas for a very special effect, but he does follow Pindar in working against the grain of the thesis-antithesis-amplification structure of argument that is invited by the strophic triad.[6] Jonson Englishes Pindar's three terms in a way that not only preserves their derivation from choral dancing but also stresses their affinity with both rhetoric and dialectic: "Turn," "Counterturn," and "Stand." (His Pindarically correct Turns and Counterturns are ten lines long in each triad, and his Stands are twelve lines long.) With the printed text blazoning the invariability of these labels, Jonson proceeds sometimes pointedly to exploit the dialectical potential of the triad in his argument and sometimes, just as pointedly, to avoid doing so, but there is no superimposed pattern discoverable in his sequence of choices. This defect of pattern is only the most visible of the many ways in which the poem subtly declines the temptation of symmetry.

In the first triad, the three stanzas are fully end-stopped, but the relation between Turn and Counterturn is not antithetical, while the relation between Counterturn and Stand *is*, or distinctly seems to be, antithetical. This asymmetry can be elaborated. In the Ashmole MS of the poem, the Counterturn is called the "retourne" (VIII. 243n.), and in the first triad this heading reinforces one of the strangest crossings of form and argument in the poem. The position of the Counterturn marks the "returne," in the last line, of the Infant of Saguntum to the womb. What is not at first clear from Jonson's text is that in Pliny, whence the anecdote is borrowed, this return marks a monstrous birth. At least for the moment, Jonson's "Brave Infant" seems commendably prescient in retreating from the jars of the world. Even in the reader's retrospect the infant seems a model of wisdom exceeded only by the higher model of Morison's activism. Still, Jonson's handling of this return is, to my ear, distinctly ironic:

> Thou, looking then about,
> E're thou wert halfe got out,
> Wise child, did'st hastily returne . . .
>
> [5-8]

The infant acts like an animal, like a marmot; as well he might, since Pliny's *infans* is, in fact, a hippocentaur and is mentioned only because he *is* a monster.[7] It was a dramatic convention of Jonson's time to use Pliny's assertion that monstrous births were portents (we would say metonymies) of civic discord, and Jonson himself must clearly have understood that his alleged motive for the infant's return completely changes the accepted meaning of the event. Pliny's text reads: "est . . . exempla in uterum protinus reversus infans Sagunti quo anno urbs deleta ab Hannibale est"; there is no mention of recoiling from the horrors of war. "Reversus" would remind Jonson of his own dialectical "versus," and could thereby return the monstrosity he has suppressed outward to the plane of form: a Counterturn, in that case, is a monstrous birth, a deformation of what Barish identifies, again, as Jonson's "ideal of stasis." The Counterturn has "summ'd" a chimerical circle, and the lines that follow those quoted above are therefore still more ironic: "How summ'd a circle didst thou leave mankind/Of deepest lore, could we the Center find" (9–10). This circle has no center because it has no circumference: the inarticulate *infans* can scarcely "cleare" his mystery,[8] and has no significance except rather violently to challenge the formal dialectic Jonson has chosen for his poem. It remains to be seen whether the infant's circle will give way plausibly to the figure of Morison, "of Humanitie the Spheare" (52),[9] which, being perfect "in measure, number, sound," must hence be fully articulate.

In letting us notice the virtual irrelevance of the first Turn and Counterturn to what follows, Jonson imitates Pindar's habit of starting, as if spontaneously, with a digressive apostrophe. The beginning of the Stand—"For what is life, if measur'd by the space,/ Not by the act?" (21–22)—introduces the main didactic strain of the poem, but it has little to do with the preceding monstrous "life" that has no "space" at all except the negative space of the womb. The indecorum of this gap in the argument, which Jonson could have played down as the thematic correlative to the space between stanzas, is underlined mockingly by the word "For," a phantom transition that insists on consequence without cause. "For" follows from nothing, from the nothingness of a phantom circle, and is itself a *lusus* or monstrous issue.

However, the word "For" returns the reader to a second conceptual play in the first two stanzas that does introduce the rest of the poem, namely, the concept of issuance, of "comming forth" (2) or being "brought/To light" (61–62). The entire poem identifies prodigy (both good and bad) as an aspect of "immortal memorie." In this context, the tacitly prodigious "comming forth" of the infant and "Prodigious *Hannibal*" (3) are not contrasted but the same, both monstrous births "hurried forth" (15) into the world as avatars of disorder; and yet it is these ugly prodigies that make Saguntum as "immortal" (4) as the elegant friendship of Cary and Morison. If poetry itself gives birth to immortal memories, then everything depends on the quality of its own coming forth: is it a monstrous or harmonious (measured) prodigy? The studied indecorum of this ode's beginning shows how candidly Jonson permitted himself to encounter this question, which is also the question—since the poem insists on the analogy between poetry and life—of whether the assumed norms of harmony in nature and society are actually possible or only formal illusions. These two prodigies, the infant and Hannibal, turn out to furnish the only causeway between the first pair of stanzas and the second pair. The worthless *senex* who is satirized in the Stand and the second Turn was in his youth another prodigy who "entred well" (33), unlike the infant and Hannibal, but was soon "sunk," like the infant, into a hollow place, "sunke in that dead sea of life/So deep" (40–41).

This depth, like the "deepest lore" of the infant's return, is only a bathos,[10] a sinking of poetry that anticipates "Thou fall'st, my tongue" (44) in the second Counterturn and contrasts in advance with the self-constellating flight aloft of the Pindaric eagle and the Stoic standing ("Hee stood") of the fallen Morison. The first four stanzas of the ode constitute a series of formal and thematic collapses of form. There is no antithesis, again, between the first Turn and Counterturn, whereas the first Stand perversely takes up a new position. The second Turn claims to "enter well" (these being nearly its first words), to be a fresh beginning of a new triad, and yet it carries forward the satire of the Stand with no thematic caesura.[11]

At the same time, however, all this indecorum amounts to a negative decorum.[12] The false beginning of the poem has taken a series of false beginnings for its satiric theme; hence its form is, curiously enough, a mirror of its sense. But it remains to be seen whether this arguable coherence in the opening will join smoothly with what follows. From the atmosphere of Pliny's natural and historical orders (which seem more like disorders), the poem will now move into the purely formal atmosphere of the Roman moralists, especially Cicero and Seneca;[13] but this movement in itself illustrates, as we shall see in a moment, the distance between reality and formality. The test, then, of Jonson's totalizing metaphysic will consist in whether these four stanzas can be called a negative *unit* that is linked by contrast with the greater unity of the ensuing argument.

The second Counterturn proposes itself as the crucial counterturn of the whole poem. (We may add provisionally that the third Counterturn, beginning "Call, noble Lucius, then for Wine," opens the Stand of the whole poem.) The tension of its prominence is marked by its sudden flurry of ascents and descents, and is further marked, perhaps fatalistically, by the "Alas" (43) that ushers it in. That the antithesis is indeed more fragile than it seems may also be shown in thematic terms. The means of transition from negative to positive, from the old "Stirrer" (30) to the young Sir Henry and Sir Lucius (Jonson's patron and later Viscount Falkland) is "the Corke of Title" (42). Now, this ode is preceded in *Under-wood* by an "Epigram," assumed by most scholars to be addressed to Cary, on the subject of flattery. Jonson knew, of course, that title is the cork of panegyric, and he would not have been surprised to learn that for the next two centuries the most buoyant of all corks for patrons would be the pseudo-Pindaric ode. Jonson's correct Pindaric ode deliberately puts the questions in advance that make nonsense of nearly all later encomiastic flights: What is the relation between "comming forth," or noble birth, and a person's entitlement to the qualities of virtue? Is nobility naturally prodigious (abnormal by blood), or is it culturally prodigious (abnormal by breeding)? Or, finally, is nobility perhaps merely the airy swelling of ode-like utterances, furnishing the world with "immortal memories"?[14]

The compression of Jonson's lines on the old man's youth forces these questions to the surface:

> He purchas'd friends, and fame, and honours then,
> And had his noble name advanc'd with men;
> but weary of that flight . . .
>
> [35-37]

"Had . . . advanc'd" of course means "would have advanced," but that only steadies the balance of sense: because the old man fell despite his entitlement, it does not in the least follow that he rose, despite his entitlement, on merit alone. We know, indeed, from the birthday ode to Sydney that until the attainment of majority (a year after the death of Morison and the decline of the old man), genuine worth is "measured" as promise, the promise of what in itself is still absent, and not as the presence of achievement. So, then, just as nobility is either a condition of substance or an empty entitlement, poetry likewise, the record of nobility, either embodies its topic or vainly entitles it. Because it highlights this parallel, the ode form entails a crisis of presentation.

Morison died at twenty, and the whole burden of his praise, as of Poe's praise of the short poem, depends on the brevity, the anti-Ciceronianism, if I may, of his life. We assume that the pattern of Morison's life will stand forth in contrast with that of the old man, and yet Jonson has already written of the old man: "How well at twentie had he falne or stood!/For three of his foure-score, he did no good" (31–32). At twenty, that is, the *senex* would have died a Morison. Is Morison, then, like the "Brave Infant," immortalized only by proving mortal before his time? If precocious death is, in part, what allows one to be an "early man" (125), what moral view are we to take of the survivors? What of Cary, calling for wine in elegiac resignation but also with anacreontic and triumphal relish, the perfect Cavalier in a single gesture? And what of the scarcely *integer* "Ben/Jonson," split between the bonhomie of his first name, his actual or present life, and the impersonal record of his last name, his afterlife that is *not* present but imagined, rather, in a tense that looks like the accomplished past but significantly expresses the conditional future perfect?[15]

The prolonged closing movement of the poem runs the risk that similarly threatens poems about cultural "progress," the risk of suggesting that worth is by nature "early" and then absents itself from life, henceforth to be represented only by Patterns. It is disturbing that winter comes after one has "got the harvest in" (128), but it is even more disturbing that, in a poem about being "in season" (61), "early men" like Morison and Cary are seasonal aberrations, reminiscent of Jonson's first *lusus*, the Brave Infant of Pliny, "Who, e're the first downe bloomed on the chin,/Had sow'd these fruits, and got the harvest in." The end of Jonson's ode to premature autumn is indeed in its beginning, but it is there in a way that surely parodies the idea of circular structure rather than confirming it.

But "fruits" are living spheres, not ghostly circles, and in this degree Jonson's study of growth may be said to have developed from his "Plant, and flowre" (72). It is not at all my purpose, nor Jonson's, to overshadow his celebration with its troublesome undergrowth. If I have pursued what amounts to an antithetical interpretation, I do not wish to cancel or efface any just paraphrase. I would suggest, merely, that Jonson has not only far exceeded the perfection of "short measures" (74) in this rather distended ode, but also that he deliberately frays and overlaps the measures he retains. In any case, after much delay, I have now moved forward too quickly, and must return to consider several other aspects of the ode's enforcement of absence.

The success of Jonson's *epideixis* depends on our willingness to believe that virtue and friendship, once firmly located, can be transmitted from figure to figure and, by extension, from person to person like blood through arteries: that is, that they are "written . . . with the heart, not pen" (123–24). The poem must trope what it admires into life. Its first containments of worth were geometric— a worthless circle replaced by an elegantly measured sphere. These figures belong to the Plinian or natural-historical phase of the poem; hence there is a tacit discord between an organic, turbulent setting (the sack of the town, the busy "acts of strife" performed by the *senex*) and the foregrounding of geometric orders. The next and central movement of the poem, by contrast, plays off figural containments of worth that are organic (the lily, the plant and flower, even the inert oak log) against a backdrop of serene homiletic formality. These first and second movements are linked, then, by a chiastic exchange of functions between nature and artifice, an exchange that serves at first glance to redeem nature from its entry into the poem as a chaos. But the exchange is not fully accomplished. If nature and art are properly to be contrasted in the first, negative movement, where it is clear that figuration is meant to fail, would not an exchange of roles (with nature now figural) imply an undiminished distance between them in the second movement? A way must be found of merging the beauties of life with admirable forms.

Jonson tries two ways. First he imagines a "flowre of light" (72). This image, fine sounding but impossible to envision or figure out, looks forward to the transcendent aster-ism[16] that can be envisioned but also leaps, like Morison, "the present age" (79). This is leaping too far, as we shall see when we trace the course of light in the poem.

Jonson's second attempted merger of life and form brings the circle and the plant together as "this garland." This attempt seems to work smoothly because the garland is a conventional metonymy clearing the way for the last assertion of the poem, that friendship's garland is the crowning poetry of life:

> Where they might read, and find
> *Friendship*, in deed, was written, not in words:
> And with the heart, not pen . . .

[122–24]

The garland, then, seems a very effective containing frame of value, and, lest we complain that it is emptily circular and not spherical, Jonson insists that it is rooted in its center, the living mind: "Accept this garland, plant it on thy head" (77).

One can ask no more of figural logic than Jonson's garland supplies, and if he had seen fit to end his poem at this midpoint, he would indeed have seemed to close a circle. But necessarily there is more to say; for the eschatological mind, presence cannot be posited as a value apart from permanence, and Jonson must therefore raise presentation to the transcendent site of a "bright eternal Day" (81). The light of the "flowre" does not suffuse the garland. Garlands die, like Morison, yet Morison must live: Jonson's figure must embrace Morison (as the garland of Jonson's praise and Cary's memory does not) or else it is merely a Pattern, alienated not from life, the friend and poet being alive, but from its originary center, Morison himself. Or, if the poet is the originary center, then *he* is excluded from the garland. The poet's self-presence must properly be the containing figure of both Morison and Cary; he must at once comprise his magic circle and stand within it if the circle is to contain rather than exclude presence. He must

> taste a part of that full joy he meant
> To have exprest
> In this bright *Asterisme*.

[87–89]

In the absence of light, the garland fuses too little, and the figural sequence of this third Counterturn therefore abandons the garland and returns to the "flowre of light,"[17] now duly constellated.

Instantly, however, Jonson reveals the "schisme" (90) that will break open the third Stand and forfeit the unity of friendship's garland even when it is raised to the sky: "that full joy" in the future is dependent on Jonson's death, just as the awarding of value to Morison's life has required *his* death; hence, "that full joy" is not contained in "this bright *Asterisme*," as the antithesis of "that" and "this" frankly confesses. The ambivalently enjambed "twi-/Lights" (92–93), "that in heav'n" and "this light on earth," "must shine" (96) always in different places and times and can never be present to each other. One or the other of the Dioscuri will always be obscure; furthermore, persons cannot even be fully present to themselves, since "Ben/" alive is separated by the abyss between stanzas from "Jonson" dead, and "thy Morison" (78; this is the moment when the garland is bestowed) is no longer "Harry" now that he is constellated. Full presence requires the prevenience of death, and shines only in the realm of the dead.

Little by little, Jonson comes to terms with the necessity of incompleteness through the use of the Pindaric format. Every flaw in his circle is a dip of the eagle's flight, either where the stanza interrupts the argument or where the enjambment required by stanzaic compression makes a leap stretch too far. "Dig a long pit for my jump from here," boasts Pindar,[18] whose sublimity has always been imputed to his long leaps, concealing transition, from one figure to another. The name for this sort of leap is metalepsis, which Lanham has defined as the "omission of a central term in an extended metaphor" (*Handlist*, p. 67). Jonson's hoped-for illumination of the garland as a crowning constellation is a metalepsis that omits the present by soaring above and beyond it, and he cannot resist calling attention both to his trope and its failure when he says, at the most triumphant moment of the poem, that Morison "leap'd the present age"(79).

The last triad is more self-contained than any of the other three. It fills out the twelve stanzas that equal the twelve lines of each Stand, perhaps pointing to the involution of a twelvemonth that witnesses the harvest before the bloom. (One could go on in this vein,[19] but no intricacy of holistic evidence can suppress this poem's even more intricate self-deformation.) This last triad begins as a peroration, that is, as a proper ending: "And shine as you exalted are;/Two names of friendship, but one Starre" (97–98). But then, because there is still more to say, it trails off in a new direction. The false peroration has recalled the problem of naming. The previous triad had attempted the transmission of qualities in figures and seemed briefly iconic, but the failure of this effort made the distance between figure and presence explicit. After this noble failure no symbolic logic will seem likely to succeed, as the relatively subdued tone of the final Turn and Counterturn and the rather feeble gathering of force in the final Stand may suggest. But Jonson's dénouement does have a lesser assertion of its own to put forward, that words, at least, if not substances, may still have a certain currency or value, and that the first analogy (48–52) between poetry and life may still hold good.

The anticlimax after the peroration consists of a catalog of aristocratic excesses that defines Cary and Morison by exclusion. If the presence of the two friends to each other, to the poet, and to the world is now seen to be impossible, their absence can at least be glorified as a fortunate absence from the decadent vortex that had swallowed even the name of the *senex* earlier in the poem. As friends, Cary and Morison live in this happy absence to become "surnames,/And titles"—not mere "corkes of title" but talismanic words "by which all made claimes" (114). Cary and Morison are reified names, like Lucy, Countess of Bedford: "Such when I meant to faine, and wish'd to see,/My *Muse* bad, Bedford write, and that was shee" (VIII. 52). The phrasing, however, of "Nothing perfect done, / But as a CARY, or a MORISON" (115–16) tends to undermine itself. Morison being gone, and Cary too (since this latter outcome is suspended in an indefinite future), perfection now exists only in their names. The last stanza recoils from this new self-betrayal and turns from the "stile" and "Copie" (111–12) of written names to the writing of a concept—*Friendship*—that is not written as a word but carved as a feeling on the heart. But the poet cannot have his poem both ways, written and unwritten, just as he cannot have his asterism in the sky and in the garden at once. Proudly, then, he reaches his last, diminished Stand, refusing to end with a trite antifigural figure about the heart's writing, and reposes instead in his role as chronicler of absence and witness of emptiness. The "lines" of Cary and Morison are the "rowles" and "records" of a departed "early" race that harvested and used up its transmissible nobility. The "immortall memorie" of Cary and Morison, like that of the Brave Infant who never entered life, begins with the coming forth of their death in words.[20]

II

The form of the "sublime" ode is more certain than any other form to bring a poet's presentational ambition to grief; but the ambition of most odists is as emptily conventional as the form itself. That is why all the "Descend, ye nine" detritus of English literature need not be mentioned with any prominence in this study.[21] It is worth glancing briefly, though, at a few minor odes that are very early in order to show that the ode's necessary betrayal of its vatic calling does not arise historically as a case of generic overwork.

Since these odes are all experiments with forms of address or of avoiding address, a word or two on that topic may be in order. Much can be learned about the possibilities of address in an ode from titles. The Ashmole MS of the Cary-Morison Ode, for example, which appears from the editor's notes to be remarkably careless, nevertheless has a title that is more intelligible than that of the 1640 Folio: "Ode on the death of Sr: Henry Morison to the noble Sr: Lucius Cary." It is both an ode *on* and an ode *to*. (The Folio title is very differently addressed "to" memory and friendship, twin numina.) Whereas an "ode on" simply announces a topic, sometimes carrying in its title the lapidary suggestion that it is literally inscribed on its object, an "ode to" claims to be a poem of address: it will apostrophize some hearer who may not be, nominally at least, the topic of the poem. We shall see in a moment, though, how characteristic it is that the hearer and the object of description merge together in odes of address; an "ode to" is apt to recognize that its occasion, whether nightingale or patron, is also its inspiration. In an ode of address the hearer is elsewhere, and if he is not merely apostrophized but actually invoked, he is being called in to serve as a Muse. The hearer is the figure who must be made present in an ode. In the Cary-Morison Ode there are several apostrophes, including one to Cary, who is named as the hearer in the Ashmole MS; but there is no proper invocation, and this omission may help confirm my feeling that the poem views memory as a dead letter, a chronicle of time lost, and friendship as a departed Genius.

A possible simpler reason for the omission, though, is that Jonson was leery of Pindaric invocations after his disastrous attempt at one in the early Desmond Ode, to which I now turn. This poem is nearly half invocation, mainly because the invocation is itself a mirror image of the absent object, the exact identity of which is never clarified and keeps changing because it frustrates the poet's understanding. Thus the invocation is prolonged as it gropes toward a clearer notion of what it is calling for and a clearer understanding that its own structure, as an invocation, embodies its highest value. If the prisoner Desmond is confined in the Tower, the invocation implies, so the poet's intricate pseudo-Pindaric strophes similarly wall off the poem,[22] and both prison and poem are towers of invention:

> Where art thou, Genius? I should use
>   Thy present Aide: Arise Invention,
>   High, as his mind, that doth advance
> Her upright head, above the reach of chance,
>   Or the times envie:
>   *Cynthius*, I applie
> My bolder numbers to thy golden *Lyre*:
>   O, then inspire
> Thy Priest in this strange rapture; heat my braine
>   With *Delphick* fire:
> That I may sing my thoughts, in some unvulgar straine.
>
>   Rich beame of honour, shed your light
> On these darke rymes; that my affection
> May shine (through every chinke) to every sight
>   Graced by your Reflection!
> Then shall my Verses, like strong Charmes,
> Breake the knit circle of her Stonie Armes,
>   That hold[s] your spirit:
>   And keepes your merit
> Lock't in her cold embraces, from the view
>   Of eyes more true . . .
>
> [VIII, pp. 176–77]

This is poor verse, not just because its heat is so very cooling, but also because it is full of badly governed pronouns. However, the idea that is half masked and half revealed by the drift of Jonson's pronouns is not uninteresting. In the second strophe, the female "mind" of Desmond, now called a "Rich beame of honour," supplants the sun god so unobtrusively in the invocation that the change is easy to miss. Desmond's intellectual light shines through every chink in his tower more assuredly than Apollo illumines the towering (q.v., 4) Babel of Jonson's verse. Not only Desmond's mind, but also the verse and the tower are female. The poem is a

welter of absent light sources and looming walls that blend or ex-
change their functions androgynously whenever the poet's con-
fidence wavers in himself or in his imprisoned and imprisoning muse.
All these figures are soon usurped by the enigmatic Elizabeth, "oure
faire Phoeb[e]" in the last strophe, the "stonie Armes" of whose
Tower had earlier embraced the prisoner sans merci:

> oure faire Phoeb[e]'s shine,
> Shall light those places
> With lustrous Graces,
> Where darkness with her gloomie-sceptred hand,
> Doth now command;
>
> [58-63]

The "rich beame" of Desmond's mind, which formerly lit the Tower
and these verses with no aid, has now darkened and become depen-
dent on that inconstant moon, his Queen.

All these quite genuinely Pindaric transferences disclose, perhaps
as a code of sorts, a political riddle: either Elizabeth is unjust (an
oppressive wall) or she is not; but if she is not unjust and shines with
a true grace, then Desmond is no rich beam of honor but darkly
guilty. The closing exhortation is charged with doubt:

> O then (my best-lov'd) let me importune,
> That you will stand
> As farre from all revolt, as you are now from Fortune.

I would suggest that the Desmond Ode is a seditious coterie poem
that resorts to the indirectness of Pindar to mystify prying readers,
but that a measure of private doubt about the prisoner led Jonson to
choose the ode form for other reasons as well. Jonson's ode con-
ceives of itself as a formal wall ("these darke rymes") that dams up
the lucidity of expression, as if to insist that even normal, unam-
biguous discourse cannot encircle or illumine the otherness of
truth. This redoubling of lyric isolation parallels Jonson's problem
as a political reporter: his ignorance of the facts is as great as his
fear of the censor.[23]

The swervings of Pindarism are like the zigzag of consciousness
between external and internal censorships. These facing walls, which
squeeze the poet inside their stony arms, are themselves traces of the
repressed; of the coldly beautiful and regal muse as she appears
daemonically. Tyrant, traitor, and devouring mother, she is essen-
tially the same figure as the "Wiser Nature" who swallows her child
in the Cary-Morison Ode. The source of antithetical meanings in an

ode is the repressed, insofar as the poet has not forestalled the operation of the repressed by staging the breakdown of his own holistic defenses.[24] The later Cary-Morison Ode reflects the mastery of that staging, while the Desmond Ode, written at least thirty years earlier, reflects the confusion of being taken by surprise. In either case, Jonson turns to the Pindaric form, to the idea of a sublime ode at once exacting and frenzied, as an emblem of the psychic conflict between order and anarchy, steadfastness and betrayal.

III

It is unlikely that Michael Drayton read Pindar, but the preface "To the Reader" of his 1606 *Poems Lyrick and Pastoral* shows that he knew what the idea of Pindar represents, thanks to Horace and to a tradition of Pindarism that extends from the Italian Humanists[25] through the Pléiade to late Elizabethan England. Pindar, Drayton knew, rushes like a mountain river that floods its banks, "numerisque fertur/lege solutis" (Horace, *Carm.* IV. ii [Loeb ed.]). No English poet until Cowley tried to free poetry from the laws of number, but Pindar's precedent did allow, as we have seen, for other more subtle anarchies: the abrupt phrase without transition, the sudden shift of perspective, and a syntax so tightly squeezed by the twisting of meter that obscurity is unavoidable. All these effects are also produced by the short, Skeltonic line that Drayton improvised for his odes. As Kathleen Tillotson remarks, "His method is generally Procrustean: the limbs of syntax (especially relative pronouns) are removed. . . . Yet these jerks and ellipses seem at times calculated rather than compulsory."[26] This description is equally well suited for Jonson's Desmond Ode; and indeed Drayton, in "Ode XVIII: To the Cambro-Britans, and their Harpe, his Ballad of Agincourt" (II. 375–78), edges close enough to sedition to require, perhaps, in common with Jonson, a "calculated" clouding of sense. Since Drayton was not nearly as intelligent or self-conscious a poet as Jonson, it is doubtful whether he knew precisely how the ode form undermines his celebratory themes, but its subversion is all the more devastating in not being, as we may suppose, fully governed.

"Agincourt" is a poem that struggles to achieve address in its own voice, but the pastness of its subject is so absolute that Drayton can only manage a proper address in a surrogate voice, that of King

Henry, whose ode-within-an-ode is, as will appear, an inaccessible model of presentation. In his own voice Drayton tries only one apostrophe, "Well it thine Age became,/Oh noble ERPINGHAM" (65–66), but the ambiguity of "thine Age" instantly opens the abyss across which no apostrophe can reach out to touch what Schlüter suggestively calls its "Kontaktaufnahme" (*Die Englische Ode*, p. 33). This martial poem is a struggle with the pastness of the past that is signaled more than once in a disagreement of tenses brought about by the need for quick rhymes: "Faire stood the Wind for *France*,/When we our sayles advance" (1–2). Drayton cannot long keep up the dizzy logic of being on the ship both now and two hundred years ago, but for two stanzas the illusion lingers: the wind comes up, "we" hoist sail, and, as the fleet enters the Seine and camps near Agincourt the action still seems to be carried out and recorded simultaneously. Present tense returns later only once, where the meaning of another couplet is distorted by rhyme; here, the deviant verb itself announces the burial of the present: "They now to the fight are *gone*,/Armour on Armour shone" (57–58). Defeated as a verb, the presentation of the past becomes possessive and passes over to the fiercely proprietary "our," but tense fore-closes that illusion also, at line 88: "Our Men were hardie."

Henceforward "our" carries Drayton's hint of sedition. At line 89, "our Noble King" is an Englishman linked to his own past, not the Scottish intruder now on the throne whose pacifism is in part what divides Drayton's attempted address from any fit audience.[27] The ode-within-an-ode has been introduced in a manner that is also possessive—"Quoth our brave HENRY then" (26)—but at that point the seditious contrast is muted by the narrator's still seeming to be a member of the army. It is Henry's exhortation and his character as its speaker that reveal decisively, however, what is missing from Drayton's own poem and character. Henry is a new Tyrtaeus,[28] a bard-hero who sets his own example (how different is James, bard of Tobacco!), proving that he deserves to speak of "our skill" (44) when later he sallies out to "ding" (91) the French. What farther deepens Drayton's alienation from the past is his realization that Henry too has a past, but that his is still a living past. Henry stands already at the end of his age, but as yet there is no gap between him and the exempla he cites; he is the descendant of "our Grandsire Great," Edward III, who fought and won at Crécy. Today, the King is a Stuart, and Drayton, the gentleman's gentleman, is no veteran foot soldier of the sort who conventionally sings (and at first appeared here to sing) eyewitness ballads.

Henry's heroic age is known by the Elizabethan antiquaries—Camden, John Weever, and Drayton himself—to be a time when much poetry was vocal, happily illiterate and improvised for the harp. In this setting, what Drayton understands an "ode" to be could flourish spontaneously. "Agincourt" is addressed "to his harpe," and its short lines are meant to be sung, but its ending shows that in the present, just as acculturation has dried up the bloodlines of valor, so the arterial flow of voice has been replaced by the dead ink of writing:

> Oh, when shall English men
> With such Acts fill a pen,
> Or England breed againe,
>   Such a King HARRY?
>
> [117–20]

Drayton's ode cannot be an ode, since its short, "vocal" cadences are themselves, when represented in writing, the cause of overstrain, anomaly, and absentation.

The confinement of voice to prehistory is what dooms the Progress-conventions of "To Himselfe, and the Harpe" from the start. The poet asks a question that answers itself proleptically in the negative:

> AND why not I, as hee
>   That's greatest, if as free,
> (In sundry strains that strive,
> Since there so many be)
>   Th'old *Lyrick* kind revive?
>
> [*Works* II. 347–49. 11. 1–5]

Perhaps Horace is "hee/That's greatest," but the stanza's implications make him seem too urbane to be a proper forerunner: Drayton takes his "lyric" literally, as we know, and "strains" does not chiefly refer to either genres or meters, as would be the case in most poems, but rather to modes of playing the harp.[29] The phrase "if as free" appears to imply everything it would imply for a street minstrel today: lack of inhibition, innocence of learning, and defiance of law. When Drayton later writes that the Muses "be such coy Things,/

That they care not for Kings" (16–17), one thinks partly of this privileged lawlessness and partly of the political discontent of "Agincourt," but his sentiment also expresses the more general discontent of being simply too civilized.

A degree of repression seems always to govern Drayton's thinking about kings, and it is worth pausing over one of the exempla in this ode to identify what is repressed. That "King" is synecdochic for the whole social fabric is shown most clearly in Drayton's misreading of the story of King Pyreneus from Ovid (*Metamorphoses* V. 11. 274–93). The way Drayton tells it, the fate of Pyreneus seems to represent one of the many conventional warnings against challenging the Muses in song: Pyreneus "Fell, as he with them strove" (24), and his crime therefore seems no different from that of the magpies in Ovid's next story. The moral is simple and implies no self-examination: the Muses dislike anyone, even a King, "That is not borne a Poet" (20). But it is Ovid's own account of Pyreneus that reveals the main concern of "To Himselfe."

What Drayton leaves out is not, in fact, that Pyreneus's actual crime was attempted rape. That much he makes clear: the Phocean's "foule Lust did move / Those Mayds unchaste to make" (22–23), and the marginal gloss describes him "attempting to ravish the Muses." But Drayton wants to understand this rape allegorically, as a hubristic attempt at *vocal* "ravishment" by a poetaster who does not come to his task "with hands pure" (13). Ovid's own allegory, however, has a broader meaning. During a storm, his Pyreneus lures the Muses into his "house" on the pretext of letting them dry off. He has removed them, that is, from their wild natural element, and thus his attempt on their virtue is at bottom an attempt to domesticate them. "We wished to go on our way," recalls one of Ovid's muses, "but Pyreneus barred his home. . . . By taking to our wings, we escaped his assault."[30] Pyreneus tries to follow them, but people who live in houses cannot soar aloft, and he falls from his presumptuously artifical "high tower." His Fall is the bathos of an ode that comes too late in the history of culture. This moral underlies Drayton's terse version of the story.

In this and other ways, the formal Progress that now begins has been negated in advance. Since the harper David is the "best of Kings," in contrast with Pyreneus, Drayton would appear to have advanced the "lyrick" into a state of society, but that is because, still compulsively skewing the topic of kingship, he has suppressed David's more visionary role as a shepherd in a nomadic culture. The Amphion story (45–50) brings the "Progress" to the threshold of civilized culture, but Amphion is, precisely, a threshold figure who raises the walls that henceforth domesticate and naturalize his magic. Instead of moving on to the already civilized art of Pindar, Drayton then swerves to the Druids (51–60), whose genius he surrounds with an atmosphere of savagery that includes human sacrifice. The Druids' harps were strung "diversely," but this is scarcely dispraise, since the opening of the poem has already implied that to be "free" is to be irregular. Pindar and Horace then appear, allegedly to teach crude Northerners to "Finger . . . aright" (63) their lyres with "Strokes divinely cleere" (77). It is implied, however, that Pindar "retayn'd" his lyric "power to strike" *despite* his emphasis on craftsmanship; and if Horace is a writer whose "Ayres we all imbrace," the very ubiquity of his influence must in itself disqualify him as a model for a poet who wishes to "revive" a long-forgotten mode of lyric. Clearly preferring the freedom and strength of prehistory to the formal clarity of advanced cultures, Drayton makes his stanzas on Pindar and Horace a single sentence that rushes the poem from the Druids back to other artless avatars, the Irish and the Britons.

The fruit of this native strain is the hapless John Soothern, author of the first Pindaric ode in English, which is possibly the worst poem in any form that has ever been printed.[31] Drayton tries to admire "Southerne" (though the compression of "I long thee spare" yields yet another ambiguity) for harping "neatly" (85), but surely Soothern could only be admired for his primitivism, for "erring from the right" (89) far more than his "Judges" do; and the underlying sense of the poem as a whole would suggest that indeed Drayton does admire Soothern as a neo-Primitive who has learned nothing whatsoever, ironically enough, from the metrical art of Pindar and Horace. "Nor is't the Verse doth make" (91): this echo of Aristotle, a Renaissance commonplace, has unusual force in Drayton, who believes not just that versification maketh not a poet, but that, in fact, versification signals the decline of lyric into the decadence of writing. "Ryme" (95) is a different matter, and more praiseworthy, because it is the verbal equivalent of the harp's closely spaced repetitions. Fearing that his 1606 audience had failed to see that Skelton was a valuable forebear because he was primitive in manner, Drayton in the 1619 edition makes Skelton seem older than he is; pretending that his readers have a short memory, he notes learnedly in the margin—as if referring once more to some ancient source book—that Skelton is "An old *English* Rymer."[32]

Drayton's choice of Skeltonics for his odes is a wise one; he does vigorously "revive" a special lyric kind, but the very success of his overcrowded phrasing, its resonant power of countersuggestion, continuously undermines his faith in the Progress that his own example helps to confirm. Heroic and lyric greatness belong to a buried past that cannot be represented; or if they are freed from the past, these qualities then leap into the future, as in "To the Virginian Voyage" (*Works* II. 363–64). The "brave Heroique minds" apostrophized in this poem are brave because they are leaving England, while those who stay are "loyt'ring Hinds." (The reader hears his own staying behind in the epithet.) The voyagers are just now disappearing, still within earshot of apostrophe, but Drayton's vision of their heroism can only arise from what the poem gives us reason to call their "absolute" absence from England:

> when EOLUS scowles,
> You need not feare,
> So absolute the Deepe.
>
> [16–18]

Since Virginia is a new Eden, it cannot be reached fluently through space or time, but only through a leap placing the voyagers outside the cycle of history that began with the loss of paradise.

I would explain the crux at lines 16–18 by saying that Drayton sees the Atlantic as a kind of time machine; the promise of being drowned (for that, incredibly, is what line 18 seems to offer[33]) forces its way into the poem as a baptismal prelude to rebirth in paradise. Once through this abyss, the absent voyagers enter a Saturnian pastoral: "the Golden Age / Still Natures lawes doth give" (37–38). From this new beginning a second history can develop[34] that leads toward the "absolute" past of "Agincourt":

> And in Regions farre
> Such Heroes bring ye foorth,
> As those from whom We came . . .
>
> [55–57]

In this heroic age new poets will emerge, but they will sing in an absolutely absent radiance, "Under that Starre/Not knowne unto our North" (59-60). In this ode, then, as in the other two, Drayton subversively denies, as if against his will, the absence of everything worth invoking from the England of his own day. With such an undertheme struggling to be expressed, he would understandably have recourse, like Jonson in the Desmond Ode, to the Pindarically sanctioned obscurity of an ode.

It should be evident from this sampling of early odes in English that the way poems have of subverting themselves and their themes is not a symptom of recent origin. It is not least the purpose of this book to show how poetic forms overburden what might be called the conscience of discourse. The strain is most apparent where the forms chosen are most extravagant, and it is from this correlation that the special nature of the ode appears. One reason why I shall not carry this study beyond the Romantic period (to include, for example, some consideration of Tennyson) is that increasingly during the nineteenth century, as doubt and self-consciousness more and more openly marked the artistic intelligence in general, so also the element of form in poetry came to be more and more openly experimental, more self-justifying than hitherto, and hence the form of *all* poetry came to serve the subversive function that it had once served, from the time of Jonson and Drayton onward, most notably in the ode.

2

Milton's Light-Harnessed Ode

Our poets must understand that a prayer is a request made to a god, and should therefore be scrupulously careful not to ask for a curse in mistake for a blessing.

—Plato, *Laws* VIII. 801

Milton's Nativity Ode is written under a novel radiance that resembles the star of Drayton's Virginians. The Nativity Ode is offered in the presence of "Heaven's youngest-teemèd star"[1] as it now appears, but is also offered as though in the presence of the star's first rising—or so Milton's bewildering array of tenses, recalling those of "Agincourt," would cause us to believe.[2] Like Drayton's odes, the Nativity Ode is suspended between great events of the past and future, but Milton's poem can still spare praise for the actual present as a time of the soul's betterment in a state of grace that will finally give way, without relapse, to a state of eternal glory. Milton uses both doctrine and rhetoric to avoid suggesting that the heroic age is irrevocably past, and if we hear a note of humanistic nostalgia in his rebukes of heroic romance and pastoral, in his rout of the pagan idols, or in his chastisement of the lawless natural order,[3] we still cannot pretend that in this poem the Christian promise is in any sense subverted. Like Drayton, Milton heralds a brave new world that must be entered through an "absolute" change, in this case the Conflagration, but Milton also claims, again, that the auspicious star of the new world has been steadily present since the day of the Incarnation.

Written in the same year as the Cary-Morison Ode, Milton's ode also shares important figures with that poem: the speechless infant, the sphere, the "twilight shade" (188) of qualities and stars eclipsed by absence (Jonson's "twi-/Lights" are ostensibly very different, but I have suggested that they, too, are elegiac), and above

37

all the figures of constellation that insist on a transcendent site for what Jonson calls "full joy" and Milton calls "our bliss/Full and perfect" (165–66). In addition, there is a masquelike quality about the form of both odes (anti-masque/masque: Turn/Counterturn), and both also have in common the masque theme of Descending Virtue's redemption of Nature grown monstrous. In the more quiet staging of an ode, the presence of a redeemer who has come ex machina is tested by each poet through the logic of univocal figuration: can a poem incarnate what once mysteriously incarnated itself, and if so, Milton will go on to ask, can that achievement be viewed without anxiety, with proper humility, as a triumph of holy inspiration?

It is tempting, and up to a point it will be fitting, to show that a diminishment of stellar "influence" (71) commits Milton's ode to the eloquent outer darkness where I have placed Jonson's and Drayton's odes, and to show further how its form hastens its departure from the light. But these matters are only incidental, I think, to a disturbing factor of quite another sort in Milton's poem that is no less crucial to an explanation of what makes the ode in general a treacherous undertaking. Although Jonson in the Cary-Morison Ode questions the scope and powers of his vocation, he has no doubts about its dignity and benign function. Milton's nervousness about his vocation is far more radical; his ode is certainly about its own scope and powers, but it is even more crucially about what it means for one's voice to be "touched with hallowed fire" (28). The gift of prophetic authority, for Milton, must be used with trepidation, not because in itself it will prove illusory but because, once given, it may promote illusion. The universe of the Nativity Ode teems with stars and choirs of every origin and magnitude, each with its own influence, and what disturbs Milton's celebration is his concern about his own place, and that of Christian hymnody, in the "maze" of light and sound he has imagined. As the reticence of his title and the confusion of terms within his poem would indicate, he cannot decide whether he has written a hymn or an ode. The decision must nevertheless be a momentous one, because it determines which choir he has joined,[4] and under which influence.

As James Nohrnberg has remarked, Satan in *Paradise Lost* "is the victim of a course in 'the Bible as Literature.'"[5] Being a syncretist, Satan knows no final authority but his own. So it is with "Lucifer" in the Nativity Ode, who will not settle for his role as a leader among equals. He had been one of the "sons of morning" (119; Isa. 14:12)[6] who sang cosmogony, but then he fell, not willing to quire it with the rest, and reached a worse eminence than he had wished for. Now, like a bad shepherd, he tries to herd the stars away from the light, begrudging them their "precious influence." I begin with this fragmentary comment on "Or Lucifer that often warned them thence" (74) in part because it has been the object of rather heated debate, and also because it will be possible to clarify Milton's subtly registered hesitancies as a hymnodist by tracing the influence of this passage elsewhere in the poem.

Many critics[7] have given Milton's play on "Lucifer" its due, or at least confessed their perplexity at finding a name out of place in the work of a poet who is a master of controlled allusion. A. S. P. Woodhouse rests his case against them, and against all perversity of interpretation, by quoting the *TLS* review (12 July 1951, 428) of Brooks and Hardy's edition, with commentary, of the 1645 *Poems*: "'Now, poetically, the intrusion of Lucifer-Satan into this part of the "Nativity Ode" is just what is not wanted; it detracts from the charmed air of peace the poet is in the act of creating. And it is hard on a poet if critics, in their eagerness for an ambiguity at all costs, thrust on him a secondary meaning which, though possible theoretically, he never intended.'"[8] I myself find "the intrusion of Lucifer-Satan" to be handled too cautiously by those who notice it, handled in a way that rationalizes and synthesizes too quickly; but these critics have at least confronted that which disturbs, as well as that which preserves, the "charmed air of peace" in poetry. Surely "it is hard on a poet" to round off the sharpest edges of his text. Against the *TLS* passage one might set the following, also on Milton:

My purpose . . . is not, primarily, to establish the decorum of an image. The theory of criticism does not seem sufficiently advanced to solve problems even of this elementary kind, since two quite opposite types of justification could be entertained: one demonstrating that the image is in its place, and is a link contributing to the poem's unity; the other that it is displaced, yet expressive of some extraordinary feature of Milton's poetry or mind. To rule an image out of order might suggest, of course, a new order accommodating it; but one feels that poetry, like religion, cannot be ruled this way, and that Milton's idiosyncrasy is of the essence.[9]

"Lucifer" and its context point to the idiosyncrasy of the Nativity Ode.

Envious once before at being merely a witness to Creation—one of many "sons of morning"—Lucifer is now only too willing to fall away from the new Prince of Light, who reconfirms the faintness of his, Lucifer's, always compulsively contrary influence. Once more he is envious, this time of his inferiors, insignificant in "their glimmering orbs" but "precious" in their combined influence, because they stand "fixed" (like Abdiel) in their admiration of unquestionable brilliance. The fixity of this scene, contrasted with the restlessness of Lucifer, is paralleled by later contrasts between harmony and dissonance: the angelic choir, the lower Music of the Spheres, and the still lower "base" of human hymns, all these harmonies supplant the harsh noises that hurry countless heathen lights to their eclipse. Lucifer happily joins the other, more reluctant sun and moon gods who were lights unto themselves. By contrast, the stars "bending one way" (71), the "full consort" (132) of the choirs, the "order serviceable" (244) of the attendant angels, even the "rustic row" of the shepherds—all these conform, all bend themselves univocally. These voices "will not take their flight" (72); they are not Pindaric, since they all submit to a prior sublimity that is universally commanding.

The other morning stars are like hymns, not odes. They will not imitate Lucifer or accept his command, but when "their Lord [bespeaks]" them, they efface themselves. The speechless "infancy" (151) of Christ's incarnation shows that his Word is reified above and beyond the articulations of language; as sheer presence, "infancy" is the object of both hymns and odes. The song of the angelic choir itself aspires to the state of infancy: as in "Lycidas," its notes are "unexpressive"—a coinage that means, I think, just what it seems to mean. Language only exists, in fact, in the sublunary world, that being the sole region where nothing is its own object, and all discourse is dress.[10] At the beginning of the "Hymn," Nature's need to dress her guilt is at once echoed and expressed in an invocation that resembles a poet's to the wind: "Only with speeches fair/She woos the gentle air" (37–38).

Nature's predicament, and her invocation, anticipate a passage in *The Reason of Church Government* that may, in turn, gloss other relevant passages in that same text. Even a didactic poem, says Milton there, must offer "delight to those especially of soft and delicious temper who will not so much as look upon Truth herself, unless they see her elegantly dressed,"[11] unless, that is, they see her looking like themselves. Such persons, as Sidney had said earlier, are the special beneficiaries of poetry, but the need to serve them unfortunately endangers poetry, whose "elegant dress"—or rhetoric—exposes it to Platonic censure. Plato, however, had not criticized the authors of hymns that justly praise gods and men, as Milton, of course, knew: "Or if occasion shall lead to imitate those magnific odes and hymns wherein Pindarus and Callimachus are in most things worthy, some others in their frame judicious, in their matter most an end faulty" (Hughes, p. 669).[12] The parallelism of clauses in this passage shows Milton to observe the distinction between odes and hymns, since Pindar was understood in the Renaissance to have written the former, and Callimachus gave his own addresses to the deities the latter title. Even as a hymnodist, though, Callimachus is only "in most things worthy" because he praises false gods. All these poets fall short in some degree ("some others" are no doubt Anacreon and Horace), owing to the distance between their "frame" and their "matter."

This distance does not frustrate the prophetic "holy sages" of the Nativity Ode because they are inspired witnesses. Milton continues the above-quoted passage: "But those frequent songs throughout the law and prophets beyond all these, not in their divine argument alone, but in the very critical art of composition, may be easily made appear over all the kinds of lyric poesy to be incomparable. These abilities, wheresoever they be found, are the inspired gift of God rarely bestowed, but yet to some (though most abuse) in every nation. . . ." The best kind of lyric poetry, then, can assuredly join the "ninefold harmony" in concert, though only one of the nine muses, Polyhymnia rediscovered as Urania, can be present. But there remains a grave danger of writing the worst kind of lyric, the kind that does not "inbreed and cherish in a great people the seeds of virtue and public civility" or "celebrate . . . the throne and equipage of God's almightiness" (ibid.). The "Hymns devout and holy psalms" of mortals ("At a Solemn Musick") are subservient because they are communally, rather than mystically, participatory; because, that is, they are both secondary and collective. Hymns must invoke their aid and subject just as Nature invokes the air in "fair speeches," and above all they must suppress idiosyncrasy, encouraging the conformance they practice. I would venture to suggest in this context that

Lucifer is a writer of odes not hymns, and return to consider Milton's ode or hymn with this notion in mind.

The part of the poem that is called a "Hymn" celebrates the exorcism of darkness by light, yet in the sequence of its unfolding, darkness tends to succeed light, at least until the last stanza. In the proem, Christ's descent to man is a movement from "the blaze of majesty" downward to "the darksome house of mortal clay." Indeed, whenever they are dynamically represented, Descent and Progress appear as movements, both sacrificial and punitive, from light to dark, and from the freedom of the skies into some "darksome house": the snow-covered face of Nature, the "dark foundations deep" of the universe, the "oozy channel" of the waves, the "dolorous mansions" and "straiter limits" of Hell, and the many nether jails of the pagan gods. As I have suggested, the paradigm and crux of this basic movement, its prolepsis, is the disappearance of the morning stars and their influence. In each new figural shift, the expansive freedom of light and "unexpressive" harmony is replaced by enclosure in some wished-for or involuntarily inherited prison-house. That is, the ode keeps describing the disappearance of full presence into embodiment. This is hardly surprising on the anniversary of the Incarnation, but the steady repetition of that sacred figural descent at every level of experience seems almost compulsive. "Lucifer," then, is not an isolated disturbing factor but the signal of a general oddity.

Milton does not concede easily, though, that descent is diminution, and that is what makes the design of his poem so brilliant.[13] Just now I contrasted the Father's "blaze of majesty" with the Son's "darksome house," but Milton's own more local and balanced contrast is between the house of clay and "the courts of everlasting day." Heaven, like the well-composed "songs throughout the law and prophets," is by no means amorphous. Its "courts" comprise a first palatial figure that points toward the wide-open "gates" of Heaven's "high palace-hall" and on to the infant's "courtly stable" at the close of the poem. Such relays of figures seem meant to show emphatically that formalization is not diminution and that the "Trinal Unity" is unbroken despite separation. (One is reminded of Jonson's three-part "asterism," with one of its stars above, one below, and one excluded.) The persistence of the palatial figure is weakened, however, by the fact that its middle appearance, as the opening of Heaven's gates, takes place during the merely hypothetical return of the golden age. The Day of Judgment, on the contrary, will not open the highest and lowest strata toward the center ("peering day") but will move upward from "middle air" (164) toward the transcendent site that thenceforth will close off nothingness.[14] Already, in token of this moment, the old Dragon "Not half so far casts his usurped sway" (170).

Judgment Day will repeat, then, on an ascending scale, the originary descent to formal closure that is described as follows:

> the Creator great
> His constellations set,
> And the well-balanced world on hinges hung,
> And cast the dark foundations deep
> And bid the weltering waves their oozy channels keep.
>
> [120–24]

This carpenter's reduction of energy to *ousia*, unwillingly sung by at least one son of morning, recalls the restraining of the Dragon by the repetition of the word "cast," a word that has troubled commentators on line 123. Earlier, Satan, still at liberty, had "cast" his sway after the manner of a Pindaric leap, whereas here "cast" is a containing verb that forms a sculptor's or mason's "earthly mold."[15] In *Paradise Lost*, Milton recalls this figure for the grounding of the universe (and also recalls the "wisest Fate" of this poem) as the setting for the Fall of Lucifer:

> Hell heard th'insufferable noise, Hell saw
> Heav'n running from Heav'n, and would have fled
> Affrighted; but strict Fate had cast too deep
> Her dark foundations, and too fast had bound.
>
> [VI. 867–70]

The strain of the word "cast" between opening out and enclosing is repeated in every new figural replacement, and it echoes the dramatization, in the introductory stanzas, of the poet's attitude toward his calling and toward the choice his calling offers between unfettered freedom and obedient form.

We may now turn to those first stanzas in order to consider the poet's postponement or suspense of choice more closely. In this proem the Son's descent from Heaven to the body, a second fortunate fall, is repeated in the poet's request that the muse descend from the moment of inspiration into poetic form. The invocation to the star-muse Urania hectors her a little, as if sensing her reluctance to rechannel her "sacred vein" below. The invocation is uttered at a moment of natural darkness mixed with unnatural brightness: or, more accurately, at a moment when the imminent arrival of natural light is suggested in advance by supernatural figures.[16] The sky un-printed by the Sun's team (a classical and therefore improperly inspired image) anticipates the more numinous "radiant feet" of Mercy (146), and the personified "spangled host" of stars looks forward to the "globe [i.e., troop] of circular light" in the "Hymn." In each of these cases the degree of difference between light in the proem and light in the "Hymn" is controlled and significant; the anticipatory figures of the introduction carefully avoid *witnessing* the supernatural, stressing by this decorum that prophecy (as eye-witness testimony) can only begin when the "Hymn" begins, at the moment of Urania's implied entry into the poet. The introduction suspends the poet between nature and the divine, and so too it suspends the scope of his vocation.

He calls: "Hast thou no verse, no hymn, or solemn strain,/To welcome him to this his new abode . . . ?" (17–18). Here is yet another house, where the poet also dwells, and from whence he arro-gates a "hymn." But the word "abode," which only slantingly rhymes with the undomesticated words "God" and "untrod," is pulled out of its place and toward the rhymes of the next stanza, there to be walled in further, first by "the eastern road" and then by "humble ode." The significance is clear: in Milton's humble abode, far removed from the palatial heavens, he is not sure that he can rise to a hymn.

But this modest fear wholly conflicts with an even more troubling thought that also appears in the proem. A hymn, however exalted, is, as I have said, still and always a choir-poem that harmoniously effaces the individual; it is really a *hymn*, therefore, that is "humble," and an ode that stands alone, voluntarily in the dark but independent, like Lucifer. One of the chief sources of the Nativity Ode, Tasso's "Nel giorno della Natività," ends by comparing its *"humil"* offering to the *"odori"* of the Magi,[17] hoping in effect that all birthday songs will blend as one hymn. In one sense, Milton intensifies Tasso's cooperative stress by linking the sound of his Magi's "odors sweet" to the sound of his "humble ode," and this humility paradoxically improves his prophetic hopes. But it is difficult not to read these lines dramatically, in a way that stresses rivalry (not least perhaps with Tasso) rather than cooperation:

> See how from far upon the eastern road
> The star-led wizards haste with odors sweet!
> Oh run, prevent them with thy humble ode,
> And lay it lowly at his blessed feet;
> Have thou the honor first thy Lord to greet . . .
>
> [22-26] [18]

"Wizards," we know, are simply wise men, and "prevent" means to come before—which meaning itself is troubling enough. But it is hard not to recall these wizards when later one encounters the "timbreled anthems dark" of the "sable-stolèd sorcerers" of Osiris, since their chosen darkness in contrast with the sometime brightness of their sun god is just that of Milton's "darksome . . . mortal clay." The wizards in any case are "star-led" partly because they are astrologers, like the Egyptians. [19] They, too, have their star-muse, in other words, and who is to say it is not Lucifer, who still stands in the dawn next to the new star of Bethlehem? Or, conversely, how is the poet himself to know whether, in his haste to forestall his rivals, he has really invoked the harmonious Urania and not some more baneful influence? Having wished for priority, it is perhaps too late for him to "join [his] voice unto the angel choir," even though that union would usher him into the presence of light. The beautiful allusion to Isaiah's seraph, "From out his secret altar touched with hallowed fire," cannot quite satisfy the reader (possibly because the moment is as secret as it is sacred) that the seraph's coal is not sparked at the wrong furnace. It is disturbing that, having invoked Urania in the third stanza, Milton then steadily apostrophizes himself, in an "ode to himself," on the threshold of the "Hymn." [20]

Many readers have noticed that the "designed asymmetry" or "intellectual core" [21] of the poem is the eclipse of the pagan gods, each of which, tradition states, is a devil in disguise. I hope to have shown from my own point of view why it is important for Milton to insist with disproportionate emphasis that "The Oracles are dumm" (173): in that case only one vocal oracle would remain, his own. Each of the ensuing tableaux dissipates a false enlightenment in darkness, and a false hymnody ("breathèd spell," "service quaint," the invocation of Moloch [209], "timbreled anthems") in a cacophony of groans and shrieks that has at least the virtue of sincerity. It is difficult not to identify to some extent with the creatures in this nearly universal rout. The first tableau, indeed, the rout of Apollo, which Keats will take as a dubious model for his own priesthood in the "Ode to Psyche," invites comparison with the secretly housed altar and twilit setting of Milton's own call to witness in the proem: "No nightly trance, or breathèd spell,/Inspires the pale-eyed priest from the prophetic cell" (179–80).[22] It would not be easy to void the world of its local and accidental energies without a pang, or a qualm. I am not urging that the Nativity Ode is "really" a skeptical and syncretistic poem but only that Milton is alerted by his own resonances to the knowledge that true inspiration is difficult to recognize and dangerous to engross to oneself.

If it is difficult to part with the gods of nature cults, it is still more difficult to forfeit the vitality of fallen Nature seen simply as nature, as Milton shows in his miniature elegy on "the parting genius."[23] Here the darkling prosopopoeia merges gently with the natural scene it mirrors: "With flower-woven tresses torn,/The Nymphs in twilight shade of tangled thickets mourn." Nature disinspirited, like "Amaryllis in the shade" ("Lycidas," 68), is even yet a "maze" that bears traces of daemonic sportiveness: "the yellow-skirted fays/Fly after the night-steeds, leaving their moon-loved maze" (235–36). Between the grandly airy formality of Heaven and the imprisoning forms of the lower regions, there is an informal zone that Milton most regrets forsaking: the labyrinth of Nature, with her "gaudy trim" and tangled tresses. This place is covered with "speckled vanity," yet it is also the place of Earth's summer, and must go the way of the "age of gold," snowed over by a happier winter "month, and this the happy morn" (1).[24] In deference to the vast unities of light and sound he celebrates, Milton gives up the plurality of fancy's maze: "moonèd Ashtaroth" being plural, for example, the world before the incarnation must have been as lavish in moons as in those Tyrian maids who now must mourn their wounded fertility god.

The choice against Nature is the Penseroso choice, and it also reflects the turning from youthful pleasures to Orphic asceticism in the "Elegia Sexta," which ends with Milton's report to Diodati that he has written the present poem. The Nativity Ode entertains the hope, however, that all the lost pleasures of the natural world can be restored without moral or generic sacrifice. Necessarily in imitation of the "usurpèd sway" cast by the Dragon, Milton's "Hymn" aims to cast itself outward by keeping open the portals of its palatial form and urging the reentry of all that it has rejected by reforming the sublunary world on new foundations. Nature is recalled in a state of covering grace.[25] The native strains of pastoral and folklore return through the quaintness of tone and subject in the penultimate stanza.[26] Martial poetry returns in the last stanza with the militant angels for its new heroes. Nature and her arts return, then, by celestial dispensation, unclear though it is whether the new nature will grow more like heaven, or heaven more like the new nature. This question recurs, with special force, when on comes to read the Intimations Ode of Wordsworth.

The redemption of nature does not afford Milton's conclusion the exuberance one might have expected. In the last stanza the tone of the humble ode writer unexpectedly returns, as if to let the Child sleep. This quiet accompanies a sudden narrowing of Milton's baroque panorama,[27] just at the point where the poem becomes truly a hymn, no longer restive or individualistic. Everything stabilizes. Angels remain in the scene, bearing witness and bearing out the poet's continued witness, but their stable configuration is represented as a curiously stolid "order serviceable." The new star, unlike Isaiah's star of the morning, is a magnificent servant, "with handmaid lamp attending." The poem's last equipoise is an oxymoron, "courtly stable."[28] All powers, influences, and graces shrink down, like Lybic Ammon's horn, fixing themselves in submission to the unexpressive Word, and Milton's suddenly more "tedious song" bows down as well, extinguishing the last spark of Lucifer, whose presence had even touched the title of the poem.[29] As its morning closes, the Nativity Ode is more than an ode, and less.

Even at the risk of unearthing the old disputes about Milton's sincerity, I have tried to indicate that the Nativity Ode is as much preoccupied with the vocation of the poet as "Lycidas," for example, is commonly understood to be. My reading has been decidedly a "Romantic" one, committed to the insistence that ("without knowing it," as one does certainly assume) Milton was of the party of Lucifer the light-bearer. The Nativity Ode celebrates the birth of an authentic voice, and the end of speechlessness. It is most crucially about its own coming to be, and in this respect it preconditions most odes until Keats's "Ode to Psyche." It is this inwardness at the heart of Milton's public occasion, however, this virtual eclipse of an old birth with a new, that exposes the poem to the surprising subversions of tone and structure that must go unremarked by any deliberately solemn interpretation.

Still, the Nativity Ode is not at all breezily or simply a "Romantic" poem. (Not, of course, that good Romantic poems are either.) To the question, What is the nature of inspiration? Milton's ode offers a very complex but also rather old-fashioned answer. In Milton there is no easy correlation between transcendence and inspiration; indeed, there seems to be something that *is*, precisely, "nature" in the conception of a poem, something not so much the Devil as the old Adam. Hence the poignancy of having to abandon, even temporarily, the "tangled tresses" of Nature, and hence the fitness of her having uttered, "with speeches fair"—though speciously enough—the first invocation of the "Hymn" proper. The sources of light are celestial; we share them, and perhaps finally even become them, like stars, and like the "base" notes sung in unison with the music of the spheres. But the poet, struggle as he may with conscience and the call of humility, cannot and will not join the choir. His *imitatio Christi* is nowhere plainer than in his wish to enter the "darksome house" of his own motives and resources, to eclipse the light with a darkness, perhaps even an ominous darkness however strangely conceived and borne, a darkness that is prevenient, preventative, and makes the light much more unstable than the handmaid lamplight of Milton's hymnic conclusion.

3

"Alexander's Feast" and the Tyranny of Music

The diminished last stanza of Milton's Nativity Ode is a "Dying Fall." In some degree, Milton's ode is Pindaric;[1] it also has something of *pictura* about it, and perhaps even more of the masque;[2] but its dominant theme, as the "resolution" of the last stanza helps to show, is *ut musica poesis*. The Nativity Ode, together with Milton's "At a Solemn Musick," looks forward to the Odes for Music that include Dryden's "Alexander's Feast."[3]

Before Milton, the elevated ode had not been closely associated with music. Drayton's odes may have been sung to the harp, as he wanted them to be, but they are not choral, nor do they attempt to re-create the festive settings of Pindar's Epinicia. The etymological precision of Jonson's stanzaic titles alludes to the dance of his mind and not to a possible choreography for his ode; his ordinarily keen interest in music is confined in the Cary-Morison Ode to a pun on the word "ayre" at line 64. In the early seventeenth century the alliance of poetry and music was represented in large part by songs and airs for the lute. When Shakespeare's Dumaine (*Love's Labour's Lost*, IV. iii. 93) mentions "odes," he is thinking of songs and airs, as is Gabriel Harvey when in a letter to Spenser he complains of a recent vogue for the "amorous odious sonnet." (Harvey's phrase is thus interpreted by Shuster, *The English Ode*, p. 31.) Stanzaically more adventurous songs for music first appeared in Francis Davison's *Poetical Miscellany* (1602), and they continued to appear in the (often very fine) congregational devotions to which I have confined the word "hymn." Unlike the hymn, the secular ode moved away from its musical antecedents.[4] At the same time, though, its musical imagery steadily increased, drawing on Orphic *topoi* and their Christian adaptations, with special stress, as in the Nativity Ode, on the kindred figures of World Harmony and Soul Harmony. Indeed, the fact that musical imagery and musical adaptation are mutually exclusive in lyrics of this period is extremely significant. A poem that sustains musical figures claims to *be* music, and therefore, of course, to need no accompaniment. Poetic language, such a poem implies, can move its own trees and raise its own Thebes.

Harmony is featured in the Nativity Ode to persuade us that the speech of the Infant has the unique self-presence of music, whence he derives the infallibility of his command—of that power that "bespake" the departure of all inferior influences. The eloquence of Schopenhauer on music as self-presence (as command or Will) is already to be found in the earliest poetry about music, but thereafter civilized poetry gradually submitted to an outlook that is, as the learned treatises of Milton's time fashionably put it, "syntagmata," or analyzed into parts. For Milton, sound coincides with the will only when it joins intelligible words. Thus he weakens the purely acoustic summoning power that is awarded to music in all mantic cultures.[5] From this standpoint, the various myths attesting to the power of music change somewhat in meaning. Amphion raised Thebes either with his lyre or his voice, it is not clear which, but it does not matter, since his voice was *lyric*, was enabled by its lyricism to speak words that in themselves could not have raised a straw. Or again, David's musical cure of Saul's madness typologically represents salvation through the Logos, but as instrumental sound it is not in any sense miraculous. The rise of the Ode for Music after Milton, as John Hollander has shown and as Dryden everywhere seems to admit, accompanies the collapse of the belief that either poetry *or* music can have mantic properties. This belief was impossible to sustain after poetry and music had been torn asunder by the recognition that they are not identical to each other, and therefore require each other's accompaniment to fulfill any possible notion of completeness. Thus the later seventeenth-century revival of the collaboration between poetry and music results in a "trivialization," as Hollander puts it, of musical imagery that marks "the untuning of the sky."[6]

Milton proclaims that creature-music, the hymns of man, are the "base" note of the universal diapason—or at least were so at the Nativity and will be so again. Milton seems to feel that this is still a vital figure, but he taints the figure, as if to concede the coming of rationalism, with his grim play on the word "base," which English had not yet salvaged for music by respelling. An Ode for Music cannot accomplish Milton's ideological poise. Its text points away from itself to the Phrygian flutes, Lydian strings, Dorian brass, and so forth, leading finally to Cecilia's organ, which "brought an angel down" (says Dryden) and so supplanted celestial music instead of joining it.[7] Like the Nativity Ode, "Alexander's Feast" is a Descent that routs pagan sounds; but it also imperils Christian sounds of the sort that Milton could still evoke.

I shall be concerned mainly with the language of "Alexander's Feast," but there is still more to say of a theoretical nature about the music of Odes for Music; that is, about their "harmony." During the seventeenth century the word "harmony" became specialized. It came to refer, as it does today, to chordal relationships, and lost its antique acceptation as a proportionate sequence of sounds. A scholar like Milton could, of course, recover and admire what "harmony" means in Pythagoras, Plato, or Aristotle, with all its old suggestion of political and social as well as celestial order; but precisely because he had two ideas of the word, he must have had a difficult time imagining what either the harmony of the spheres or the soul's harmony actually sound like.[8] I would speculate that in the Nativity Ode, during most of the "Hymn," harmony is imagined as chordal—organlike—because Milton so strongly insists on the simultaneity of its music at every tier of the Creation. The "rustic row" of singing shepherds, by contrast, might suggest polyphony, while the final "order serviceable" of the angels, which I have interpreted as a measured loss, could be understood as harmony in the Greek sense. However profoundly attuned with the stars, Greek harmony might well sound impoverished alongside the rich resolution of sequence in simultaneity of which the organ alone is capable: "The air, such pleasure loth to lose,/Still prolongs each heavenly close" (99–100). Dryden's Cecilia similarly "added length to solemn sounds" (165), and hence we may assume that Dryden, too, leaned toward the modern idea of harmony. If so, then he would have felt a discrepancy between his idea of harmony and the contrapuntal score that Signor Baptist had prepared for his earlier 1687 ode.[9]

In a written score, the impression of simultaneity is not, of course, auditory but visual. But music is also silent in profounder ways. As Kretschmar tells Leverkühn in *Doktor Faustus*, referring chiefly to the scores of Bach, sound has a visual component, an "appearance" that raises the question whether the true objective of sound may not be its own sublimation and silencing as "theory." However fanciful it may seem in reference to Dryden and his contemporaries, this observation reveals an unquestionable irony in any celebration of the "Power of Musick." The "theoretical music" that is immutable, and therefore merits the praise of ascetics from Plato to Stephen Gosson, is just what odes for music can never celebrate.[10] "What passion cannot Music raise or quell?" is Dryden's keynote for his 1687 ode, and it suggests that "practical music" is not the stable sound of truth but rhetoric. Practical music orchestrates "The various Turns of Chance below" ("Alexander's Feast," l. 86) and determines the soul's sequence of affections. Because it commands the will rather than *being* Will, practical music can be shown from the several standpoints reviewed above to be as subversive and secondary a medium as poetry. A combined critique of music and poetry is the purpose, I believe, cheerfully and tolerantly framed, of "Alexander's Feast."

II

Among all the forms of lyric, the ode is most jealous of its command (by invocation) of Voice. The ode is designed, as Roman Jakobson says in a somewhat different context, "to check whether the channel works," to "attract the attention of the interlocutor or to confirm his continued attention. . . . This set for CONTACT, or . . . PHATIC function, may be displayed by a profuse exchange of ritualized formulas."[11] Still, however, we have seen a tendency among the great odes of the seventeenth century (and nothing sets them apart more clearly from the "Pindarique" effusions of the same period) to approach invocation with extreme caution and in some instances to avoid it entirely. They have another means of commanding Voice at their disposal, which is more plausibly effective because it establishes the hegemony of the addressed power without seeming to demand its immanence. This alternative is the pars epica,[12] or etiological narrative, which is a sleight of presentation: through the intercession of Mnemosyne, it places the poet in the originary scene where breath first entered the numen or Voice that, in turn, by a tacit extension of the channel, inspires the poet himself. In St. Cecilia odes, the etiology of the organ, powered as it is by inhuman breath, is well suited for this line of transmission.

It is to the convention of the pars epica that Dryden alludes, in "Alexander's Feast," when he says that Timotheus's "Song began from *Jove*" (25). The song, in other words, is like the moment of birth chosen by Milton for his inaugural ode. Itself set within Dryden's own narrative, the mock narrative of Timotheus redoubles the distance between the human and the divine, just as King Henry's interpolated exhortation redoubles the pastness of the past in "Agincourt." Etiologies, like everything else that pertains to the ode, are subject to ridicule from the instant of their first appearance. One cannot disregard Euripides' contempt for Tiresias's etiological pendantry in *The Bacchae*; and the narrative of Callimachus's "Hymn to Zeus" is decadent at the least, if not decidedly mock hymnic. The birth of Euphrosyne in *L'Allegro* may also be mentioned, as may Sin's autobiography in *Paradise Lost*. The absurdity of Timotheus's story and the dramatically enforced further absurdity of its eager acceptance by Alexander and the rest of the audience point to the self-analysis that overspreads Dryden's entire poem. For one thing, Timotheus discredits in advance the etiological convention that Dryden himself must rely on to show, in the last stanza, that Cecilia and her organ really did begin "from Jove."

There is also a complex structure of topical allusion set in place by Timotheus's narrative when it is viewed as panegyric. If Dryden himself had been the Timotheus of the Stuarts, and if his Alexander has qualities that are recognizable in King William[13] and also in Milton's Satan, then clearly the Alexander story *ab ovo* was chosen for this libretto, which Dryden only reluctantly agreed to write, for his own compensatory delight and instruction. "Ye Princes, rais'd by Poets to the Gods,/And Alexander'd up in lying odes,/Believe not ev'ry flattering Knave's report," wrote Dryden in his late Chaucer translation, "The Cock and the Fox." Fulsome odes to "great Nassau" were rife, but it is, in fact, with regard only to the better of them that Dryden could envision the poet as a Fox, and therefore suggest to himself that "music" is a menace to society in proportion as it is excellent: that is, as it is persuasive.

The "Preface to Fables" (1700) shows that Dryden was unable to shrug off Jeremy Collier's invective against the immorality of his plays. Collier's *Short View* appeared in 1698, a year after "Alexander's Feast" was written, but what he would probably argue against the profane arts may already have occurred to Dryden from reading Collier's essay "On Musick," reprinted in 1697, which contains a précis of the Timotheus story. Although Collier laments that the music of the ancients could "command" more powerfully than that of the moderns, this sentiment (an old convention of the *laus musicae* that gained new force, in Dryden's time, from the Battle of the Books) is offset by another that sounds more like Collier's own: "to have our Passions lie at the mercy of a little minstrelsy . . . is a sign that we are not so great as we might be."[14] In "Alexander's Feast," Dryden agrees with Collier that the Power of Music exposes the weakness of the human will, but, in effect, he also agrees with Collier's more conventional sentiment, that the weakness of will is paradoxically protected, nowadays, by the weakness, the loss of "command," that characterizes modern music. For Dryden as for Milton, redemption and nostalgia for imperfection are inseparable.

There is no need to suggest, though, that the sentiments of "Alexander's Feast" are new to Dryden, and amount merely to the palinode of a dethroned laureate. Much earlier, in the powerful irregular ode "To the pious Memory of . . . Mrs. Anne Killigrew" (1685), Dryden had questioned the ethics of hyperbole. Having addressed the young lady's *"heav'n-born mind"* (34), just as his banqueters will later immortalize Alexander (" 'A present deity!' "), Dryden turns soon after to a very different sort of apostrophe:

> O gracious God! how far have we
> Profan'd thy heav'nly gift of poesy:
> Made prostitute and profligate the Muse,
> Whose harmony was first ordained above
> For tongues of angels, and for hymns of love!

[56-61][15]

Dryden was, of course, a connoisseur of attitudes, as his plays and his great *Essay on Dramatic Poetry* attest, and his scholars have long warned against committing him to any one attitude. But their caveat should not extend, as it seems to me, to the assumption that for the sake of decorum or generic experiment he is prepared to adopt naïve attitudes. Rather he exposes naïvetés by seeming to adopt them, and it may be said that no genre is more suited to *that* kind of experiment than the ode.

Most readers have agreed that "Alexander's Feast" harbors a slight irony, which they have placed in the service of the Arms versus Letters topic: heroic poetry, this reading concludes, is a greater thing than heroic action.[16] As I experience the poem, though, neither of these vocations is given much to recommend it, and the characters of Alexander and Timotheus do not seem, in any case, merely typical.[17] Dryden sets his tone with his first words: " 'Twas at the royal feast," echoing the jaunty opening of *Absalom and Achitophel*, suggests the vicinity of satire, and, more specifically, prepares for a satire like that of *Absalom*, which is directed not against heroism per se but against the unwarranted "assumption" (cf. l. 39) of heroism. Perhaps the liveliest character in *Absalom* is Milton's Satan, whose example continually shapes Achitophel. So in the present poem, Satan sits in Alexander's place:

> Aloft in awful State
> The God-like Heroe sate
> On his Imperial Throne.[18]

If Satan is an errant son of God, and in that sense not a true son, so "Philip's warlike son" (his mortality thus firmly established at line 2) is a spurious offspring of Jove—who is himself a false god descending in the form of Milton's "old Dragon." Dryden's Satanic Alexander, however, is a buffoon, like the outwitted Satan made physically ludicrous in Milton's later Books. Dryden divides the Miltonic Satan between Alexander and Timotheus, who is also "plac'd on high," and whose "tuneful Quire" follows his command just as the "valiant Peers" follow Alexander's. Bard and Hero together span the whole of Satan's nature, as sycophantic seducer and seduced prince. So much, then, on this view, for heroic action *and* heroic poetry.

Whether Thaïs is related to Milton's Sin is doubtful, but she does share her name with the prostitute in Terence who told her lover of the moment that he was her favorite.[19] For this remark Terence's Thaïs became the heroine of Dante's pocket of Flatterers in the *Inferno*, where her profession links her with the neighboring pocket of Panders and Seducers. Alexander's Thaïs is clearly enough identified in Diodorus Siculus (XVII. 72) to make this extra allusion seem needless, but Dryden does need it, I think, to make his entire cast of characters demonic and his feast a Pandemonium. The irony of Thaïs's sitting "*like* a blooming Eastern Bride" may be elaborated. Thaïs in Dante is the last flatterer the Pilgrim meets before he reaches the pocket of the Simonists; he has had a vision, in other words, of the corrupted Church (the Eastern Bride of Christ) before he encounters its corruptors. If Dryden's Thaïs offers a similar preview in simile, then she becomes an ante- and antitype of "divine Cecilia," mother of the church-loft organ, who will supplant *both* of Alexander's seducers, Thaïs and Timotheus, in the last stanza. Alongside this view of Thaïs may be placed Prynne's description of the contrapuntal obscuring of words by composers (*Histriomastix*, 1633) as a "whorish harmony to tickle the ear," so that "the authority and power of judgment is taken away both from the minde and the ears utterly."[20]

Cecilia's enlargement of "the former narrow bounds" is not only an expansion of Timotheus's "breathing flute" into the many pipes of her own "vocal frame," but also a moral enlargement that extends government from the state to the soul—or at least, as we shall see, this is what it *should* be. From this viewpoint the affinity of Dryden's ode with the Nativity Ode can be clarified: just as Peace in Milton heralds the coming of Christ, so here Cecilia "drew an angel down," and just as "the wedded maid and virgin mother" of Milton's proem contrasts with the sexual violence of paganism (stanza twenty-two configures battery, mutilation, and fertility), so the pacific "sweet enthusiast" Cecilia leads down her angel in contrast with the violent magnetism of her antitypes:

> *Thaïs* led the Way,
> To light him to his Prey,
> And, like another *Hellen*, fir'd another *Troy*.[21]

Like Milton's ode, "Alexander's Feast" is an attempt to exorcize demons; but Dryden also resembles Milton in waiting too long to subdue the color and excitement of his narrative. His last stanza is a comparatively weak aftermath, though it is by no means dull. Dryden has borrowed the structural principle of his poem, not from the idea of sacred music, which is fixed, one, and suited by nature to fill only one stanza, but from the rich feeling of plurality that is represented by the Greek modes.[22] Once committed to the modal scheme, therefore, by far the greater part of the poem must celebrate the pleasures of vicissitude, leaving too little space for the grander vocality of the organ to "frame" the "changes" (also in the musical sense; see line 72) that it has allegedly "Enlarged" upon. The subversive logic of these contrasts is tellingly present in the final epigram: the music of Timotheus is expansive, whereas that of Cecilia contracts the universe. In these ways, then, the affective experience of Dryden's ode, enhanced by the variety and duration of the music, undermines its attempted rout of the Passions. Whereas the 1687 ode had framed its review of the Passions between two choral stanzas on universal harmony, which are inspired by Milton's affirmations of this theme, Dryden in the present poem no longer seems interested in offsetting the mutability of his stanzaically sprawling "epic middle." But his irregular structure, while it may overwhelm his moral, nevertheless does allow the enlargement of his satire. In gauging that enlargement more precisely, we can come to recognize what disrupts both celebration *and* satire in Dryden's ode.

Timotheus's deification of a mortal is mocked by Dryden's setting for it: "A present Deity, they shout around;/A present deity the vaulted Roofs rebound." This walling off of the sky, which creates the acoustics of the fable's "lofty Sound," represents the unanswered invocation of a poet whose song does not "begin from Jove" any more than his subject does.[23] An echo fills the space from which the god is absent. (The vaulted roofs intervene only for thematic reasons; later, "The many rend the *Skies*, with loud Applause.") Timotheus's myth, like his invocation, is a false currency: it makes Alexander a bad coin purchased by a too deeply impressed crowd as soon as Jove "stamp'd an Image of himself, a Sov'raign of the World." Not *the* sovereign, that is, because sovereigns are as cheap as crowns.

Alexander is, of course, "ravish'd," not least by the lubricious account of his begetting, and plays the fool; but it is not only he who is open to ridicule. His Jovian "nod" only "*seems* to shake the spheres," in part because the fable that has ravished him has nothing in common with the music of the spheres from which the vaulted roofs exclude it. It is as unwarranted for the bard as it is for the hero to "assume the god." After an anacreontic visit to the bottle in the third stanza, the poem returns to its analysis of the Power of Music, having now established the close collusion of Bacchus and Venus with Timotheus. From this point onward Dryden sustains a joke that deprives Timotheus even of his right to be called a seducer.[24] For a while, "The Master" (69) seems still to have the exclusive honor of controlling his master: "Love was Crown'd, but Musique won the Cause." But even before this, his wizardry has become superfluous: "At length, with Love and Wine at once oppress'd,/ The vanquish'd Victor sunk upon her Breast." There is little praise, or even respect, in these lines for the wholly superseded Power of Music. If it be objected that Alexander was encouraged to drink by music—music in this case remaining the formal cause of his over-throw—one can only answer that thirst has proved sorcery sufficient for most emperors. Only the complete lowering of taste and resis-tance allows the sheer madness that music allegedly causes in the sixth stanza. "War," sings Timotheus earlier, blithely innocent of plagiary, "is Toil and Trouble;/Honour but an empty Bubble." But the real witch in this play is "Lovely *Thaïs*."

Alexander pities Darius, who is "Fallen, fallen, fallen, fallen,/ Fallen from his high Estate," but he soon "sinks" himself, since "Pity melts the Mind to Love." Self-pity, however, is chiefly involved: Timotheus has aroused pity for Darius in order to contrast the loyalty of those present, especially his own loyalty, with the treachery of the Persians against their king. The irony of Alexander's reaction is all-encompassing:

> With down-cast Looks the joyless Victor sate,
> Revolveing in his alter'd Soul
> The various Turns of chance below;

The revolutions are not his own, they are his "master's," and the "turns of chance" stressed pointedly by Timotheus summarize Dryden's critique of the Power of Music. The next stanza reveals further that Timotheus is equally subject to turns of chance and that these are not just the capricious whims of his emperor. Timotheus is not master of but mastered by the conditions and conventions of his own medium: "The Mighty Master smil'd to see/That Love was in the next Degree." Here is another seducer seduced; the slyness of his "changes" is only the sleight of modality itself. Submissive to his five modes of persuasion, Timotheus himself is "Fallen, fallen, fallen, fallen,/Fallen." When the last "change" is reached, one senses that Alexander has turned, not to madness, but to his essential character, inspired by Timotheus's favorite genre, the martial ode. The course of music's power is revealed as a cycle of formal determinacies beyond the control of audience or artist: what raised Thebes razes Persepolis. Yet it is doubtful, at the same time, whether "music" itself accomplished either the beginning or the end of the culture in question: "Thaïs led the way."

The last stanza closes the satire where it began, with the *Absalom* opening: "Thus, long ago/Ere . . ." But then, at the turn to Cecilia, a difficulty arises that confirms the irreversible tyranny of modal sequences. "Ere priestcraft did begin," begins *Absalom*. Cecilia, who enters legend with the rise of priestcraft, does not herself appear at the beginning of the last stanza, but an awkward image does appear that makes one wish for the speedy return of the "breathing flute" and "Sounding lyre" of the heathens: "'Ere heaving Bellows learn'd to blow,/While Organs yet were mute" (155–58).[25] This sudden tone-deafness on Dryden's part is not a "controlled irony." It is simply a mistake, a failure to make the turn, owing, as it were, to the gathered momentum of the poem's previous direction, and it reveals, as mistakes usually do, the bias that the "frame" of the poem cannot contain: an imbalance favoring the number and exuberance of the Passions, even of passions that have been ridiculed. Like a comedy heroine, Cecilia is a faceless lady in whose behalf the plot alone, and not her own charisma, can rescue the stage from a host of energetic Vices.

Dryden recovers from his lapse of aural sympathy, and there is much grace in the rest of the stanza,[26] but traces remain of the difficulty that now stands revealed. Cecilia's music, "With Nature's Mother-Wit, and Arts unknown before," significantly differs from the poetry of Anne Killigrew, who "Art had . . . none, yet wanted none:/For nature did that want supply" (71–72). "Wit" sharpens the simplicity even of Cecilia's "nature," and the resulting impression that her art reflects a new and newly confining commitment to form (like that of Milton at the close of the Nativity Ode) is deepened by her capture of the angel. This drawing down signals yet another defection of Will; this time in a region where the will is said to stand firm, and thereby recalls, in this last instant—Satan. He returns to occupy the space that is vacated by the uninvoked Cecilia's quiet lack of presence,[27] and he may stand as my final emblem in these first chapters for the self-disordering of the ode. He is the force of disruption, the freedom of music, and the bane of composers, and he is simply too unruly to fit the vocal frame.[28]

III

> Give ample room and verge enough
> The characters of hell to trace.
>
> —Gray, "The Bard"

The difference between seventeenth-century odes and nearly all later odes is very great. The ode from Jonson through the time of Dryden remains a poem for public or publicly shareable occasions; its mode is oratorical and its purpose epideictic. Some later odes will retain all or part of this civic-mindedness, and some will not, but henceforth in this study a great divide will have been crossed, with occasional backtracking, into a region where unashamed self-communion is held to be as dignified and, in its own way, as sociable as public speech. Akenside, a transitional poet between these regions, actually put the question in his "Ode XII, To Sir Francis Drake, Bart.": "wherefore should we part / The public and the private weal?"[29] It has been important to show, however, that odes before and after this watershed have much in common; generally understood, the form, ethos, and occasional nature of the ode are unaffected by change in the history of thought and taste.

Even the distinction with which I have here begun must be qualified. Seventeenth-century odes are meant to be public, meant, that is, to be hymns, encomia, funeral orations, and so on; but, in fact, they are already personal and dissident, in one or another of these words' many senses. However distinctly heard, they harbor a residue that must be overheard. I do not really mean by this that they are "ambivalent," because that characterization would imply a vacillation that is controlled by a triumph of form. They are not ambivalent, because their residue is a violence against form that is not steadily subdued. Whether they are covertly antinomian like the Nativity Ode, colored by sedition like "Agincourt" and the Desmond Ode (Marvell's Cromwell Ode and Dryden's panegyrics would notably enlarge this group), or simply drawn to an imagery of dwindling and misshapenness like the great odes of Jonson and Dryden, odes also subvert the persuasive power of their formality. Their circles are empty and broken; they roof over their figurations of light and the sky; they institute sea changes between the present and the absent, all in the service of some excluded force that keeps returning, uncannily, from within. When this interior force yields to some established power from without, the ode diminishes toward its end, scales itself down for its occasion, which is, invariably, the glorification of some power or authority not its own.

The theme of the ode, like that of tragedy, is the dialectic of death and birth, presented in one of two patterns: either something is born to replace a loss or something is destroyed to make room for a birth. Perhaps this theme is simply what one means when one speaks of an "occasion" or event: the fall of an arrival. The theme of the ode, in any case, is always its occasion; in an "ode to" the theme is the object of ceremony and in an "ode on" the theme is the ceremony itself. In the text of an ode these two sides of its occasion appear as invocation (the ceremony) and etiological myth (the object of ceremony). As we have seen, invocation may be latent in many odes but it is never uninvolved, since the myth of descent that informs all odes is itself, like invocation, a calling down to the present. Invocation and myth are signifier and signified; the text of an ode, like a sign, is manifest only at the level of the signifier; hence, the latency of invocation and the predominance of myth is precisely what I have been calling a "sleight of presentation," an insistence that the signifier is the signified. The elevated tone required of invocation rises to meet its object, which is meanwhile descending like the Dioscuri or Christ, being drawn down like Cecilia's angel, or even, as in a funeral ode, lowered into a grave. But the numen can only appear as the myth of its being and having come to be; absented by the necessity of being referred to, it is *always* buried. Hence, to restate the dialectical theme of the ode, whatever dies or is figured as absent is the object of celebration, and what is born in its place is the celebration itself. All that remains for an ode to invoke with success, therefore, is its own existence.

The excluded force reenters the poem through the necessary gap between its buoyantly rising celebration and its descending, or condescending, celebrity. This force is endlessly elusive because, as the repressed, it appears only in symptoms. Once its point of entry is remarked, though, its traces will be seen to overspread and scar the text. These traces are the written component of the ode, the *design* that stabilizes both invocation and inspiration, only to confirm their differences from itself. The irregularity of the ode stanza, which is meant to represent the frenzy of inspired speech, instead betrays speech to writing by drawing attention to the stanza as a shape. Every detail of the shape reproduces this betrayal. The rhythms of speech are constantly at odds with the graphic distortions of meter, of enjambment, of stanzaic closure, and of rhymes that either recur too quickly or are too obliquely and widely spaced to leave an audible impression.

It is only when one thinks of the ode's nostalgia for voice and its "vocal" tone that one can notice that the writing of the ode is itself a trace of disruptive force. As a displaced symptom, writing differs so extremely in character from force itself that its origin is wholly disguised: when we speak of "form" we mean writing, the very opposite, we assume, of force. However different it may be from its traces as writing, though, the force of disruption is itself obscurely figured forth in the ode. Thus far its identity has seemed devilish: a wise infant that chooses oblivion, a Druid, a light-bringing star that is impatient for darkness, a tangled thicket, a grounded serpent-god. But to associate this force with demons personifies it excessively, and too quickly domesticates it as part of a figural plan. That which disrupts the ode is indifferent to command and formality, and it is its indifference, perhaps even more than the mystery of its identity, that mars the calling of the poet even while it inspires his most stubborn affections. It is not finally a question of demons but of the daemonic, and writers of odes in the next two centuries will challenge the indifference of the daemonic by calling it Nature. Nature: the force that returns in writing, as we shall now see in the odes of Gray and Collins, just when it seems that the ode has supplanted every mode of being but its own.

4

Thomas Gray's Feather'd Cincture

Selima, Horace Walpole's favorite cat, has no sense of distance:
"Again she stretched, again she bent,/Nor knew the gulf between."[1]
Unlike Gray's more knowing creatures, she thinks that she has only
to reach out in order to possess "The genii of the stream" (15). She
thinks this partly because she is a "nymph," and belongs, like Milton's
tangled nymphs in their tangled thicket, within the compass of the
half-natural, half-figural object of her desire. The comfortable wealth
of Walpole's fish, their "golden gleam," discloses to her classicist's
eyes a familiar vestige of Apollo—of an Apollo in "armor" like the
more brilliant figure Gray elsewhere introduces for the use of many
future ode writers: Hyperion, with his "glittering shafts of war."
But Walpole's fish only vouchsafe a last glitter; their scaly armor is
defensive not militant, and they are deeply overlaid by the japanning
of civilized comfort. Their living artifice recalls the morning-room
atmosphere of natural illusion in the opening lines of the poem:
"'Twas on a lofty vase's side,/Where China's gayest art had dyed/
The azure flowers that blow." This deftly poised figure, with its
evocation of the mixed hauteur and frivolity of Walpole himself and
its merger of death, breath, and blossoming, distills the culture in
which Gray finds himself trying to be a bard. Selima parodies Gray's
Bard in advance; she expresses her desire despite "the gulf between,"
and plunges to a watery grave:

> Eight times emerging from the flood
> She mewed to every watery god,

> Some speedy aid to send.
> No dolphin came. . . .
>
> [31–34]

Arion's power of music is no more, and the single remaining muse that is not, cannot be, invoked by Selima's eight mews is Polyhymnia.

The gulf that Selima does not know until she fatally discovers it to be the "slippery verge" of self-consciousness is the *abîme infranchissable*" that Count de Bonstetten (Gray's last Walpole) described as yawning steadily between the poet and all his efforts to join the stream of life.[2] Gray's irony about his own alienation is reflected in his having devoted most of his rare poetic attempts—for he neither "stretched" nor "bent" very often—to the "vocal transports" ("Bard," 120) of the ode. That he took the term "ode" seriously is most evident, as is usual with Gray, from his good-humored disclaimers, as in this complaint about Walpole's indiscrimination of titles: "You have talked to [Dodsley] of six *odes*, for so you are pleased to call everything I write, though it be but a receipt for apple-dumplings. . . . I don't know but a may send him very soon (by your hands) an ode to his own tooth, a high Pindaric on stilts."[3] Before "The Progress of Poesy," to which he here refers, Gray had worked only with Horatian meters and tonalities, but from the first, he had used the ode in one form or another to explore his unvarying personal theme, which concerns the impossibility of narrowing "the gulf between."

It is true that the speaker's isolation is pervasive not just in the odes but also in the "Elegy," where the world of action is forfeited "to darkness and to me." The speaker of the "Elegy," alienated from his locale by virtue of his "Fair Science," remains anonymously mysterious in the eyes of his anonymous neighbors. But although the tone of the "Elegy" reverberates from the speaker's solitude, the poem still differs significantly from any of Gray's odes. Even the quality of solitude itself in the "Elegy" is different: it is voluntary, a Penseroso choice intimately uniting the speaker with darkness in a way that is suggested by the quiet zeugma of the fourth line.[4] In the ensuing lines, solitude in the *locus sanctus* becomes a jealously guarded tryst between the melancholic and his gloom: "The moping owl does to the moon complain/Of such as, wandering near her secret bower,/Molest her ancient solitary reign." Solitude has become an identity, a mark of identification, and results in what is rare in Gray until "The Bard," the charismatic visibility of the speaking subject: " 'Oft have we seen him. . . . ' " He is alienated not toward oblivion, then, but in order to become visible, and he can therefore conclude with confidence that he has been seen by "his Father and his God." Without touching upon the modulations of social sympathy in the "Elegy" (which are also dutifully rehearsed in the odes), one can see that in that poem solitude is ultimately a triumph of communion, and that in this respect, again, the Elegy stands apart from the odes.[5]

For Gray, the letter *o* (the vocative, the vowel of the ode) is most often an empty circle: "I have struck a medal on myself: the device is thus O , and the motto *Nihilissimo*" (*Walpole's Correspondence* XIII. 228). This is an apt device for Gray's experiments with invocation. The slightest and least memorable of these, but in many ways also the most subtle, is the "Ode on the Spring."

Although there will be a great deal more to say about the metaphysics of seasonal poetry, for the moment it may suffice to suggest that seasonal odes (and topographies like Thomson's) occupied an increasingly prominent place in poetry at a time when subjectivism was also gaining ground, and when, therefore, it would become possible to question what it means for the conscious subject to be "present to" or determined by the changing weather, which seems, at first blush, virtually to constitute consciousness. The climatology of Montesquieu in Gray's "Alliance of Education and Government" looks forward in some ways to the rise of nationalism, but metaphysically it is already a little archaic. Johnson's refusal to admit that we need be affected by the weather is a subjectivist's attitude that is quite inconsistent with his abhorrence of Berkeley and Hume, and that inconsistency betrays the unsettled ontological atmosphere of his period.[6] (Johnson himself had written youthful odes to the seasons.)

Gray's "Ode on the Spring" is about alienation from the weather. The title of the poem was not his own, but Mason's instincts in choosing it were sound. It certainly is not an ode *to* the Spring. It was written in response to Richard West's "Ode to May," definitely an "ode to" that begins, "O join with mine thy tuneful lay / And invocate the tardy May."[7] That is just what Gray cannot do, and his "ode on" should in fact be seen as a counter-ode.

Called "Noon-Tide. An Ode" in Gray's Commonplace Book, the

poem evokes the idleness of the Hour of Pan, not as a condition of nature but as a state of mind. The Horatian moral of the poem wittily turns the speaker's contempt for the uselessness of human bustle against himself, since quietude, we are told, is just as useless. This peripety, which is what has caught the attention of most readers, fully parallels the more metaphysical peripety that I wish to stress: Gray is alienated from the weather because he wants to be, in hopes that a condition approaching solipsism will preserve him from time.

The opening sentence anticipates the course of the whole poem:

> Lo! where the rosy-bosomed Hours,
> Fair Venus' train, appear,
> Disclose the long-expecting flowers,
> And wake the purple year!

Time stands across the way, a stranger whose appearance in the distance seems to startle the poet, who enforces the reassuring safety of that distance through the echo of "where" in "Hours." Rosy-bosomed Time *is*, by the transference of an epithet, the pinkening of buds from within as well as the glow of sunshine. Not an agent in itself but an effect, Time is drawn into being by the Lucretian eroticism of *natura*. Gray has begun, then, waiving invocation, with an etiological myth:[8] Venus begets Time, which begets the Year. But he keeps his myth veiled, distancing the myth itself as well as its content, behind a screen of epithets. His "poetic diction," here and everywhere in his poetry, is his way of indicating that he can "see, not feel" the force of nature that Wordsworth took to be wholly absent from his manner; and of indicating, furthermore, that he rather prefers distance to intimacy. Textuality in Gray, the dense layering of allusion and syntax, is a deliberately pronounced emblem of his isolation.[9] The logic of poetic diction combined with allusion weaves a tissue of mediations. Every predication cancels the others, so that no one prosopopoeia can finally be held responsible for the presence of an atmosphere.

Since the "year" in the above passage is awakened by the hours (which in turn are led forward by Venus), the year itself cannot be a part of temporal existence. As indeed it is not: "purple" is no color at all in Gray but rather a sense of luxuriant brilliance, a linguistic sense that is brought into play by the sound of the Latin *pur-*

pureum.[10] Thus modified, the year is reduced to an occasional and intricately derivative text "on the spring" that is disunited from time's rosy blossoming. The violently transferred epithet "long-expecting," which modifies the flowers and the poet in different ways, marks this disunity while seeming to effect a fusion: either the flowers are purely rhetorical flowers that bloom prematurely in the poet's discourse or else, in the key of elegy, they are long expected but never come.

West had urged Gray to "invocate the tardy May." Both he and Gray would have felt that request as a prayer for the return of that "cool zephyr" ("Spring," l. 9), the health of the feverish West, whose coterie name was "Favonius."[11] The most Gray can do, though, is to feign an invocation by planting specious imperatives in the midst of his predicative syntax: "appear,/Disclose." In fact, this speaker can command nothing, since Nature, the tutelary numen from which Gray is distanced by temperament and by having read too many odes to Spring, responds only within her own charmed circle:

> The Attic Warbler pours her throat,
> Responsive to the cuckoo's note,
> The untaught harmony of spring;

The poet is excluded from this exchange just as he will be excluded, in "The Progress of Poesy," from the intermingling of Greek melody with the native strain of "Nature's darling," Shakespeare. In the present passage Gray blends allusions of two kinds: first, to the elegiac mode of Propertius and Ovid that longs for the spontaneous voice of Spring, and second, to the world of Milton before the Fall— to the warbler of native woodnotes in *L'Allegro* and the "'celestial voices'" that are still present in Eden (Adam reduplicates them by explaining them to Eve), "'responsive to each other's note'" (*PL* IV. 682–83).[12]

The last stanza draws out as a moral what was implicit in the opening. Sitting apart "in rustic state" (an oxymoron that weakly reassociates the poet with the regality of the purple year and the enviable artlessness of the cuckoo), and sitting apart also from the rosy brilliance of the spring light, the poet in his "browner shade" has only slightly felt the breezes' synaesthetic dalliance with the unshaded world: "whispering pleasure as they fly,/Cool zephyrs through the clear blue sky/Their gathered fragrance fling." At the end of the poem his hearing is just as faint as his other senses have been: "Methinks I hear in accents low/The sportive kind reply." He must strain to hear himself admonished by characters from the world of Satire and the Moral Epistle because he has already told himself everything they can say in the more inward accents of thwarted invocation.

In part, then, Gray cannot be heard because he in his turn chooses not to hear. He typically reserves a clearer admission of what inhibits him as an odist for a comic moment, in the fragment called "Hymn to Ignorance": "Oh say—she hears me not, but, careless grown,/Lethargic nods upon her ebon throne." The poet apportions much of the blame to the goddess, whose name bespeaks the indifference toward human desire of all departed numina. But the poet is still confessedly at fault; he approaches the cloud of unknowing "with filial reverence," and his opening lines are, in fact, a specifically directed self-parody: the "antiquated towers,/Where rushy Camus' slowly-winding flood/Perpetual draws his humid train of mud" transfer to Cambridge the topography of Eton's "antique towers,/ That crown the watery glade," in another and more famous poem of 1742 that ends: "Where ignorance is bliss,/'Tis folly to be wise."

The keynote of the "Ode on a Distant Prospect of Eton College" is struck in the title and in the "distant spires" of the first line.[13] Like the "Ode on the Spring," this poem presents a lively scene that is far removed from the poet's present outlook and opens a vast distance between the sportive kind and the gloomy moralist. The second stanza apparently proffers the claim that things were not always as they are now, and seems to anticipate The Intimations Ode of Wordsworth in so doing:

> Ah, happy hills, ah, pleasing shade,
> Ah, fields beloved in vain,
> Where once my careless childhood strayed,
> A stranger yet to pain!
> I feel the gales, that from ye blow,
> A momentary bliss bestow,
> As waving fresh their gladsome wing
> My weary soul they seem to soothe,
> And, redolent of joy and youth,
> To breathe a second spring.

But in truth, as the poem at large and details even within this passage will indicate, there was never even a first spring. Gray's "poetic diction" does indeed mark the difference between him and Wordsworth, and does so very tellingly. It was not the poet himself who was a happy child but rather, more tautologically, his "careless childhood" —a personification taken from countless Ages-of-Man allegories that underscores its own irrelevance to any actual childhood. This device, together with the bold and un-Wordsworthian prolepsis "in vain," reveals the private theme embedded in Gray's universalizing diction: the childhood of the person who writes the speaker's lines was, as far as he can realize it, empty and vain, and no more full of joy—whether social or spiritual—than is the present.

Childhood itself is the etiological myth of the Eton College Ode, as of the Intimations Ode, but Gray presents his myth self-consciously *as* a myth, as a fiction of the soul's fair seed-time. If such a time ever existed, the poet is too distant to recognize it.[14] In this context, the premature present tense of "all are men" is significant: taken at face value, as I believe Gray's diction usually should be, the expression "all are men,/Condemned alike to groan," suggests that children themselves are not exempted from adulthood and its misery. Gray's motto from Menander, "I am a man . . . ," contains no hint of a prelapsarian myth and anticipates the calculated self-absorption of a poem in which all conditions that are distant from the place and voice of the speaker are known only as touchstones of homiletic discourse. The notorious "chase the rolling circle's speed,/Or urge the flying ball" is overwrought to warn the reader that the distant speaker knows nothing of the reality that his phrasing buries; he is as ignorant of cricket as is the Latin language from which *urgo* is borrowed. The eighteenth century, which certain of its partisans are fond of calling "adult," does seem wanting in an authentic poetry of childhood. Gray's calculated distance is nothing to Shenstone's effusion in his "Ode to Memory": "Bring me the bells, the rattle bring,/And the hobby I bestrode."[15]

Actuality, whether that of childhood or of any present that is not distant, is what cannot be invoked or evoked in Gray's odes, not only because of his temperamental aloofness, but also because he seems committed to the awareness that presentation in language can only be undertaken in blissful ignorance. It is best to assume this awareness, in any case, when one interprets the passage from Gray's

Correspondence (I. 192) that is often cited by apologists for his diction as if it were transparently self-justifying and needed no explanation: "The language of the age is never the language of poetry." This gnomic utterance and the argument that follows are not in the least persuasive, and richly deserve to be ignored by all the polemicists for naturalistic diction from Wordsworth to Williams, unless the whole passage be reinterpreted as a critique of presentation. "The language of the age," in this case, would be language that spontaneously presumes contact with the actual.[16] What I am suggesting is that the Eton College Ode, written six months later, requires no palinode in the unfinished "Hymn to Ignorance"; it is its own palinode, undermining the sententialousness of the gloomy moralist by denying that there ever was a world from which—and toward which—his prospect was not "distant."[17]

The first five stanzas beguile the reader into thinking that the poet converses in the presence of beings of all kinds. Although nothing that is addressed ever answers, Gray's phantom invocations seem to build from the quiet of apostrophe to the strength of command: "Ye distant spires"; "Ah happy hills"; "Say, Father Thames." Having addressed the landscape without even telling it anything, much less being answered, the speaker then commands the river, a poor substitute for Mnemosyne borrowed from "Lycidas," to give him information, which "Father Thames," as Johnson said, "has no better means of knowing than himself." Being nearly as ruthless an opponent of "vicious" diction as Wordsworth, Johnson is nearly as little qualified to appreciate Gray. The artifice of Gray is the ornamentation of an empty circle, a private way of remarking that one chases the rolling circle's speed "in vain."

There is only one moment when the poem suspends its elegant variations on the device **O**, and that is the moment Wordsworth might well have acknowledged in his Preface as a hint for the transitional stage of his own childhood in "Tintern Abbey":

> Still as they run they look behind,
> They hear a voice in every wind,
> And snatch a fearful joy.

Here alone "voice" enters the poem as a point of contact with the human; more furtive and fruitless than for Wordsworth, and also perhaps more complacently distanced by the clink of oxymoron, the "joy" here imagined nevertheless opens the thought of the poem to a region of "vocal transport" (or transmission) that is not absolutely absent but absent only from the circle of the poet's neurotic defenses. His childhood still haunts him after all, but is it not the "careless childhood" he had wanted to describe. As a trace of guilt about the recollected pleasures of childhood surfaces in this passage, we again witness the revenge that an ode carries out from the depths against its author. Gray's ode has been disrupted by the forces of nature despite his poetics of distance: what he invokes will not come, but what he refuses to invoke is already present, writing his lines.

II

Childhood in the Eton College Ode races past with depressing speed. As soon as the punningly intended "sprightly race" appears, it speeds, flies, runs, snatches, and greets the morn fresh from the fly-ing hence of "slumbers light." As soon as this race begins, however, a variety of retardations appear also. There are riverbanks and paths, the water is a solid that must be cloven in swimming, the captive linnet is enthralled (a capture of uninvoked voice that goes un-remarked),[18] and the little reign of the children has "limits." Most important, there are "graver hours, that bring constraint/ [like this enjambment] To sweeten liberty." Here Gray interjects the moral paradox that concludes his "Ode to Adversity," one that will persist in later odes until Keats's "Ode on Melancholy": the paradox govern-ing the interdependency of oppression and freedom, pain and pleasure, sadness and joy. In having suggested that Gray's verbal artifice em-broiders an empty circle, I mean that his mode of writing, in drawing interest to itself, gains opacity, density, and thus more effectively entraps meaning than does the naturalistic diction that allows mean-ing to slip through its transparency; even if it captures nothing, Gray's writing still has the happiness of being formal. In my remaining remarks on Gray, I shall trace his early figures of circularity forward to later figures of weaving and texture, suggesting finally that in the later odes an accommodation is brought about between vocality and the medium of writing—an accommodation that results, as for the ode writers of the seventeenth century, in a fortunate loss.

In a letter written nine years after the "Ode to Adversity," Gray called the poem a "hymn," which designation appeared in the editions of his poems in the fifties and sixties. In 1768, Gray asked Dodsley to change the title back to "Ode." This Dodsley failed to do, but in the same year James Beattie saw to it that in the Glasgow edition Gray's wish would be honored. "Adversity" meanwhile had readily become a "hymn" in the minds of all concerned because of its apparently impersonal deference to moral norms and its close adherence to the structure of the classical cult hymn: invocation, myth, petition, and at least the hint of a *votum* in the closing lines. It may be conjectured that religious scruples led Gray to prefer the title "ode" late in life; they would be understandable, since the poem must be read allegorically if it is to be taken for a Christian prayer, and it retains the pantheistic atmosphere for which its structure is designed, however firmly demythologized into psychic attributes its pantheon may be. Gray knew that "Adversity" was the sort of poem that proponents of the "sacred ode" from John Dennis to Bishops Lowth and Hurd would characterize as a "secular ode."[19]

It would seem at first that, barring its author's scruples, "Adversity" might well quality as a hymn. It invokes a norm of moral restraint that matches its own formal limits, the "rigid lore" of Gray's moderately intricate Horatian stanza: *a b a b c c d d 6*. The Alexandrine is not directly indebted to Spenser, I believe, but to Milton's Nativity Ode stanza, in which, as Louis Martz has aptly said, the Alexandrine "draws his poem . . . into the larger area of this poet's predestined goals."[20] For Gray, each stanza with its Alexandrine is an emblem in miniature of his poem's goal, namely, the increased latitude of Adversity's bondage and of the poet's sympathies. Gray's motto, from the famous chorus on suffering as the origin of wisdom in the *Oresteia*, gives the cue for these expansions by recalling the whole of the source text to mind, including the conversion of the Furies to Eumenides. Altered from nemesis to "form benign" by the end of Gray's poem, Adversity seems to affirm, by this change, the course of self-discipline that may revive "The generous spark extinct." Gray's etiological myth in the second stanza appears smoothly to bridge this conversion by assigning Adversity as governess to Virtue, whose reciprocal influence softens the "Stern rugged nurse" for the rest of the poem. Interpreted thus far and no farther, the poem indeed appears to resemble the sort of choral hymn that supplies its motto.

There are, however, a good many gaps in this pleasant reading, and when these are considered, the poem becomes an ode again. In the first place, it is clear that the "Ode to Adversity" attempts without success to repudiate the psychology of distance that governs the other odes of 1742. In Gray's myth, the role of Adversity is that of the "gloomy moralist" ("Spring"), whereas the role of Virtue, with "her infant mind," is that of the boys at Eton and the "untaught" birds of Spring. Governed by this contrast, Virtue is not far removed from "Folly's idle brood," and it may fairly be questioned how she will find the strength of character to put herself to school. Again owing to the predicative fracturing of personification, there is no "aspect" that can properly be called Virtue's own, not even the power of sympathy: taught to recognize "sorrow" by Adversity, "she learned [from her own woe] to melt at others' woe."

Despite the inessentiality of Virtue, it appears to be her, and not Adversity, whom the poem honors with its myth of origin. Invoked patronymically, Adversity becomes an older sister who seems to have no childhood. Like her cousins the Furies, she has always existed. Virtue, on the other hand, is one of the more lightly conceived offspring of Jove's later years. One reconsiders these kinships as allegory only to reach strange conclusions about the psyche that the allegory shadows forth.[21] Recapitulating the philogeny of cultural history, human consciousness is born to itself, comes to know itself, as a feeling of savage imprisonment, of self-laceration in chains. This condition crushes the "proud" and the "purple tyrants" who are rejected as parental models ordinarily at the height of a child's autogenetic fantasies.[22] Belated Virtue, herself empty of content, is the sublimation of precisely these tyrannical origins, while Adversity is the disruptive force that is not, in fact, external but is rather the firstborn of the psyche itself. Gray's poem shares with the early odes of Collins an Aristotelian theory of catharsis; but the coupling of Adversity's "frown terrific" with Pity's "sadly-pleasing tear" cannot purge the original tragedy, consisting as it does simply of having been born, that is somewhat more stoically acknowledged in the other odes of 1742. Having annotated the *Republic*, Gray was well aware of Plato's warning—evaded by Aristotle—that the deliciousness of pity weakens the psyche's defenses and results in self-pity (*Rep.* X. 606b).[23]

The pressures that undermine this poem's attempted resolution and independence are reflected in Gray's having realigned the pantheon of the poem that Johnson was the first to name as its source, Horace's ode "To Fortuna" (*Carm*. I. 35). Not the scourge but the patroness of "purpurei . . . tyranni" (12), Fortuna is not at all the same goddess as Adversity. Horace feels no need to rationalize the amorality of her power, and he finally petitions her, therefore, not to chasten him gently but to bring the Empire victory in an offensive war. The "iron scourge" of Gray's beginning is deliberately blunted during the course of his poem, whereas at the end of Horace's poem Fortuna is implored to resharpen the "retusum ferum" of Rome. As befits her ethical neutrality, Fortuna is flanked symmetrically by evil and benign forces. The wholly evil force, "saeva Necessitas,/clavos trabales et cuneos manu/gestans aëna," is none other than the scourge-wielding Adversity of Gray's invocation.

The logic that preconditions Gray's poem will not permit the Aeschylean conversion of Adversity; her coming first binds everything that follows within a deterministic chain. Gray struggled all his life to free himself from this chain. "That we are indeed mechanical and dependent beings, I need no other proof than my own feelings," he writes in 1758 and then gamely continues: "and from the same feelings I learn that we are not merely such." Unable to end complacently, however, he therefore adds, referring to the more skeptical *Philosophes*, "I can be wretched enough without them" (*Correspondence* II. 582). For once, in the "Ode to Adversity," the gesture of invocation succeeds; Gray summons Nemesis and cannot make her go away. Having chosen "I am a man. That is reason enough to be miserable" for the motto of another poem in the same month, Gray now actually petitions Adversity (so helpless is he before her) to be taught how to "know myself a man." By allusion, perhaps, this ending is meant to recall the more redeemably bipolar Man of the *Essay on Man* and Young's *Night Thoughts* ("A worm! a god!" I, 81), but it remains closest to the Man of the Eton College Ode.

Horace's ode is a poem on an affair of state; Gray's has entirely to do with a state of mind. He seeks the protective coloring of Milton's Penseroso, whose patroness appears in Gray's poem as one of Adversity's mediators, "Melancholy, silent maid/With leaden eye that loves the ground." But the force of Gray's dilemma changes Milton's sense along with Horace's. Melancholy does not soothe and abet Gray, but grounds him like a leaden plummet and binds him to the influence of Adversity. Self-cloistering may paradoxically result in liberty for the melancholic—"leave us leisure to be good"—but the mere protection from evil could never have satisfied the Milton of, say, the *Areopagitica*. The urge to expand Gray's limited freedom is one motive of Wordsworth's "Ode to Duty," which may be considered here to complete the synchronic setting, bounded by Horace and Wordsworth, of which Gray's "Adversity" is most fully to be understood as the center.

Wordsworth's open reconciliation with Gray in the "Ode to Duty,"[24] which takes over Gray's stanza as well as an aspect of his theme, fittingly accompanies Wordsworth's own prolonged farewell to "unchartered freedom." The "Ode to Duty" is so full of self-restraint that it is easy to overlook the idea of freedom that is meant to lend it a compensatory dignity:

> Through no disturbance of my soul,
> Or strong compunction in me wrought,
> I supplicate for thy control;
> But in the quietness of thought:

Once duly registered, however, this passage then demands to be taken more seriously than it can be. Far more than in the case of Gray's "leisure to be good," the integrity of this moment depends on our believing that the Penseroso's chosen rigors precede the mere reflexivity of cloistered habits. Wordsworth seems to be on safe ground, since his Duty has the appearance of a volunteer, whereas Gray's Adversity comes before she is called. But Duty, according to Wordsworth's motto from Seneca (added in 1837), *is* "Habit," and the notion that habits can be taken up and left off at will exposes Wordsworth to a psychic anomaly that is as intractable as Gray's.

An example of the formalism that Wordsworth newly proposes to embrace and be embraced by is set forth in his invocation, which violates every tenet of his 1800 poetics in two lines. Wordsworth doubles the distance of Gray's invocation; whereas Adversity is the "Daughter of Jove," Duty is the daughter of "the Voice of God." (The increased importance of mediation for Wordsworth may be seen yet more clearly if one compares this phrasing with its closest source, *Paradise Lost* 9:652–53.) She is twice removed, and it is rather difficult, in fact, to trace her descent from her mother, Voice, since she is not at all vocal, except perhaps as a permanent echo. The

venerable *quocunque gaudes nomine* of the second line also out-
Grays Gray and bespeaks a humble remove of such great distance
from Voice that the numen is no longer audible as a name. Words-
worth's ode recommends a religion, and implicitly a poetry, of
precept, and seems more plausibly entitled to the name of hymn
than does Gray's ode. It is a High Church poem that turns against the
inner voice of antinomianism.[25]

However, there is one critical lapse from this intention:

> I, loving freedom, and untried;
> No sport of every random gust,
> Yet being to myself a guide,
> Too blindly have reposed my trust;
> And oft, when in my heart was heard
> Thy timely mandate, I deferred
> The task. . . .

The nostalgia that lurks in this passage briefly confuses Wordsworth's
new perspective and effects the disruption of his poem. Duty is here
imagined in a former aspect, not as The Daughter of Voice but as
Voice itself; resident in the heart without discipline, in those days she
was scarcely to be distinguished from Conscience; or, for that matter,
from consciousness and inspiration. This nostalgia offers a much
more crucial challenge to the affirmative cast of the poem than the
one presented by the rather impersonal recollection of glad animal
movement in the second stanza. The Tom Joneses and Winander
Boys of the world have not ceased to exist, but the vogue for benevol-
ism has passed, and the hint of an etiological myth in the second
stanza is prelapsarian without reason. Wordsworth's most important
genealogy is contained in his invocation, and its divine origin is
subtly and tellingly in conflict with the human past that is rejected
in the fourth stanza. If the "mandates" of Duty have always been
present in the heart, as who can doubt, what motivates their super-
fluous invocation at this moment?

The poem does not come upon Duty for the first time, but rather
warms for the first time to what the eighteenth century would have
called the Pleasures of Duty; pleasures, perhaps, that anaesthetize
pain. Wordsworth's kerygmatic gesture[26] gains him nothing, since
nothing can be demythologized and replaced that has always existed
in its present form. It is too late, in the fifth stanza, to repeat Gray's

fleeting impression that self-restraint is less oppressive than "un-
chartered freedom" (37). The first word of this phrase is as puzzling
as it is in Blake's "London," but its primary sense is probably "un-
charted," a too long delayed figuration of the past as a formless
chaos. One can observe how perfunctory Wordsworth's myth of the
past has become by tracing palinodic echoes of the Intimations Ode
in the next stanza:

> Flowers laugh before thee in their beds
> And fragrance in thy footing treads;
> Thou dost preserve the stars from wrong;
> And the most ancient heavens, through Thee, are fresh and strong.

Duty universalized as natural repetition, as a beaten path for flower
beds and astral orbits, here becomes a kind of Christian *Themis*.
However profound this concept may be, it offers even less individual
initiative than the diminished philosophic present of the Intimations
Ode, when splendor is still in the grass and glory in the flower, when
the heavens are not harmonized by custom but by "the primal
sympathy/Which having been must ever be," and when "strength"
comes not from duty but from a "timely utterance" of the poet's
own voice that "again has made me strong." The "Ode to Duty"
completes the inland journey of the earlier poem.

It is important to notice how clumsily the Alexandrines of the
"Ode to Duty" are handled. The weariness of the first of them is a
mild triumph of imitative form effected by its elegiac echoes of
"Tintern Abbey" and Gray's "Elegy," but after that the Alexandrines
are dull ("Yet seek thy firm support, according to their need"), and
they seem compulsively to stutter: *"for a re*pose;" "through thee"—
a phrase that forces duty upon the stars through the fence, as Homer
would say, of their teeth. Wordsworth's "Adversity" stanza is averse
to its own opening out, and refuses to miniaturize the thematic pull
of the poem. Duty offers no latitude, and the last stanza recalls the
insistent narrowing of the Nativity Ode, where an "order serviceable"
harnesses the bright beginning of the last Alexandrine. Wordsworth's
last Alexandrine is lit by Milton's "handmaid lamp," but "tru*th thy*"
stutters between the light and its Bondman, signaling the implicit
betrayal of Voice in every predication of freedom as bondage. Like
the designed allusion to Pope and Young at the end of the "Ode to
Adversity," the designed allusion at the end of Wordsworth's poem

also misfires. We are meant to hear the close of *Il Penseroso*: "These pleasures, Melancholy, give,/And I with thee will choose to live." But instead we are reminded of the reluctantly hymnic closure of another ode, where pleasure has been "fixed" in an order that is no more than serviceable.

Both Wordsworth's and Gray's odes about discipline are corrupted by disclosures that make them odes rather than hymns: Wordsworth's by the inadvertent discovery that the past requires no new birth as a supplement, and Gray's by the discovery that a force supposedly from without is in fact a force from within. Gray's discovery could be said to be Wordsworth's also, since Wordsworth surprises Duty in his heart: but even in the "Ode to Duty" Wordsworth far surpasses Gray in his power of turning the "mandates" of psychic force to complex advantage. We now leave him with that advantage and return to witness Gray's struggle with his more "adamantine chain."

III

"... nor seek from me a loudly resounding song. It is not for me to thunder; that is the business of Zeus." And indeed, when I first placed a writing tablet on my knees Lycian Apollo said to me: "... poet, feed the victim to be as fat as possible; but my friend, keep the Muse slender."
                                        —Callimachus, *Against the Telchines*

Roger Lonsdale has a persuasive theory about what may have happened to Gray after his "Elegy" made him famous: the rusticated poet in that poem was anonymous no more, and the "Long Story" recounts, not without anxiety, a comic invasion of his crippling but addictive distance from the madding crowd. Gray's next ode and first Pindaric, "The Progress of Poesy," was intended to estrange his new public.[27] It has a motto in what Gray hoped was the unintelligible language of Pindar that means "Vocal [*phonanta*] to the Intelligent alone." Gray's later affectation of surprise at the witlessness of his readers extended to the circle of scholars to whom "Intelligent" presumably refers. "I converse with none but the dead," he once wrote half-flippantly (*Correspondence* I. 202), leading me to suspect that "the Intelligent" are the voices of dead poets, a fit audience though few toward whom his "distant way"

(121) urges him. Reassured of his distance from present admirers, Gray sets out along new paths to lessen his distance from the well-springs of vocality.

There could be no more ironic purpose for a Progress Poem; Gray's Progress is written steadily under the shadow of that purpose, and of the related but more generalized irony that recent critical approaches to progress poetry from Gray to Keats have made familiar.[28] For Gray, however, the problem of belatedness takes an unusual turn: in his writing, the burden of the past is an *audible* burden that he wishes not so much perhaps to carry forward as simply to hear. Even that modest wish will open a new and difficult distance that is not wholly conceded by its first admission in the "progress"—"But ah! 'tis heard no more" (111)—or even by the later admission, in "The Bard," that "distant warblings lessen on my ear" (133). It is unwise to assume that Gray wishes to add so much as a grace note to the vocal harmony of his precursors; what he does wish to do, as I shall attempt to show, is to "capture" them, as though they were the warbling linnets of an earlier poem, in the enthrallment of writing. This capture will result in an altogether surprising and atypical exaltation of the self.

The prevenient doom of Gray's Progress appears at line 4: "A thousand rills their mazy progress take." Both as periphrastic birthplaces for poets and as fonts of inspiration (if these are separable), rivers crisscross the "Progress" but not always with equal fluency. The departure of the Muses from an enervated Greece is foreknown by the landscape, "Where Maeander's amber waves/In lingering lab'rinths creep" (69–70). The waters that flow from Helicon have thickened since the origin of poetry, but their pattern remains the same: it is not a fluency but a texture that captures the channeling of sound through time in a grid, and makes a stasis of progress. The maze of Helicon's thousand rills is an emblem of the hermeneutic palimpsest that Gray calls an ode.

The perfunctoriness of the invocation to Pindar's and the Psalmodist's lyre, which reminds one of "Hail, Muse, etc." in Byron's almost-epic, is appropriate for an almost-ode. Gray's metonymy ignores Pindar and calls down the *technique* of Pindar's odes—their triadic form, profusion of epithets, and dialectical progression. There is no sustained vocative energy in Gray's poem, nor is meant to be. His emphasis on lore rather than logos is the reverse of the purely

vocative emphasis of Blake's Progress Poems, the five odes to the
seasons and the evening star in *Poetical Sketches*, of which Geoffrey
Hartman has written: "The primacy of the invocational-prophetic
mode suggests that this progress is linked to the very energy of
anticipation, to a poetry that can envision what it calls for" (*Beyond
Formalism*, p. 195). Nearly all of Gray's ode is what Scaliger would
have labeled a "genealogical hymn," with Poesy the absent numen
who is uninvoked but still traced philologically to her source.[29]

The major turns of Gray's argument, unlike those of Jonson's
Cary-Morison Ode, appear as skillful transitions between triads,
with each triad therefore containing a more or less continuous block
of composition. What syncopates the triadic form is the coming and
going of confidence in Gray's argument. As the lassitude of his in-
vocation shows, he is strangely unable to register excitement and
unhappiness in the right places, and the most significant shape of
his poem is created by this formally decentered ebb and flow of
response. At the level of the stanza and also at the level of the triad,
the highest pitches of confidence appear roughly at a midpoint,
rising out of a blockage, lull, or note of absence carried over from the
fall of preceding lines. As I shall now argue in detail, this stanzaic
framing of sonority uncannily becomes a wordless commentary on
the enthrallment of voice.

The brief invocation and the foretaste of "mazy progress" start
the first strophe uneasily. Early songs then begin to resonate, build-
ing toward the confident "Deep, majestic, smooth, and strong"
at line 8, the tone of which gathers the "thousand rills" into a
"rich stream of music" (7). But the strophe ends disturbingly by
recalling the exclusionary communion of Nature with herself in the
"Ode on the Spring": "The rocks and nodding groves rebellow to the
roar." Early lyricists, in other words, the descriptive naturalization of
whom culminates with Horace's image of Pindar as a mountain
torrent (10–11), *are* Nature: they speak only to each other, and
Gray's first attempt at capture closes him out of the net. The first
antistrophe renews the invocation to the lyre, this time with more
apparent enthusiasm; the trouble is, however, that an initial com-
mand has now been replaced by a purposeless apostrophe, no longer
conative. This loss of command just when the river's momentum
casts up the first epithet that is sonorous enough to be worth com-
manding amounts to a confession: by the end of the strophe the

speaker has awakened voices that are engaged in speaking only to each other in a genial place and time.

The rest of the antistrophe reviews the Powers of Music, stressing only the power of music to *quell* the passions, in contrast with Dryden's emphasis in "Alexander's Feast." The antistrophe rises to its sonorous midpoint at the superb "On Thracia's hills the Lord of War/Has curbed the fury of his car": but this curbing begins to restrain the stanza. The continuation of textbook-sublime rhetoric contributes to the present theme, which is the anodynous effect of music, and as the speaker nods he suddenly blunders: "thy magic," he assures the enchanting shell, "lulls the feathered king." It is permissible for Pindar to say this, as he does in *Pythian* I, but when the present speaker says it the subdued bird becomes Pindar himself, the Theban Eagle. In the second antistrophe we shall find the "feathered king" transformed and redeemed in a rather remarkable way, but for the moment the epithet is a witty blunder: Gray has borrowed a progress of dulness or art of sinking from the *Dunciad*, and presented the false sublime in the act of reducing itself to the "dark clouds of slumber."[30]

So much, then, for orotundity. The epode turns gratefully to the more spritely airs of *L'Allegro*; but if sublimity is dull, gaiety is trivial and touches nothing. The figure of "mazy progress" returns, again in reference to the more ephemeral modes of lyric: "Now pursuing, now retreating,/Now in circling troops they meet." These "Sports and Pleasures" attendant on their absent queen, Venus, are like children chasing the rolling circle's speed at Eton College. The very flirtatiousness of the elusive circle bespeaks absence, and the tone of the epode modulates richly, but also sadly, toward the Ionian mode, the "Slow melting strains" that prolong through the Alexandrine a figure of desire: "O'er her warm cheek and rising bosom move/The bloom of young desire and purple light of love." The movement of each stanza in this triad has been repeated in the triad as a whole; random and indistinct voices swell toward a sound that stupefies itself, giving way to fairy measures that fail to encircle the object of desire. The triad concludes its summary of the lyric modes in a state of restlessness, then, having captured none of them.

Still in the grip of this frustration, the second strophe begins bitterly, rehearsing Gray's usual litany of evils. Gray's 1768 note speaks of the "real and imaginary ills" in this passage, and in the poem he declares his intention of showing that poetry can cure the "fond complaint" of melancholia. He mounts as usual in mid-strophe to a peak of confidence, borrowed here from Milton and Pope, aligning his Progress with the Fortunate Fall in order to "justify the laws of Jove." We shall see in a moment the curious way in which this boast is modestly fulfilled. Meanwhile, though, a difficulty arises in this second strophe, the same difficulty that has closed the first strophe. Hyperion is introduced to purge the black bile of "Man's feeble race," but he fails to do so, as we see from the series of horror-gothic images that darkens nearly all the rest of the stanza and completes the hypochondriac catalog of the first lines. The too long delayed coming of Hyperion is magnificent but troubling. Why not Apollo? Apollo is more civilized and westerly than his predecessor, who had come "down the eastern cliffs afar." Perhaps Apollo is not called upon because he verges on the effete, the hellenistic: an urbane god, like Walpole's fish, he is made too much in the image of a feeble race to cure its ills. Therefore, the supplanted Hyperion is invoked, but he also fails. There is too much distance between the ailment and any possible figure of cure: Hyperion is, in fact, a figure of desire, not cure, confined by myth to the energetic cultural dawning of the first strophe. The second strophe therefore ends just where the first one did, and also where the first triad ended. There has been no progress—but the rayed phalanx of Hyperion's arrival fixes itself for future use as a new labyrinth.

We come now to the midpoint of the poem, the second antistrophe. Here the dilemma of belatedness is stated in the most extreme terms, yet this statement in itself supplies the trace of a solution. First, the inaccessible primitivism of Hyperion is taken a step further, "beyond the solar road," and the speaker reviews the extremes of climate and savagery where poetry and liberty, according to tradition, always appear together.[31] The stanza is initially expansive, warming to the theme of boundlessness: "beyond the solar road," "The Muse [like Hyperion] has broke the twilight-gloom," not of melancholia in this case but of bestiality; in "Chile's boundless forests," "loose numbers wildly sweet" are repeated in the "savage youth" of culture and poetry graces "the unconquerable Mind and Freedom's holy flame." But the stanza is only partly committed to the praise of boundlessness. At this moment of maximum freedom, the imagery of the labyrinth begins to accumulate, and to constitute a progress of its own. Texturation begins hesitantly with "shaggy forms." The "native's dull abode" is certainly not promising, but the "odorous shade" of the forests begins to suggest a pleasure, not of wildness, but of repetition; the total experience of the youth's repetitions by rote is regular, bounded by the sameness that ensures the continuity of a culture.

What began "beyond the . . . road" is now reduced to a "track," and the binding image of this reduction, I think, is that of the "feather-cinctured chiefs," which has much the same central and operative effect as does the garland "planted" on Cary's head in the Cary-Morison Ode. In the first antistrophe, Pindar, the figure of voice, was a "feathered king." Now the bird is dead, but traces of its vocal existence engirt man, a covering zone of quills usable for writing that is linked synecdochically with vocal origins. Now, "feather-cinctured chiefs" is not, I confess, a very exciting epithet. The speaker fills out a line with it, giving it no more heed than he gives dozens of other epithets, and furthermore it is a Wartonian commonplace—not even distinctly identifiable as Wartonian, in fact, but simply a scrap of jargon cast up by the fashion of noble savagery. No doubt this would be Gray's own view of the phrase I have not *yet* finished magnifying, except that he would know that the commonplace is not, distinctly not, Wartonian. The Indian is Wartonian, but not the epithet,[32] which is taken from Milton's simile for the covering of nakedness after the Fall:

> O how unlike
> To that first naked glory. Such of late
> *Columbus* found th' *American* so girt
> With feather'd Cincture, naked else and wild
> Among the Trees on Isles and woody Shores.
> [*Paradise Lost* IX. 1114–18]

For the moment, in Milton, Adam and Eve have no solace; this simile encounters them precisely at their nadir. The feather-cinctured chief for Milton is man fallen but unredeemed; but for Gray, whose temperament was more timid and decorous than Milton's, even Adam and Eve themselves, without their covering, would be "naked else, and wild," with no attendant glory, and hence a cincture of feathers would in itself go a long way toward redeeming Gray's Indian. As I have said, there is no seriously entertained prelapsarian myth in Gray. His cincture of feathers covers the savage body and transcends the savage mind because it bears traces of the vocal elegance of the Theban Eagle's writing, which is Gray's model for this poem. What is "commonplace," then, is not this epithet but rather—and perhaps deliberately so—the *rest* of the second antistrophe. It is hard to imagine the gloomy moralist and learned prosodist writing "She deigns to hear the savage youth repeat/In loose numbers wildly sweet" without pausing to consider that the savage youth cannot write. Perhaps it is true, as the poet might go on to tell himself, that his ultracivilized "joys no glittering female meets" ("Spring"), but he, at least, can write. Writing, as I began to suggest in my last chapter, is a screen, a displaced symptom of man's inner "nature," and in Gray's poetry the displacement of nature in writing (of the eagle in the quill) actually becomes a substitute for the forfeited "responsive notes" of sexuality. Writing is Gray's fortunate fall, an unquestionable loss and a binding, a labyrinthine sign of self-consciousness, but still an accomplishment.[33] It is at this point only, and not before, that Gray's actual Progress of written poetry from Greece to England can begin.

Gray rushes through his Progress once he has launched it, arriving in England by the beginning of the third triad. His treatment of Greece and Rome mainly concerns the Muses' departures—fittingly enough, since originary inspiration has already been shown to have fled before the progress of writing begins. "Inspiration breathed around" can only be reported *after* sound has departed from the Maeander. The Pindaric indirection of diverting the sense of an argument into landscape figures that Gray has used as a sign of self-exclusion in the first strophe continues here, as the "boundless forests" of antipodal life are centralized in a bounded canopy of "Woods that wave o'er Delphi's steep." As it emerges from the state of nature, space is covered and partitioned. Nature becomes landscaping. "Maeander's amber waves/In lingering lab'rinths" intensify the artifice by alluding, as Roger Lonsdale points out, to Ovid's comparison of the Maeander to the labyrinth of Daedalus (*Met.* VIII. 162–66).

Artifice, then, which I am identifying with the artifice of writing, governs the Progress from the first. It is clear in retrospect that Gray's chosen voice for an ode always subtly jars against his chosen mythology: in the rather quietly measured "Ode to Adversity" the etiology led inadvertently to a savage beginning, whereas now, in Gray's more rapturous "high Pindaric," the etiology is decorously screened off at the origin of *techne*, which saved man from the Minotaur. Jonson's hippocentaur, the Infant of Saguntum in the Cary-Morison Ode, is a far more candidly encountered monstrous birth than anything that appears in the tidier Pindarics of Gray. It can be said with some precision that for Gray, art is sublimation. Not repression, however, since Gray is a paradigm of what Harold Bloom would call a "weak poet"; what Gray screens out in order to re-formulate his psychic distance is not the consciousness of strong origins, but rather the threatening idea that originality is strength. I call this screening "sublimation" because it involves forgetting that there is any connection between writing and the disruptive force of nature—which the Victorian Pindarist Coventry Patmore called "the Unknown Eros."

Sublimation this extreme becomes a stern decorum that submits even the most hackneyed praises of spontaneous energy to its censor-ship. As the third triad begins, even Shakespeare, the little prattler of *L'Allegro*,[34] warbles his woodnotes rather too much like a "savage youth," and Gray ushers him in through an ominous darkness, "Far from the sun and summer-gale." But this unease is enclosed in new cinctures that represent the comfort of coming home from the Mediterranean to the "sea-encircled coast" of Albion and the even more reassuring "green lap" of England's inland. With these frames in place, there is no need for the river Avon to stop flowing and begin meandering, but it is still kept from flowing rapidly. It is inclined to "stray," like Shakespeare's irregularity, but its being "lucid" keeps it clearly in view. Shakespeare's originality is held further in check by Nature, who teaches him to paint the passions by numbers. Still, however artificial it may be, Gray's catalog of the passions recalls the persistent desires and ills that Hyperion could not banish. Shakespeare remains a troublesome figure by daedal stand-ards, and the strophe repeats the emotional parabola of the earlier stanzas, rising from darkness to the sounding epiphany of Nature's "awful face" and sinking back to the faint thrill of vicarious passions.

The apotheosis of Milton in the third antistrophe is held in place to the front by the hesitant "Nor second he" and to the rear by the coming of Dryden's "less presumptuous car." Milton, like "th' *American*" borrowed from him for Gray's second antistrophe, passes "beyond the solar road": "He passed the flaming bounds of space and time."[35] There is little apparent sense of psychic unease in this description. If we compare Milton's blinding "with excess of light" to an early passage in Gray's *Correspondence*, we can see that the "presumption" of Milton need have no personal reference at all: "Must I plunge into metaphysics? Alas, I cannot see in the dark. . . . Must I pore upon mathematics? Alas, I cannot see too much light; I am no eagle" (I. 57). Milton has ventured on truths as absolute as mathematics, and Gray has screened out that region so thoroughly that he retains—or so it appears for the moment—no urge to compete for it.

Dryden is the only poet in Gray's ode who is not named periphrastically, in part because without a proper name his characterization could fit Pope equally well. But Dryden's name appears also because it is the first *nomen* that carries no unruly excess of numen. Dryden's political verse is vocal, thundering and "long-resounding," but since his "Two coursers" are couplets, a visual harness constrains his heroic resonance. Dryden's odes for music (Gray's note shows that he has "Alexander's Feast" in mind) retain only the faintest echo of sound in "Thoughts that breathe." Such odes belong chiefly to the visual and tactile borders of Horace Walpole's fishbowl:

> Bright-eyed Fancy hovering o'er
> Scatters from her pictured urn
> Thoughts that breathe and words that burn.

If there is a funerary hint in Keats's urn, so here also. Even though in *pictura* the nymph tipping an urn is often a figure of inspiration (Fancy was painted in this posture, as were Naiads standing at the source of their brook), in print the coupling of "urn" and "burn" unfortunately suggests cremation, words that self-consume. Dryden's "lyre," in any case, is not vocal but pictorial, and not surprisingly " 'Tis heard no more."

The topic of Dryden has spanned two verse units, this being the first time any topic has done so, and it forces the final topic to be an unequal quantity. It is Gray's self-portrait, designedly shorter than the portraits of his predecessors but still surprisingly ample. After the matter-of-factness of "Dryden," the denomination of Gray is once more periphrastic. The numen has returned, just where we would not expect to find it, carrying with it the last surprise of this maddeningly difficult poem. The self-portrait describes the "distant way" of a poet who is not vocal but who captures voice, and it will be important to notice how little pride is lost through this diminishment. Gray's is the first ode I have paused over that curbs itself willingly, with no apparent daemonic resistance, yet it is also the first that ends with an upsurge of confidence, at the last minute breaking the pattern of terminal decline that has hitherto been the structural norm of this poem and also, with respect at least to endings, of the ode in general. Only the last Alexandrine of Milton falls; only the first in Wordsworth's "Ode to Duty" rises; only the last rises in Gray, for reasons that reward consideration.

At first the self-portrait seems as modest as we might expect it to be. The "lyre divine" is no longer Aeolian, and the speaker, who began by commanding it to "Wake," is reduced to asking who wakes it now. Clearly the vocal expectations of Gray's ode have been lowered. As the lines on himself begin, Gray does not have to admit outright that in his art he has confined himself to merely lapidary craftsmanship, since that admission is accomplished by the allusion of the whole concluding passage to the "ego parvus" of Horace (*Carm.* IV. 2), with whom Gray throughout his poem has spun variations on the oxymoron "operosa carmina fingo." Horace, then, only one of whose odes was written to be sung, appears to have silently supplanted Pindar as Gray's presiding lyrist. This substitution, supposing it to have taken place, is not without dignity: "Though he inherit/Nor the pride nor ample pinion,/That the Theban eagle bear," the present speaker still has a cincture of quills.

The course of the ode has prepared and pared the self-portrait, but the self-portrait also rewrites the course of the ode: each former crux reappears, measured this time according to its place in abstract autobiography, and then, having absorbed the periphrastic identity of each forerunner in turn, the self suddenly inflates and rises beyond any of them. Pindar has appeared and then apparently been abandoned, "Yet [Gray] shall mount . . ."; the babe Shakespeare has appeared and then disappeared under censure, "Yet oft before [Gray's] infant eyes would run/Such forms . . ."; Hyperion's "glittering shafts of war" on their eastern cliffs have dispelled no gloom, yet now "Such forms as glitter in [Gray's] Muse's ray/With orient hues, unborrowed of the sun"—*visionary* forms—exist within the poet's frame of experience; Milton, finally, who also surpassed

Hyperion in passing beyond the solar road, has nevertheless been dismissed, blinded by hubris, yet now Gray himself shall "mount . . ./ Beyond the limits." Here, then, is an extraordinary return of the dead to exalt the living; the artifice of sublimation effects a mediate decorum that allows even the most timorous psyche to witness the sublime.[36] Through unresisting self-limitation, Gray uncannily soars beyond limits and writes the most boastful ending to be found in any major ode in English. I do not say "the strongest ending," since Gray's pinions are never his own; what I have taken to be the figural turning point of the poem was stolen nearly verbatim from Milton. But that theft, and the application of alien figures to the self in the final epode, exactly bear out the definition of the sublime that Gray knew best: "as if instinctively, our soul is uplifted by the true sublime; it takes a proud flight, and is filled with joy and vaunting, as though it had itself produced what it has heard" (Longinus, *On the Sublime* VII). It is Horace who is effaced at the last minute after all, and through Milton the voice of the braggart Pindar lives on record, as it were, captured by the glittering shafts of his own feathers.[37]

The last line is supposed to lay the subject of poetry to rest in favor of the subject that the progress of poetry is everywhere said to promote, human virtue flourishing in a state of liberty.[38] The structure of the line supports our readiness to assume that this transition does occur, since it is the only line in the ode that resembles the chiastic conceit of an Augustan moral essay. But the two subjects, poetry and virtue, *are* closely related; the thematic drift of a whole poem cannot be canceled in a single line, and the controlled, privileged referent of a trope cannot completely supplant the uncontrolled logic of the trope itself. It *must* be concluded, then, that the poet's assertion of his moral independence carries with it, willy-nilly, his surprised and surprising assertion of being "far above the Great" voices he has captured. What it would mean, in this context, to be "Beneath the good how far," has to do, once again, with the sorts of disorder that a presentational ode in itself and also the arrogance of undertaking an ode are apt to bring to the surface.

IV

The noble art to Cadmus owes its rise,
Of painting words, and speaking to the eyes;

He first in wondrous magic fetters bound
The airy voice, and stop'd the flying sound.
—"On the Invention of Letters," Dodsley's *Collection* (1756) IV. 297.

"The Progress of Poesy" demands cautious respect, but it is not a
wholly likable or even readable poem.[39] Popular taste and scholarly
taste agree very closely about Gray. His most readable poems *are* the
"Elegy," "Eton College," and the "Favorite Cat." But a serious
approach to Gray does unearth certain anomalies about the relation
between readable poetry, which may be defined in part as well-
ordered poetry, and the balance or well-ordering of psychic forces,
anomalies that popular taste may find uncomfortable. Running
through Gray's most elegant poems there are delicate disturbances: a
tryst with darkness to "snatch a fearful joy," "the gulf between," the
return of the Furies. "The Progress of Poesy," which Johnson
called a "cucumber," is a painfully overworked and in some ways
grotesque poem, but its very intricacy begins to seem like an expedi-
ent cure that sublimates the Minotaur. Its philology is a coming of
age that protects both civilization and the psyche from the "savage
youth" of its origins. The therapy is writing, but in "The Progress,"
the real and imaginary ills of civilization taint the art of writing too
deeply for its suppression of voice to be entirely happy. In 1755,
with the writing of Gray's next ode, "The Bard," perhaps already
under way, we find him still exercized about the difference between
voice and writing: "setting aside the difficulties, methinks [the
equivalence of meter in strophe and antistrophe] has little or no
effect upon the *ear*, wch scarce perceives the regular return of metres
at so great a distance from each other. To make it succeed, I am
persuaded the stanza's must not consist of above 9 lines each at the
most. Pindar has several such odes" (*Correspondence* I. 420-21).
Strophe and antistrophe in the "Progress" have twelve lines, in "The
Bard" fourteen. Gray designedly gives up the vocal in his Pindarics,[40]
but in so doing he at first increases the strain of writing.

The original and translated antiquarian odes release some of the
strain by projecting writing backward onto the mantic vocality of the
past.[41] Now writing becomes a metaphor for speech itself. These odes
take their cue from the runic metaphor for prophecy, "weaving a
spell." "The Bard" and the Norse odes represent themselves as vocal
texture, at once pro-phatic—in the presence of voice—and spellbinding.

They are woven incantations. Johnson felt something peculiar in this fusion, and objected that "theft is always dangerous: Gray has made weavers of the slaughtered bards, by a fiction outrageous and incongruous." In "The Fatal Sisters," the imprinting or charactering of voice is like the shuttling of space and time by the spears of warriors:

> Glittering lances are the loom,
> Where the dusky warp we strain
> Weaving many a soldier's doom,
> Orkney's woe, and Randver's bane.
>
> See the grisly texture grow,
> ('Tis of human entrails made,)
> And the weights that play below,
> Each a gasping warrior's head.

Death falls in a dense pattern; it writes history in advance and each new stroke expels a last breath.

This writing is not in fact designed to know the future. All of Gray's bardic odes, including the "versions," self-consciously follow the wholly literary precedent of Horace's "Prophecy of Nereus" (*Carm.* I. 15),[42] of Virgil in Hell (*Aen.* VI), and of Dante in Hell. Dante's Farinata explains the limits of infernal foresight on grounds that the author of the "Distant Prospect" must necessarily accept: "'We see, like those with faulty vision, things at a distance from us,' he said, 'so much light the Sovereign Lord still grants us; when they draw near or are present our intellect is wholly at fault and unless others bring us word we know nothing of your human state. Thou canst understand, therefore, that all our knowledge will be dead from the moment the door of the future is closed'" (*Inf.* X. trans. John Sinclair). Gray's "grisly texture," then, is not prophetic but an infernal prospect. It is a mark of absence from the light that screens out and thus prevents the becoming and full presence of things, and yet literally *is* the end of things—a fatal prolepsis. Gray's antiquarian odes could have been published together under the title "The Loom of Hell" ("Fatal Sisters," 2). The ease gained from narrative and dramatic situation in these poems makes them more fluent than the mazy "Progress," but they are also far more extensively suffused with loss. The upsurge at the end of the "Progress" is countered in "The Bard" by a plunge "to endless night." "The Bard" can be read as an allegory of Gray's unceasing theme of distance as absence, and of his awareness that an ode is always its own palinode.

In "The Bard," the texturing of voice is a far more continuous process even than in the "Progress."[43] The third antistrophe, for example, rearranges several figures from the first epode of the "Progress." In "The Bard," the triumphal march of the Tudor monarchs forms a circle around Queen Elizabeth, and these monarchs in turn are cinctured by their retainers, "Girt with many a baron bold." Inferior rank makes the outer circle secondary, but it easily surrounds its royal center. Within this inner circle of kings, secondary in their turn, the numen stands contained: "In the midst a form divine!" This Elizabeth, then, seems concertedly opposed to the elusive figure of "Cytherea" in the "Progress," where the "queen's approach" is closed off by the morris dance of her Graces: "Now in circling troops they meet." When this Venus, whose earlier giving way to her "train" of Hours in the "Ode on the Spring" heralds her absence from all of Gray's poetry, moves toward the center of the tableau in the "Progress," she is surrounded, not by the dance but by a sign of her absence, "The bloom of young desire." By contrast, Elizabeth in "The Bard" is surrounded from the instant of her appearance, in fact preceded, by the circle that contains her "form divine," and she is then surrounded latterly by a figure of voice as encirclement:

> What strains of vocal transport round her play!
> . . . .
> Bright Rapture calls and, soaring as she sings,
> Waves in the eye of heaven her many-coloured wings.

These wings are the wings of Longinian rhetoric, the iridescently woven "colors" of oratorical design.

Gray's "antiquarian enthusiasm" appears to have a rather surprising bias in his essays and in the extant fragments of his planned History of English Poetry. Repeatedly he praises the Welsh bards, not for their wildness, as one might expect, but for "that excellent prosodia . . . which is perhaps the finest that any language affords," and which is "admirably suited for assisting the memory" (Works I. 381). What plainly interests Gray about oral poetry is its mnemotechnics, its capacity for interlocking and preserving voice. Although he asserts that the Welsh were the first British race to use rhyme, when he sorts out the history of rhyme by dates in his "Observations

on the Pseudo-Rhythmus," the Welsh in their third niche on the list
seem strangely belated and post-urbane:

At Rome before the Introduction of Christianity	137
In the Latin Church	420
In Use among the Welch	590

[*Works* I. 371]

When Gray proceeds to discuss the surviving texts of the Welsh bards,
he begins with a hypothetical objection that is exactly the one
leveled by criticism to this day against Gray's own poetry: "it may
naturally be thought that their verse is clogged with so many rules,
that it is impossible to write a poem of common sense in their
language" (*Works* I. 382). By the time Gray's Bard appears on his
rock, then, seven hundred years after his ancestors had begun to use
rhyme, and howls into the void a language that Edward I cannot
understand, he represents not the youthful vitality of culture but a
cultural endpoint. His last words delay the disappearance of voice,
like Gray's last words in the "Progress," by means of the inter-
texturing of memory.

"The Bard" narrates the death of the Last Poet. In the sequence
of events as they occur in the text, though not in history, his death
comes after the future poets whose coming he predicts, poets whose
voices "lessen on" his ear. Even before his death there is a "gulf
between" him and his auditors, who pass far below his rock, as well
as between him and his poetic predecessors, whose ghosts sit "on
yonder cliffs." He can only begin to prophesy when he joins the
voices of these ghosts to his; they sing through him, just as dead
poets sing through the speaker of the "Progress." The bards are no
sooner joined in "dreadful harmony" than they weave and finally
print the coming of death:

> Weave the warp and weave the woof,
> The winding-sheet of Edward's race.
> Give ample room and verge enough
> The characters of hell to trace.
> Mark the year and mark the night . . .

[49–53]

Line 51 could be an instruction to the printer of irregular Pindaric stan-
zas, after which, as the image develops, death is dated and published.

When the fatal phase of the prophecy is over, the harmony ceases and the ghosts vanish. Left alone, the Bard is briefly inspired with a happy independence, and sings in solitude the progress of the Tudors and their Bards. But, in fact, he is alone only in spirit; the Renaissance poets who are outlived by his power of hearing fill his voice with phrases from their poems (125–33). They are as much his ghostly inspiration as his mantic predecessors were, and when their voices cease to resound, he has no further voice of his own. He has soared on their wings, as Gray soars at the end of the "Progress." In the present poem, though, the dead do not return. They are woven too deeply into the past, into the textured winding-sheet that has drawn even "vocal transport" into its pattern. The only way the bard can join the circle he has created is to plunge into the silence of having finished fabricating speech, of *having been* a poet. It is well known that when Gray was asked what he felt when writing "The Bard," he replied, "Why I felt myself the Bard!" (*Correspondence* III. 1290). He may have meant this rejoinder more pointedly than has been realized; I have tried, in any case, to bring into relief a pattern in "The Bard" that shows it to be a deadly serious parody or sixth act of Gray's own apotheosis in "The Progress of Poesy."

V

After "Odikle"—Gray's unvarying name for "The Bard" in his letters to friends—Gray as a writer of odes very nearly maintained the silence of his last protagonist. The 1769 Installation Ode for the Duke of Grafton's Chancellorship at Cambridge was written to repay obligations, and it could be argued that Gray got himself through the task by alluding as often as possible to his Cambridge mock-ode, the "Hymn to Ignorance." When the parodies of the Installation Ode began to appear—"Hence, avaunt, ('tis venal ground)," and so forth—Gray was of course hurt, but he could take comfort in knowing himself to be the author of his own best parodies. All of his odes flirt with parody; one imagines that tipping his hard-won phrases over the edge must have afforded a steady recreation from becoming the poet unsympathetically described by Wordsworth as "more than any other man curiously elaborate in the structure of his poetic diction." I am persuaded, indeed, that there is a strain of internal parody in all of Gray's odes, visible to anyone who has accepted their constant concession that they are not "vocal."

Among considerable English poets, only Collins and Keats can be said to have conducted an experiment with the possibilities of ode writing that is as sustained and as dialectically alert as that of Gray. It has seemed proper in this place to take up Gray's odes for the most part in sequence as answers to, or at least as extensions of, questions raised in his own previous odes, and to consider each ode, furthermore, as a theoretical assessment of its own generic identity. (In this last respect, for the present study, Gray's odes are significant beyond his own concerns.) This emphasis has not been meant to show merely that Gray's odes are "about poetry," but to show, more specifically, that they are about being odes. From the outset, Gray appears to have approached the ode as a confrontation with compulsion neurosis; as evidence, that is, of the need to repeat constructively, and thereby for the nonce to mediate, the chronic sense of being cut off from the self and from others that was so obviously the ground of his personal anxiety.[44] The ode is a good choice for meeting this need, because its conventions force the poet to "purple" his discourse beyond any possibility of presentational illusion. Such is the motive, I have argued, for Gray's "curious elaboration." We need not go to the extreme of asserting that Gray has "a distinct and human voice" (e.g., in the "Elegy" and certain early odes) that he juxtaposes with a cold "public" voice[45] in order to believe that he was not merely a hapless victim of his diction; he was unquestionably, in my view, the deliberate master and obscurantist of a current mode that he found ready to hand. This is not to say, however, that he was master of his neurosis, or of all the random implications created by the dense local texture of his diction. But then, all odes, not just the odes of Gray, come at last to betray their design; no text can masquerade as voice without betraying, as does "The Bard," the very idea of vocality to oblivion.

Absence, neurosis, writing: fashionable themes. But these were also fashionable themes in the mid-eighteenth century. I refer not only to the Gothic revival, to the outpouring of nostalgic treatises on the origin of language, poetry, and metaphor, to the high incidence of the word "nervous" (partly meaning sinewy) in criticism, and to the longing for noble savagery and nature's simple plan; I refer also to the ontological paradoxes that the fashion for ode writing in itself brought to the fore. John Cunningham, an altogether representative weather vane, wrote an amorous ode "On the Late Absence of May,"[46] which fails to convince the unhappy reader that that oft-invoked genius has yet returned or will ever do so. Thomas Parnell's well-known "Hymn to Contentment" (Cunningham wrote one also) invokes that condition, calls it heaven-born and everlasting, and then describes its absence for the rest of the poem; *if* the poet could only find contentment, he would sing the "Source of Nature" like "the ancient prophets," but alas, *non beatus ille*, and his poem has no content. It is true that in *The Gift of Poetry*, Parnell is delighted to report, having invoked Time, that "my call is favour'd"; but since Time needs no calling, this success is simply a travesty of invocation from an opposite direction.

An extremely intelligent approach to these difficulties, and a tentative association of them with neurosis, can be found in Anne, Countess of Winchelsea's long poem in pseudo-Pindaric strophes called "The Spleen."[47] Having first lamented man's absence from paradise and from the soul's "native sky," Lady Winchelsea then characterizes spleen as a downward pull upon the soul by the body, causing a "dullness" that subverts the flight of vocative poetry: "I feel my verse decay, and my cramp'd numbers fail./Through the black jaundice, I all objects see." This poem is a satire against its own Pindarism, "cramp'd" in large part by its chosen form; and Lady Winchelsea's analysis of the megrims later suffered by Gray in his Pindaric "Progress" is more dispassionate, perhaps, than Gray's would ever be.

Aided further by Matthew Green's poem on the same subject, spleen became a popular complaint during Gray's age of "imaginary ills."[48] Hobbes had long before blamed spleen for the apparition of ghosts, and in Gray's odes the ghosts have completely vanquished the living. Gray fools his ghosts, though, by merely pretending to invoke them, and then, just when they think they are free from his curiously elaborate calling (since being called is what absents them), he en-thralls their distant voices in the very "winding-sheet" that proves them merely to be signs of the dead. I have called this enthrallment writing. "The origin of allegorical expression," wrote Collins's first editor, John Langhorne, "arose from the ashes of hieroglyphics,"[49] because, he argued, writing must at first have been as close as possible to picturing. The extravagant artificiality of Gray's and Collins's

odes arguably had, then, a rather startling rationale: it is not natural-
ness but rather the trappings of poetic diction that bring writing as
close to being coeval with voice—mediated only by hieroglyphic
"natural signs"—as arbitrary signs can ever come. Thus close, though,
was scarcely close enough; Gray did not write, nor would Collins
have written, the lost poem that Edmund Gosse called "the supposi-
tious *Ode on the Liberty of Genius*" (*Works* I. viii).

5

The Tented Sky in the Odes of Collins

The last Cavalier poet, Charles Cotton, wrote his "Contentment. Pindaric Ode" from a temperamental standpoint that is closer to Ben Jonson than to the Poets of Sensibility. He insists sturdily that discontent is a vapor of the mind: "'tis ourselves that give this frailty sway." For Cotton, contentment could be called down, with a proper effort of the will, to become a genuine *content* of the mind. For Gray, as we have seen, contentment is containment, a truly "formal" education by the goddess Adversity that brings peace in the form of impersonality; and this is also true, to some extent, for Collins and for any formalist poetics.[1] But the tendency of Collins is more radical. Rather than dwelling among the textures of containment, Collins sets out to explore, and also to restore, the origin of contentment. His odes invoke the ground of freedom rather than the impersonality of form. They are meant, I think, to reassert the freedom of the creative will in times that are hagridden by spleen.

The personified virtue that is called upon to bring about this resurgence, a virtue that figures more strongly in Collins than in any poet since Spenser and the Milton of *Comus*, is Chastity, the state of freedom from tyrannies that are indeed sensual, but are also political and poetic.[2] Chastity, though, is not only an untouchable state but an untouching one; it is therefore an emblem, at one and the same time, of originary freedom and of absence from natural origins. Chastity is a state of apparent freedom that is actually subordinate to the sexual origin that, by providing life, is of course what allows the living to be chaste. This paradox disrupts the new mythology of each new ode of Collins. Although his odes differ in purpose and design from those of Gray, they are doomed, like Gray's, to chase the rolling circle within which, alone, questing ceases and contentment is contained. I shall return to these issues after some first remarks on the form of Collins's odes.

Norman Maclean and Jean H. Hagstrum anticipate Schlüter's master plot of the presentational ode in the course of describing the typical ode of Collins.[3] An invocation beginning "O Thou" is followed by a genealogical myth, which gradually changes into a narrative outlining the addressed power's contributions to history. This Progress leads to the assertion of the present need for the addressed power at once in the self and in England, and this assertion, in turn, naturally introduces a concluding petition and vow. As Hagstrum says (*The Sister Arts*, p. 269), "the entire ode is presented as a prayer, which becomes the unifying metaphor of the poem" (perhaps "structure" would be a more precise term than "metaphor"). Just as the attitude of meditation informs a devotional lyric, so the attitude of prayer rationalizes the structure of a vocative ode. The narrative portion of an ode should be seen as a necessary part of the final petition: thou *canst* do all these things (description), and furthermore thou *hast* done them in the past (Progress). Does it not follow, then, that if I am worthy (vow), thou wilt do something for me as well (petition)?[4]

To an unusual degree, clearly, the prayer is a form of verbal exchange that must be read backward to be fully intelligible: *pro quo quid*.[5] Keats's "To Autumn" strikes most readers as "pure poetry" because it seems to be a prayer without a motive. All the preliminary rituals are in place, but there is (or seems to be) no petition. Poems of this sort are, in fact, as old as the ode itself and are often simply called "Invocations." They are apt to be mysteriously stirring poems, but there is no longer anything that seems mysterious about them as rituals once it is understood that by convention the entire structure of prayer, not just the petition, proleptically utters its request. The actual petition, then, can go without saying.[6]

The business of the invocation, the description, and the vow is to create a listener who is willing and able to answer the petition. Unlike a prayer, the ode does not depend for its success on the speaker's worthiness but on whether the addressee has ears to hear. The speaker's worthiness in fact resides precisely in the creation of an auditor, in the grand illogic (perhaps the most fundamental illogic that poetry and pathology have in common) of projecting from the self a precedent other who will then be willing to take the self seriously. The clever mendicant stages this same projection: despite his complete ignorance of our Thou-ness, he addresses us as Thou and tells us that we are generous and sympathetic beings, working this vein for some time before he puts his request. The odic vow, the resolution henceforward to be worthy ("for a cup of coffee"), completes the panhandler's petitionary formula.

The supplicant has a better chance of creating his donor through self-criticism (I am not worthy) than through self-pity (I deserve a break). Undiplomatic mendicancy has its own genre, the Complaint, which Johnson singled out for censure with reference to Cowley's ode called "The Complaint." Shelley's "I fall upon the thorns of life, I bleed" has always been considered by his detractors to be a falling away from Ode to Complaint. As most love poetry attests, we are likely to experience the Complaint as a falling away from the devotional to some masochistic form of the erotic; the passionate hermit becomes a dismembered swain. One motive for our praise of Collins's finest odes is our feeling that he never complains but only chastely regrets. He is "elegant," he is "pure." So indeed he may satisfactorily seem to be, but the ensuing interpretation of his odes will suggest that purity in the ode is an extremely unstable quality.

Chastity, when it becomes what would clinically be called the "overvaluation of chastity," reveals its symptomatic nature in promoting the assertion that creativity is autogenetic; in the chaste moment of Collins's odes, the *intacta virgo* supplants the Lucretian Venus as a channel of origin, but eroticism returns again and again to mar the exquisitely evasive form of the "nymph reserved." The "Ode to Evening" is a beautiful poem, one feels, but—"chaste Eve," indeed! The revision of Milton is not ordinarily thus bold, and cannot be sustained, because "lyric poetry," as Jonathan Richardson remarks in his "Observations" on Smollett's ode "To Independence," "imitates violent and ardent passions" (Chalmers, XV. 589). In every ode Collins must rediscover that the creation of a "new pantheon"[7] is also a begetting. With so many numina jostling for priority in Collins's hymnic genealogies, there are bound to be doublings and kinships that interrupt the will to independence and the fundamental monism of his vision.

It is the purpose of the descriptive portion of hymns and odes from antiquity onward to reduce all the warring powers of nature to the sway of the invoked deity. Just as, arguably, a tendency toward monotheism underlies the pyramidical structure of any pantheism, so in the cult hymn the proper appeasement of the god flatters him by insisting that the whole of life submits itself in "order service-able" to his precedence and presence. Both of the Hymns to Con-tentment I have mentioned above follow this design, awarding the numen (if she would only "come") a monopoly over all modes of influence. Among the Anacreontea, there is an early, affectionate parody of this monopolism in a poem called "A Cicada":

We bless you, Cicada, when, having sipped a little dew, from the tops of trees you sing like a king; for yours are all things that you see in the fields; all that the woods grow is yours; you are a friend of the farmers, for you damage nothing. And you are honoured by mankind, the sweet prophet of the spring. The Muses love you, and Phoebus himself—for he gave you your shrill song. Old age does not weigh on you, wise one, earth-born, lover of song. Undisturbed, of bloodless flesh, you are almost like the gods.[8]

Collins himself, hindered by that "almost," seeks to discover in his odes a poetical character that resembles the cicada, presiding every-where but bloodless, prophetic but undisturbing and undisturbed.

Although the quest for the monistic center is most intense in Collins, it is everywhere in progress during the historical period that preceded his *annus mirabilis*, 1746. By mid-century the usual business of invocation in the ode was to expand some subjectively deified force, a psychic or environmental influence, to occupy all space. "Health!" exclaims the younger William Duncombe of Cam-bridge in Dodsley's fourth volume, "to thee thy vot'ry owes/All the blessings life bestows" (p. 268). The challenge for the ode writer is to reconcile the mutability of experience with the prevailing unity of the invoked force. Either the force is single but protean, as in Thomson's "Hymn to Solitude" ("a thousand shapes you wear with ease"),[9] or else it is multiple because it stands in place of the one force that is understood to be originary, as in Thomson's "Hymn to the Seasons," where the seasons are "but the varied God." The invocations of Collins take a middle course between the protean naturalization that would eventually characterize the Romantic ode and a more hymnodic monotheism, uneasily blending elements of both these mutually distinct psychological and ideological stances.

The twelve odes that comprise Collins's 1747 volume pose a number of interlaced questions that are all forced upon him by the structure of prayer, questions having to do with the hierarchical precedence—or "unity"—of his pantheon. Who is Fancy? Who begot her and whom does she beget? Does her cooperation then restore the vocality of the ode to its antique power of building walls as well as texts—temples in the navel of Albion (see the odes to Pity and Liberty) that are fit to house the genius of Liberty? These questions are troubling enough in themselves, as we shall see, but underlying them are two even more recalcitrant difficulties.

The first can be generalized as follows. Trapped both by history and by temperament in a transitional phase between impersonal and personal voicing, Collins must find some bridge from private to public concerns, some leaping trope across which the poet's desire for power may be carried to join with and virtually to become the desire for liberty that inheres in the consciousness of his race. Curiously enough, the bridge from genius to heroism collapses most noticeably in Collins's most perfect poem, the ode beginning "How sleep the brave": the "hallowed mould" of the heroic dead is "a sweeter sod/Than Fancy's feet have ever trod." The poem succeeds, in part, because it lacks the arrogance of a presentational ode; its moving admission that the ground of valor is not the ground of genius (the figure of Aeschylus at Marathon had represented the opposite view in the "Ode to Fear") becomes in itself a genial patriotism.

The second difficulty, which I have touched upon already, is even knottier, and its undeniable vividness in Collins justifies the bias of Thomas Weiskel's psycholinguistic reading of his poems in *The Romantic Sublime*. This is not just Collins's difficulty, however, but arises, as I have suggested, with the writing of the first ode that is cut off from the collective sanction of the hymn. It is the difficulty of the Nativity Ode: Will the pagan gods—the daemonic, the bad seed—stay routed or will they return?[10] Every ode, again, is at once *occasio* and *adventus*: the falling out of a coming forth that inevitably, in the dialectical pressure of the moment, causes what is fallen and repressed in darkness to return and eclipse the poet's "latest-teemèd star." In Collins's odes this difficulty recurs as a dramatic conflict between the independence of chastity and the intricate pattern of incest that begets his "new pantheon." I shall begin to describe this conflict by attempting to unravel the "Ode on the Poetical Character."

II

> Uriel, no wonder if thy perfect sight,
> Amid the Sun's bright circle where thou sitst,
> See far and wide: in at this Gate none pass
> The vigilance here plac't, but such as come
> Well known from Heav'n.
> —Paradise Lost IV. 577–81

"Pale Fancy dropt a tear," wrote a magazine poet of Collins in 1766, "to see her son o'erpowered by her charms."[11] If Collins's predicament was already clear in his own day, it must require a peculiarly heroic decorum of perception for any modern reader to deny the implication of incest in the "Ode on the Poetical Character." I should imagine, in fact, that even the most restrained reader simply filters the incest motif through such parallel metaphors as he takes to be more rewarding.[12] Collins's second editor, Laetitia Barbauld, was the first to suspect that some misconduct may have passed between the Creator and his "lov'd Enthusiast," and Collins's "Romantic" critics have been amplifying her distress signal ever since. In its first stages, my own approach overlaps those of the modern Romantic critics,[13] but my argument finally differs from theirs in taking the incest motif to be a point of repetition from which both the structure and the unstructuring of the ode *as an ode* may be derived, and which also serves, in the antistrophe, to dethrone Milton.

The tryst in the mesode at lines 29–32, every phrase of which except the one about the Creator's *mens divinior* has a long history in erotic literature, is only the most prominent repetition of what touches every moment of the poem. The Eden or Bower of Bliss of the antistrophe, guarded by "strange shades" that are "tangled round the jealous steep," is "curtained close . . . from every future view." This is an almost clinical description of repression, of the re-creation of the primal scene in a screen-memory that hides its own origin. It is as though Fancy had never recovered from her helpful gesture ("Fancy lifts the veil between") that had starkly revealed the crime of Oedipus in the "Ode to Fear."[14] Once we have adjusted ourselves to the intricate withholding of Collins's conclusion in the "Ode on the Poetical Character," the self-proclaimed misreading that launches the poem takes on, in hindsight, the proleptic force that first words should be expected to carry. Spenser and his Elfin Queen represent the first of many encounters of a father with "Young Fancy, to me divinest name," and Collins's inexact representation of Spenser and his Queen's offspring, *The Faerie Queene*, may show him wilfully to have absented himself from the probable scene of its begetting.[15]

Collins holds a great deal back in revising Spenser's allegory of the magic girdle. In Spenser, the girdle did fit Amoret, and yet it was borne off by the false Florimel, whom it did not fit. This omitted chain of events, which returns constantly to shape Collins's ode, represents the impasse that is reached by the double quest of any ode for a pure source and for an unbroken, fitting form. Amoret or the false Florimel: a perfect form that will not materialize, or a disruption of form, a bursting free from a temperate Zone that is nevertheless a birth of the actual. The possibility of sexual corruption at the source of creation, the *possibility* of it, not the certainty, is the secret burden of the poem. Cosmogony, whether poetic or divine, either is or is not chaste; it is either a free and independent formalization or a foreordained energy. Collins's song, like Dryden's, "began from Jove," but it is hard to say whether his myth has not implicated an Olympia, a Thaïs, or even a Cecilia who has been corrupted by the angel she drew down.

The passage that most openly defies this impasse in Collins's ode will remind us of the sublimation that marks Gray's "Progress of Poesy": "The dangerous passions kept aloof,/Far from the sainted growing woof." The rich-haired youth of morn has sprung forth from, or at the behest of, an originary "sound," but the sound comes in turn from a "veiling cloud." The youth's latterly described hair brightens this veil but still repeats its shape, and with it forms a circle around the "magic notes" of his begetting, a circle that anticipates the vocal weavings of Gray. Creation throughout the mesode is a reverberant texture: wove/called (24–25); tented/laughing (26); sound/veiling (34–37); notes/rich-haired (38–39); woof/thunder (42–44); vest, braided dance/murmurs (45–48). The last act of the Creator before he joins his celestial paramour to produce the eloquence (magic notes, flowers) of human consciousness is to pour "the main engirting all." This framework for life is like the River Ocean that borders the shield of Achilles; it is both a channel for energy and a defense. We shall have to turn to the plot of this ode in order to substantiate further the sense of cosmic[16] discord that already seems apparent from Collins's insistent circles: there is no continuity between Being, which is univocal sound, an autogenetic and concentered source that is screened from view, and Becoming, which is the screen itself, a textured layering of concentric circles. Every successive personage of this richly peopled poem is barred from an inspiring bower by some defense, and it will become evident that no figure, chaste *or* passional, can actually enter the garden—not even Milton.

The entire narrative of the ode is encoded in nearly every epithet, most clearly, perhaps, in the lines about the disappointed contestants:

> Happier hopeless fair, if never
> Her baffled hand with vain endeavour
> Had touched that fatal zone to her denied!

The repetition of hopelessness overrides the logic of the fable, which holds out the hope that some "few" will win the prize. (These few are later to be reduced to "one alone," and ultimately, I shall argue, to none.) But even if there are winners, the contest will have been falsely advertised, since the chastity of their girded loins will reduce them to onlookers, voyeurs gazing at what takes place in the mesode, and perhaps, even then, seeing little or nothing. Both the ladies who preside and the ladies who compete merit close attention.

The strophe is an analogy: as "Some chaste and angel-friend to virgin-fame" is to the rival fair, so Fancy is to the poet. Most readers have erred, I think, in assuming that the angel-friend and Fancy are not themselves dependent figures. What tells against this sensible assumption is the compulsively genetive character of Collins's epithets. (We know from Warton—*Poems*, p. 412—that he was "perpetually changing" them.) The unseen angel and Fancy are both doubles of rather more powerful predecessors. The angel who blesses chastity is a derivative Elfin Queen, a diminished version of the muse who "blessed" the School of Spenser—Fairfax, one supposes, and the Fletchers[17]—but did *not* bless Spenser himself, because she was "His," possessed by him and creative through him. All the epigones, including the angel, are indeed merely chaste. Similarly, "Young Fancy" has charge of the cest of amplest power, but it is not hers. She is pure enough, "prepared and bathed in heaven," but she is not the maker of the cest; someone gave it to her, a more potent double who is none other than the loved Enthusiast of the mesode. (The resolute wooer of the Creator is not the sort of Pre-Raphaelite Iphigenia who will lie still, like Young Fancy, to be prepared and bathed as if for a ritual offering.) Even before we descend to the thrice-removed scene of rivalry among the mortals, it is already clear, on both sides of the simile, who is Amoret and who is the false Florimel. Amoret, protégée of the androgynous Britomart, is the epigone; her face, in Spenser, is "The heavenly pourtraict of bright Angels hew" (*FQ* IV. v. 13); and the false Florimel, both "idole" (IV. v. 15) and daemon, is the Dark Ladye, "some celestiall shape, that flesh did bear" (IV. v. 14).

What Fancy and her favorites witness, or seem to witness, is the mesode. We would not expect such modest persons to have "wild" visions, and indeed the first line seems merely to promise the sort of thing their gentle minds would be likely to take in: "The band, as fairy legends say . . ." Only after this first line is the poet overtaken by a vision that is more dynamic than the "unmixed flame" of the strophe had promised. His sudden access of power comes from an echo in the first line itself, which is not from the cosmogonic Milton, patron of the mesode, but from Spenser. Spenser too had assigned a former owner to the magic girdle:

> Whilome it was (as Faeries wont report)
> Dame *Venus* girdle, by her steemed deare,
> What time she used to live in wively sort;
> But layd aside, when so she used her looser sport.
>
> [IV. v. 5]

Venus leaves the girdle behind for the true Florimel to inherit, and Spenser locates the inheritance in a scene that is curtained close, "her secret bowre,/On *Acidalian* mount." So it is that the chaste cest of amplest power, the "zone" that literally *becomes* every phase of Collins's cosmogonic event, is forfeited in advance, by allusion, to the muse of Lucretius: Venus, the unfaithful wife and sister[18] of the great daedal artificer, Vulcan.

Commentators have not ignored the echoes of Lucretius—via Dryden's translation—in the mesode, but the dynamism of Collins's description is perhaps better reflected to the reader of English in a more literal translation:

Mother of Aeneas and his race, delight of men and gods, life-giving Venus, it is your doing that under the wheeling constellations of the sky all nature teems with life. . . . Through you all living creatures are conceived and come forth to look upon the sunlight. . . . For you the inventive earth flings up sweet flowers [Dryden: "For thee the Land in fragrant Flow'rs is drest"] . . . into the breasts of one and all you instill alluring love, so that with passionate longing they reproduce their several breeds.

Since you alone are the guiding power of the universe and without you nothing emerges into the shining sunlit world to grow in joy and loveliness, yours is the partnership I seek in striving to compose these lines. . . .[19]

The "Ode on the Poetical Character" is one of the three odes in Collins's 1747 volume that are overtly mythopoeic rather than devotional; it wants to persuade us that an invocation has already succeeded—that a chaste muse has been found and is now being celebrated—and for this reason there is no invocation in the poem. But an invocation lurks near it, Lucretius's invitation to Venus, repressed but not untraceable.

Collins's footnote at the beginning of the ode is significantly worded: "*Florimel.* See Spenser Leg. 4th." Not just the solemn tourney but the whole story of the true Florimel, her birthplace, tutelege, and inheritance of the belt that "*Cestus* hight by name" (*FQ* IV. v. 6), is the myth that Collins's ode distorts in order to prefer its own myth of power as chastity. "Cestus" is from *caedo*, "to fall," and more directly from *caestus*, "a boxer's gauntlet or defense." There is no real etymological linkage between "Cestus" and *castus* (chaste), or between "Cestus" and its phantom opposite, *incestus* (incest), but the spelling of both Spenser and Collins forces these coincidences into view. "The cest of amplest power" is a psychic defense that protects the vision of an unfallen begetting even as its daedal workmanship screens out a primal scene.

In the mesode, the Creator is a prototype for an ode writer because he has *invoked the universe,* "called with thought to birth,/Yon tented sky, this laughing earth." This gesture, as Earl Wasserman has shown, is Platonic:[20] the object is constituted as a representation by the subject and so, with that Idea in mind, brought into existence. Just so, the maker of odes constitutes an other for his invocation. The cest, which "was wove on that creating day," the Creator uses as an ad hoc blueprint for his tenting, dressing (27), engirting (28), and veiling of phenomena. From the standpoint of the reader, however, it is difficult to keep the invocation and the weaving separate, just as it has been difficult to find the poet's tacit invocation embedded in his mythology. The poem at every level presents the Logos as a woven voice.

For the first few lines of the mesode, Creation seems certainly not to be bisexual (even though the mindlessly vital world the Creator calls to birth is just what Venus inspires in Lucretius). Giving birth by thought, however, sounds not unlike giving birth to Athena. Perhaps I am mistaken in allegorizing the event thus far, for an identification of Nature with wisdom seems not to make sense, unless the wisdom-figure is the biblical Sapience who joined with God in the Creation;[21] but unquestionably the dressed and laughing earth is already a feminine presence against which the loved Enthusiast must be seen to enter as a rival. The Enthusiast represents a novel creative principle. The "diviner mood" of the Creator may be seen as a transference of affection from reason to imagination, as an indication of the change in taste from Pope to the School of the Wartons. The Creator's mind *needs* to be diviner than it was, because his new paramour is enthusiastic, "with the god," in contrast with the earlier figure, or ghost of a figure, who was no sooner born with thought than she lapsed into the unreflecting self-sufficiency of the natural order.

The result of this fresh union is at first hard to distinguish from what happened before; and indeed at bottom the whole cosmogony is, simply, the repetition of a single act. But there remains a difference between these first and second creations. The Enthusiast (who is, again, related to Fancy but is a far more dynamic figure) peoples the formerly uninspired landscape with genii and other Miltonic figures: Angels, Passions, Wonder, "all the shadowy tribes of mind." Unlike the Creator himself, who constituted the earth as an object, the Enthusiast projects her own protean identity throughout its compass. Henceforth, the universe is an Idea "charactered" by enthusiasm, a triumphant embrace of reason and the imagination.

Neither of these faculties, however, can represent themselves to themselves; they are both unreflexive, pure utterance, and they are both also absent from their own voices, "uncircumscrib'd retired," like Milton's God, who spoke through the Holy Spirit. The Creator and the Enthusiast need a luminous image of themselves to reflect them, and so they conceive and give birth to a herald at the climax of their creation:

> And she, from out the veiling cloud,
> Breathed her magic notes aloud:
> And thou, thou rich-haired youth of morn,
> And all thy subject life was born![22]

The sun-poet (it is not easy to see how anyone could insist that he is either sun or poet exclusively) is both creator and created, and hence he is the first scion of an already lengthy family tree who can be said to mediate selfhood and the "subject life" of the self, to retain his natural primacy, that is, while achieving self-consciousness. His rayed hair is at once the phallic concentration of creative strength (like the streaming meteor of the Bard's hair in Gray) and a sunscreen that protects him from a withering excess of self-knowledge.

Divine presences continue to multiply; each of them is both a witness and a thread of the expanding fabric, like the rich-haired youth. Then suddenly the poet's ecstasy ceases, and he seems to deny even that it ever happened:

> Where is the bard, whose soul can now
> Its high presuming hopes avow?
> Where he who thinks, with rapture blind,
> This hallowed work for him designed?

It would seem reasonable to go through the lines just preceding these in search of some motive for Collins's recantation. Possibly he is unhappy, for instance, about the distance between sunny Truth and "shadowy" subjectivity; possibly he is overtaken by timorousness in the face of grandeur; or, conversely, by fears of flagging inspiration when his vision encounters wonders, like the angelic "powers" and ambrosia, that are less mythopoeic and more conventionally sacrosanct than what he saw earlier. Certainly these are plausible and not irrelevant observations, and certainly the poet's sudden change is a cumulative reaction: I suspect, though, that the afflatus is not ended by any one point of doubt. It is quite appropriate that there be *no* transition between the vision and its denial, and this not merely because the leap between moods is properly Pindaric. The absence of transition tears apart the "growing woof" of Collins's presentational tapestry; it points to the anxieties that have shadowed his affirmation from the beginning.

Collins's emphasis on "now" has led nearly all readers to assume that the decrescendo beginning at this point is a deferential bow to

Milton, the continued echoes of whose writings are meant to show, on this view, that the inferior Modern at least still tries to follow in the master's "guiding steps." I would suggest, on the contrary, that the disappointed visionary is playing a more insidious game—but also a far healthier one that involves a subtle critique of Milton. No poet in history, as I read the antistrophe, has ever "witnessed" the primal scene because no poet has ever had a sufficiently transparent medium of vision. Collins has decided that the nature of expression itself is responsible for the screening of vision; this is apparent from his having thematized the texturing of his own text ever since he introduced the daedal talisman that was supposed to help him see but instead neatly excluded him from its circle. If one's medium is to blame, then there is no point in disparaging oneself and exalting other poets such as Milton.

What can a text see? Neither chastity *nor* incest. If we weigh the unequivocal evidence of the text as a text, we must agree with A. S. P. Woodhouse[23] and disagree with the followers of Mrs. Barbauld. We have no solid evidence about what passed between the Creator and the Enthusiast because it is not in the nature of a text to give us such evidence. In a text, as in a psychoanalytic case study, an implication or symptom (as of incest) is an "infolding" which in itself screens off what we consider to be implied. I would not belabor this rather fruitless issue were it not that Collins's text itself appears to be doing so. If it is not doing so, then no sense can be made of Fancy's wholly anomalous role in the closing lines: "Heaven and Fancy, kindred powers,/ Have now o'erturned the inspiring bowers."[24] Why should Fancy wish to assist in her own disabling? Surely the answer cannot be historical; if Fancy had grown weaker since the time of Milton, she might confess decline, but she would not thus eagerly engineer the decline herself. Not, that is, unless she is secretly a guardian and not a pioneer of psychological borderlands, a timid sorceress of vocal presence who fears her own calling and finally refuses to invoke beings whose response she dreads. Even the creative imagination itself, Collins must finally admit, screens its own workings from consciousness.

If we go back to the suspect creation scene, we shall find that what we thought we saw is "curtained close":

> Long by the loved Enthusiast wooed,
> Himself in some diviner mood,

> Retiring, sat with her alone,
> And placed her on his sapphire throne.

If he was "with her alone," no one saw what happened. The fourth line in this passage does record an event that can be visualized, one that tends to happen before an audience, but in narrative the playful enthroning of the concubine would be, at most, a metonymy of the evidence the reader thinks he has found. If there is something of Dryden's Alexander and Thaïs in the mesode, there is also something of Milton's Sin, who sprang, "a Goddess armed," out of Satan's head:

> familiar grown,
> I pleas'd, and with attractive graces won
> The most averse, thee chiefly, who full oft
> Thyself in me thy perfect image viewing
> Becam'st enamour'd, and such joy thou took'st
> With me in secret, that my womb conceiv'd
> A growing burden.[25]

With the burden of these demonic echoes weighing against his own pure cosmogony, Collins will be especially concerned to put the question, What can Milton's text see? The mediation of epic narrative, with its leisurely temporal distances, lessens the personal shock of recognition that lyric consciousness must endure in bearing witness to scenes like the one Sin cheerfully recalls in Milton. Epic therefore will always appear to have seen more than Lyric, but the presentational claims of its "trump," Collins will show, are no better founded than the claims of the chaster and necessarily more re(com)pressed lyre.

Far from being the "one alone" who knew paradise at firsthand, then, Milton in particular is the target of Collins's assertion that the visionary act is self-blinding. In this dubious light, Collins will appear to have performed what Harold Bloom calls *kenosis*, or the annihilation of the precursor's sublime.[26] Something like this doubtless does occur, for certainly the grapes of paradise have soured for Collins. I shall prefer, however, to arrange the evidence to show not only that Collins has staged a psychic defense but also that his defense is consistent with the reality principle—that is, that his resentment against Milton is well founded.

The impasse of an invocational poem, as I have suggested, is that its calling upon its own sources must be thwarted by ignorance of what those sources are. The hope that they are chastely free or primary is undermined by the fear that they are wantonly duplicitous or secondary. Clearly, however, an impasse is not created by the knowledge of what is beyond itself but rather is, in itself, the fact of not knowing. The ode writer comes to realize that his impasse is his medium itself. He must face this recognition more squarely than he would if he had written an epic, and for this reason an ode about the progress of poetry, as we have seen also in Gray, will constitute not only its own critique but also, more openly and stridently, a critique of rival genres. The writer of a Progress ode reminds the usual heroes of his poem, the great dramatists and epic poets of the past, that their own creations were in some measure theogonic and, therefore, displacements or even evasions of the ode's more immediate, high-pressured calling. As Eli Mandel writes concerning the mid-century ode, "A miracle of compression condenses the vast and comprehensive plan of epic into the flashing power of creative phrases or insights."[27] This covert attack in behalf of lyric[28] may result in the strange and unexpected personal apotheosis of Gray's "Progress," or it may, as in Collins, simply supply an underlying consolation. Bloom has called this moment *askesis*,[29] at once an inwardness and a narrowing of generic scope that reduces the large-mannered motions of epic procedure to the tropes of lyric. Thus it is not without irony that Collins follows Milton's "guiding steps" and repeats Milton's vision of the earthly paradise on a lyric scale.

The evidence against Milton may be assembled as follows, beginning again at "Where is the bard." In Milton's time as much as in the present, the hopes of such a bard are "high," but also "presuming." The difference between then and "now" is not the difference between achievement and failure but between "rapture blind" (the low blow against Milton is hard to ignore) and crippling insight. To reinforce his charge of presumption, Collins begins his antistrophe—or *anagnorisis*[30]—by imitating the thwarted approach to paradise of Milton's own Satan:

> Now to th'ascent of that steep savage Hill
> *Satan* had journey'd on, pensive and slow;
> But further way found none, so thick entwin'd,
> As one continu'd brake, the undergrowth

> Of shrubs and tangling bushes had perplext
> All path of Man or Beast that passed that way . . .
>   [*Paradise Lost* IV. 172–77]

This is the impasse I have mentioned. Can the "Man" Milton get by, and enter Collins's "Eden, like his own"?

Collins makes a point of laying personal claim to this place, and he *now* makes the assertion he avoided making outright in the supposedly visionary mesode, namely, that he is really seeing something: "I view the oak, the fancied glades among." Again, however, Fancy taketh away what the ego giveth; these glades, we are very pointedly told, are not real. Collins claims, in any case, to see the inspiring bower (that is, in the vulgar but also the Addisonian sense, to have a vivid image-ination), whereas he allows Milton in his day only to have heard the last echoes of the divine presence there:

> his evening ear,
> From many a cloud that dropped ethereal dew,
> Nigh sphered in heaven its native strains could hear.

It is important to recall what is being repeated in this beautiful passage: "And she, from out the veiling cloud,/Breathed her magic notes aloud." Once more, the primal scene is invisible, especially to the blind and aural Milton.[31] He did not pass Satan's impasse and, to his credit, he was no cormorant, but merely "lay" still, a supine oracle under a Dodonian oak that he, Milton, never mentions among the trees of Eden.[32] He does not mention it among the evergreens on the mountainside either, but an oak is a noble tree, iconically poised between pastoral and the symbolism of hardihood in northerly storm poetry, and it could easily augment the "Insuperable highth of loftiest shade" (*PL* IV. 138) that screens out Satan's view. Collins's own "glades," even in Fancy (or rather precisely there), are never definitely placed within the gates of paradise.

The "Ode on the Poetical Character," then, finally offers its title character the choice of residence under two obscuring shadows: that of Milton's oak or "Waller's myrtle shade." The latter choice, to which Collins says that he is for the most part confined, is by no means easily to be dismissed. Milton himself was once tempted to sport with Amaryllis in the myrtle shade.[33] Collins's epithet, though, is not apt to refer exclusively either to amorous verse or to the couplet style founded by Waller, since Collins never seems to have been much tempted either by the genre or by the style in question. The necessity of often going back to a place one oft retreats from suggests the compulsion to repeat that I have taken to govern the overall structure of Collins's poem. This compulsion stems unquestionably from the erotic sources that can be found in the poem itself, but it has nothing to do with the pretty pastoralism of *vers de société*. Collins is simply incapable of writing that sort of poem. His exquisite "Sonnet" (1739), for example, begins with a *concetto* that is overwhelmed almost immediately by an awed vision of the birth of Venus, and the bizarre inscription "on a Paper which contained a Piece of Bride Cake" frightens the reader away from a darkened and hallowed place under the poet's pillow. For Collins, eroticism cannot be lighthearted because it is much too profoundly alluring.

Who can say, in truth, having read Collins's ode, with its genealogical myth of sport in heaven and its secret invocation to Venus, whether the myrtle shade might not be a more godlike and cosmogonic choice (however unsettling and disillusioning) than Milton's oak? An ode cannot answer this question without belittling itself, and so it keeps temptation just out of view, turning aside with jealous leer malign to its last and most diminished calling. Collins's ode, like many other odes, ends with an Alexandrine of loss, having determined by way of compensation that the "one alone" to whom the bliss of paradise was known was certainly not Milton, nor was he the creator of the Bower of Bliss. As the text states so plainly that no one can quite believe it, the one alone was Adam.[34]

III

For the attentive reader of the "Ode on the Poetical Character," the famous opening lines of the "Ode to Evening" are full of implications that challenge without wholly spoiling Collins's triumph of purity:

> If aught of oaten stop or pastoral song
> May hope, chaste Eve, to soothe thy modest ear,
> > Like thine own solemn springs,
> > Thy springs and dying gales,
> O nymph reserved, while now the bright-haired sun
> Sits in yon western tent, whose cloudy skirts,
> > With brede ethereal wove,
> > O'erhang his wavy bed;

The purification of Waller's myrtle shade in the "Ode to Evening" is Collins's pastoral choice. Perhaps as a result of his struggle to confront the poetical character, he decides that the praise of chastity in the ode may fairly be local and superficial as well as archaeological. He is resolved no longer to worry about what the sun is doing in his wavy bed, though doubtless fables of Tithonus and Aurora have their music too; he no longer tries to lift the sky's "cloudy skirts" but calmly walks in their shadow. There is loss in this temperance and a new cordiality toward inhibiting screens, but the result is no shallow complacency. In this ode, the persistence of the erotic becomes a haunting.

Both the descriptive "Evening" and its allegorical companion poem, the "Ode to Simplicity," belong to the ancient genre of the idyllium, sacred to Hesperus and to Philomel but also to erotic love. Of all traditions, this one has probably contributed most to the lyrics that we call "haunting." It marks the meeting place of ode and elegy, and it effects a vocational compromise that makes up for the loss of passion by embracing temperance. The Hellenistic lyricists are the acknowledged fathers of this tradition, but all such poetry in English is more nearly indebted to the elegiacally rendered lines that precede Adam's address to his chaste Eve in *Paradise Lost*, "Now came still Evening on" (IV. 591-609).[35] Because this evening falls before the Fall, thenceforward the Miltonic scene is irrevocable, but not for want of being reinvoked.

An exemplary poem of transition between the tryst-idyll and the lonelier serenade of Collins is Akenside's "Ode to the Evening Star,"[36] in which, on the occasion of a pilgrimage, the poet laments the loss of "fair Olympia" in her "virgin tomb." Led at first by the inferior light of the evening star (the moon is "retir'd" with Endymion, no doubt reflecting the sun's misbehavior in other poems), the poet journeys down a slippery bank. The impression that he is falling, or at least stumbling, is increased by the name of Adam hidden in the description: "Down the red marl [i.e., clay] with moss o'ergrown." On this far slope of life, the poet needs more guidance than a faint light can afford, and relies more and more on the vocal guidance of the nightingale. Thanks to the necromantic voice of the bird, he enters a haunted circle, there to regain with increment his power of sight. Here the oak of the *locus sanctus* and the myrtle shade of the *locus amoenus* are perfectly reconciled, and, with the evening grown much later, a haunting occurs:

> See the green space: on either hand
>   Enlarg'd it spreads around:
> See, in the midst she takes her stand,
> Where one old oak his awful shade
> Extends o'er half the level mead
>   Inclos'd in woods profound.
>
> Hark, how through many a melting note
>   She now prolongs her lays:
> How sweetly down the void they float!
> The breeze their magic path attends:
> The stars shine out: the forest bends:
>   The wakeful heifers gaze.

This is a confused poem on the whole that will not survive interpretation; it is enough to say that into these two stanzas Akenside has pressed nearly all the raw material that makes up the evening ode in English. "She now prolongs her lays" recalls both the prolonging of heavenly closure by golden-age harmony on the morning of the Nativity Ode and also the length added by Cecilia to solemn sounds in Dryden. All these delays stubbornly extend the power of music into the silent void of natural science; they are like the late overhearing of Milton's "evening ear," and like the ode itself.

Collins's "Ode to Evening" is built out of these same materials, which are warranted in the 1747 volume by the ideological gloss that Collins provides for them in the "Ode to Simplicity."[37] That poem must be attended to, because while it is not confused, like Akenside's, it is not at all simple. The "Ode to Simplicity" is a modest conjuration that forswears high presuming hopes and calls upon a "chaste unboastful nymph." She is invoked "by" all the places and times that can be associated with her. The formulae of conjuration draw the descriptive stanzas of the ode perilously close to the orbit of black magic;[38] this set of devices is called into service, in fact, by the poet's hope that Simplicity will find a new "haunt." The force of Collins's will to purify does very nearly succeed, however, in keeping passions and primal fears aloof. The remaining difficulty is that a figure like Simplicity calls attention to all the problems associated with personification, problems that troubled Collins's contemporaries as deeply as they trouble modern readers. Simplicity is an empty subject, an affect and not an intending object or content. If she is to be conjured into visibility, therefore, her allegorical attributes must necessarily reflect the phenomenal ground on which she cannot appear without ceasing to be simple. Thus when the poet conjures by the simple nightingale he instantly calls up instead, by periphrasis, the experience of Euripides' nightingale—the agonies of absence, sexual loss and dismemberment that are too painful to be "simple" and belong rather in the odes to Fear and Pity:

> By her, whose love-lorn woe
> In evening musings slow
> Soothed sweetly sad Electra's poet's ear:

If Simplicity belongs to the ground of being, she is not simple, but if she transcends that ground, she will not appear in her own right. Like the mesode of "Poetical Character," this poem forces one to inquire how the Idea of nature is to be distinguished from nature itself. It was the business of eighteenth-century personification to maintain that such distinctions exist and should be observed. To recast Gray's pronouncement on the language of poetry from this standpoint, the semiabstractness of poetic diction should never descend to the atomism of ordinary language.[39] In Collins's odes, however, there is a strong urge to dissolve the distinction between idea and ground in order to discover the ideal in some local habitation. The "Ode to Simplicity" invokes a quality "by Nature taught/To breathe her genuine thought." Simplicity *is* the warble of birds and the hum of bees, and her chastity remains in question because we only know her as a procreative sound.

For this reason, Collins knows better than to confine Simplicity to the strain of a virgin birth, and hedges (as does Milton in his etiology of Euphrosyne, the amenable genius) regarding her provenance in his mental pantheon: Simplicity "first . . ./In Fancy, loveliest child,/Thy babe or Pleasure's, nursed the powers of song!" The chain of tutelage is clear, but it cannot be reconstructed genealogically. The quest of this poem is somewhat paradoxical; it is the quest for a place of contentment that would put an end to desire without rejecting the objects of desire: "I only seek to find thy temperate vale." In this Saturnian bower, where the climate is even and the distraining passions are unknown,[40] every Jack still has his Jill, and Nature is as lavish as ever in "sons." As usual, however, prolepsis has forestalled the quest. The Albion of the mind has already been declared lost to every future view in the seventh stanza, which decries the tyranny of an opposite climate in society, contaminated by a "servile" poetry of the enervated libido. Collins's vision of Albion's daughters is obscured by the glittering reign of fair Chloé.

The request for relocation (take me here, place me there, bear me to yon grot, and so forth) is one of the most tiresome conventions of the sampler-odes spawned by L'Allegro and Il Penseroso; not until the "Ode to a Nightingale" is it properly dusted off. Collins cannot fully reconcile the reader to this device, but he handles it better than any of his contemporaries because he is able to make it a functional sign of a presentation crisis. In this respect the "Ode to Evening" is undoubtedly his masterpiece. Evening is the descriptive equivalent of Simplicity, a genius so intricately grounded in her successive locales that she grows transparent, a scene in the shape of a nymph, like Keats's Autumn. Her mission is to restore content to contentment and to banish desire from her mild zone, which engirts every English locale in which Evening may appear transparently as Albion.

Temperance and Simplicity, who are near allies if not twins, are the qualities that encode, merely in being mentioned, the immense ideological variety of the Whig aesthetic. In politics, in morals, and in poetics, they represent the difficult ideal of liberty without license. Limited monarchy and squirearchical benevolism, warm but innocent love, irregular gardening, a flexible and in some cases openly dissenting view of the sacraments and the Articles of Faith; a leaning toward romance rather than epic, elegy rather than satire, complaint rather than panegyric, and, in poetics, toward pleasure rather than instruction—all these qualities accompany the growing fashion for an ode that falls midway between the conventions of Pindarism and Horatianism. A typical ode of this sort adapts a moderately elevated or "rapt" tone to the celebration of what it would be like to live soberly in a liberal climate. But neither Pindar nor even the Horace of the retirement odes can wholly account for the Whig tone of the mid-century ode. The Greek pastoral elegists

and the early Virgil come closer, but it is, of course, the minor poems
of the dissenting Milton, and the descriptive interludes of his major
poems, that supply nearly every cadence of the Warton School.

One finds the steady and clear-sighted disapproval of all these
ideological signs everywhere in Johnson's *Lives.* An ideologue him-
self, he knew how intimately the most disparate strands of opinion
are interwoven; the contexture of his own simplest pronouncements
is nowhere clearer than in his repeated rough handling of Milton and
of the ode as a genre. Among the Whig Gray's odes, he admired only
"Adversity," which he evidently read as a hymn.[41] Collins he treated
leniently because he had known and liked him, but he could find
little to say in praise of the odes, and his censure of their too fertile
imaginings is a Tory censure. The patriotism that Johnson called the
last refuge of scoundrels has too rarely been recognized for a specific
kind of patriotism: Johnson believed that the praise of a Saturnian
climate of affairs was an escape into unreality, an illegitimate patrio-
tism with no known historical precedent or father. As Lord Lans-
downe comparably complains in his *Essay Upon Unnatural Flights in
Poetry* (Chalmers, XI. 27), any poet who is "driven with ungovern-
able fire,/Or void of art" will deliver "monstrous births." So it is,
in politics and poetics alike, when moral topographies turn utopian.

An early personification of the spirit that lurks in Johnson's
"last refuge" or unnatural womb appeared in a low, vulgar, and
disgusting poem that mentions "the genius of the shore." This
spirit reappears in Collins's temperate vale of Simplicity and comes
finally to reign in Blake's green and pleasant land. Such a sacred and
pleasant place as this is the goal of containment in the mid-century
ode; it is the "fairy circle" (T. Warton, "Ode to Fancy") where the
Druids exercized their mantic voices, the place and hope of the
Whig poet's invocation. Compulsively, though, as we have seen, hope
turns to elegy, as in the beginning and end of Collins's "Ode
Occasioned by the Death of Mr Thomson": "In yonder grave a
Druid lies." The poetic moment of Whig patriotism is a meditation
among the tombs that invariably finds the temperate vale in dark-
ness, curtained close but still haunted, as in the Death of Thomson
Ode:

> And see, the fairy valleys fade,
> Dun night has veiled the solemn view!

—Yet once again, dear parted shade,
　　Meek Nature's child, again adieu!

The shade is parted, but "Remembrance oft shall haunt the shore."[42]

The reader will have wondered what the difference is between an elegy and the odes that I persist in reading elegiacally. The two kinds are mirror opposites: the compensatory turn of elegy is ode-like, while the final movement of the ode is elegiac. As soon as it is agreed, however, that lyrics have a way of miniaturizing their holistic self-conception at every moment of their course, this distinction will seem too schematic. Both kinds juggle gain and loss too swiftly for the schematic eye—or indeed for their own intentions—to follow. There is still an area of difference, however, that I should wish to defend, and that has to do with the presence in each kind of its ideal self-identification. It is at this level that I would expect daemonic laughter to overtake each kind from opposite directions. The elegy longs for the grinning and inscrutable dead who refuse recovery. The ode is haunted by death against its will, by the death-like prefigurativity of the movement from nothingness to origins that mocks any celebration of living orders. Possibly if one were to carry even this distinction a step further, only one mode of self-betrayal would stand revealed in either kind. But then one would have arrived at a level of sheer textuality that makes of the concept "ode" in any guise a false denomination. Since I have chosen as my subject an experiment with vestigial shapes (making an ode of my own discourse), deliberately clinging to a kind that current *Gattungs-theorie* assumes to be "merely formal," I am not prepared, for the moment, to take this last step.

My approach will be found, however, to entail its own trans-generic concept, a concept that appears on consideration of an ode's intertextual bearing. The arrogance that modifies even the ode's concession of presentational failure is most prominent, as I have shown, in Progress odes such as "Poetical Character," which I part company from most readers in *not* elegizing. The ode effects a strange distortion of all the texts it commemorates and absorbs: *it makes them all odes*,[43] either by stressing their theurgic moments or by showing that in sidestepping the challenge of mantic invocation with its reductive pars epica, epics and plays are merely weak-jointed odes that yield to the pluralism of their cast of characters.[44]

Thus Gray's reservations about the daemonic or monstrously born infant Shakespeare may be glossed from Johnson's "Preface": "[Shakespeare] seems to write without any moral purpose." And thus some imp in Collins rebukes Milton: the sprawl of epic is unchaste. An ode trims monsters to its own decorum, but with this dialectically emergent result: the sprawl and, as it were, the erotic multiplying of occasions and affects that suit the loose decorum of the more expansive genres *must* be subdued in support of the ode's commitment to oneness—to univocity, to monotheicity, and even to the Hartleyan associative principle that unifies "irregularity"— but this necessary repression can never be complete, because the djinni of the other genres will not stay bottled up.

The dead return to the ode, then, with a libidinous overcharge; and this they will not do in elegy because it is in the nature of elegy to absent the dead by calling for them. In contrast with Gray's "Elegy," which leaves "each in his narrow cell for ever laid," and in contrast also with Collins's "Song from Cymbeline," where "No wailing ghost shall dare appear" to "vex a virgin tomb," the Death of Thomson Ode is haunted without effort. What causes the ode to be haunted, as we have seen in Jonson and Milton, is its ambiguous attraction to "twi-/Light," to the too early or too late hour of its calling:

> Ne'er be I found, by [Fear] o'erawed,
> In that thrice-hallowed eve abroad,
> When ghost, as cottage-maids believe,
> Their pebbled beds permitted leave.
>
> ["Ode to Fear"]

We may test some of these new axioms by returning at last to the tonally elegiac "Ode to Evening." The ghosts in this poem are two texts of Milton, the translation of Horace's Pyrrha Ode, from which Collins takes the meter of "Evening," and the evocation of evening in *Paradise Lost*. If my impression of generic monopolism in the ode is correct, the Pyrrha Ode will prove to anticipate the bottling or distillation of Collins's evening, whereas *Paradise Lost* will be the rebuked rival genre that overturns Collins's bower.

"Plain in thy neatness" is how Milton smooths over Horace's near-oxymoron for Pyrrha's hair, "*simplex munditie.*" This phrase in Latin well describes the paradise that is vainly sought in Collins's companion poems, "Simplicity" and "Evening." Pyrrha herself, unlike her temperate hair and exactly like Akenside's moon or Collins's "lov'd Enthusiast," is fickly "retir'd" on business that Horace can only suspect; she is curtained close in a bower that in both Horace and Milton may faintly anticipate the sun's "wavy bed" in Collins: "What slender Youth bedew'd with liquid odors/ Courts thee on Roses in some pleasant Cave." By allusion, then, Collins's "nymph reserved" is two-faced, gone west perhaps with the sun to leave the natural evening a void of hope, or else far more deeply involved with the forces of nature than her transparency and the detachment of her presiding would have us believe. These are the direst possible outcomes of the fusion of "spirit and place" that Hartman has called a "prothalamion" (*Beyond Formalism*, pp. 323–24).

Horace is so badly shaken by the discrepancy between the complex Pyrrha and her memorably simple hair that he vows from now on to keep to the lee shore and avoid all treacherous experience. From the beginning to the end of his ode the element of danger is "liquid," a Cytherean and fluxuous ocean; his renunciation consigns Pyrrha to her wavy bed. The only bedtime in Collins's "Ode to Evening" is that of a bright-haired *puer*, the sun, and Collins can only hope to keep his neatly plain Evening (whose sounds are nature's homeliest) away from that dark bed as long as possible. The trouble is that all the other firmaments are rivals too. The evening star, with his nuptial torch, traditionally keeps watch when greater stars are preoccupied elsewhere, but here he seems to light the way to his own bed when the poet concedes Hesper's possession *by* Evening, "thy folding star," implying that when the shepherd (or sheep) returns to the fold it is not he who will be folded in Evening's embrace. The ode evokes a long evening, diverted by as many "Pensive Pleasures" as possible and finally made to span the whole year. These delays, like the prolonging of heavenly closes, postpone an unsanctified nuptial. Like Horace, Collins hopes to screen out the storms of passion:

> O how oft shall [the new lover]
> On Faith and changed Gods complain: and Seas
> Rough with black winds and storms
> Unwonted shall admire.
>
> [Milton's Horace]

> But when chill blustering winds or driving rain
> Forbid my willing feet, be mine the hut
>   That from the mountain's side
>   Views wilds and swelling floods.
>
> [Collins]

In this hut Collins finds himself just where Satan-Milton was stationed in "Poetical Character," but now he looks in the opposite direction, downward toward the future perils of fallen man and away from the evening of *Paradise Lost* IV. An important result of the Fall in Milton was the axial slippage of the planet that brought on the Seasons, "else had Spring/Perpetual smil'd on Earth" (X. 678–79); the effect of this event on Adam reminds one of the effect of storms on Horace and also on Collins in his "hut" and "sylvan shed":[45]

> The growing miseries, which Adam saw
> Already in part, though hid in gloomiest shade,
> To sorrow abandon'd, but worse felt within,
> And in a troubl'd Sea of passion tost,
> Thus to disburd'n sought with sad complaint.
>
> [X. 715–19]

All this because of Eve. Collins takes Milton's evening in paradise as a model ode, but he cannot reduce its epic aftermath to a serenade. As if under compulsion, Collins includes decay and Winter in Evening's neighborhood:

> While sallow Autumn fills thy lap with leaves,
> Or Winter, yelling through the troublous air,
>   Affrights thy shrinking train,
>   And rudely rends thy robes.

At this point, when Evening is most threatened, Collins for the first time guards her honor without innuendo, because she is raped against her will.[46] It follows, however, that in an intemperate climate the will to chastity must no longer be free. The unhappily abrupt transition between winter's ravishment of evening and Collins's cheerful conclusion marks the gulf between desire and the temperate vale of Simplicity. Evening is a haunting "influence," like the grave of Thomson, but only her "name," with all its attendant confused echoes, can be hymned. Her absence must be written, not in a hymn, but in an ode.

To the ode, again, all of literature is an ode, or would be, at least, if the ode could purify its sources. In the "Ode on the Popular Superstitions of the Highlands of Scotland," Collins accomplishes the task of purification by lowering his standards. In this loose string of Spenserian romance stanzas, Collins less elegantly realizes Keats's later conclusion that it is wisest for the ode, as a shrine or altar, not to seal itself off too tightly, but rather to "leave a casement ope at night,/To let the warm Love in." Accordingly, Collins begins in the key of the "Ode to Evening." John Home, like Evening, has been "lingering, with a fond delay" in the temperate south. Quickly, however, the newly robust and loose-limbed Collins swerves from evening's delay to welcome an approaching nuptial, even though, once more, it is not his own: "Together, let us wish [Thomas Barrow] lasting truth,/And joy untainted with his destined bride." This first stanza is so disjointed, indeed (it seems genuinely to have been written for a private audience), that it could almost be called an epistle and not an ode. But its thorough handling of the irresolution about origins to which Collins devotes his odes is evidence enough that this poem is a new approach to an old kind.[47] Its purpose is to subsume the greater genres by enlarging itself.

John Home is a pity-full tragedian, a "gentle mind" like Otway in the "Ode to Pity," who may hope that someday an audience will "melt, perhaps, to hear [his] tragic song." No one to my knowledge has noticed how licentious it is, even for Poetic Diction, to call a play a song; it was, of course, commonplace to do so, but I shall try to show that in Collins this commonplace is significant. Collins's envoi advises Home to ransack Scottish folklore for tragic subjects. What is strange, though, is that not one of the subjects canvassed in this poem is suitable for a tragic plot. Everything in the poem is suffused by Romance, the traditional faerie genre; Home will hear "Strange lays, whose power had charmed a Spenser's ear" (39), and the annals of fierce war will be "some sounding tale of war's alarms" (49). But although this poem meanders enough almost to become a romance itself, even that congenial genre will finally yield to the ode's monopoly.

By way of assuring Home that witching tales are not really "false themes," Collins points to their use in sophisticated genres. But even though Shakespeare is "with every garland crown'd," Collins evokes only one of them, the druidical crown that empowers hauntings in

Macbeth: "There Shakespeare's self . . ./In musing hour [evening, the hour of Euripides in the "Ode to Simplicity"] his Wayward Sisters found,/And with their terrors dressed the magic scene" (176–78). Shakespeare "sung" (179) this scene, and also sang the scene where "The shadowy kings of Banquo's fated line,/Through the dark cave in gleamy pageant passed" (181–82). These are scenes, not from theatre, but from the runic and the allegorical ode, respectively, of the mid-eighteenth century. Of *Macbeth* as a whole, Collins says only that it is a "bold design," recalling the "high presuming hopes" of epic in the "Ode on the Poetical Character." Romance undergoes a more lenient reduction; what is unquestionably a proper romance episode from Tasso is given room to breathe life into a magic world where "each live plant with mortal accents spoke." (The fact that Collins could as easily have taken this miracle from Virgil or Dante shows that he is not merely reducing but in fact ignoring indisputably sublime narratives.) For the poet himself, however, the experience of Tasso is altered in genre as well as language in having been translated, as the phrasing suggests, into a British lyric: "How have I sat, where piped the pensive wind,/To hear his harp by British Fairfax strung."

Unlike tragedy, Romance can be sung, and so it nearly keeps its identity when its genre is changed. But still, to Collins's evening ear, *Jerusalem Delivered* has no sound if it does not sound like an ode. Every poem of every kind seems in retrospect to have been sung by "Old Runic bards" who "shall seem to rise around/With uncouth lyres" (41–42), the same bards who rose for Drayton and who will soon rise for Gray. Clearly Collins cannot be seriously advising Home to look for tragic subjects when he says, "to my ear transmit some gentle song" (159). No matter what the intrinsic nature of Home's "native legends" may be, "To such," the poet exhorts, "adapt thy lyre." On the contrary, it is a question of adapting the legend to the lyre, and Collins in this ode has furnished a model adaptation. His ode is a "choral dirge" (45) that mourns the passing of superstitions, of the greater genres, and of the poet's "absent friend" from England; but at the same time the ode easily absorbs and transforms all these ghosts, especially the ghost of John Home, whose "new scenes" are "touched with love like" that of the univocal Collins. They are no longer the scenes of a dramatist but the "magic scenes" of an apprentice bard.[48]

All these reductions are weakly managed, depending as they do on the patchy phrasing and halting logic of this ode, his most uneven by far. But the relation to be inferred from this example between structural laxity and the reduction of anxiety is highly significant for the student of the ode. It was in the eighteenth century, after all, with its epic and tragic vacuum filled by cartloads of odes, that it first became a habit to call Shakespeare "The Bard." When Shakespeare and Milton were most narrowly constricted, as poetic ideals, by the audacious formalities of the best odes, they turned daemonic and burst their bonds. A poem that was lax enough, on the other hand, but still tenuously an ode, could tame any number of kelpies and other spooks merely because it was not "rapt" enough to miss their footsteps in the dark.

> At those mirk hours the wily monster lies,
> And listens oft to hear the passing steed,
>   And frequent round him rolls his sullen eyes,
> If chance his savage wrath may some weak wretch surprise.

In the poetics of the ode, weakness is unpreparedness, inflexibility. The loose-jointed ode, clumsily mounted on its wingèd steed, has nothing to fear or gain from the uprising of monstrous births. Unrepressed, as in this passage, they circulate freely and trivially. Everyone expects them on Hallowe'en.

IV

> It lies in the nature of poetry to be always straining towards a plenum of consciousness, and of knowledge, which (if achieved) would bring about its own destruction, that it is, as has been finely said, "a ship that is wrecked on entering harbour."
> —Owen Barfield, *Poetic Diction* (1952), p. 26

The structure of prayer will always seem a little arbitrary in a secular context, as any student will notice when he tries to apply the notion of "lyric development" (learned from the study of poems like "The Extasie" and "Tintern Abbey") to sustained evocations like the "Ode to Evening." It takes an effort of relearning in order to see that in the ode, generally speaking, repetition and recurrence are more important semaphores than the drift of argument, and that often, in fact, repetition nullifies the semantics of argument altogether. What I say here of the ode has often been said of all texts whatsover. The

text qua text can be seen as a tissue of repetition that feigns break-
throughs into absolute difference, with the reiteration of a dilemma
staging itself as a happy movement from dilemma to cure. The
present study of a literary kind cannot accept this final reduction
without reserving for itself the idea that between the kinds there are
irreducible distinctions of occasion and stress. This reservation re-
treats, not to intention, but to intentional structure, to what I have
called the self-conception of a text, with the still more cautious
proviso that a structure of this sort can never harden in place but
proves rather to be a generically distinct point of unstructuring. The
occasion of the ode is vocative, presentational, yet what it repeats
over and over is the dispersion of voice and presence from the text
that stands in their place. This is true of all odes, but nowhere more
clearly true than in Gray and Collins, who show unexampled daring,
if I may, in their willing submission to the conventions of "vocal"
writing. What their odes repeat, as I have tried to show, is an imagery
of that submission, a circumscriptural imagery based on the central
paradox of formal achievement: the more a circle closes, the more it
closes off its content from the viewer.

   Collins always writes essentially the same poem. In "The Manners.
An Ode," a poem about forsaking the "magic shores" of abstruse
thought and joining the stream of life, a poem surely intended by its
author as a corrective to the other odes, we nevertheless find the
whole plot of the "Ode on the Poetical Character" and the "Ode to
Evening" repeated:

> Farewell the porch, whose roof is seen
> Arched with the enlivening olive's green:
> Where Science, pranked in tissued vest,
> By Reason, Pride, and Fancy dressed,
> Comes like a bride so trim arrayed,
> To wed with Doubt in Plato's shade.

The inept anti-intellectual satire of this passage presents once again
the wedding at which Collins is always a reluctant but fascinated
guest and thwarted voyeur. Under the porch, the roof, the tissue, the
shade, where a neatly plain nymph and a bold rival sequester them-
selves, it might be possible to witness conception, but the poet,
whisked off in rapture blind, is never wrapped in the scene's em-
brace.[49] His farewell to such forces is appropriate because he is not

in their presence, but it is not a dismissal because he has never been in their presence.

The eighteenth-century ode never claims to have known a prior state of bliss, even though it evinces a constant voyeuristic wonderment about what such a state might be like. There is no childhood for man or culture in Gray because he fears the "fearful joy" of childhood and screens it out periphrastically. Collins is bolder; he nervously confronts the screen, tests its density, and finds himself repulsed, never quite becoming a "Youth of quick uncheated sight" ("Manners"). In this and the previous chapter I have discussed odes (all but Wordsworth's "Ode to Duty") that claim no more than to suspect where they came from. The remarks that follow are meant partly to review the nature of this confessed impasse, with its attendant rewards, and partly to cast a theory of the ode some way farther ahead.

Like modern criticism, Gray and Collins are text-obsessed, and the intertextual play of their odes is no less self-conscious than our commitment to the idea of interpretation as palimpsest. Their odes imply a theory of writing, "charactering," printing, as the demarcation of absence, or, in short, as death.

> Leave ample room and verge enough,
> The characters of hell to trace.
>
> [Gray]

> Heaven and Fancy, kindred powers,
> Have now o'erturned the inspiring bowers.
>
> [Collins]

In screening voice, the circumscriptural ode sacrifices the aural as well as the visual knowledge of conception and birth, sacrifices the knowledge that Collins conceded, through many mediations, to Milton's evening ear. Without a persuasive figure for vocal priority at one's disposal, there can be no Crocean distinction between receiving and creating a stamp; that is, between impression and expression. Inspiration itself becomes chirographic, a sexless imprint upon Locke's sensorium that simultaneously enables and unmans Collins's ideal of chaste independence. As a result, Collins's experiments with the personified fusion of spirit and ground reduce all signification to a single plane; there is no difference between blueprint and building, or between "calling with thought" and weaving the birth of the universe. This reduction is what also eliminates the difference between childhood and adulthood, as well as the difference between freedom and determinacy.

If there is a loss of mythic variety in these reductions, there is a consoling gain in poignancy that derives from the poet's prescience about the closeness of death in the haunted silence of writing. This intuition seems in itself to be an adequate motive for the powerfully sophisticated odes of Gray, and also for Collins's finest achievement with "poetic diction":

> Now air is hushed, save where the weak-eyed bat
> With short shrill shriek flits by on leathern wing,
> > Or where the beetle winds
> > His small but sullen horn,
> As oft he rises midst the twilight path,
> Against the pilgrim borne in heedless hum:
> > Now teach me, maid composed,
> > To breathe some softened strain,
> Whose numbers stealing through thy darkening vale
> May not unseemly with its stillness suit;
> > As musing slow, I hail
> > Thy genial loved return!

Clumsily artless and sightless nature casts up its dogged, unintelligible sounds, vocal to itself alone, and ushers consciousness into the atmosphere of dying. Perhaps the most religious instant in Collins is his pilgrim's encounter with the beetle, "borne in heedless hum" by something beyond its own motor. Evening is the vehicle, the same nymph whose being composed prolongs the "dying gales," but death is the high tenor, whose shrill shriek decomposes into silence.[50] Collins's death wish, compulsively repeating the genial loved return of Evening, is part invocation and part welcome, since Evening is one of those powers that comes whether we will or no.

Not death, of course, but an advance sense of dying is what writing preserves, and with that sense, as in this passage, an attenuated experience of voice, "some softened strain," is preserved as well. The most haunted knowledge of evening belongs to early youth, and so childhood does have a modest place in the evening ode; but the innocent voice of childhood ("Now teach me") is overawed by premonition and speaks dryly, like the beetle, or like the anacreontic cicada. Nature's most sadly comforting sounds are thin repetitions, not "swelling" like the magic notes of the loved Enthusiast, or like the "swelling floods" that the retired speaker only "views" (l. 36).

Water, with its flooding force and resonant voice, is a dangerous region where the sun sleeps in Gray and Collins. Gray's solidified, unresponsive, and labyrinthine rivers check the energy of change, and Collins's odes are almost wholly wanting in awareness of the flood.[51] The "youth" in Collins represses, or tries to repress, the liquid trill of his conception and his immersion in the heedlessly humming current of time since the deluge. Writing, in one of its aspects—its textured appearance—almost successfully accomplishes this repression: "o'er all," Collins tells his gossamer Evening, "Thy dewy fingers draw/The gradual dusky veil." But the dew, like the homeopathic *uvida vestimenta* that Horace in the Pyrrha Ode hangs up to keep Neptune from the door, cannot be omitted, and Evening breaks out in a cold sweat that belies the composure of her hands.

Another aspect of writing, its potency as an act, more boldly negates the possibility of composition. If writing is to remain pure, it cannot be influential, as Matthew Green graphically insists, in *The Spleen*, when he vows conformity to impersonal orders:

> I rail not with mock-patriot grace
> At folks, because they are in place;
> Nor, hir'd to praise with stallion pen,
> Serve the ear-lechery of men;
> But to avoid religious jars
> The laws are my expositors,
> Which in my doubting mind create
> Conformity to church and state.

Because it conforms, *The Spleen* is not an ode; it is a Tory poem that chooses a sociable yet cloistered virtue. Collins, as I have argued, dedicates his odes to a Whig conception of freedom that Addison heralded when he said of landscaping (*Spectator*, 412) that "a spacious horizon is an image of Liberty." The open field that the ode proposes to clear for itself, purified of determinacy, requires that not only childhood but the historic past be ignored. The text of the ode before the Romantic Period is a repository of the past that cannot evade the poetry of the past and endlessly invokes the past; and yet it has no sense of the past. It does not unequivocally constitute itself as a falling away because its periphrases screen out the immediacy and pain of recollecting high origins. When one remarks the strong elegiac tone of the ode before Wordsworth, one must also remark that in the endlessly repetitive odes of Gray and Collins nothing has ever changed, or ever will.

Akenside, whose odes always deliberately retreat from personal themes to the shareable values of the classical topoi, can seem to recover the past as an otherness by appealing to common experience:

> When Hesper gilds the shaded sky,
>> Oft as you seek the well-known grove,
> Methinks I see you cast your eye
>> Back to the morning scenes of love.
>>>> [*Odes* I. 3. "To a Friend"]

But in the mid-century ode, in contrast with all the great elegies from Milton to Tennyson, the dialectic of evening star and morning star is never persuasive. Under a shaded sky, the figure of the lost Venus avails nothing, and no "scenes" materialize. Akenside is the poet who claims in another ode that the muse has returned to him just as she was in his youth—as the happy result of his rereading Milton (I. 10. "To the Muse"). Gray never composed without first reading Spenser. Collins, as Bertrand Bronson unsympathetically but in substance truly remarks, never rids himself of the "collegiate air" of an unreliably informed imitator.[52] An ode that remembers the pastness of others and not the otherness of the past can have nothing to say of fallen experience as a distinct phase. Gray's chirographic bards and censored precursors, Collins's disparadising of Milton and eclipse of the major genres—all these sublimations of envy in counterstatement persuade me that the mid-century Progress ode should be read, as it were, naïvely. How else can we take "poetic diction" if not at its word? A language of poetry that is not the language of the age is never the language of the past either. Original in the mode and insistence of its repetitions if in nothing else, the ode devises its own continuous present.[53]

Repetition is what unlearns the genealogical knowledge of the ode, which creates a world and a god with every stroke of the pen, only in the same movement to absent these creations from the poet's field of vision.[54] Nothing fully exists for any ode except in the act of being called on, but the odes of Gray and Collins are the first important odes that are impelled by the total vacancy of received, hymnically authorized worlds constantly to create their figures ex nihilo. I have tried to argue that, among other figures, these odes create their forerunners, both persons and genres, as though they had never before existed. Epic, tragedy, romance, all are odes, and earlier odes are trial invocations. These reductions make possible the monotheism toward which all odes bend themselves. Brought to being by the poet, "conceived" in whatever chaste terms his ode will allow, the single numen is never other than the singular formality of the ode itself.[55] In the woven or circumscriptural ode, the creation of the numen is a self-creation. Dissatisfied with the pluralistic mythology of divine *or* natural origins in the past, the ode supplies itself instead with an autogenesis that is always present.

The eighteenth-century ode is as antinomian in occasion and self-conception as the seventeenth-century ode, if not more so. Left by choice to their own devices, the odes of Gray and Collins, as much as those of Jonson, Milton, and Dryden, must continuously allay the fear that self-conception may yield a monstrous birth, "called with thought" from dark and uncontrollable sources that are not past (because there is no past) but present. The invocational poet must steer carefully between the danger of calling up demons and the bombast or hysterical pregnancy of having appeared to call up nothing at all—between the terrors of Faust and the absurdity of the yokel conjurers in Marlowe's *Doctor Faustus*.[56] The daring of the ode is described by Edward Young as an embattlement; having remarked that the Pindaric must be "immethodical" and may easily become "an involuntary burlesque," Young concludes, in the "Essay on Lyric Poetry" that prefaces his own disastrous odes: "It holds true in the province of writing, as in war, 'The more danger, the more honour' " (Chalmers, XIII. 403).

Once it is perceived that Collins's Pindaric "Ode to Fear" is not about tragedy but about tragedy as an ode, that poem appears clearly to be written in the spirit of Young's simile, with Aeschylus, hero of Marathon and writer of choral odes, as its most significant hero. This ode begins by compelling Fancy to do what she never does elsewhere—to lift the veil, with terrifying results:

> Thou, to whom the world unknown
> With all its shadowy shapes is shown;

Who see'st appalled the unreal scene,
While Fancy lifts the veil between:

One recalls the gloomy shadows that Gray failed to scatter with Hyperion's "glittering shafts of war" by rewriting epic as lyric; but the more circumspect Gray never thus clearly associated his "imaginary complaints" with repressed scenery. Collins's Fear, fear of nothing but his own hobgoblinry, is really anxiety.[57] Having once identified himself with the "fear" that is designated as a creative principle in the *Poetics*, he then shudders to view its (his) conceptions: "like thee I start, like thee disordered fly./For lo, what monsters in thy train appear." These monsters may be identified rather colorfully by *implication*, but if one carefully attends to their role in the language of the poem, they appear to be nothing other than Pindaric odes; their author "starts," like an abrupt transition in Pindar and also like Pindar's abrupt beginnings, and then retreats in the state of disorder that had malformed the ode since Cowley.

But Collins knows himself to be a better poet than Cowley; he is a regular Pindarist whose power of imaginative compression creates a more serious, and, psychologically speaking, more appalling tension than Cowley ever managed. The first monster in the train of Fear, a giant who couples with other monsters to "prompt to deeds accursed the mind," is Danger, the patron of lyric courage in Young. Collins's odes court Danger with a more brilliant extravagance than appears anywhere in Gray; but one should add that Collins's odes are rarely free from the hysteria that is elegantly subdued to resignation in nearly all of Gray's encounters with "the gulf between." Collins knows his limits, I think, and envisions a power less desperate than his own and more energetic than Gray's (whose Theban eagle lulls himself to sleep, and who never ventures too near the edge of his "gulf") when he reports that Danger "throws him on the ridgy steep/Of some loose hanging rock to sleep." This happy carelessness at the edge of the abyss is what one misses, and finds most openly envied, in the tense, "nervous" odes of the mid-century. Experiments with naturalization in the Romantic ode will seem somewhat to reduce the anxieties of Gray and Collins, but the ode will never, in any era, become truly insouciant in the face of what it comes to know, through constraint, about its own imperfectly contained monsters.

6

Wordsworth's Severe Intimations

As I arrive at the period when genres begin to be "naturalized" along with poetic diction, my continuing to read odes as odes may call for a few further words of defense. In the eighteenth century the genres still comprised a "cosmic syntax"[1] that had its place in an articulate and more or less legible universe. Generic thinking prevailed in most quarters, even though there was often disagreement about the proper hierarchy of the genres: epic was still highest in the criticism of Pope's followers, but a lively minority from John Dennis to Watts and Bishop Lowth placed the "sacred lyric" highest. Johnson was rather unusual in viewing the genres with some disapproval. He opposed the strict decorum of any generic approach to poetry for fear of encouraging insincerity and distorted observation. As one pieces together his strictures on pastoral and the ode, his defense of Shakespeare's mixed genres, and his attention to the local rather than the larger structural features of poetry in all the modes, one realizes how fully he anticipates Wordsworth (though, of course, in behalf of a far more generalized sense of reality) in viewing poetry as the "real language of men."

The challenge to the taxonomic view of literature arose from a resurgence of epistemological trust in what Gray had contemptuously called the "language of the age." A genre, from Aristotle onward, had always been understood to be a fictive solution to the problem of untidiness in the real world, but no one had ever claimed that "history" is not itself far tidier than life. History was more accurate, perhaps, than poetry; but no critic in the line of

Aristotle ever confused verbal representation with objective presentation. As Aristotle himself put the matter in his seminal grammar, the *Categories*, "Substance cannot be predicated."[2] Discourse, in other words, always defers and specie-fies the thing in itself, proceeding necessarily in referential categories. Since generic thinking is therefore inescapable, the Aristotelian might argue, it may as well be cultivated, especially because it does seem to correspond to the several great forms that inhere in nature. Although in the Neoplatonic variant of this tradition that Sidney follows, the generic fictions were understood to merge with a transcendental ground (the Ideal) insofar as they purged the dross of their material ground (the phenomenal apparitions that Plato was right to abuse poets for imitating); and although even among empiricists opinions differed concerning the degree to which genres should realign the nature of things, there was still an implicit belief at the root of every generic theory until 1800 that poetic space is what we largely perceive and moderately re-create according to received models given either by nature or by nature's best metonym, Homer, whose *Margites* and "Homeric Hymns" made him the father of every genre that exists.

A Wordsworthian poetics leads to the new conclusion that poetic space is what we half perceive and half create on the basis of an ad hoc symbiosis of mind with nature. Thus the cosmic syntax or taxonomy formerly given ready-formed to the creative faculties of the poet becomes in Wordsworth a unitary principle that appears in changing ways, according to the pressure of the moment, at the joining place of mind and nature. This powerful reduction to "the one Life within us and abroad" (Coleridge) undermines all gross classification even as it promotes the unique selfhood or substance of "the meanest flower that blows" within the imagined unity of things. The atomistic and the cosmic fuse under the pressure of imagination, leaving the illusion of difference to linger only among intermediate quantities:

> the one interior life
> That lives in all things, sacred from the touch
> Of that false secondary power by which
> In weakness we create distinctions, then
> Believe that all our puny boundaries are things
> Which we perceive and not which we have made.[3]

On this view, symbolism is available to all the arts of expression, symbolism being the making-present of some universal power that is universally absent until by magic the *nomen* grows numinous. This faith in the symbol is meant to quiet our obstinate questionings, whether of sense or of the supersensuous, by waiving altogether the question of the existence or nonexistence of the physical referent. The triangulation of word, thing, and spirit by the "symbol" effaces the thing by sublating its newly glorified selfhood.[4] Only the symbol, as Coleridge might say, "is that it is," an articulate Presence, like the Word. This antigeneric faith, be it said now, is none other than—the faith that typifies the genre called the ode. Were it not antinomian, defiant of determinacy by externally given origins, this faith would attach itself to the office of prayer.

When genre theory reappears in the organization and the Preface of Wordsworth's 1815 *Collected Poems*, it is based in good part on subjective distinctions. The cosmos is still one, but our different faculties (e.g., fancy, imagination) with their different predilections (affection, the need to name, and so on) and phases of perception (e.g., "early youth") will present the "one Life" in various guises that truly are different from each other. Not absolutely but in tendency, Wordsworth transfers the science of genres from cosmology to psychology.[5]

It is only very recently that the idea of a random field of signification, irreducible to any well-ordered syntax of faculties in the conscious subject, has challenged classification of all kinds. According to this view, both objective *and* subjective generic thinking are attributes of a naïve epistemology, or rather of the naïve faith that an epistemology is possible. I think that this Pyrrhonism has always been perceptibly registered by the presentational lyric, despite its generally idealistic aims. The ode, that Great Auk among the birds that are themselves objects of the obsolete science of ornithology, the ode of all forms, has always known the ruptures of dissemination. The sheer textuality of the ode, its re(com)pression of alien generic structures as the daemonic traces of lyric metaphor, yields a skepticism about the contentments of form that belies both occasion and vocation.

Perhaps there is room for yet another sentence in the current debate about periodization, a sentence that would defend my own approach to literary history: *The theoretical discourse of any period lies waiting and implicit in the discursive forms that precede it.* Thus one could support the observation of Fredric Jameson, for whom origins are material and diachronic agencies, that "the new is to the old as latent content working its way to the surface to displace a form henceforth obsolete."[6] Periodization might properly map the passing over of knowledge from its encodement in structure to the discourse about structures: from code to statement, which in turn becomes a new code, harboring anxieties that will force their way into the open in yet later statements. This dialectic would somewhat exaggerate the incidence of change in the series of poems I am studying, however. The knowledge I am tracing in the ode remains partly encoded and partly discursive knowledge in any ode to this day, but periodic changes in the ode can nevertheless still be recorded as topological shifts, irreducibly different, in the near-utterance or dissemination of the repressed. Thus, concerning the great Romantic odes to which I now turn, it will gradually become apparent that in them the sublime, here understood as the uncanny element of lyric inspiration, has been conceived in a way that differs wholly from its conception in the eighteenth-century ode.

I

Wordsworth's early "Remembrance of Collins"[7] reflects a complex and alert reading of Collins's odes. Beginning as Collins once did with Spenser, Wordsworth's "Glide Gently, thus for ever glide,/O Thames!" recognizes Collins's desire to write the poem of his own chaste marriage. Very possibly, therefore, Wordsworth numbers among the motives of the mad "Poet's sorrows" (20) the epithalamic failure of Collins's odes. Interweaving images from the Death of Thomson Ode and the "Ode to Evening" (and also from Thomson's "Hymn on Solitude": "Descending angels bless thy train"), Wordsworth tries to purify Collins's typically mysterious haunted moment by arming it with holiness and scattering the daemonic, as did Milton in the Nativity Ode, with a militant poise:

> How calm! how still! the only sound,
> The dripping of the oar suspended!
> —The evening darkness gathers round
> By virtue's holiest powers attended.

Wordsworth's prayer that the "child of song"(19) be attended by a vision that lightens our falling toward darkness, a vision of the high birthplace both of ourselves and of our virtue, is offered in order to restore the otherness and innocence of the past to the odes of Collins; and, on a far more difficult occasion, it is also the prayer of the Intimations Ode.

The happier past, as a sign of poetic election and of life after death, can be recovered only through that most ontologically treacherous of faculties, memory. Recollection in "calm weather" can never be facile; indeed, it may be wise to assume, upon careful reading, that recollection in the Intimations Ode is recognized to be an exhilarating but futile exercise. In itself, however, the quality of difference between present and past that is given by memory as a newly refined poetic topic[8] — "and, oh! the difference to me!" — enables the odes of Wordsworth and his major contemporaries to represent change more plausibly than any of Gray's or Collins's resources had permitted. But only *more* plausibly. The Romantic ode writer hopes that one change—from past to present—will imply the coming of another, the redemption of the present. But the disappointment of that hope cannot be avoided, owing to the continued necessity of repetition, which insists upon the immutability of the present. No naturalizing of vocative devices can ever completely suppress this immutability because, after all, the presupposed existence of some indivisible and unchanging power is just what an ode is written to celebrate. The ode bends the quality of difference in all experience to its mono-myth, which is only speciously genealogical.

All the great odes I shall discuss from now on are evening odes.[9] The veils of Gray and Collins are taken over by the Romantics as a sober coloring of clouds and tropes at sundown that still conceals the "wavy bed" (Wordsworth's "mighty waters") of the sun-poet's origin. That the sense of evening in the Romantic ode is yet more intense than in earlier odes can be shown in a rough way even by comparative biography. Whereas eighteenth-century poets, even Swift, began their careers by assaying the vocational challenge of Pindarism, Wordsworth and Coleridge "began" (if we disregard their school exercises) in the quieter keys of the topographical poem and the slighter lyric modes. M. H. Abrams's inclusion of the Intimations Ode and "Dejection. An Ode" in his persuasively described unifying

genre, "the greater Romantic lyric" (encompassing the common
themes and structure of the sublime ode and the Conversation Poem),
may be questioned simply by appealing to dates. Nearly all the
major Conversation Poems of both Wordsworth and Coleridge were
written well before the Companion odes that were begun in 1802,
begun in response to growing intimations of loss.[10] If the eighteenth-
century poet proved himself to be a poet by writing an ode, the
Romantic poet proved himself *still* to be a poet by writing an ode,
but no longer a poet gifted with unmediated vision. The turning of
Wordsworth and Coleridge to the unnatural conventions of ode
writing is itself a farewell to the natural holiness of youth.

II

> L'ode chante l'éternité, l'épopée sollenise l'histoire, le drame peint
> peint la vie. Le caractère de la première poésie est la naïveté, le carac-
> tère de la seconde est la simplicité, le caractère de la troisieme, la
> vérité. . . . Les personnages de l'ode sont des colosses: Adam, Caïn,
> Noé; ceux de l'épopée sont des géants: Achille, Atrée, Oreste; ceux
> du drame sont des hommes: Hamlet, Macbeth, Othello. L'ode vit
> l'idéal. . . .
>
> —Victor Hugo, *Preface de Cromwell* (1827)

From its publication to the present, the Intimations Ode has had the
reputation of being Wordsworth's most confused poem.[11] In this
respect it is appropriately an ode or, more precisely, an irregular
Pindaric. What Wordsworth dictated to Miss Fenwick, "To the
attentive and competent reader the whole sufficiently explains
itself" (*Poetical Works* IV. 463), curiously recalls Gray's "vocal to
the intelligent alone." As we have seen, from Jonson through Collins,
the Pindaric form is a refuge for confusion; it both reflects and
deepens uncertainties that will not lend themselves to forthright
treatment. As a final preface to the Romantic ode, we may review
here, in the form of a summary typology, the confusions that lie
beneath the unending hope of the ode to stand purely, through
invocation, in the pure presence of what its presentation always
stains and darkens.

Here, then, is the normative course of an ode. Some quality of
absolute worth is traced back to its conception, where it appears as
a fountainhead, sunrise, or new star. But the landscape of dawning,

inescapably twilit, is instinct with regional spirits that misbehave and will not be reduced to order. It is impossible for the compressions of syntax and figure to avoid implicating these dark spirits in the ur-conception of the ode and of its numen alike. Such spirits are "kept aloof" at first, like Collins's "dangerous passions," by the ode's shifting of its etiology from the spiritual to the sublunary plane— from theogony, in other words, to the earliest stages of recorded history or childhood. This descent from the divine is halted and in some measure reversed by the poet's location of a primitive society or early selfhood in a region that he still calls sacred (the magic circle, garland, manger, shrine, or temple). The history of poetry, meanwhile, is imagined as one great ode, sacralized by the analogy between the holy place the ode describes and the circle of its own form. Hence, the transcendent pastness of the past is lost almost completely in the defensive act of exorcizing its false, daemonic, and generically diverse oracles. Once great Pan is pronounced dead, the oracle grows nearly silent, and the vocal occasion of the ode, con-secrated to the celebration of the present, is mediated and muted by all the formal defenses that writing ritualizes.

In violent denial of this loss, the ode now loudly reasserts its divine calling: it hazards the frenzied tropes of identification that we call "enthusiastic"[12] and then quickly collapses into self-caricature. This is the brief noontide phase of the ode, envisioned as a Phaeton-myth of flight followed by blindness and a fall into or toward the sea. The sun has been placed once more too squarely in view, so that the excessive bright of its cloudy skirts becomes an ominous darkness, like the darkness of dawn. To avoid the bathos of Phaeton's death, the poet reins in ("Stop, stop, my muse," exclaims Cowley in "The Resurrection," "allay thy vig'rous heat!") and adjusts himself to the light of common day. In the decline of this light toward evening, the ode accepts a diminished calling, often movingly and even cheerfully embraced as the hymning of a favorite name, and never reasserts its enthusiastic mission. Even this dénouement is marred, however, by the regathering and haunting of twilit forces.

We may adapt some of these outlines to the Intimations Ode in order to establish a viewpoint from which its confusion may then be reconsidered more carefully. Wordsworth's ode opens with the recol-lection of a pastoral dawn[13] when the sun, in place of the poet, had a "glorious birth." This happy scene is peopled by the usual denizens of the vernal ode—songbirds, frolicking animals—from whose jubilee the speaker is excluded. In content the scene is that of the "Sonnet on the Death of West" abused by Wordsworth in his 1800 Preface. In earlier life the speaker's spontaneous vision helped "apparel" the scene he now adorns more conventionally. In order to make himself present to his own childhood, as he attempted to do by evoking the Boy of Winander in *The Prelude*, Wordsworth now invokes and petitions the happy voice of the Shepherd-boy. His identification with a better self, which is wholly fitting in an ode, seems for the moment to yield rewards. The Babe leaps up, as Wordsworth's heart had leapt up the day before, to nestle closer to Mother Nature. But— and here the voice of the original four-stanza ode turns downward after the blindly exclamatory "I hear! I hear!"—but, the poet seems to wonder, does paradise have a mother only? The lost Tree and single Field suggest an Eden that was begotten by a Father, and the adult poet can only partly keep from knowing that his visionary birth, though too noble for pastoral, was nevertheless still erotic. The Pansy at his feet recalls Milton's Pensive Nun, who always keeps her head pointed toward, if not in, the sand. Thus far Wordsworth's expression of loss has simply followed the convention of the amorous vernal ode whereby the speaker looks about frantically for his absent mistress.

Wordsworth does have a glimpse of her, though, and is not pleased, as the fifth stanza reveals. The maternal earth from which he feels alienated has "pleasures of her own," and it is her natural yearning to possess her foster child and make him forget his epic and patriarchal origins, "that imperial palace whence he came." Following exactly the scenario presented by Otto Rank,[14] she interferes, in her lowly role, with the poet's myth of his birth as a hero, and her interference is as erotic as that of the Nurse in *Romeo and Juliet*. Even as we pass the poem thus schematically in review, we should note that there is a degree of voluntarism, even relief, in the adult's alienation from his childhood. The "Child of Joy" is given pause in so designating himself, and feels a hint of Gray's "fearful joy."[15] We shall see in the long run, however, that this impure intimation is vastly preferable to those purer ones that come to replace it. From stanza five onward, the poet will strive to imagine a self-conception that is not an earthy anecdote from the pastoral tradition, to imagine a birth-myth that is not an earth-myth or failed autochthony. At first this seems a good idea. By bringing about a reconciliation of his mortal being with "the light of common day," with the ordinariness of earth, the poet can once more invest with the appearance of dialectical truth the assumption that his immortal being must derive from a region that is *not* common; the animation of the soul seems to depend on the disinspiriting of earth.

The figure of the imperial palace carries the sun's "glorious birth" across the increasingly dualistic chasm of the poet's logic while alienating the sun from the landscape it formerly graced. The poet remembering himself as a bright-haired youth or sun-child now identifies with the Father, through the metalepsis "God, who is our home," in a higher region that is set apart from natural kindness as the sublime is set apart from the beautiful. This brief intimation (his first of immortality) makes up the subsumed epic phase of the ode. In Victor Hugo's terms, Adam has become Orestes. Shaking off the mother, by whose possessive kisses he is fretted (like a brook fretting in its channel [l. 94]), the hero descends from his epic to his dramatic phase, recalling Aristotle's derivation of theatre from child's play in the *Poetics*: "As if his whole vocation/Were endless imitation." Here the Father stands back, the one apart from the many, no longer identified with the son but still tendering the sunlight of his gaze. Now the child becomes the chameleonic Hamlet, trapped in a "prison-house" (68) of nature and changed into a different player by each attention from the mother whose yearnings in her natural kind have caused him so much anxiety. Little actor though he is, however, he is still a solitary and a soliloquist, like John Home in Collins's Scottish Superstitions Ode: "unto this he frames his song." He acts odes.

Hamlet calls the world a "prison" (II. ii); but in *Hamlet* the world is only one of two prisons, the other being identified by the ghost of Hamlet's father: "I am thy father's spirit . . ."

> But that I am forbid
> To tell the secrets of my prison-house,
> I could a tale unfold whose lightest word
> Would harrow up thy soul.
>
> [I. v. 9, 13–16]

This discordant intimation Wordsworth records in his next stanza:

> Mighty Prophet! Seer blest!
> On whom these truths do rest,
> Which we are toiling all our lives to find,
> In darkness lost, the darkness of the grave;
> Thou, over whom thy Immortality
> Broods like the Day, a Master o'er a Slave . . .

For the child's domination by Mother Earth, then, there is an equivalent master-slave dialectic between son and father.[16] Immortal regions are suddenly as much like prisons as mortal ones; and the ode's noontide, its most high-flown rhetoric, having seen too much reality, falls back to the theme of blindness, which could be an ode's address, thus stated, to its own self-blighted celebratory mandate:

> Thou little child, yet glorious in thy might
> Of heaven-born freedom [as a Slave?] on thy being's height,
> Why with such earnest pains dost thou provoke
> The years to bring the inevitable yoke,
> Thus blindly with thy blessedness at strife?

In singling out the main point of repetition in this poem (crucial repetition being typically revealed, as we saw in the "Ode to Duty," by a stutter or gaffe like this one about the slave's heaven-born freedom), we have perhaps come to see why no blessedness is visible that is not in some wise tainted. The child must be admitted to know what he is doing in choosing blinders.

Having absorbed the rival genres in the child's progress toward his earthly prison and then reacted frantically back toward its displaced theme of originary magic, only to discover a different prison in that theme, Wordsworth's ode now lapses into its final, elegiac phase, giving notice of this change with a verbal allusion to "Lycidas": "Not for these I raise / The song of thanks and praise." Here begins Wordsworth's evening retrospect and its attempt to overbalance the heavy weight of custom with the philosophic mind's conversion of remembered joy into "natural piety." The ode becomes a song in praise of sublimation, and it has some sublime moments remaining. It distances the Deluge (into which an ode, like Phaeton, is always falling) from the standpoint of calm weather, thus belatedly justifying the suggestion of a covenant in the rainbow that comes and goes; it returns to the vernal festival of earthy childhood "in thought" only; and finally it returns to the landscape of the first line, adding the word "Fountains" to the initial list because, through the sublimation of dangerous waters, the philosophic mind is now able to recognize a seminal source as well as an Edenic foster mother. All these qualified returns make up Wordsworth's "Stand." The irregularity of all the previous stanzas is reduced to uniformity, with the exception of an odd line out that refuses the eclipse it appears in: "Is lovely yet." Wordsworth's hymnic epode, like Collins's homiletic harvest at the end of the "Ode to Evening," joins the common produce of the common day in an order serviceable. The necessary sacrifice of godlike autochthony for natural piety brings on silence, an unutterable pathos that is vastly different from the shouts of the Child of Joy. The question of immortality is mooted in the end, and we must reconsider it if we are to discover why this is so.

III

> that dubious hour,
> That twilight when we first begin to see
> This dawning earth. . . .
> —*The Prelude* V. 511-13

Is the Intimations Ode, in Lionel Trilling's deft phrase, about growing old or growing up?[17] It is hard to know how or where to enter this dispute. It seems to me that the poem is about not knowing whether childhood, adulthood, or yet a third state of complete disembodiment is best; that it is, in short, about confusion. In the Fenwick note Wordsworth confesses having experienced the opposite "subjugations" of idealism and materialism in childhood and adulthood, respectively, and seems to imply that the purpose of his poem is to thread its way between prisons, or rather to find a restful expansiveness in their mutual collapse. In this modest aim I think it succeeds, despite serious flaws of coherence that will appear. Deliberately an ode, the poem experiments with presentation, the presentation in this case of an elusive nimbus called a "glory." The experiment fails, but in place of ecstasy the poet gains knowledge, a new awareness of the role played by determinacy in consciousness.

Wordsworth's apology in the Fenwick note for his chosen myth of a prior existence reflects the etiological anxiety of any ode, the fear of dark places, and also recalls the antinomian relation of an ode to orthodoxy. His myth, he says, "is far too shadowy a notion to be recommended to faith." Still, however, as he also clearly implies in the note, he knows no proof of immortality that is not in some way shadowy; this despite the fact that for Wordsworth, as for Coleridge, autonomy of thought cannot be demonstrated without proof of the mind's original participation in an eternal cause. This necessary priority of the spirit is termed by Wordsworth in the note an Archimedean "point whereon to rest" what would be, otherwise, the dreary machine of Associationist psychology.

Although the lack of such proof may cause some anxiousness, it is not really the belief in immortality, however founded, that the ode questions, but rather the nature of immortality. By allusion and repetition, Wordsworth's ode clouds over what in religion are foregone conclusions about the sources of life and death. It is disturbing, for example, that "Nor man nor Boy,/Nor all that is at enmity with joy,/Can utterly destroy . . ." alludes to the speech of Moloch in *Paradise Lost* that calls the Creator a destroyer, like Collins's Fancy. Or again, it is difficult to understand what blindness is if the Child is at once "an eye to the blind" and "blindly with his blessedness at strife." As was also apparent in Collins's "Ode on the Poetical Character," a poet cannot merely decree a difference between Vision and vision that his poem fails otherwise to sustain.

To cite another troublesome passage, where is the guilt and on what ground is the misgiving in the following lines?

> Not for these I raise
> The song of thanks and praise;
> But for those obstinate questionings
> Of sense and outward things,
> Fallings from us, vanishings;
> Blank misgivings of a Creature
> Moving about in worlds not realized,
> High instincts before which our mortal Nature
> Did tremble like a guilty thing surprised. . . .

The solipsism of the child is obstinate, and his experience of a lapse is the opposite of Adam's: not a corruption of soul but a falling away of the flesh. Immortality is intimated by the child as a state of emptiness and vertigo, a Melvilleian blankness that is duplicitous for all its vacancy, since it has more than one habitation ("worlds")—perhaps a true and a false zone of antimatter. The bodily "Creature" would appear to have been created as a companion for the soul's loneliness. The song that is raised, in sum, shows every sign of being a song of thanks for the gift of mortality.[18]

This is not to imply, however, that the entire burden of the song is a foolish critique of immortality. The main point is, rather, that memory harbors phantoms. Whatever immortality may be like, mortal discourse is confined to what a child can know about it, or, yet more mediately, to what an adult can remember of childhood knowledge.[19] The child's recollections are indeed "shadowy," both because adult memory is busy securing the present by darkening the past (in this sense the poem *is* "about growing up" and being happy with the present) and also because, as "be they what they may" rather sheepishly concedes, what the poet remembers is not really the "high instincts" of childhood but the phantom Underworld of the Greeks. The confessed Platonism of Wordsworth's preexistence myth comes chiefly from the Myth of the warrior Er, who "coming to life related what, he said, he had seen in the world beyond" *(Rep.* 614b). Er describes souls struggling to be born between two worlds, governed, like Wordsworth's Slave, by the Spindle of Necessity. But the feeling of Wordsworth's intimations is, in fact, more Homeric than Platonic; it is "impalpable as shadows are, and wavering like a dream" (Fitzgerald's *Odyssey* XI). Wordsworth's ode may be seen as a moving failure of perspective; called forth to be condemned, mortal Nature reasserts its vital strength and beauty.[20]

By comparison, immortality is a dream. In the third stanza there is a crux of remarkable compression, "The Winds come to me from the fields of sleep." Many a hapless recitation of this line has produced "fields of sheep," a slip that is prompted by the surrounding gleeful pastoral in which no creature sleeps during the rites of spring. The fields of sleep belong to an earlier time and place, the threshold of birth which is, later, "but a sleep and a forgetting." Wordsworth's winds bring news of birth, then, yet seem imagistically to recall an even earlier moment, the classical fields of asphodel and poppy.[21] In contrast with the jollity of a child's landscape, the winds of adult memory recollect the stupor of immortality, or what Homer calls the "shores of Dream" *(Od.* XXIV).

In approaching the designedly binding and blinding symbol of the ode, that of the "glory," we must pause over metaphysics a little longer. The prolepsis that the ode never moves beyond is the ambiguous apposition of line 5. Presumably "the glory and the freshness of

a dream" modifies "celestial light" in the previous line; but the gram-
mar does not prevent reading the line in apposition to "every com-
mon sight." One's total impression of lines 1–5 is that the glory
summarily modifies both the common, with which the poem con-
cludes, and the celestial, with which it has begun. Hence either the
common itself is glorious, properly viewed (like the cuckoo and the
lesser celandine of the 1802 period), or else the glory is a nimbus, a
frame of celestial light that leaves the framed common object un-
illuminated in itself. This sliding apposition looks forward to the
confusion of the whole text. The word "dream" belongs to the
rhyme group "stream-seem,"[22] and thus its presumptive modifying
power over "sight" and "light" is further weakened. Having been
spread too thin, the glory is only faintly visible. To parrot the in-
escapable question of Wordsworth interpretation, does the glory
come from without or within?

Since the glory is now absent, and since it is recalled by an *ubi
sunt* that is also, at the same time, an indirect invocation, this ques-
tion is doubly difficult. To disregard for the moment where the glory
comes from, even though that is the motivating question of any ode
and plainly an important one, it may profit to go on asking what it
is. Here an answer is forthcoming. The glory is an "Apparel," a
dressy appearance that is Wordsworth's equivalent of Gray's tapes-
tries and Collins's veils.[23] It is worn by every common sight as a
covering for nakedness: "not in utter nakedness,/But trailing clouds
of glory do we come." The glory screens out the indecent as well as
the quotidian commonness of things and poses an obstacle to the
kindness of natural yearning. Perhaps it is already clear where the
glory comes from. Once more the Fall proves indeed fortunate, as it
lends a needful covering to an original state of nakedness. In this
poem death is not only the context of intimation, but also, it seems,
the context of intimacy. By allusion to Collins's "sallow Autumn fills
thy lap with leaves," Wordsworth's imagery of mortality turns
autumnal long before his evening ear takes command of the ode.
"Earth fills her lap with pleasures of her own" is a covering of Eve's
nakedness that unites the pleasures of life and the glory of afterlife
in a common veil. Man *wears* "Earth" even before we are told that
he is her inmate, exchanging as he grows up "the glories he hath
known" for new apparel.

If we compare the mortally colored imagery of the celestial that the adult remembers from the time of glad animal movement in early childhood with the otherworldliness of the celestial that he remembers from the time of solipsism in later childhood, we can see the distance between two glories, between the festive dress of a young world and the phantom light of interstellar vacancy. Concerning this second glory: Wordsworth could love a clear sky, and in the second stanza we cannot yet feel uneasy about the sky's undress, as "The Moon doth with delight/Look round her when the heavens are bare." But the region of the Moon is absolutely separate from that of man, and her delight cannot be merged with Earth's pleasures. Later, when pleasure has palled, the bare sky will mirror a blank misgiving. In "Dejection," Coleridge will seem to narrow this gulf by giving the moon her own nimbus from the outset, "a swimming phantom light," and he will transfer Wordsworth's earthly pleasure to the sphere of the moon's delight: "I see the old moon in her lap." In "Dejection," as we shall see, it is not the immortal skies that are lonely, but the poet.

Both "Dejection" and the Intimations Ode sometimes touch upon subjects that are too intimate to remain within a shareable sphere of reference. For both poets, but for Wordsworth especially, the daemon of an ode is an unreconstructed and thus far "strong" egoism. What poet before Wordsworth admitted to being relieved and made strong by his own timely utterance? As we have seen, Akenside read Milton for inspiration, Gray Spenser, and so on. Although the position of the sounding cataracts between "I am strong" and "No more shall grief of mine" might indicate that Wordsworth has found his timely utterance in Revelation,[24] one feels that too many more griefs succeed this one to confirm any gospel. Earlier odes have mottoes chosen from the classics; Wordsworth's utterance and his motto (starting in 1815) are all his own. The drawback of this strength is that Wordsworth's allusion to his own uncanonized oeuvre leaves the ordering of his present text in a muddle. It is not possible to say with certainty what Wordsworth's timely utterance was, nor what his thought of grief was. But if a note on the subject in Wordsworth's own hand were discovered, that would be a positive harm. In the text, the grief and the thought are significant because they are unspecified. They remain simply implied presences, emblems of what Coleridge termed the "flux and reflux" of the whole poem. They are impure signifiers—symptoms. Perhaps their presence in the text can be understood, then, as a near-utterance about the idea of repression, about the apparel of the repressed that veils an ode. To refer again to the Fenwick note, what Wordsworth most vividly remembers about writing his ode is frustration. He needed a fulcrum, a prior content without which his form, "the world of his own mind" (*PW* 4. 464), would follow its own irresolute course. The preexistence myth provides inadequate leverage, but the timely utterance, because unspecified, can stand behind and beneath the text as a buried originary voice.

One may wonder about the deference of sound to sight in this ode,[25] noting that elsewhere Wordsworth explored aural areas that have more profound mystical roots than does the (mainly Western) visionary idea. Like Dionysus "disguised as man" in Euripides, this written ode travels daily farther from the East because pure voice would be naked, a too immediate experience of "God, who is our home." This is the experience an ode cannot risk. The prophetic child must be "deaf" in order to read "the eternal deep." The visual blankness of eternity is also an "Eternal Silence," and sound is relegated wholly to "our noisy years": birdsong, the tabor that syncopates the vernal heartbeat,[26] the outer-ance of speech that relieves solitude, the trumpets sounding from the Salvator-fringes of the regenerate landscape, the shouts of happiness. After this outburst, there are no more sounds until the pygmy turns actor; however, even his "song," is not sung but written down, "a little plan or chart."

Sound resonates beyond the setting for pastoral joy only once in the poem, at the end of the ninth stanza, in the song of praise for the adult's recollection of the child's recollections:

> Hence in a season of calm weather,
> 　Though inland far we be,
> Our souls have sight of that immortal sea
> 　Which brought us hither,
> 　Can in a moment travel thither,
> And see the Children sport upon the shore,
> And hear the mighty waters rolling evermore.

This magnificent passage, the pivot (or fulcrum) of the poem, culminates in another unspecified utterance. It is also the key to Wordsworth's version of Milton's resurrected Lycidas, the "genius of the shore." It *is* a pivotal passage, yet it is not easy to discover a context for it. It is not clear by what logic the celestial descent has become an aquatic emergence; nor is it clear, though we happily accept the transit, just how we are carried from sight to sound.

I have suggested that the genealogical phase of the ode before Wordsworth leaves out, or tries to leave out, the Deluge, which appears in nearly every scriptural cosmogony in the history of culture and recurs in Jung's belief that the materials of the dream-work are oceanic.[27] Until his personal tragedy concerning a death by water in 1805, Wordsworth, unlike his predecessors in the ode, was a willing voyager in strange seas of thought and loved sonorous waters. The dream-vision of *Prelude* V (88–97) offers up the sort of apocalyptic "Ode" that Wordsworth could have been expected to write:

> "This," said he,
> "Is something of more worth;" and at the word
> Stretched forth the shell, so beautiful in shape,
> In colour so resplendent, with command
> That I should hold it to my ear. I did so,
> And heard that instant in an unkown tongue,
> Which yet I understood, articulate sounds,
> A loud prophetic blast of harmony;
> An Ode, in passion uttered, which foretold
> Destruction to the children of the earth
> By deluge, now at hand.

One might then certainly expect the Intimations Ode, considering its subject, also to leave the shore for deeper waters. But the "Waters" at line 14 are merely lacustrine, and the jolly "sea" of "Land and sea" (30) is, one suspects, only present for the sake of rhyme. For the most part, the movement of this ode is inland and downward, until it comes to rest in a place that is "too deep for tears." Traditionally, the ode takes an aspiring flight but fears Phaeton's plunge, and with partial success avoids the risk of drowning by curbing its flight. Wordsworth's ode bows to this tradition, with the result, however, that this passage, with its seaward direction, seems isolated from the argument of which the passage is meant to be the center.

"Lycidas," not an ode but an elegy, makes room for a drowning. Milton recalls a happy pastoral setting, "by fountain, shade, and rill," to which Wordsworth alludes in lines 1 and 189; but with the death of its pastor, the *locus amoenus* will have fallen silent except for mournful echoes unless Milton can reanimate the strain. Wordsworth's first revision of "Lycidas," then, is to fill his own pastoral site with noise and to locate the noise only there, hoping to imply that the silence of higher places is preferable. However, the errancy of his intimations points to some awareness on his part that Milton was right, as was Sophocles in the *Coloneus*: if the vital and benign genius cannot be given a home within the budding grove, its possible course among the stars can offer little consolation. "Lycidas" announces the return of the genius from water to land through the intercession of one who could not drown. Wordsworth describes the return of memory from land to the shoreline where genius had been left behind.

Or rather, where genius *appears* to have been left behind. Wordsworth's ninth stanza, with its key in "Not for these," begins to look homeward, back toward the starting places of the ode that will be reviewed in stanzas ten and eleven. Wordsworth's journey to the shore begins this review of inland places because, in fact, the journey only seems to have been undertaken. He is and remains inland far; it is only in moments of vacancy, seasons "of calm weather,"[28] that he counteracts his fear of the eternal abyss with memories of "sport" among a community of children who have nothing in common with the solitude of infinite space. The children emerge *from* the "immortal sea," happy to be born, and steadily move inland themselves toward the pleasures of the Shepherd-boy.[29] Immured in our adulthood, our souls seem to want something else, something other than what children want, when they listen to the conch shells of their inner ear. They zoom directly back to the sea itself, and only afterward notice the children playing with their backs to the water. Unlike the ignorant child, the soul of the adult has intimations of death; they are not quite the intimations he was meant to have, but they still induce a state of mind that is preferable, as Jonson's Cary-Morison Ode also insisted, to "listlessness" and "mad endeavour."

The soul's hearing death for the first time, then, is an intimation of voice, of aural immediacy, not as a beginning but as an end. The children's audition, which is permitted by the grammar if not by the parallelism of syntax, is quite different; it is not nostalgic but strains forward, and smooths their passage from the deafening roar of death, which they no longer hear as such, to the companionable shouts of their coming joy. Lycidas our Shepherd-boy is not dead, because the morning star of his return replaces the evening star of his having sunk elsewhere. For Wordsworth's Child we rejoice, as in "Lycidas," because he has been born, not because he was previously drowned:

> The Soul that rises with us, our life's Star,
> Hath had elsewhere its setting,
> And cometh from afar:

The child has returned, fortunately, to be Nature's Pastor once more. His "vision splendid" arises from his own glorious birth, when Heaven is no distant bareness of the sky but an immediate environment that "lies about us in our infancy."

"Our birth is but a sleep and a forgetting," the line that precedes those just quoted, wavers uncertainly between two famous counterstatements about life and death in *Measure for Measure*. One of them, Claudio's "Ay, but to die, and go we know not where" (III. i. 118-31), is worth quoting at length, not only because it juxtaposes the two prisons of both *Hamlet* and the Intimations Ode, but also because it expresses the fear that Wordworth's frostlike weight of life is, in fact, a condition of the afterlife as well:

> or to reside
> In thrilling region of thick-ribbèd ice,
> To be imprisoned in the viewless winds
> And blown with restless violence round about
> The pendant world. . . .
> . . . .
> The weariest and most loathèd worldly life
> That age, ache, penury, and imprisonment
> Can lay on Nature is a paradise
> To what we fear of death.

This is the body of imagery that Wordsworth's shadowy recollections cannot dissolve, however much his ode may aspire to the otherworldly viewpoint of the Duke's counsel about sleep and forgetting:

> Thou hast nor youth nor age,
> But as it were an after-dinner sleep
> Dreaming on both.
>
> [III. i. 32-34]

The Duke's utterance is not strong enough to be "timely," though; it is merely Stoical, and itself contains the repetition that negates transcendence: "thy best of rest is sleep,/And that thou oft pro-vok'st, yet grossly fear'st/Thy death, which is no more" (III. i. 17–19). Among these less than reassuring attitudes Wordsworth must himself have felt compelled to waver, "when having closed the mighty Shakespeare's page,/I mused, and thought, and felt, in soli-tude" (*Prelude* VII. 484–85).

The conclusion seems inescapable that Wordsworth's Intimations are best forgotten; and forgetting is what the last two stanzas in effect achieve. Stanzas ten and eleven seek images for the continuity that was hoped for in "The Rainbow":

> The Child is father of the Man;
> And I could wish my days to be
> Bound each to each by natural piety.

In these lines, the wish for existential continuity is weakened by having been spoken conditionally, and also by the impious bid for autochthonous independence of being that here and elsewhere undercuts Wordsworth's homage to the adult father.[30] Perhaps these slight discords are enough to warn us that an ode for which such a passage is the best available motto will not be smooth going; but they are nothing to the discords that any ambitious presentational ode will engender in itself. In any case, the poet's days are bound each to each at the close of the Great Ode in an altogether "natural" way that is *pius* if not pious; but his piety is *not* founded in any visionary or eschatological intimation.

From his and Coleridge's Conversation Poems, perhaps from the Meditative Lyric of the seventeenth century,[31] and certainly from instinct, Wordsworth had formed the habit of concluding with a benediction, which typically, as in "Tintern Abbey" or "Dejection," transmits the boon of gladness in nature to a beloved friend who is less burdened than the poet with the heavy weight of adulthood. The hesitation with which the pronoun "my" is introduced in "The Rainbow" may itself imply the replacement of the self by an-other in a benediction: *my* days and perceptions may prove dis-jointed, but perhaps yours will not. So in stanza ten of his ode, Wordsworth confers his generalized blessing on unself-conscious youth from the detached and newly acquiescent standpoint of "thought." However successful the tone of this blessing may be thought to be, it must still be stressed that there is no scope for benediction in the cult hymns after which odes model themselves. The ending of a hymn leads by nature in quite another direction, toward a petition. In a hymn the petition may possibly involve the blessing of others,[32] but in an ode it is primarily for the self, a request that the poet's egotistically sublime vocation be confirmed. Not just Wordsworth's but nearly all thoughtful odes, however, swerve away from the formula of petition toward benediction and other forms of self-sacrifice that are all essentially vocational disclaimers. At least in this last respect, then, the endings of hymns and odes are similar.

Wordsworth's heart no longer leaps up; rather it goes out, in "primal sympathy," to others, to the whole sphere of those Creatures whom Coleridge's Ancient Mariner learned to "bless" (see the Intimations Ode, l. 37). Henceforth there is little to be heard of the immortality theme and nothing of substance about the "one delight" (192) of joyous childhood that the poet has now "relinquished"— pretending, with the active verb, to have given it up voluntarily. What now appears, rather, is the severer compassion of the Eton College Ode, the "Ode to Adversity," and Wordsworth's "Ode to Duty": "the soothing thoughts that spring/Out of human suffering." As in the "Ode to Duty," the healing power of Nature is itself now hallowed as routine, as Nature's "more habitual sway," and the sober coloring of the clouds no longer needs to serve as a repressive veil, since the troubled mysticism of the poem is now silenced, apparently by choice. Until the final line of Wordsworth's evening ending there is no hint of immortality, no effort even to carry over or restate the phantom imagery of immortality. Natural piety in these lines is a secular reverence moved by the pathos of mutability:

> The clouds that gather round the setting sun
> Do take a sober coloring from an eye
> That hath kept watch o'er man's mortality;
> Another race hath been, and other palms are won.
> Thanks to the human heart by which we live,
> Thanks to its tenderness, its joys and fears,
> To me the meanest flower that blows can give
> Thoughts that do often lie too deep for tears.

This is a grave ending, full of allusions to Gray: to the "race" and the "fearful joy" of the Eton College Ode, to the frail blossoms in the Death of a Favorite Cat. Also, as in so many great odes, there is a final "gathering" of the mind's humbled thoughts now rendered as congregational homilies, a gathering that willingly stands far below the cosmic gathering of clouds or twittering swallows. A conclusion of this sort is a service rendered, a graveside hymn to man's mortality, without intimation but with something that would seem to achieve collective intimacy were it not for "To me," a last gift of special knowledge awarded to the self by the odic voice.[33] To the famous question, "Where is it now, the glory and the dream?" we may answer in behalf of Wordsworth's "me": Aye, where is it? Mortality alone has its music.

Intimations apart, then, the question remains, Which is better, childhood or being grown up? It may be of use to measure the Intimations Ode in this respect against a passage from "In Desolation," by a poet whom Wordsworth would have been less than human not to have reperused attentively in the summer of 1803, his new acquaintance Sir George Beaumont's Renaissance ancestor Sir John Beaumont:

> If solid vertues dwell not but in paine,
> I will not wish that golden age againe,
> Because it flowed with sensible delights
> Of heavenly things. . . .
>
> [Chalmers, X. 25]

Like Beaumont, Wordsworth is never quite easy about the glad animal movements of his little pagan selves, though it would be an exaggeration to insist that his nativity ode exorcises them; early childhood, for him, is simply incomplete. The later stages of childhood, however intense, are already projected by present memory toward the double imprisonment of the adult, the state of being shuttled to and fro between the burden and the absence of the flesh; but the difference remains that late childhood lacks the solace of adulthood's deliberative resources. At bottom, as it seems to me, the speaker of the Intimations Ode prefers himself grown up, or just as he is, in fact, at the moment.

Wordsworth's choice of the Pindaric format would mean that he could scarcely have composed the poem on his customary walks, chanting aloud. In attempting the vocality of an ode, Wordsworth would have needed to stay at his desk, weighing meters and blocking stanzas in writing. In facing this paradox, a highly relevant passage may be enlisted from Jacques Derrida: "Writing is that forgetting of the self, that exteriorization, the contrary of the interiorizing memory, or the *Erinnerung* that opens the history of the spirit."[34] Wordsworth's ode is more crucially a forgetting than an attempted reconstitution of any earlier self; it celebrates forgetting in celebrating birth, its own birth ultimately, and does so by entering a poetic shape that imitates the constant discontinuity of being alive and suffering. "Pain," says Nietzsche, "always raises the question about its origin while pleasure is inclined to stop with itself without looking back."[35] Childhood has no myth of childhood, and no fund of suffering to be projected as a benediction. (It goes without saying, I hope, that concerning actual childhood these assertions are probably false; we are speaking here, though, of what the overstrained figures of memory can know about a child's memory in an ode.) The failing powers of adulthood are necessary, like the fading of Shelley's coal and the secondariness of Coleridge's secondary imagination, for the dissemination of voice in the writing of poetry, which starts, like a mortal stroke, as a severance from the Logos, and then, over that very fissure, takes its stand against the "severing of our loves."

IV

> To the last point of vision, and beyond,
> Mount, daring warbler!—that love-prompted strain
>
> . . . .
>
> Thrills not the less the bosom of the plain:
> Yet might'st thou seem, proud privilege! to sing
> All independent of the leafy spring.
> —"A Morning Exercise" (1828)

The Intimations Ode is uncharacteristic of Wordsworth. It is a poem that appears openly to espouse the attitudes that partisans of the sophisticated Wordsworth take to be important but only covertly present in his poetry (longing for apocalypse, hatred of nature), but that actually favors, presumably against the poet's design, the wise naturalism that partisans of the Simple Wordsworth take to be everywhere intended: faith in and through nature without clear revelation, whatever "faith" in this context may mean. The Great Ode loses the power of grounding spiritual knowledge in physical experience, the power which had made "Tintern Abbey" a less confused poem, "well pleased to recognize"

> In nature and the language of the sense
> The anchor of my purest thoughts, the nurse,
> The guide, the guardian of my heart, and soul
> Of all my moral being.

This passage, which redeems even the troublesome foster mother of the Intimations Ode, represents what can with most propriety be called Wordsworth's "unified vision," though needless to say there are rifts in the ground near the Wye as well. Speaking only of "vicious" poetry in his "Essay, Supplementary" (1815) to the 1800 Preface, Wordsworth identifies the quality of "confusion" that Cleanth Brooks was the first to emphasize in the Intimations Ode itself: "the realities of the Muse are but shows, and . . . her liveliest excitements are raised by transient shocks of conflicting feeling and successive assemblages of contradictory thoughts."[36] Wordsworth seems to have felt that bad poetry is full of contradictions in terms—oxymorons—yet his own most contradictory poem is his Great Ode. In these concluding remarks I want to reconsider the oxymoron "natural piety" from the standpoint of Wordsworth's lesser odes[37] in order to show that the confusion of all his odes is peculiar to what he would have termed the "mould" in which they are cast (1815 Preface).

It may be remarked, though, before turning to other odes, that Wordsworth could always handle intimations of immortality more positively in poems that were not odes. Unless "The Mad Monk" was written by Wordsworth himself,[38] the clearest forerunner of the Intimations Ode (as of "A Slumber did my spirit seal"), doubtless printed as the first poem in the 1849 edition for this reason, is not an ode but a quieter sort of poem, "Written in Very Early Youth":

> a Slumber seems to steal
> O'er vale, and mountain, and the starless sky.
> Now, in this blank of things, a harmony,
> Home-felt, and home-created, comes to heal
> That grief for which the senses still supply
> Fresh food.

This passage affirms a "blank" vision without being troubled about its blankness; it is quite possibly referred to directly in the compromised affirmation of the Great Ode, lines 145–51, where a blank misgiving condemns the eternally dead to roll round earth's diurnal course with shadows. Another convincingly positive treatment of "this blank of things" appears in an untitled poem of 1800, in which a Solitary forsaken by his beloved exclaims:

> I look—the sky is empty space;
> I know not what I trace;
> But when I cease to look, my hand is on my heart.

This is indeed an intimation, lesser than, but comparable to, the moments of surprised revelation in lassitude that are featured in *The Prelude*. An intimation thus suggestive cannot appear in an ode because its quiet tenor openly founds knowledge in ignorance and avoids afflatus. Perhaps this distinction alone is enough to indicate that an ode can never be characteristic of Wordsworth.

Wordsworth's odes and ode-like poems constantly reject mysterious knowledge. The apostrophe called "To H. C. Six Years Old" (1802), for instance, offers an unambiguous view of the semi-transparent "glory" that confuses the Great Ode:

> O Thou! whose fancies from afar are brought;
> Who of thy words dost make a mock apparel,
> And fittest for unutterable thought . . .

Here the "glory," like Wordsworth's "home-created" harmony of 1786, is the opaque apparel by expression of sights both common and uncommon. "To a Skylark" (1805) summarizes without reversing the values of the Great Ode: strength of song in despondency, joy divine, the "banqueting place in the sky," "Joy and jollity," and the "hope for higher raptures, when life's day is done." This slight poem, which may play in the background of Keat's Nightingale Ode, petitions the bird to "Lift me, guide me, till I find / That spot which seems so to thy mind," but then admits failure, lacking as it does "the wings of a Faery," and at last reposes solely in hope.

In "To the Cuckoo" (23–26 March 1802), which plays in the background of Shelley's Skylark Ode, the poet asks, "shall I call thee Bird, / Or but a wandering Voice?" Clearly the latter, since only when invisible does the bird bring back childhood; the poet listens, "till I do beget/That golden time again." This poem, like the Great Ode, deprives spiritual knowledge of any material ground:

> O blessèd Bird! the earth we pace
> Again appears to be
> An unsubstantial, faery place;
> That is fit home for Thee!

Metric stress drives home the point: for thee, but not for me, and never for both of us at once. Only a much later bird poem, now fully shackled by the sense of "Duty" that overrides an ode's wish for immediacy, can return, though weakly, to the balanced tropes of earthbound freedom that sustain "Tintern Abbey." "To a Skylark" (1825; very possibly written in response to Shelley's "Skylark") concludes with the sort of nonvisionary emblem of continuity that characterizes the later Wordsworth: "Type of the wise who soar, but never roam:/True to the kindred points of Heaven and Home!" Here Donne's compass is lamentably overstretched, as Wordsworth's figure pays homage to the elastic metaphysical grounding that was available to Donne but is now unavailable, given the dualism on which the dialectic of presence and absence in an ode depends.

In the "Vernal Ode" (1817), a lumbering Pindaric, a "Stranger" descends from the sky and is compared to "the sun,/When it reveals, in evening majesty,/Features half lost amid their own pure light." Hence we are not surprised at his apparel: "there the Stranger stood alone;/Fair as a gorgeous Fabric of the East." This angel then delivers a homily to the harp that exactly recalls the dilemma of perspective in the Intimations Ode; what should have been a condescending account of mortality by an Immortal takes itself by surprise and gives way to envy of the lesser condition:

> Mortals, rejoice! The very angels quit
> Their mansions unsusceptible of change,
> Amid your pleasant bowers to sit,
> And through your sweet vicissitudes to range!

This passage is yet further sullied by its evocation of the tarnished angels (as interpretations of Genesis 6 often made them out to be) who wooed "the daughters of men" before the Flood. The poet tries in vain to undo what the Stranger, perhaps one of those angels himself, has done, and hopes to evoke a "golden time again" by studying the providential anatomy of the bee. But since that time *has*, after all, departed, man's intimations of any higher state are now a mockery, and the angels are perhaps a little too cozy when they appear even in man's least postlapsarian memories:

> We were not mocked with glimpse and shadow then,
> Bright Seraphs mixed familiarly with men;
> And earth and stars composed a universal heaven!

Nothing could confess more clearly what was missing from the "glimpse and shadow" of Wordsworth's earlier intimations.

The last line of the "Vernal Ode," like that of the 1825 Skylark poem, effects a clumsy and confessedly conjectural liaison of ground and sky that is amplified, again within the pleasing chains of Duty, in the long ode "On the Power of Sound" (1828):

> Ye wandering Utterances, has earth no scheme,
> No scale of moral music—to unite
> Powers that survive but in the faintest dream
> Of memory?—O that ye might stoop to bear
> Chains, such precious chains of sight
> As laboured minstrelsies through ages wear!
> O for a balance fit the truth to tell
> Of the Unsubstantial, pondered well!

This passage concedes the necessary failure of vocal poetry to unite the material and the immaterial worlds in the single liberating prison of a secular scripture, a minstrelsy "laboured" as writing but still not absent from vocal sources. The ode concludes hymnically, as the poet defers to a single and inimitable Maker, denying once and for all the priority of vision—which is nevertheless the only intuitive sense at the disposal of man, bounded as he is by space and time:

> A Voice to Light gave Being,
> To Time, and Man his earth-born chronicler;
> A Voice shall finish doubt and dim foreseeing,
> And sweep away life's visionary stir;
> . . . .
> O Silence! are Man's noisy years
> No more than moments of thy life?
> . . . .
>   No! though earth be dust

> And vanish, though the heavens dissolve, her stay
> Is in the WORD, that shall not pass away.[39]

This poem is yet another critique of the hopes that Wordsworth now imagines his Intimations Ode to have embodied. His critique leads him to give up the idea of an ode altogether and to welcome in its stead the idea of a hymn. Wordsworth plainly understood a hymn to be a collective service, inspired only by faith in common and commonly shared truth. His two "hymns," "Hymn for the Boatmen" (1820), which begins "JESU! bless our slender boat" and ends "All our hope is placed in thee;/*Miserere Domine!*" and his "Labourer's Noon-Day Hymn" (1834), are both written as if for rote use by the unpoetical faithful. In Wordsworth, as in most other ode writers, the idea of a hymn is confined to the end of an ode. So "To the Small Celandine" (30 April 1802) ends by pledging a duty: "I will sing, as doth behove/Hymns in praise of what I love"; and since this flower or its equivalent is the "meanest flower" of the Great Ode, the decision in that poem's close for the renunciations of hymnody may be seen yet more clearly.[40]

In "Composed upon an Evening of Extraordinary Beauty and Splendour" (1818), called an "ode" in Wordsworth's headnote, aural childhood and an obscurely visionary present once more appear contrasted. The "Time"

> when field and watery cove
> With modulated echoes rang

is now supplanted by

> This silent spectacle—the gleam—
> The shadow—and the peace supreme!

On the present evening, the speaker claims to have had an unqualified renewal of Joy, at which he is too surprised not to wonder peevishly about the purpose of the experience: "This glimpse of glory, why renewed?"[41] To prepare him (he may suspect) for some unappareled horror? Or is it rather that he has grown accustomed to his earthly prison, to the "precious chains of sight" required for "laboured minstrelsies," so well accustomed in fact that he actively resents the recurrence of the boundless, of the unutterable sublime that mocks the ever-narrowing boundaries of his craft? Plainly he considers the Intimations Ode, not this one, to have been peevish, and he now accepts visionary loss as a wise Providence protecting him, perhaps, from a dangerous and heretical possession: "Oh, let thy Grace remind me of the light,/Full early lost, and fruitlessly deplored." The Great Ode's lament as much as its petition, he now feels, was fruitlessly undertaken for what already, in "Peele Castle" (1805), he had called "the gleam,/The light that never was."

If, as we now have seen, the dualism of a Wordsworthian ode is given as part of its "mould," so that its oxymorons cannot be sustained or illustrated without turning hymnic, we may reconsider "natural piety" as a gloss on the Intimations Ode, assuming that the oxymoron can be resolved only in ceasing to be a contradiction in terms.[42] Perhaps a literary source for a piety that *is* "natural" can be suggested: *The Aeneid*, by the author from whom Wordsworth took his punning and evasive first motto, *paulo majora canamus*. Wordsworth's sober coloring is quite Virgilian; it consists in the discovery of personal strength through reverence for an absent father who can *only* be revered in strength when he is absent. Wordsworth's tears (still tears, though "too deep" for them) are tears for the passing of *things* in their gay "apparel." In the conversion of spiritual loss to earthly sympathy, Wordsworth's Great Ode stages its limited triumph—and triumph of limits. The watch it keeps over mortality betrays its calling but recovers humanity. The moment when the ode writer crosses from the heroism of *pius Aeneas* to the profounder but far more melancholy heroism of *pater Aeneas*, having left the originary father forever among the Shades, is also the moment of relieved self-conception that purifies the earthly nature of Aeneas's mother, Venus. Thus much concerning nature in Wordsworth's natural piety; at the end of the next chapter I shall reconsider natural piety yet again, as a more truly oxymoronic threshold between nature and the preternatural.

7

The Wedding Guest in "Dejection"

I write melancholy, always melancholy: you will suspect that it is the fault of my natural Temper. Alas! no—This is the great Cross in that my Nature is made for Joy—impelling me to Joyance—& I never —never can yield to it. . . .

—Coleridge, *Notebooks*, 1803

My discussion of Coleridge's "Dejection: An Ode" will make use of the text printed in *Sibylline Leaves* (1817). For this choice among the many existing variants, a choice that might seem to lead us farther from the poem's kinship with the Intimations Ode than need be, I would allege several reasons. First, the 1802 "Letter to Sara" is aptly so named; it is a lover's complaint, a loosely organized address to an individual. When the poem became an "ode" later in 1802, it kept traces of its epistolary (or "Conversational") origin by addressing a clearly specified, more or less nonsymbolic, personage, "Edmund" or "William." Not until Sara comes to be called a "Lady" does the poem become more like an ode; the Lady is still a person addressed, as in a letter, but now her vaguer identity can be so closely connected with the wedded earth, with the domain of the wind, and also, vestigially, with the idea of a muse, that Coleridge's apostrophe is no longer split apart—no longer half invocation and half address, with each half bringing imperfectly related entities into play.[1]

The 1817 text differs in few other important respects from the one published in the *Morning Post* on 7 October 1802, the day of Wordsworth's wedding. No great distance is implied, then, in speaking of "the 1817 text." Although it had been Wordsworth's example, we assume, that had purged the nakedest moments of masochism from the "Letter," "Dejection" had already become, by the autumn of 1802, what it was to remain: a vehement counterstatement against Wordsworth's four-stanza Intimations Ode, hurried forward by an untenable logic to become a palinode against itself, and to find

162

that it is *not* radically in disagreement with Wordsworth after all.

Despite the importance of the dialogue with Wordsworth, however, the subjects of the two odes are not the same. Whereas Wordsworth defers the immortality he claims to desire, Coleridge puts off a wedding he claims to desire. As I remarked earlier, the skies are not lonely in "Dejection," but the poet is. Unlike Wordsworth, he has no doubt that the heavens are companionable places, that the sphere of immortality is intact and exciting. But he himself is barred, he says, from weddings that may occur either in heaven or earth. He claims to be kept from the festival of life by the "dull pain" of dejection, a pain he ascribes to the failure of his "shaping spirit"; but we shall have occasion to see—indeed this matter will occupy most of our attention—that the logic of the poem refutes this claim and proposes instead, rather grimly, that the poet's dejection is the sole and necessary origin of his creativity.[2]

Unlike the fastidious Wordsworth coming to terms with his "foster mother," the poet of "Dejection" is ready and willing to embrace the earth on any terms. Precisely because of its candid distress about the absence of everything desirable, this poem does not at first enter upon the dialectic of presence and absence that marks an ode. In saying this I do not mean simply that it starts in the noncommittal registers of the "middle" or "conversational" style, but this factor does contribute to my point. The atmosphere of the Conversation Poems prevails in "Dejection" until the speaker can summon strength to launch his invocation and petition; his thus needing inspiration in order to invoke inspiration reflects, as will appear, the poem's subversion of its own values. What Coleridge invokes, in contrast to Wordsworth's various joys, is turbulence, a sublime tragic atmosphere at the opposite extreme, among the varieties of unhappiness, from dejection. Despite "Hence, viper thoughts," there is no real exorcism; the poet shows no desire to drive hence the disbarring clouds, but wishes rather to draw them to the ground, uniting consciousness and cosmos in a single moment of agitation. When the storm comes, and the presence of a force is then asserted, a dialectic of presence and absence can properly begin, leading finally to the poem's eclipse as the ode it has only tardily become. Or rather never become at all, since there is really *no* dialectic in "Dejection." The storm does not directly affect the poet's consciousness. In part because Coleridge's ode constantly disputes with Wordsworth's and

hence never fights free of Wordsworth's frame of reference, the poem
never actually refutes the Wordsworthian injunction to cultivate a
wise passiveness. Coleridge's storm fails to arouse any emotion
except Wordsworthian pathos, a despair expressed by others to
which the poet defers, and which is therefore only obliquely related
to his own despair. The mad lutanist and the dull sobbing draft are
all one wind, even though the former is absent and the latter is
present. These conclusions are offered now as an admittedly gnomic
introduction to provide a framework for the succession of details that
will augment and, I hope, explain what I have here asserted.

    To begin with the motto: after 1815, when Wordsworth substi-
tuted "The Rainbow" for the phrase from Virgil's Fourth Eclogue at
the head of the Intimations Ode, Coleridge's motto from "Sir Patrick
Spens" took on a new combativeness. Coleridge rebukes the egoism
of Wordsworth's new motto by hanging on to the old convention of
heading an ode with a tag from the classics. "Sir Patrick Spens" is a
new classic, however, a ballad from Percy's *Reliques*.[3] It represents
a compromise between the old moon of Classicism and the new
moon of Romanticism.[4] This motto also anticipates the ode's under-
lying question: Is there, can there be, any meeting place between
Nature's emblems of family inheritance (the new embracing the old)
and the apocalyptic moment that puts an end to isolation and yet at
the same time sunders the Family of Man? When Coleridge's longed-
for storm arrives, he imagines that Wordsworth's Lucy, far from her
parents, is about to drown, like Sir Patrick Spens. Wordsworth's
Lucy ballads (see especially "Three years she grew") and the often
interchangeable plots of ballads by Bürger, Scott, and others all
seem to raise Coleridge's question: Can there ever be a wedding that
does not mark a death? "Ours her wedding garment, ours her shroud."
In Coleridge's own great ballad, it is a disbarred wedding guest who
unwittingly reminds us of the likeness between the ribs of the death
ship and the rib cage of the ghostly mariner. Thinking of the barred
clouds in "Dejection," still hoping for a wedding, Coleridge may well
have remembered that the wedding guest's simile ("And thou art
long, and lank, and brown,/As is the ribbed sea-sand") was com-
posed by William Wordsworth, now betrothed to Sara Hutchinson's
sister. To be sure, a *bridegroom* can speak of continuity (between
days, between persons, between his own poems) and see a covenant
in the rainbow; but an alienated man, more weather-wise, sees a glow

around the moon, some other poet's moon, and knows that it is no covenant but a forecast of death in a dreadful storm.

Coleridge's motto, then, was "late yestreen," not too long ago to be irrelevant but still the ballad evening of another day, and he turns to wrestle with his own evening, a late beginning that he opposes to Wordsworth's pastoral dawn. Wordsworth's first sky was bare, Coleridge's is lazily flaked; Wordsworth's moon was brilliant, Coleridge's is also brilliant, but its radiance has a lambency that fills the surrounding atmosphere with "glory" more persuasively than any comparable figure in the Intimations Ode. The moon's glory exists, then, but it purports to be self-supplied, with no contribution from the human imagination. Unaware that its pale fire is a plagiary of sunlight,[5] Coleridge's moon proposes itself as an instance of giving without receiving. Self-enlightenment is not sympathy, however; Coleridge's moon does not look round itself with delight like Wordsworth's but exists in and for itself, "fixed as if it grew/In its own cloudless, starless lake of blue." The creative initiative in man, by contrast, should be mixed with sympathy:

> from the soul itself must issue forth
> A light, a glory, a fair luminous cloud
> Enveloping the Earth—

Unlike this projected embrace of imagination and world, the moon's rain-forecasting nimbus does the Earth no service. But this happy contrast is not sustained. Elsewhere the poem confesses an autonomy, even a solipsism, in human imaginings that corresponds to the solipsism of the moon. The need of an ode for self-creation, which appears stealthily in Wordsworth's ode as an autochthonous myth, is more freely recognized by Coleridge:

> And from the soul itself must there be sent
> A sweet and potent voice, of its own birth,
> Of all sweet sounds the life and element!

A poet who is not self-begotten is merely an "Aeolian lute," and so it is, Coleridge claims, with himself, left without creative initiative in dejection.[6] In fact, however, his self-pity is itself a "dull sobbing draft"; hence it is parallel not to the passivity of the lute but to the autonomous motion of the wind. Unhappiness alone comes "from the soul itself," and the poet is therefore preconditioned by everything except his "Dejection." Because this dejection lacks an external cause (in the "Ode," not the "Letter to Sara"), it is clearly a kind of anxiety. The logic of the wind imagery, then, locates creativity in anxiety and only there, and sets in place the firmest paradox of the poem: If the disablement that allegedly follows upon dejection, here opposed to a "potent voice," is in fact the only possible self-birth of the soul, will not the coming of Joy, brought about by a wedding with another, eliminate the poet's last trace of self-presence and prove that all gifts are prior and given from without? In dejection of spirits and only then, the poet's light is cast from within, more completely so, in fact, than the moon's. Coleridge's first positive wish in the poem (it can be read as an invocation), would seem not to strengthen the soul in selfhood but to scatter it abroad, alienating its feeble integrity:

> And oh! that even now the gust were swelling,
>   And the slant night-shower driving loud and fast!
> Those sounds which oft have raised me, whilst they awed,
>   And sent my soul abroad . . .

"Dejection" conceives the paradox of being an ode from a standpoint that is new to our study. Not covertly but at once openly and unwillingly antinomian, this poem yearns for the community that would make it a hymn, however secondary and obeisant. It discovers its identity as an ode, its witness of self-presence, in the pathology it sets out to exorcize. Coleridge's daemons or pagan oracles are depressive, like the Countess of Winchelsea's Spleen, and not erotic. In Coleridge the erotic, the irritation of desire, is wholly unrepressed (until stanza five), and furnishes the hymnic content of a prothalamion. It is by no means the "crowd" in this poem that is "poor loveless ever-anxious."

The 1817 text more or less successfully buries the real-life occasion of the "Letter," but the paradox of the "Ode" is still wholly analogous to that of the "Letter." An unhappily married person wants a new marriage. He tries to will the marriage by saying that its coming to pass is in his own power, and he further strengthens his infantile control of the situation, his sense that in his life alone fulfillment lives, by saying that the will to marry is not easy to achieve. If he can only work up enough interest, then, the marriage is as good as celebrated: "I may not hope from outward forms to win/The passion and the life, whose fountains are within." At the same time, however, his poem steadily denies this assertion, which sounds like despair but is actually a comforting regression; in fact, his desire is not in the least wanting, and there will be no marriage unless the object of his desire takes the first steps toward the consummation he devoutly wishes. As W. J. Bate reminds us, the corollary of "we receive but what we give" is that "'nature will not give to us.'"[7] The "friend devoutest of my choice" is not his to choose. The absent object of the ode's calling is not spirit but flesh, not an idea haunted by impurity but a body that could perhaps be brought to delight in impurity. What "Dejection" repeats against its will is the pretense that the person wooing is being wooed. The poet writes "in this wan and heartless mood," wooing the landscape into his poem as he does so, yet he puts all this in the complaining language of one who is "to other thoughts by yonder throstle wooed"—to thoughts of love, sweetness, benignity. It is not until long after the thrush has stopped singing that the poet, no longer wooed, turns freely to these "thoughts," shaping them out of his own weary sleeplessness. The reason behind these several anomalies is the suppressed theme of "Dejection": imagination, born of desire, and wedded joy, fulfilled in sympathy, are opposed and incompatible states of being.[8]

The goal of Wordsworth's early and late poetry is tranquility, whether animal or spiritual. What his poetry tries to subdue is busy-ness, like that of London, a mighty heart lying still in his famous sonnet. We see, then, how calculated Coleridge's rivalry with Wordsworth will be when he writes: "This night, so tranquil now, will not go hence/Unroused by winds, that ply a busier trade." Something we tentatively assume to be the pathetic fallacy devalues the passivity of the poet's current state and gives preference to the busy-ness of a trade wind or profitable energy.[9] We are led to assume that this scale of values is operative because the poem seems to be written in praise of energy. We must admit, though, that the usual values attached to tranquility and bustle cannot be reversed merely by a wish. After all, the man from Porlock came on "business." We have read this inversion into the opening lines of "Dejection" not so much at the behest of the pathetic fallacy as from having decided too soon that we understand the values of the poem as a whole—a mis-reading, this, that begins on rereading. It is in a state of enervation that Coleridge composes what is most original in him, the landscape of his evening eye and ear from the mid-1790s onward, with its bars, flecks, and graceful chiaroscuro.[10] What by contrast is the storm of stanza seven? Quite deliberately a pastiche of other poets' poems. One need not claim that the opening landscape is the best writing in the poem: enough that it is the most like Coleridge and the least like Wordsworth of anything in the poem. It describes a sullen tranquility founded in pains that are far more intense and more inward than the "human suffering" of Wordsworth's ode.

At length Coleridge says that his great darkening evening-scape is "excellently fair." And then: "I see, not feel, how beautiful they are!" The visual pathetic fallacy, never fully in effect, is now fully revoked, because the poet's plan depends on his inability to identify with anything in nature. But in the audible realm, the pathetic fallacy continues unnoticed.[11] The sad winds that "mold yon cloud in lazy flakes" are a shaping *spiritus* that composes the landscape, a voice that begets light. The poet projects his dull sobbing into this dejected wind even as he laments the loss of his shaping spirit. The personalization of the wind goes unchecked, then, and the light it helps to organize has a Coleridgian appearance also. Its "peculiar tint of yellow green" is the color of vipers, and also of a jaundiced complexion. Coleridge's wind composes with a jaundiced eye that is peculiar to the poet.[12] If this landscape is excellently fair, so too is the art of the speaker—as long as he is depressed.

As we have seen, every ode, burdened with the awareness that the "power of music" cannot keep its magic much longer, tries to "prolong" some evening strain, to stretch its vocation into the merely scientific world where vaticination is called superstition. So during the drawing out of Coleridge's "long eve" among ever more nocturnal skies, he complains that though he "should gaze forever/ On that green light that lingers in the west," he still "may not hope from outward forms to win" the passion he wishes. And yet, again, the outward forms of this distended landscape are not really outward forms; they are the peculiar articulation of his calling. True, he cannot hope to win a marriage from such jaundiced forms, whether outward or inward, but then, an ode is not a marriage poem. The divorce between lyric fulfillment in desire and human fulfillment in satiety is what "Dejection" tries without success to gloss over.[13]

It is a tribute to the surviving power of music that the absurdity of Coleridge's

> stifled, drowsy, unimpassioned grief,
> Which finds no natural outlet, no relief,
> In word, or sigh, or tear—

has given very few readers pause, despite being, of course, itself a "natural outlet." To be sure, this passage is ambiguous: *human* or *merely* "natural" grief in desire cannot be relieved by commonplace talk, and he who is no poet "better far were mute." But this ambiguity only deepens the gulf between the ground of poetry and the ground of emotion. In his submerged argument, Coleridge concedes that Wordsworth's opposition of emotion and tranquility was perfectly justified, and that storms and sigh-tempests are out of place. Each "visitation" of affliction "Suspends what nature gave me at my birth,/My shaping spirit of imagination." Suspends: keeps it hanging in suspense, keeps it lingering in play as long as the visitation is no less becalming than it is this evening.[14] Here is yet another ode that devours the past, that praises the virtues of the past, and then consumes it to sustain the present.

II

The first acknowledged borrowing by Coleridge from Wordsworth had been the phrase "'green radiance,'" which appears quoted in "Lines at Shurton Bars" (1795), one of the poems Coleridge wrote to persuade himself that his first marriage was happy.[15] Like the "Letter to Sara," "Shurton Bars" was an "Answer to a Letter," and one may suspect that he had this early poem vividly in mind when he wrote the first sobbing draft of "Dejection." "Shurton Bars" begins in evening, with the poet watching the glowworm "Move with 'green radiance' through the grass,/An emerald of light." Here certainly is a light that receives what it gives, illuminating the daedal earth that makes it green. In "Dejection," Coleridge means to describe an outward form of green radiance that imagination has not shaped, and thus to retract the influence of Wordsworth; but imagination *has* shaped the greenness of "Dejection," and stays vigorous, paradoxically, in failing to refute Wordsworth's timely utterance.

The contentment of "Shurton Bars" is achieved during a temporary absence from the beloved, a secure loneliness; in 1802, Coleridge wishes to contrast that comfort with his current plight. In the early poem, with his wife present in apostrophe, he marks the distance between their happiness and human vacancy: "And hark, my Love! The sea-breeze moans/Through yon reft house." In stanza seven of "Dejection," house becomes harp; the whole image is transferred from human shelter to the housing or medium of poetry, and that transference—from local habitation to name—makes all the difference. "Shurton Bars" is a shared utterance, not an ode, and therefore huddles with humanity against the wind, which soon rises in Fancy and becomes a storm:

> When stormy midnight howling round
> Beats on our roof with clattering sound,
>   To me your arms you'll stretch:
> Great God, you'll say—To us so kind,
> O shelter from this loud bleak wind
>   The houseless, friendless wretch!

This is wretched verse, truly a betrayal of imagination in behalf of humanity, the more so for its weak echoes of Thomson, Cowper, and Lear on the heath. Where the wind is, humanist Man is not; the unreal wind is the howling of the unattached and destructive signifier, blown through us and not spirited by us, that humaneness represses and poetry becomes. Even "Shurton Bars" itself presents the alternative of a still earlier self, a foolish melancholy Jaques whose morbid creativity will reappear in "Dejection": "Time was, I should have thought it sweet"

> in black soul-jaundiced fit
> A sad gloom-pampered man to sit,
>   And listen to the roar:
> When mountain-surges bellowing deep . . .

This verse is still very poor, but it subverts in advance the premise of recovery in "Dejection."

So also does "The Eolian Harp," a much less contented poem about marriage that stands in even clearer relation to "Dejection." Coleridge's lines on the "Aeolian lute" in 1802 effect a contrast in pathetic fallacy with those of "The Eolian Harp," which stress embrace rather than abrasion:

> And that simplest Lute,
> Placed length-ways in the clasping casement, hark!

> How by the desultory breeze caressed,
> Like some coy maid half-yielding to her lover . . .

But this poem moves away from the embrace of the wife beside the Cot, arriving on "yonder hill" where, at the safe distance of solitude, the poet can conceive of the "one intellectual breeze" or demon lover that writes the poetry of the world by animating nature's organic harps. Inspiration comes not during excitement or high passion or the warmth of passion fulfilled, but only to "my indolent and passive brain."

Against these anti-epithalamic marriage poems, then, Coleridge entirely fails to write a palinode in unwilling solitude, and instead rewrites the poem he has written all along. This time, however, he writes it as an ode, in the form, that is, that traditionally accompanies poetry's highest claims to enter the embraces of transcendent consciousness and of the world. The presupposition of any ode is ironic, but Coleridge's ode is the first, apart from the parodies of which Coleridge himself numbered several in his juvenilia, that deliberately features an irony.[16] It is for this very reason, so inexorable is the antithetical sense of words in the wind, that "Dejection" is the first ode that is *not* at bottom ironic, the first to discover, however unwillingly, the basis of voice in desire, not presence.

III

What may be called the theoretical stage of "Dejection," which begins at the fifth stanza, describes the hermetic pursuits that jaundice the soul, and it brings the Lady into its sphere of address in a complex way. It is at this point that Coleridge shows the strongest influence of Collins. Like Collins's Fancy, Coleridge's Lady must be at once pure and ready for marriage. Herself the essence of Joy, she therefore need not ask the poet what Joy is, unless, as the ensuing sermon implies, she is too naïve to know her own nature. The Lady is a figure of Chastity, yet gives a regenerate sensory realm to the poet "in dower." Here the genealogy of the ode can begin, and here also begins the dialectic of sublimation, bringing with it what Harold Bloom has called "The dangers of idealizing the libido."[17] Joy is given sexually, yet it is a self-conceived gift, a glory autochthonously born from "A new Earth and new Heaven" of one's own making: "We in ourselves rejoice!"

After John 21, drawn into the ode here to add prophetic afflatus to its trial flight, the gloss on these lines that will first occur to mind is from *Hamlet*, a touchstone that seems to affirm the transcendental realm: "There are more things in heaven and earth, Horatio,/Than are dreamt of in your philosophy." "Undreamt of," that is—to be grossly unfair to the gentle materialist Horatio—"by the sensual and the proud." But *Hamlet* is no very sound anchor for a poet's faith in the pure origin of the transcendent, since Shakespeare's plot starts with a cankered wedding. A passage in *Hamlet* of a wholly different sort, a passage that interrogates the prisons of both heaven and earth, more subtly informs Coleridge's ode. In this passage Hamlet's too, too sullied flesh has cast him into a suicidal dejection, a grief without a pang that is "weary, stale, flat, and"—in contrast with Coleridge's "busier trade"—"unprofitable." Here the flesh is unregenerate: "Things rank and gross in nature/Possess it merely." The first King, like Coleridge in "Shurton Bars," was "So loving to my mother/That he might beteem the winds of heaven/Visit her face too roughly." But the Lady, the idea of a Lady for Coleridge, was corrupted by her very virtue, by the growth of the poetic faculty of desire even in fulfillment:

> Heaven and earth,
> Must I remember? Why, she would hang on him
> As if increase of appetite had grown
> By what it fed on . . .

If Joy is "cloud at once and shower," potency and act, repressing veil and manifestation, it is, like Collins's Fancy, an unstable possession, corrupt if creative and useless if chaste.

Collins's Fancy appears in her own person in the next stanza, where "Dejection" turns, as odes do, from a metaphysical to a personal myth of origin. "There was a time." Coleridge contrasts Wordsworth's boyhood pastoral with his own immemorial suffering. In days of yore Joy-Fancy was coquettish and throve, like Keats in his "Ode on Melancholy," on life's imperfections:

> There was a time when, though my path was rough,
> This joy within me dallied with distress,
> And all misfortunes were but as the stuff
> Whence Fancy made me dreams of happiness.

This stuff that dreams are made on gave rise to the creative moment at a time of life when no representational obligation held the poet's dreams in check. The contrast in stanza six fails, since by its own terms nothing has changed: the rememorized youth of the speaker is subsumed in the present, the continuity of absence being, at the same time, the continuity of self-presence in the careless signifier. So absolute was this continuous self-presence, indeed, that in the past all textuality seemed one, and the hope invested in the freed signifier resulted in spontaneous plagiary: "Fruits and foliage, not my own, seemed mine."[18] This is what it feels like to be the moon.

What is this continuous self-presence if not, precisely, "abstruse research," the tracing of discourse as it unfolds its inspirational sources?[19] This habit of soul certainly does destroy the natural man, but the natural man, as Coleridge insists in the *Biographia*, is no poet. Wordsworth's "man speaking to men," speaking the "real language of men," is, as Coleridge indicates, a fallacious being. Poetry is inconceivable without education, and education involves an exposure to linguistic models that mediate, distance, and finally perhaps even exclude nature. If nothing else, the articulate Rustic knows his Bible and is (so to say) well-spoken by it. This much is implied in the *Biographia* remarks, and critics have always been ready enough to affirm, correctly, that in this way, from a logical standpoint, Coleridge overthrows Wordsworth's linguistic naturalism. Why then do the same critics continue to accept the Wordsworthian rhetoric of "Dejection"? Where this ode is most Wordsworthian in intent,[20] it always pulls a glory over our eyes. The "natural man" is given in marriage, but poetry is given through the solitary researches of the signifier. Merely by loading his true calling with the imputation of pedantry, Coleridge cannot repeat "Expostulation and Reply," because his abstruse researches have made him at once too tough-minded and too "still and patient" (*not* uncomplaining, obviously, but passive before the course of the signifier): "Wordsworthian" indeed, but with the key terms of Wordsworth's creative psychology realigned.

IV

The seventh stanza presents itself as a counterturn and exorcism: "Hence, viper thoughts, that coil around my mind." We have met with this jaundiced garland already, however, in a place where we were meant to affirm it: "Hope grew round me, like the twining vine" is an earlier coiling greenness.[21] When the poet "turns" from these thoughts, then, he discovers sympathy, only to realize that sympathy and originality are opposed. Here is the first genuine change of the poem, an arousal that bodes ill. Coleridge no longer has the power of plagiary; now when he rewrites the texts of others he identifies the authors (the 1802 wedding text: "As William's self had framed the tender lay"). The seventh stanza performs a conventional function of an ode, the reduction of rival authors and genres to its own scope, but it does so weakly, like Collins's Scottish Superstitions Ode. The theme of sympathy, as in Collins, leads to a loss of focus. Coleridge has gone indoors, and hence the wind now raves "without"; the poet has lost his sole participatory channel and sign of origination in the very moment of claiming for the first time to be aroused by it.

I called the enthusiastic fifth stanza a "trial flight" because the seventh stanza, with its banishment of demons ostensibly accomplished, is reserved for a more ambitious flight. Coleridge transfers the conventional noontide flight of an ode to midnight, since he is never free of darkness and hopes only for a turbulent night in preference to the darkling plainness of evening. "Reality's dark dream" in the "Letter" (where it is "the dark distressful dream") was Coleridge's pathetic fantasy that Sara would get sick so he could nurse her. In the "Ode," though, the viper thoughts are no longer specified, and the whole exorcism is made to parallel Wordsworth's unspecified "thought of grief." What ensues will be an attempted "timely utterance." How timely it in fact is, therapeutically speaking, cannot be determined; it is only possible to pursue the ode, as an ode, to its logical conclusion.

"Reality's dark dream," again, has no basis in the poem. Be the horrors of autobiography what they may, there is no remaining evidence in the poem for reading the dark dream as, say, "the nightmarishness of my unhappy life," and it is only a little more helpful to read "the nightmarish escape from the nightmare of my life." The darkness of reality's dark dream suggests, rather, that which is but dimly seen. Reality as such is as imperceptible as a dream scarcely remembered. The viper thoughts coil because they are layers of self-involvement: the research in dejection that unmanned the natural man, the poet's present brooding about his dejection, and finally the dejection itself. His commitment to the course of the signifier (which is to say, the "life of the mind") has made the signified a dream, to be sure, but not necessarily, on the face of the matter, a *dark* dream, since pedants are as often as not cheerful souls. Coleridge's darkness may therefore be taken to open toward the maelstroms of his darkest interpreters. There is also, though, the present darkness, the bad mood founded in the sort of anxiety that is, we have seen, the foundation of original poetry, of first words, and is thus inseparable from the "research" the poet persists in reprehending.

"I turn from you, and listen to the wind,/Which long has raved unnoticed." Why unnoticed? Because the poet has been being himself, a poet, writing stanzas two through six, waiting for the gust to swell so he could write a poem of another kind, a sublime ode in tune with "Those sounds which oft have raised me, whilst they awed."[22] The first stanza had been written in spontaneous concert with the wind, which functioned there as a projection of the self in nature, a figure of self-presence, until it was finally invoked for the purpose of dispersing the soul abroad. Thus the poet was with the wind when the cosmos was most personalized but least socialized. Then he goes inside, with the wind, the emblem of his morose power, so firmly in safe-keeping that thereafter he no longer mentions it. It is no contradiction to add, though, from another standpoint, that he has also reined in the wind before it could swell to become a demiurge, an intractably *other* phenomenal music in the lute. As a force "without" (before the seventh stanza, that is), the wind would have become either an alien motion in unwedded nature or else a more stubbornly independent symbol than it was when it merely sobbed, and would have been henceforth no longer self-attuned but a symbol of determinacy that would put an end to Coleridge's myth of subjective priority. The *poem* has swollen, then, because it repressed the wind as soon as its coyly conditional invocation of the inevitable storm at the end of the first stanza signaled that the wind was getting out of control. The poet now stages his counterturn. He returns to the wind, looking for himself where he is no longer to be found, because he has nothing more to say in his own person. Self-exhausted, he needs inspiration in the least honorific sense of the word. As Hobbes would have said, he needs to be blown up like a bagpipe.

The poet's going inside, supposing it to have happened when the storm began, has freed the middle stanzas from natural competition; but now, in being mentioned after the fact, the act of seeking shelter in a house (like a "lonely house" but still humanized by allusion to the comforts of "Shurton Bars") closes a door on his power to shape the world. The wind does not play through this house; even if the lute is in the casement, the word "without" suggests a repulsion of the wind even by the lute itself. The poet's turning toward sympathy, or rather to an anthology of others' sympathy, launches his ode on the most solipsistic of an ode's traditional tasks, the eclipse of rival modes, but the modest self-effacement with which this task is carried out shows sympathy to have won the night. At this point, in preparation for the last stanza, Coleridge's ode starts to resemble a hymn.

The first noise of the wind is that of northern romance and horror-gothic reduced to the cry of an occasion: not narrative but a certain mood of narrative, namely lyric, or more specifically the ode, with its "scream/. . . lengthened out" into the spaces of silence. In avoiding narrative, this first reduction is in one sense the strongest in the series; there is no story attached to it, just as there is no story attached to "Reality's dark dream," but only a daemonic ethos in which the universe tortures *itself* without motive. Hence the poet's creative anxiety is still echoed in nature. At the same time, though, this passage reeks of sensationalism, and betrays the "degrading thirst after outrageous stimulation" that Wordsworth decried in the 1800 Preface. A storm this mannered should properly haunt high places deserted or untrodden by man; hence this first utterance of the storm moves the poem away from its communal motive as a hymn as well as from the low-lying solitude that inspires it as an ode. The storm at its height is out of phase, no nativity ode but a mountain birth signifying nothing (certainly not a black mass) by contrast with the rich seasonality of an actual late March:

> Mad lutanist! who in this month of showers,
> Of dark-brown gardens, and of peeping flowers,
> Mak'st devils' yule, with worse than wintry song,
> The blossoms, buds, and timorous leaves among.[23]

The storm is like a cartoon bogey, wildly animated but never touching the real landscape in a mixed-media film. The fruitful dejection of Coleridge's dark-brown ground, with its tentative, cautiously prospective flowers of rhetoric, is what survives his afflatus; or, if it does not, the unseasonable storm is to blame.

Because of its inauthenticity, the storm easily passes into theatre; as an "actor," it has no identity of its own. Theatre is shunted aside by lyricization in the next phrase, however, since the actor is "perfect," not in scenarios (as is Wordsworth's little con-man) but in "tragic sounds." Coleridge knew his *Laokoon*, knew that whereas a "scream" is "perfect" for narrative (Lessing's example is *Aeneid* II. 222: "clamores . . . horrendos ad sidera tollit"), the plastic arts require the subtler pathos of potential agony. Coleridge sets out in this generically diffuse passage as if to show Lessing that lyric can rival *pictura* in subtlety, but in so doing he undermines his more immediate thesis—the only thesis that would require the coming of this storm—about the need for emotional turmoil in the specifically Pindaric mode of lyric: "Thou mighty poet, e'en to frenzy bold!" This mode is simply not his own. He rushes the storm through an epic moment reduced to the sounds of martial lyric (111-13), and then, more congenially, all the mighty heart of his picture lies still:

> But hush! there is a pause of deepest silence!
>   And all that noise, as of a rushing crowd,
> With groans, and tremulous shudderings—all is over—

"But hush," the "hold, my muse" convention that ends the afflatus of an ode, is what in fact partly returns the poet to his proper identity as registrar of more delicately nuanced griefs, and brings on his first clear admission that lyric, like the presentation of "natural signs" in Lessing's pictorial arts, conforms with an aesthetic of potential, an aesthetic, that is, of the framing of desire:

> It tells another tale, with sounds less deep and loud!
>   A tale of less affright,
>   And tempered with delight,
> As Otway's self had framed the tender lay—
>   'Tis of a little child
>   Upon a lonesome wild,
> Not far from home, but she hath lost her way:
> And now moans low in bitter grief and fear,
> And now screams loud, and hopes to make her mother hear.

Once more, the pathetic focus of the scene returns us to the atmosphere of the poet's dejection, even to its very sound, the "sobbing draft, that moans."[24] But whereas the poet moans low in anxiety, in a state of nervous exhaustion that is not externally motivated, the little girl both moans *and* screams, naturally and with no thought of art, because her grief comes from "fear" of the actual. Having offered this contrast with his own state is Coleridge's triumph as a humane poet and his undoing as an odist. He has, on the one hand, confessed the pettiness of his own dejection by dispassionate standards, but on the other hand he has shown that all the passions except desire (which he has in common with the child) fall outside the compass of an ode. Somewhere between theatre and lyrical ballad, this scene returns the poem to its motto, to the otherness of a yestreen that the poet had tried to create anew with a "peculiar" voicing. Now, though, his voice is lost in Wordsworth's, to his own disadvantage. Wordsworth's Babe in the Great Ode had leapt up on his mother's arm, lusty and self-assured. In reverting away from this Babe to the child of the Lucy poems, with whom he then identifies while designating her author as his own father, Coleridge concedes, as in several painful Notebook entries, the "femininity" of his own character, the helpless passivity and lack of sexually polar magnetism that makes it impossible for him to woo nature in a great spousal verse of his own. His inability to make Nature hear increases the louder he screams.

Perhaps I may add my own conjecture, in this context, to the vast literature on why "Dejection" was Coleridge's last considerable poem apart from the excellent but all-conceding lyric "To William Wordsworth" and the deliberately hermetic "Limbo" and "Ne Plus Ultra." In early youth, Coleridge took the idea of the ode as a test of vocation far more seriously than Wordsworth perhaps ever did, as may be evidenced by the fact that in notes if not in titles he bravely called nearly all his juvenilia "odes." Before he went to Cambridge, perhaps in reaction against Dr. Bowyer's hostility to all bombast and his insistence that even "the wildest odes had a logic . . . as severe as that of science" (*Biographia*, ch. 1), Coleridge seems to have imagined that if a poem was not an ode it was not a poem. He outgrew that notion, of course, and soon fathered the quieter voice of his and Wordsworth's Conversation Poems, reserving the ode from then on to be a record of public events, as in "The Departing Year" and "France." But then, somewhere between 1798 and 1800, Wordsworth must have begun to toy with the idea that the Conversation Poem, having once naturalized the most unwieldy conventions of the sublime ode, could achieve a nobler strain, and he recorded this thought in the headnote to "Tintern Abbey" in the 1800 *Lyrical Ballads*. He would not presume to call his poem an ode, he said, but "it was written with a hope that in the transitions, and impassioned music of the versification, would be found the principal requisites of that species of composition."[25] In my conservative view of the ode, which requires the immanence if not the appearance of all its unwieldy conventions, "Tintern Abbey," Wordsworth's greatest lyric, is nothing like an ode. I think that Wordsworth himself must have realized the difference; had he not, he *would* in fact have called the poem an ode. Wordsworth was not to be restrained by modesty from attempting the "species of composition" that was practiced annually by the Laureate Henry Pye. It is most probable that Wordsworth thought "Tintern Abbey" was too good to be called an ode, and that his headnote was designed to assure his readers that the poem had all the virtues of an ode and none of the absurdities. That he then later wrote his Great Ode, to be followed by more and lesser odes, is in itself, as I have argued, an eventuality marked by self-irony and by several sorts of "confusion."

To return to Coleridge and the headnote to "Tintern Abbey." It seems likely that Coleridge was caught off guard by his impression that Wordsworth now proposed to revise upward, as it were, the lyric mode that he, Coleridge, had invented. The note would have appeared to Coleridge as a critique of the middle registers, quiet transitions, and smooth versification of "Frost at Midnight," "The Nightingale," and "This Lime-Tree Bower." It must have seemed as though Wordsworth were saying: Let us put more passion in our conversations, let us make them odes. Then Wordsworth wrote the first four stanzas or strophes of what his sister called an "Ode"[26] on the day it was written; there was no doubt in the Wordsworth Circle about what the poem was. Coleridge responded first with an impassioned epistle, which Wordsworth probably criticized because it was too diffusely conversational, with its afflatus therefore topical and unearned. At that point the revision of the "Letter to Sara" came to rival the Intimations Ode not just in subject matter but also in genre. In a sense, if my conjectures carry conviction, Coleridge in 1802 can be seen to have returned, stimulated by his having mistaken Wordsworth's confusion for confidence, to his youthful idealization of the ode as the supreme, if not the only, genre of poetry. He had only the Conversation Poems and some supernatural balladry to look back on with any complacency,[27] and he now decided once more, plagued by self-doubt of other kinds from other sources, that if he could not write an ode he would ("Cousin Coleridge," we can imagine him fearing that Wordsworth would say) never be a poet.

"Dejection: An Ode" turned out to be everything by turns: a Conversational Poem, a lyrical ballad, and—something like an ode. Coleridge could not call it an "Ode to" or even an "Ode on" dejection, because clearly his affliction was not a quality to be openly invoked, nor was it something that a celebratory poem could finally be "on" or about. Dejection had to be worked through, surmounted; hence the coming of the storm and its bravura. With the storm once evoked, the poem could with license be called an ode, but only in an afterthought, a sliding apposition. The topic stands alone, nearly its own sentence and a sentence on its author, "Dejection" colon. Coleridge's title knows what his poem knows, that lassitude and the atmospherics of quiet grief are the surest ground of his genius. But Coleridge himself seems not to have admitted this much. His poem is "not far from home," indeed it never leaves home, as the dark March gardens and the sobbing of the Child indicate, but it has unquestionably lost its way through Coleridge's fatal transvaluation of his calling into a scream.

Stanza eight falls away from the storm's mountain birth, but cannot be said (in the phrase I have used to describe the denouement of an ode) to accept a diminished calling without further disturbance; not, at least, if one hears, as I do, a note of contempt for the Lady in whose behalf its hymnic benediction is uttered. A more precise word for "contempt" here would be *mépris*, the scorn made possible by misprision. The Lady has never had fair play in this poem because the poet has praised her, symbolized her, as just what the "natural man" in the poet does not want her to be, a chaste wooer of "all things" except himself, an independent person whose wellbeing is entirely in her own hands. In the end the poet and the natural man together have their revenge by subordinating her as a "simple spirit, guided from above" (this line, significantly, is *added* to the otherwise shortened "Letter").[28] Guided, it is hoped, toward the natural man by the poet's mountain screams, the Lady is stripped of the constitutive power she has just been awarded ("To her may all things live, from pole to pole,/Their life the eddying of her living soul!"), and made to join in the singing of hymns.

The contrast between the Lady's valley peace and the poet's stormy eminence is not, however, the vehicle of Coleridge's mépris. In fact it is not fully a contrast at all. The pathos that ends the seventh stanza shows clearly enough that the storm is valuable for the pregnant lull of its eye and not for its bold frenzy. Coleridge's proper home is a valley place also. The same stars have hung over both dwellers, poet and Lady, though not at the same time or quite in the same way,[29] and it is from these slanted differences that the scorn arises. The poet is wide awake ("small thoughts have I of sleep"), while the Lady, indifferent to his calling, is an unself-conscious limb of "the sleeping earth" to which she is linked in simile. The Lady's stars "hang bright," in contrast with the poet's earlier scudding stars flecked over by hanging clouds, because in her contentment, her infuriating self-sufficiency, she cannot comprehend the alienness of the stars' duties as glorious guardians. Like a poet glorious, but also like a man or an angel sympathetically protective, only the elusive stars achieve a balance between fellow-feeling and imaginative power. Coleridge's "Stand," then, turns against his sometime muse; at once lament and boast, it is his last and grimmest stand in defense of his calling as an independent and necessarily lonely researcher, if no longer, perhaps, as a poet.

I am attracted to Humphry House's suggestion that the "mountain-birth" is from Horace's "Parturient montes, nascetur ridiculus mus" (*Ad Pisones.* 139), because, as House remarks, "Horace's line is itself about the miscarriage or failure of poetic creation."[30] It is a line that ridicule of "unnatural flights in poetry" in English is never far from quoting, and that Ben Jonson, in fearing that his ode may be a Plinian monstrous birth, perhaps therefore avoids quoting or facing too squarely. As the modern Horatian treatises gradually came to give more and more space to the ode, the Horatian chimaera (*Ad Pisones.* 1–5) of the monstrous birth was given wider and wider scope. One never wrote an Art of Poetry without a flurry of caution about odes, and finally the Art of Poetry gave way to the plain prose of an Art of Sinking. During the descent of his last stanza, Coleridge cannot but wonder about the ascent of his penultimate one, especially—for instance—about the "pine grove whither wood-man never clomb." Was that not a bathetic ascent, a clumsy Milton-ism (viz., *Il Penseroso.* 135–37) thrust into a witches' sabbath? And so with regard to the mountainous *size* of the seventh stanza, itself an inflationary device that dwindles finally to the simple trimeters, doubled but not complicated in the closing Alexandrine, which are reserved to express Wordsworth's untimely joy: By what license was it a stanza at all?

The "Letter to Sara" has: "And be this Tempest but a mountain Birth." That is not a prayer but a confession that the poet has brewed his own tempest, "lengthened out" a scream that scatters any conceivable poetic form into so many *disjecta membra poetae*. No longer self-born, the soul of the poet has been dispersed, "sent abroad" into alien regions where sympathy is bathos and the elemental life of nature is no longer subtly daemonic and subject to the voicing of mood, but merely a "devils' yule," a mountain ritual (as in *Faust*) celebrating the nativity of misrule. All this is merely "Mad." By losing his way,[31] the poet closes himself out of his properly charming circle; he is dis-jected,[32] cast out of his vocation in having misconceived it.

V

The companion odes of Wordsworth and Coleridge are "metaphysical" in a way that no earlier ode is metaphysical. Their figures occupy a border region between physics and metaphysics. Metalepsis, which is like a Pindaric leap, is now hobbled when it nears this border.[33] Pindar's "Dig a long ditch for my jump from here" is just what the new ode avoids saying. The projection or cast of figures from material to transcendent regions, which I described earlier as an invocation reaching upward toward a descending genealogy, is much reduced in distance by the Romantic invention of a threshold oxymoron in which the self is called upon as an other. Both projected and dejected, the self is invoked as that which at once emerges on earth and falls to earth. Spirit resonates or gleams in the poet-as-object without seeming to have been called, and the vital energy of desire suffuses the sky to prevent the visionary's high destiny from seeming like a tedious bliss.

Wordsworth and Coleridge understand the figurative threshold of an ode as bondage and marriage, respectively. For Wordsworth, the ode is meant to celebrate a linkage or seriality, an "each to each" so subtle that we cannot tell whether by following its course we are being teased out of thought or teased out of nature. Presence then becomes what I described in the last chapter as a psychological syntax, an articulate, just barely articulate, place imprisoned by its reification (fretted by its channel), but still infinitely extensible in theory, like a Chomskyan sentence. These metaphors could of course apply to most of Wordsworth's poetry, but I apply them pointedly to the ode because the form and dialectic of the ode lie in wait, grimly preexistent like a prior life, to invalidate them. If the ode "conceives itself," thus making invocation an invention and not a request—as in a prayer—that that which is endless enter the temporal world, then the ode knows a point before which its invention was not, and another point when it will be no more. The ode is not an infinitely extensible sentence but an irregular rondure, a parody of the full circle, broken and finite or infinite only along its faults.

How could Wordsworth have failed to consider that the topic of infinite extensibility after death for which he reserved his first Pindaric foray could only pass unanalyzed in the sort of blank verse that expands until it seems to become an immortal sea, or, at times, a blank misgiving? I do not think that he did ignore this question; it could not have been ignored during the unfamiliar act of writing, as it were, from scratch, and that is why I incline to view the Great Ode as a poem that took the poet by surprise. Too long after the last gleam has fled, the return to metric norms in the last stanza is a gesture of repentence for an enthusiastic error. The interpolation of "Is lovely yet" is a dimeter farewell to the poet's earlier, more ambitiously gnomic voicing.

Wordsworth's unsurpassable border poem, "Tintern Abbey," was already written, couched in the least constraining of forms. Edmund Burke had listed a row of trees dwindling toward the horizon among his sublime objects; in "Tintern Abbey" Wordsworth supplants Burke's trees with the barely sublime "hedgerows, hardly hedgerows, little lines/Of sportive wood run wild: these pastoral farms/Green to the very door." Like the sportive wood, no line in this sort of writing is end-stopped or much impeded. But "Tintern Abbey" has advanced only *to* a threshold, with its pastoral farms and forms poised between the georgic and the eremitic; its foregrounding suspends the question of whether and how the natural man and the visionary can dwell together. Still wreathed in smoke, the question awaits the boldness of an ode to reveal its negative answer. For his testing of limits, Wordsworth chose the Pindaric leap, and fell, not like Phaeton but like the chthonic Adam, who once worked in his garden and talked to an angel on the same day.

Wordsworth and Coleridge both understood the advantage of narrowed horizons. Nuns fret not in their narrow rooms; the bondsmanship of Duty is an opportunity; and Coleridge was soothed by the lime-tree bower that was his prison. "Dejection," however, finds the comforting prison within, among the oppressive spirits of anxiety. The outer prison is too roomy for comfort, bounded only at the height of the barring clouds, themselves transparent. Coleridge makes external space pathless and vertiginous, a place where one gets lost even if one is not far from home.[34] "Dejection" sets out to domesticate distance, to "send abroad" the soul to claim a territory in marriage. The question of immortality is irrelevant in this poem, which explores the social conditions of being rather than its ontological limits. Coleridge's liminal figures seek out a meeting place of solitude and marriage in the possibility of a visionary *society*. As "public" a poem in its own self-involved way as "France: An Ode" or Collins's "Ode to Liberty," "Dejection" projects an absent sacred place, where one sky, one wind, one soul inform all the elect in common. The signs of infantile regression in "Dejection" are the exercise of tyranny over persons through talismans and the wish for revenge against the uncontrollable; but there is also a mode of regression in the poem that might be termed "juvenile." The "green light lingering in the west" is not entirely a bilious decoction from the soul in its present state; it is also a horizon where memory lingers, the memory of a time before Wordsworth's green radiance guided the poet from above. There was a time when it seemed possible to level mountain and valley, like Isaiah, there to create a bower for the marriage without impediment of equal and equally originary souls. Even through the green light of dejection the poet can descry, though he can no longer surmise, the green banks of the Susquehanna.[35]

On that distant border, imagination and sympathy, solitude and marriage, might have seemed compatible in some more youthful ode, a "To the Pennsylvanian Voyage." But these qualities would have been contradictions in terms nonetheless. When Wordsworth's imagination, that "unfathered vapour, rising from the abyss," fully confronted immortality, nature fell away and vanished; now that he contrarily believes the child to be father to the man, he is committed to seriality and can only botanize, day after day, until even the meanest flowers turn human. If Coleridge's investment in the ode is sacramental, Wordsworth's is genealogical. He inherits its crisis of birth, and tries to synthesize the pure/impure, monstrous/miraculous conception fantasies of former odes in the single concept of the "glory," only to wedge those antinomies further apart owing to his inability to trope his glory as anything other than a covering for nakedness. The glory is his feathered cincture, or tented veil. The dialectic of repression breaks up his horizon gleam, forcing it toward the opposite conceptual poles of surface and essence, leaving a contradiction in terms to occupy the vacated border: natural piety.

The theme implied in Wordsworth's choice of a discursive structure, then, is ultimately the same as that of Coleridge: imagination and sympathy cannot cohabit. We can now identify the change in the relation between structure and theme that has taken place in the ode since Collins, whose odes show that autogenesis and biogenesis cannot be reconciled. If the ode from Jonson through Gray and Collins had undertaken to repress the indwelling of nature in imagination, the new ode tries to repress the exile of nature from imagination. This attempt has been the focus of much recent thinking about post-Blakean Romanticism. Since thinking of this kind necessarily stresses the hidden wish for apocalypse in the course of tracing the poet's conscious denial of apocalyptic intent, it has most often been attacked as an affront to Humanism. I take it, though, that if nothing is knowable without boundaries (and not even Collins, immured in Plato's dubious shade, knows very much about them), we can scarcely know what the Human is, and frame our understanding to its limits, without knowing where it is not. I am attempting to show that the ode has a special role to play in the incomparably rigorous Romantic thinking about delimitation, about the border that separates the visionary from the humane. The impulse of the Romantic ode to escape the prison-house where youth grows pale and spectre-thin and dies is always countervailed by the complex closures of its medium. Its Pindarism is a violated probation and its return to life in the natural world, now known for the first time as a walled prison yard where evening voluntaries can be spoken, is, to my mind, properly humanistic.

8

Shelley and the Celebration of Power

Shelley's "Ode to the West Wind" is a political poem. Like "Dejection," it tries to imagine a renovation of the spirit that will also renovate society.[1] Coleridge himself abandoned the hope on which both the West Wind Ode and also the long dramatic ode or closet opera called *Prometheus Unbound* are based in his rather impressive "France: An Ode" (1798). The stern argument of this poem may suffice in itself to warn readers away from the standard epithalamic interpretations of "Dejection," which was begun four years later. Part of the printed "Argument" of "France" can be quoted both in support of my view of "Dejection" and as a forecast of Shelley's noble failure, in his West Wind Ode, to accomplish the long jump from nature to consciousness to society: "*Fifth Stanza.* An Address to Liberty, in which the poet expresses his conviction that those feelings and that grand ideal of Freedom which the mind attains by its contemplation of its individual nature, and of the sublime surrounding objects (see Stanza the First) do not belong to men, as a society, nor can possibly be either gratified or realised, under any form of human government; but belong to the individual man, so far as he is pure, and inflamed with the love and adoration of God in Nature." So much, then, for the social effects of spiritual liberation.

Only at the last moment of this passage does Coleridge compromise his unbending logic and thus weaken his position. If God *does* exist in Nature, adorable and adoring, then there is no reason to think that the Saturnian "form of government," that is, the State of Nature or no government at all except individual probity, would

186

not be a "realisable" utopia. Either God is not in nature, then, and leaves in His absence the necessity of an authoritarian politics, or else if He is still present, informing the spiritual and ethical life of His witnesses, there is no reason to abandon the revolutionary hope that was still chiefly the attribute, in Shelley's time, of bourgeois individualism.[2] Shelley understands these alternatives clearly; hence it is the purpose of his political lyrics to locate a numinous principle in the natural world.

If we "see Stanza the First" of Coleridge's ode, we shall find a prolepsis that furnishes both the terms that confirm and the terms that deny his gloss of the fifth stanza:

> Ye Clouds! that far above me float and pause,
>> Whose pathless march no mortal can controul!
> Ye Ocean-Waves! that, wheresoe'er ye roll,
>> Yield homage only to eternal laws!

This passage anticipates the concluding stanza, and provides the imagery that Shelley's West Wind Ode will be forced to reinterpret. The energies of nature, high and distant as in "Dejection," cannot be controlled by the individual will, but only by a consonance (taken for granted in hymns) between eternal laws and social laws. What is implied politically in Coleridge's "eternal laws" recalls the General Will of Rousseau's *Social Contract*, which is prior to and sovereign over all private political knowledge or intuition. But what then becomes of "the love of God in Nature"—including, we assume, the love of God in the natural man? *Amor Dei:* if we are "inflamed" by God's love radiating through our natures, we should therefore behave spontaneously according to the "eternal laws." Clearing an entrance for his newly conservative myth, Coleridge would seem to have cast out man from paradise while leaving the paradise itself intact.

In order to keep the reader from making this objection, Coleridge in the first stanza proceeds not only to corrupt himself but also to malform his natural surroundings (italics mine):

> Where, *like* a man beloved of God,
>> Through glooms, which never woodman trod,
>>> How oft, pursuing fancies holy,
>> My moonlight way o'er flowering weeds I wound.

This blend of echoes from Milton and *A Midsummer Night's Dream* is again subtly proleptic. Coleridge is not liberated through Grace but only resembles or mimics one who may be. He is a melancholic, whose outstripping the woodman (see *Il Penseroso* 135–37) he will repeat in "Dejection." Outcast from the assured love of God, he can only attempt a solemn imitation of prelapsarian freedom through the discipline of Milton's anchorite, a discipline of which Nature also seems much in need, being unregenerate and full of "weeds" that flower in confusion under the same indirect light that guides the poet's wandering.

These prefigurations justify authoritarian government in revealing the corruption of nature, both human and inhuman, but they also reveal the bad faith of Coleridge's invocation. Having duly enchained the "sublime surrounding objects" he has just apostrophized, he then petitions them for a character witness they are rather apt to begrudge. In fact, as if to show that their liberty is still unimpaired, they seem to have run away and hidden from him:

> Bear witness for me, wheresoe'r ye be,
> With what deep worship I have still adored
> The spirit of divinest Liberty.

There is really no "poet's recantation" in this ode, as we are told there is in the "Argument," because the poet has never once envisioned a happy state of insubordination. The fifth stanza, which again anticipates "Dejection," simply declares, this time without indirection, the authoritarian premise that had shaped the landscapes of the poem from the beginning:

> The sensual and the Dark rebel in vain,
> Slaves by their own compulsion! In mad game
> They burst their manacles in the name   ,
> Of Freedom, graven on a heavier chain!

The concluding image of Liberty as a private, nonpolitical and even antipolitical breeze divides nature against itself, forming two camps: objects that exemplify government and divine will, like the wind and the ocean, and objects that exemplify the governed, like the pines and the threshold of the sea cliff:

> And there I felt thee!—on that sea-cliff's verge,
> Whose pines, scarce travelled by the breeze above,
> Had made one murmur with the distant surge!

> Yes, while I stood and gazed, my temples bare,
> And shot my being through earth, sea, and air,
> Possessing all things with intensest love,
> O Liberty! my spirit felt thee there.
>
> [99-105]

Because part of nature has now been re-released from bondage, this moment disrupts the unity of the ode, since the argument has not really prepared us for such a finale. Coleridge's closing landscape is an unsuccessful effort to transcend politics, then, and actually provides Shelley, who told Byron that he thought "France" was "the finest modern ode," with a political landscape that *he* can use, first in "Mont Blanc" and then in the "Ode to the West Wind," to resist Coleridge's conservatism:[3]

> Thus thou, Ravine of Arve—dark, deep Ravine—
> Thou many-coloured, many voicèd vale,
> Over whose pines and crags and caverns sail
> Fast cloud-shadows
>
> . . . .
>
>   thou dost lie,
> Thy giant brood of pines around thee clinging
> (Children of elder time, in whose devotion
> The chainless winds still come, and ever came
> To drink their odours, . . .)
>
> ["Mont Blanc," 12-23]

>   Thou
> For whose path the Atlantic's level powers
>
> Cleave themselves into chasms, while far below
> The sea-blooms and oozy woods which wear
> The sapless foliage of the ocean, know
>
> Thy voice, and suddenly grow gray with fear,
> And tremble and despoil themselves: oh, hear!
>
> ["Ode to the West Wind"]

Shelley reinterprets the last landscape of "France: An Ode" by daemonizing the symbols of authority that in Coleridge remain natural. In these passages from Shelley, whatever is precedent and authoritative in nature simply ceases to be nature and becomes

supernature, an emblem of spirit which man may share with the
daemonic wind, and which may release him from determinacy. But
this revision is necessarily fraught with difficulties and doubts. The
Romantic political ode, like its presentational counterpart, is a test
of boundaries, and it discovers at the threshold of necessitarian
doctrine that either there is really no threshold, that there are
chains everywhere (which makes Liberty an illusion), or else that
beyond the threshold things in a state of liberty return to chaos and
require government by the "codes and statutes" Shelley so fiercely
hated. This is the sphere of debate in Shelley's West Wind Ode and
in the Swiss poems of 1816:

> The wilderness has a mysterious tongue
> Which teaches awful doubt, or faith so mild,
> So solemn, so serene, that man may be,
> But for such faith, with nature reconciled,—
> Thou hast a voice, great Mountain, to repeal
> Large codes of fraud and woe not understood
> By all, but which the wise, and great, and good
> Interpret, or make felt, or deeply feel!
>
> ["Mont Blanc," 76–83]

(Most MSS have "In such a faith," as does the new Standard Edition,
but I prefer the profounder meaning of the text printed in 1817.) An
entire ideology hangs in the balance here, attendant on the question:
Whence arises the difference between these two voices? How can we
"Interpret" the difference between the rebellious murmur of pines
that are slaves, as Coleridge said, "by their own compulsion," swayed
either by doubt or apathy, and the voice of the Mountain, awful and
stern, spoken from some unchained recess of Power? The figures
of bondage are present, the figure of freedom is absent.

II

> He gave man speech, and speech created thought,
> Which is the measure of the Universe.
>
> —*Prometheus Unbound* II. iv. 72–73

As we approach Shelley's West Wind Ode, we shall benefit by
pausing to witness his struggle with the unchained recesses of power
he both needs and fears in the "Hymn to Intellectual Beauty" and

"Mont Blanc" (1816), which are both, as is commonly recognized, influenced by the Intimations Ode of Wordsworth. I suggested in my Introduction that the "Hymn" is only ironically so called. It is almost what one could wish to call a *witty* poem, not only structurally but discursively so, an analytic treatment of Wordsworth and of its own genre as well; "Mont Blanc," though very different in mode and tone, builds on the analysis undertaken by the "Hymn," and carries it a step further. Perhaps neither poem strikes us as perfectly conceived because neither quite succeeds in blending epistemology with lyric knowledge, but for the moment I wish to take advantage of that weakness. Before I attempt to lyricize my reading of these poems as far as they will permit, I want to make use of their analytic bent in offering a brief interpretation of what is meant by the "source," in both poems, "of human thought," since in my opinion Shelley cannot be understood without some understanding of that source:

> Thou messenger of sympathies,
> That wax and wane in lovers' eyes—
> Thou that to human thought art nourishment,
> Like darkness to a dying flame!
>
> ["Hymn," 42–45]

> The secret Strength of things
> Which governs thought, and to the infinite dome
> Of Heaven is as a law . . .
>
> ["Mont Blanc," 139–41]

In the "Hymn," the awful shadow *of* an unseen power is called "Intellectual Beauty," and in "Mont Blanc" Shelley's surmise deepens to touch upon the "Power" itself. Thus we have: Power→Intellectual Beauty→Human Thought, with each governing agency veiled from what it governs. Considered simply as a faculty psychology,[4] these entities may be paralleled loosely by a good many other triumvirates of Shelley's era, most closely perhaps by Kant's Reason-(Aesthetic) Judgment-Understanding, where Judgment is not a categorically separate faculty but an intermediate region, a faculty that stages a give-and-take between Reason with its a priori danda and Understanding with its sensory data. These loose parallels will be clear enough if the reader avoids confusing the Kantian Reason with the British Reason that Shelley always abused—as "Reason" in the *Defence of Poetry*, and as "human thought" in the poems of 1816. In the "Hymn" and "Mont Blanc," these three agencies, which are always analyzable into three, undergo a mystification that seems to multiply them indefinitely through Shelley's overstrain of genetive constructions. The mystification is deliberate, and the genetive cruces deliberately corrupt the convention of the hymnic Genealogy, Shelley's point being that he has no idea what begat what; and, furthermore, that it is impossible for any faculty of the mind to present a clear and distinct idea of what begat what. Shelley never believed that any faculty could achieve certainty, and from this analytic viewpoint, which many of his interpreters still wistfully Neoplatonize, he despised analysis itself as *dead metaphor*. Philosophy, on his view, can only be done in poetry, where the ambiguous genetive can be further mediated by an almost uninterrupted reliance on simile: Intellectual Beauty, Power, and later the skylark that was never a bird, are all "like" dissimilative features in a syntax that can only locate them by naming all the places where they are not to be found.

Power and its Shadow, Intellectual Beauty, both of which hover (like Wordsworth's glory) between spirit and place, are metaphors for the origin and expression, respectively, of metaphoricity; or to borrow Shelley's phrase in the *Defence*, they comprise "the colouring of imagination." Power is the imaginal force, and Intellectual Beauty is its coloring. Together they produce "before unapprehended relations of things." They are recondite sources of "human thought" in exactly the same way that poetry, in the *Defence*, is the unacknowledged source of scientific postulates and human legislation.[5] Shelley never says, as he is often assumed to have said, that poetic metaphors are true; on the contrary, metaphors are "colors," tropes of rhetoric. There is no contrast anywhere in Shelley between primitive truth and sophisticated falsehood; his crucial contrast, rather, in the *Defence* and elsewhere, is between *life and death*. What begins vitally in poetry as metaphor, as the animated linkage of things that may in themselves be dead, is pretentiously taken over by "human thought" as though it were inert, empirically given fact, and soon dies.

Shelley's "faculty psychology," then, is in many ways consistent with the linguistic psychoanalysis of our own day, especially with that of Lacan. Shelley's (unseen) "shadow of an unseen power" is the Unconscious, where the Power is a drive, and the Shadow is the operation of what Shelley's own metaphors encourage us to call the dream-work, here virtually synonymous with poetry itself, or at least with the sort of revery in which Shelley claimed to have written "Mont Blanc." "Human thought," then, is simply conscious thought. If we transfer our triumvirate now to the linguistic plane (for which there is a great deal of support in Shelley, especially in *Prometheus Unbound*), "Power" becomes the always preexistent *langue* that "governs thought," "Intellectual Beauty" becomes the *parole*, or discourse, of the signifier, and "human thought" is then the quasi-empirical notionality of conscious life that fancies itself to be the originary signified.

This formulation, which makes Shelley an avatar of those who argue today that language precedes and determines thought, not vice versa, will seem so flagrantly to violate most suppositions about Shelley's philosophy that it may be well to quote in this place a crucial passage from *Prometheus Unbound*:

> Language is a perpetual Orphic song
> Which rules with Daedal harmony a throng
> Of thoughts and forms, which else senseless and shapeless were.
>
> [IV. 415–17]

The difference between this passage and the postulate of Lacan, that the elementary structures of culture and thought "reveal an ordering of possible exchanges which, even unconscious, is inconceivable outside the permutations authorized by language," is largely a matter of tone and of Lacan's clearer understanding that, strictly speaking, nothing can be "shapeless." In Shelley's text, "Language" is Power, "Daedal harmony" is Intellectual Beauty, and "throng/Of thoughts and forms" makes up the burden of the conscious mind. Finally, then, the question of the way *objects* enter Shelley's psychology is taken up afresh in each new poem, and must abide interpretation.

If Power is the linguistic basis of knowledge, it is necessarily a code. Shelley hated codes. The chain of command I have outlined is not the view of mind he wanted to hold, and all his poems, even his *Defence*, struggle to withstand this view for reasons that will appear, reasons that have not least to do with the libertarian political hope I began by stressing. But there is an intellectual honesty peculiar to Shelley that makes one feel that the defeat of metaphor by metaphor in his poems amounts to a confession, an unhappy confession that is impossible to ignore in the "Ode to the West Wind," and that constantly subverts his attraction to the ode and to the celebratory manner.[6]

III

The "Hymm to Intellectual Beauty" begins skeptically; that is, the movement from exposition in the first stanza to invocation in the second draws attention to the poet's need to invent what he invokes. After he has explained what Intellectual Beauty is, or rather what it is "like" (it is far more like Wordsworth's "glory" than Shelley for the moment is prepared to admit), Shelley imitates Wordsworth's nostalgia for the lost coloring of imagination:

> Spirit of BEAUTY, that dost consecrate
> > With thine own hues all thou dost shine upon
> > Of human thought or form,—where art thou gone?

The glory has left our perceptual and political "state." But then, instead of prolonging the attitude of lament, as Wordsworth had done, Shelley proceeds directly to the *end* of Wordsworth's poem, as though the replacement of childhood intimations by the "philosophic mind" were a commonplace fact of life that might better have gone without saying. "Ask why the sunlight not for ever/Weaves rainbows o'er yon mountain-river," and so on, reminds one of the trite but unanswerable question-series of a riddle: tell me why the ivy twines. Shelley's second stanza, then, parodies by shrinking the prolonged movement from loss to acceptance in Wordsworth's ode, and can scarcely be said to have a burden of its own. Its point seems merely to be that Wordsworth raises questions that have no answers.

The third stanza broadens Shelley's critique from Wordsworth's ode to the ode in general. Instead of providing his Intellectual Beauty with a genealogy, Shelley mocks genealogical topoi as superstitions, laying special stress on "Heaven," whence Wordsworth's Babe had descended:

> No voice from some sublimer world hath ever
> > To sage or poet these responses given:
> > Therefore the names of Demon, Ghost, and Heaven,

> Remain the records of their vain endeavour—
> Frail spells . . .

Intellectual Beauty is Shelley's Psyche, and here he looks forward to Keats's substitution of a belated numen for an outworn and pernicious pantheon, the "poisonous names with which our youth is fed." But instead of building a temple for his preferred psyche, as Keats will do, Shelley once more buries her under a heap of similitudes, as if to suggest that the goddess or daemon is not uniquely his own, nor even known by him at firsthand. This diffidence may prompt his final choice of words for the quality that "Gives grace and truth to life's unquiet dream." Blending echoes of the Intimations Ode and "Dejection," Shelley's "Hymn" now begins to concede that its numen is literary as well as personal. This concession, which seems unwilling or accidental, forecasts the surprise at the end of stanza five. For the moment, though, the analytic Shelley is still on the attack; he converts Wordsworth's "both-and" (E. D. Hirsch's term for the logic of the Intimations Ode[7]) to an either-or, a dualism that cannot be wished away:

> Man were immortal, and omnipotent,
> Didst thou, unknown and awful as thou art,
> Keep with thy glorious train firm state within his heart.
> ·
> Depart not—lest the grave should be,
> Like life and fear, a dark reality.

This is still not quite serious lyricization. The "Hymn" continues to be an almost satiric exercise in reduction throughout most of the next stanza, which simultaneously reminds Wordsworth that the intimations given to childhood are really only received superstitions, parodies other poets' admissions of vocative failure ("I was not heard—I saw them not"), and reveals falsity in the themes of rival genres. Then, just when his debunking seems complete, Shelley is unnerved by a completely Wordsworthian sensation: "Sudden, thy shadow fell on me;/I shrieked, and clasped my hands in ecstasy!" It is tempting to say that the shadow is Wordsworth's returning ghost (a return of the dead indeed, since the younger Romantics had tried to pronounce Wordsworth dead when *The Excursion* was published in 1815); and this passage certainly is the "retourne" of Shelley's ode. Here Shelley discovers why his ode has been an obliquely expository poem about the glancing blows of an "inconstant glance": Intellectual Beauty cannot be invoked, but comes when it pleases. *Pas je pense, mais on me pense.* The coloring of imagination is that which determines "human thought." It is wholly independent of the "conscious will" that Coleridge joins to the workings of the secondary imagination, but it is equally distinct from the desirable governing force of some exteranl, transcendent spirit. For Shelley, Intellectual Beauty, or rather perhaps its motive "Power," is indeed a "darkness," and later in his career its sources are summed in the figure of Demogorgon.[8]

When the shadow fell, Shelley remembers having reacted with the gladness of a Wordsworthian child. Later, though, he has had glimpses enough of madness. Intellectual Beauty is not a poet's "frail spell" or inefficacious "uttered charm" (29), but rather a "spell" only seemingly from without and so deeply charming to the poet that he must "fear himself."[9] He has meanwhile made his dedicatory vow: to link these revelations to the hope of revolution, to the "hope that thou wouldst free/This world from its dark slavery." But here, where the poem is most indebted to "France: An Ode," Coleridge's reactionary question returns: Can "darkness" liberate its likeness, "dark slavery"? "O awful LOVELINESS," writes Shelley in haste, but the prevenient simile of line 45, "Like darkness to a dying flame," has already asserted its sway. In this doubtful light the ode rejects the noontide afflatus of its genre and reenacts the evening close of the Intimations Ode, with its passage from Joy to Philosophy:

> The day becomes more solemn and serene
> When noon is past: there is harmony
> In autumn, and a lustre in its sky,
> . . . .
> Thus let thy power, which like the truth
> Of nature on my passive youth
> Descended, to my onward life supply
> Its calm . . .

But Shelley's natural piety is permanently disturbed. He knows nothing and claims to know nothing of Intellectual Beauty, except that it is incomparably beautiful, that it comes so deeply from within that it feels like a descending shadow, and that it is akin to madness: it is a daemonic force of revolution, both psychic and political, that can be rationalized as the Marcusan Eros, as a happy synthesis of desire and love. Accordingly, the poet speaks of himself as "one who worships thee,"

> And every form containing thee,
> Whom, SPIRIT fair, thy spells did bind
> To fear himself, and love all human kind.

Intellectual Beauty turns out to have been female. In other Shelleyan —and Byronic—poems, she is a Sister or epipsyche. Can incest, Shelley's "very poetical circumstance,"[10] be Platonized, like Diotima's doctrine of the social eddying of erotic love in the *Symposium*? Shelley tries to join the tradition, a hymnic tradition, that wrestles in advance with Marx and continues in today's revisionists of Marx. This tradition maintains that revolution comes from dispassionate love and not from the deepest but still material recesses of need— from what Shelley enigmatically calls "the truth / Of nature." Already in 1816, Shelley has found something to "fear" in his revolutionary self, and from then on he hopes for a slight admixture of Wordsworth's natural piety to curb his fervor.

IV

> The aim of all life is death.
> —Freud, *Beyond the Pleasure Principle*

Few poems face the unknown as resolutely as does Shelley's "Mont Blanc." For that reason it is not helpful to speak of an underlying sense of the poem, since that sense is frankly encompassed by what might be termed Shelley's rhetoric of doubt—a phrase that would be improper concerning any previous poet, however long a shadow doubt may inadvertently cast over all poetry. On the other hand, "Mont Blanc" makes no "plain" sense either, because it is addressed to the space affectively conceived as "Silence and solitude," from which plain sense and the objects of sense arise into being. This space is *not* an origin or point of issuance: the Power that "inhabits" the mountain is not an origin but a predicative "Strength" that enables phenomena, just as the thought of nothingness enables the thought of being in dialectic even though nothingness is not necessarily the *cause* of being.[11]

The last mention of an origin in "Mont Blanc" occurs in the first verse paragraph, "where, from secret springs,/The source of human thought its tribute brings/Of waters." But this source, which has its own source in "secret springs," is not Power; it is Intellectual Beauty, whose "many-coloured, many-voicèd" presence (12) animates and populates "the daedal earth" (86). The Power is wholly different, and resides beyond genealogy and mythopoeia:

> Is this the scene
> Where the old Earthquake-daemon taught her young
> Ruin? Were these their toys? or did a sea
> Of fire envelop once this silent snow?
> None can reply—all seems eternal now.

There may have been giants or daemons or Titans, there may have been flood or fire; there may have been, but the "primaeval," possibly antediluvian Power is untouched by mythopoeic structures of temporality because such structures are willed into being by ourselves to withstand the threat of Power's sheer vacancy. We are goaded into speech by the power of silence, just as the energies of life are not necessarily the wellsprings of being but may sustain themselves secondarily as a defense that suppresses the will to die. As it is with beginnings, so also with ends: the idea of an apocalyptic covenant, itself compulsively repeating—as a violence—the will to die, is an embarrassed hope prompted by the idea of eternity, a surmised arrangement of last things that veils the "unsculptured image" of Power, just as a rainbow tropically colors the waterfall that hides the eternal bedrock (25–27). All expression, all shaping and sequence, is the discourse of Intellectual Beauty. In an ode, the main purpose of expression is to establish kinships, to affirm causality through the convention of the divine genealogy. But the subject of "Mont Blanc," which entails the irony of this ode as an ode, cannot be subdued to any cycle of birth and rebirth.

Shelley's Power is what Wordsworth called "Immortality." "Mont Blanc" passes through a stage of attempting to improve on Wordsworth's "blank misgiving" by drawing first on the notion that sleep is livelier than waking, and, second, on the notion that death is an awakening from a dream into properly full-blooded life (49–52). For a poet warned by Wordsworth's negative example, everything depends on filling life after death with excitement. But in thus gathering these speculations, Shelley is only preparing their eclipse.

He soon falls back upon the tell-me-why singsong of the "Hymn" in order to keep the blankness at bay.

Avoiding entrapment in the sharp corners of an irregular ode stanza like those of the Intimations Ode, Shelley chooses verse paragraphs like those of "Tintern Abbey" (but keeps the irregular rhyme and stanzaic numbering of the Great Ode) in order to build a landscape-rooted and therefore well-grounded mythology of being that can challenge comparison with Wordsworth's. From "Tintern Abbey" Shelley also borrows his main saving appearance, the doctrine of a constitutive interplay between self and world:

> The source of human thought its tribute brings
> Of waters,—with a sound but half its own.
>
> [5-6]

> Dizzy Ravine . . . . . . And, when I gaze on thee,
> I seem as in a trance sublime and strange
> To muse on my own separate fantasy,
> My own, my human mind, which passively
> Now renders and receives fast influencings,
> Holding an unremitting interchange
> With the clear universe of things around—
>
> [34-40]

If we are to trust the explanatory passage in the *History of a Six Weeks' Tour*, this second passage refers to the state of revery in which Shelley composed the poem. The actual topic of his musing may surprise us. The partial creation and partial perception of the universe, here adopted from Wordsworth (a universe that is not necessarily, in Shelley's case, external[12]), has afforded an equilibrium that does not survive the second verse paragraph. The reason for its demise may be found in the grammar of lines 36-37, which is easy, one might almost say desirable, to misconstrue: "To muse on my own separate fantasy,/My own, my human mind." These clauses are appositional, not genetive, and therefore "fantasy" must be the mind itself, *phantasia*,[13] and not a daydream: but the impression of daydream lingers in what amounts almost to a pun. Shelley fantasizes about phantasia: the autonomy and self-identity of the thinking subject is only (a) fantasy for Shelley, a "passive" fantasy engendered reflexively by the need for some inner strength to offset the presence of sheer power, which knows no "influencings." Shelley's fantasy steadies him while he faces the "Dizzy Ravine," which in retrospect is no longer the valley of the Arve or even its Idea, but an absolute abyss. The "human mind," then, is *invented* in meditation to countervail the vertiginous magnetism of death. Life consists in sustaining this "fantasy," which makes the "universe of things" happily "clear" —a rare transparency in Shelley that appears here as an irony. It is always the role of "human thought" to make things merely clear. In this context Earl Wasserman has finely evoked "the spirit of man at enmity with nothingness and dissolution" *(Shelley: A Critical Reading,* p. 226).

The presence of this superimposed mainstay, "the human mind," governs the difficult conclusion of the second verse paragraph, which is the turning point of the poem. Shelley's phantasia is "One legion of wild thoughts," sometimes too intuitive and too full of bright intimation for words to express, and sometimes sublunary enough to be recorded:

> In the still cave of the witch Poesy—
> Seeking among the shadows that pass by
> (Ghosts of all things that are) some shade of thee,
> Some phantom, some faint image; till the breast
> From which they are fled recalls them, thou art there!

If there were a plain sense of this passage, it would, I think, be this: Following the orthodox Neoplatonic revision of Plato on poetry, Shelley hopes to capture some indirect image of the Ravine of Arve, or rather of "ravine-ness," that will designate its permanent form or Idea. The Idea *is* "there," in phantasia, and if the poet looks hard enough he will find and capture its silhouette in communicable words, in the lower or discursive region of consciousness that is roughly equivalent to Coleridge's secondary imagination. The poet will search, then, until the witch Poesy, the demiurge or shadow-mistress whom Shelley supplies to run Ideas along the track behind the spectator in Plato's cave, recalls her toys; that is, until the poet ceases to be the spectator.

It is necessary, though, to probe this passage more deeply in order to see why the poem changes so much hereafter. The "breast" puts an end to the search because it is part of the mother whence we came and whither we shall return, namely earth itself, or death. The Idea of the ravine, itself as shadowy as an abyss, is at least potentially

Idea of the ravine, itself as shadowy as an abyss, is at least potentially "there" for the poet to grasp until he himself actually enters it in entering the ravine of the shadow of death.[14] The ravine is no longer "there"[15] from that point on because it is here and now, the river of nonbeing in which we drown. We must say rather, then, that the Idea with its shadow is absent from the poet until he dies, and then suddenly it simply engulfs him. Life itself, the daedal ravine, is what we experience in the abeyance of the abyss, the empty ravine; and hence, especially in an ode, which tries to bridge all chasms, life is also what *seeks* the abyss, seeks to be refolded in the ground. The cave of Poesy is like a tomb, and "thou art there!" needs only the loss of aspiration to become "thou art here!"

The rest of the poem, not just the next few lines, is a struggle with the presence of death, and finally yields to the bedrock "un-sculptured image," Mont Blanc itself. The mountain is never apos-trophized, just as the poem never fully confronts its vision, until the final lines. As long as possible, in keeping with the prolongation of sound into silence that marks an ode, the poet has continued to invoke his image of the ravine as a vale of life. Now, rising out of the ravine, out of the "ceaseless" activity of its bestial floor (the evasive action of the life instinct), but rising also from the various thanatological rumors of the previous lines, "Far, far above, piercing the infinite sky,/Mont Blanc appears." The effect is as uncanny as the rearing up of the mountain against the boy Wordsworth in *Prelude* I. It is as if, thanks to the veiling accomplished by the "human mind," the mountain had not been there before. Earlier, in fact, the valley stanzas did mention "the ice-gulfs" that gird the river's "secret throne," but at that point the mountain was still a source, a font of inflowing "through the mind" (2) and not an impersonal *Aufhebung* rising up to freeze all causation and "cease-less motion" (32) forever. Now, in the third stanza, the mountain gives birth to nothing, neither to bird nor bush, but "Dwells apart in its tranquility,/Remote, serene, and inaccessible." It is a "city of death" (105), like Dis in the *Inferno*, yet less distinct even than that, "not a city, but a flood of ruin" that has "overthrown/The limits of the dead and living world,/Never to be reclaimed." All speculation aside (viz., ll. 49–52), death now stands forth as the synthesis that cancels all liminal structures and all dialectic. From such a place, "The race/Of man flies far in dread," like Byron's Abbot and braver

Chamois-Hunter, both natural men; but the poet, like Manfred, stands dizzily on its brink in his mind.

The fifth verse paragraph attempts to fall back from the brink by presenting the mountain as merely one sublime object among many, and "is there" tries to bend the argument back toward the populous though deathly "still" cave of Poesy:

> Mont Blanc yet gleams on high:—the power is there,
> The still and solemn power of many sights,
> And many sounds, and much of life and death.

But this is a helpless retreat, since even its self-diminishing tone of acceptance, its evening, is ominously twilit, and admits the collapse of boundary that makes life and death indistinct. We remember in spite of these distancing, pluralizing lines that the mountain is a white and silent monolith, more absolute and far more powerful than Wordsworth's blankness.[16] The next lines superbly restore the silence:

> In the lone glare of day, the snows descend
> Upon that Mountain; none beholds them there,
> Nor when the flakes burn in the sinking sun,
> Or the star-beams dart through them. Winds contend
> Silently there, and heap the snow with breath
> Rapid and strong, but silently.

These lines are written more against than according to their model, the passing in review of the seasons in hymns to a god and in the secular ode. The sibilant snow and the aspirated winds are silent sounds that bespeak the poet's absence from Power at all times. Mont Blanc is a dome or "heap" that buries the cave of the witch Poesy, showing that the motive of articulation, its fore-ghosting, is death. Simply in being itself, code and *semblable* even of Heaven, like "language" in *Prometheus*, Mont Blanc fosters our fantasies of change:

> The secret Strength of things
> Which governs thought, and to the infinite dome
> Of Heaven is as a law, inhabits thee.
> And what were thou, and earth, and stars, and sea,
> If to the human mind's imaginings
> Silence and solitude were vacancy?

This is a question that supplies its own answer. Politically speaking, since "Power dwells apart," the allegedly revolutionary strength of the mountain's voice (80–81) is especially dubious. Even though Mont Blanc destroys nature with finality, it is not apocalyptic, as the example of "France: An Ode" had showed that it must be for revolutionary purposes; it is not a divine or daemonic presence within nature, but rather a blankness against which the life of nature appears in relief. This is why, in the "Ode to the West Wind," Shelley will seek to redefine his revolutionary Spirit as a "destroyer and preserver" that is neither separate from nature nor an absolute end in itself.[17]

V

> I do not hold that the turning over of dry brown mouldering leaves can teach the antient languages, for if that were so the autumnal wind would before the 8th of Nov. have become an admirable linguist. . . .
> —T. J. Hogg to Shelley, 30 September 1817, *New Shelley Letters*, ed. W. S. Scott (1948), pp. 103–04

Traces of Shelley's strife in prayer with the West Wind can be found in the allusive and formal properties of his ode. We may begin with these, working from the outside in. Like "Dejection," Shelley's ode begins in allusion to a lyrical fragment that is not Wordsworth's. Fittingly for a poem haunted by ghosts, Shelley in his first apostrophe, "O wild West Wind," retains only the ghost of an epigraph:

> West-com wynde when wilt thou blow
> The smalle rayne down can rayne
> Cryst yf my love were in my Armys
> & I yn my bed a-gayne.[18]

In the "Lines Written Among the Euganean Hills" (1818), also a mixed personal and political "complaint," Shelley had made the hills oceanic: his "bark" had led him to a spot among the hills from which he watched the fields ripple like waves. Life in the earlier poem was a "stream," not an airstream as yet but still fluid and all-pervasive. We have already seen that what is needed by a vocative poet of Shelley's analytic rigor even more than by most poets is a ubiquitous force, harnessed by invocation, that will abridge the double distance from

Power to Intellectual Beauty to Human Thought. In the present land-locked ode, he turns to the wind, but he takes a seafaring poem for his context, as if to link his present and past metaphors for the vital current of existence.

It may be supposed that "Western Wind" is the lament of a be-calmed Atlantic explorer, returning possibly from America. Great things are also expected of Shelley's Atlantic, as of the coming storm that his poem shares with "Dejection" and "Sir Patrick Spens." At the same time, though, Shelley's ode is a becalmed westering, like the "Ode to Liberty" he would write two years later. Shelley in Italy clings to a Hesperian hope, to the Albion of his mind's eye, in order to imagine the resurgence of joy among the Euganean Hills after the expulsion of the *Österreicher*.[19] Unlike "Western Wind," which records the effort to return home after exploration, Shelley's ode never resolves the clash of westward and eastward movement, never in fact discovers a proper home; it is not becalmed but blown hither and thither before what Shelley called the "inconstant wind" of inspiration in his *Defence*.[20]

The "Christ" of "Western Wind" is called upon conditionally, as though he, like his benison, were only a possibility, a savior or guid-ing star not yet risen above the horizon. So Shelley's ode is a tissue of allusions to Judaic prophecy before the coming of a redeemer. The last line of the ballad quatrain, with its simultaneous longing for death, for rest, and for sexual reunion, is fully paralleled in the ode, where the detritus of the dying year *may* spring forth from seed-beds (each "wingèd seed" is "like a corpse within its grave") or at least from a bed of mulch ("withered leaves to quicken a new birth"),[21] to grow into the wished-for restauration. The third line of "Western Wind," finally, furnishes Shelley with a still more com-plex suggestion. Its figure of embrace resembles the moon's embrace in Coleridge's motto, which Shelley would later use in *The Triumph of Life*. The "young moon"

> Doth, as the herald of its coming, bear
> The ghost of its dead mother, whose dim form
> Bends in dark aether from her infant's chair.
>
> [83–85]

But whereas Coleridge and his Old Bard can find some consolation in the suggested continuity of this image, Shelley always suspects that such apparent unions and infoldings are merely ghostly. Shelley's "love" is never in his arms, but is, rather, an epipsyche who is always barred from him by some high convent wall of perception.

Thus the very first sounds of Shelley's ode express regret at being in an ode, and long for their proper home in a more naïve and hopeful lyrical ballad. This ode will later perform a ritual eclipse of the greater genres (stanza three),[22] but at the outset we find it in mourning for the lesser ones. As with the lyrical ballad, so with pastoral. "Driving sweet buds like flocks to feed in air,"[23] the wind presides differently in pastoral than in an ode, where the supplicant is gored on the thorns of a grown plant. In the fourth stanza, pastoral will grace Shelley's own remembered boyhood, as it did Wordsworth's in the Intimations Ode; but Shelley reverts there to the mild scorn of his "Hymn" in order to defend the hopes of adulthood against nostalgia:

If even
I were as in my boyhood, and could be

The comrade of thy wanderings over Heaven,
As then, when to outstrip thy skiey speed
Scarce seemed a vision . . .

Following "Lycidas," most Romantic versions of pastoral make the child a priest of nature, or at least a Theocritean rival singer in nature's pasturage, rivaling the poet in his present state. Shelley's ode laments the joylessness of life in the present, but like "Mont Blanc" it accepts no alternatives; it resists the nostalgia of genealogy and refuses the eschatological comfort of a Fall; the notion of loss or exile is understood to be an illusion we maintain in order to make our desolation more painful. Shelley's boyhood, then, was *mere* pastoral, merely superstitious, driven from without by ghostly doctrine as sheepish buds are driven by the wind. Once more we find an ode that demystifies its counterturn or peripety. The present is preserved, even privileged, through its reduction of the past. If change be thus questioned, though, has Shelley more to hope from the coming storm than Coleridge had from his mountain-birth? Shelley's ode is not a lament for departed powers, but a formal invocation that repeats the wind's absence.

Yet a third minor genre, in this case a form and not an ethos, is implicated in the poem. Shelley's stanzas are the length of a sonnet, and they close with a Shakespearean couplet. That the stanzas are further divided into the visionary tercets of Dante's "Comedy" would seem an affirmative gesture,[24] and indeed it is, but it is qualified by the particular sonnet to which Shelley alludes more than once, Shakespeare's seventy-third, which shows how little of the future an evening has to look forward to. Shelley's many-colored autumn leaves, decaying and shaken from tangled boughs like the clouds, are a legion driven on by a mighty power; but their number and the force that scatters them is severely weakened by allusion to:

> That time of year in me thou may'st behold
> When yellow leaves, or none, or few, do hang
> Upon these boughs

—boughs from which no voice will be heard again. Later, Shelley's apocalyptic "closing night," with its "Black rain, and fire, and hail," must be muffled, if not put out, by Shakespeare's stormless darkness:

> In me thou see'st the twilight of such day
> As after sunset fadeth in the west,
> Which by-and-by black night doth take away,
> Death's second self, that seals up all the rest.

And finally, in Shelley's fifth sonnet-stanza, his most ecstatic prayer—"Scatter, as from an unextinguished hearth/Ashes and sparks, my words among mankind!"—a prayer that is already limited by its connection with the conceit of the Fading Coal in the *Defence*, is further checked by Shakespeare's refusal of cyclic hope:

> In me thou see'st the glowing of such fire
> That on the ashes of his youth, must lie,
> As on the deathbed whereon it must expire.

The form of Shelley's stanza, then, corresponds with the poles of dialectic in the ode: prophetic afflatus, rising out of the natural cycle with Dante, and terminal defeat, falling out of the natural cycle into nothingness with the Shakespeare of the sonnet.

Like his imagery, Shelley's form stays either above or below the habitable surfaces of earth and sea. The only region that the "Ode to the West Wind" cannot inhabit, for all its richly observed science, is the region of the familiar. To return for a moment to the long misread and underrated *Defence*: Shelley concedes there that the power of poetry is limited. The *Defence* is less confidently a celebration of imagination that a critique of the "Reason" celebrated by Peacock in his *Four Ages of Poetry*. For Shelley, imagination as it enters expression is already inaccurate, a distorted coloring of things as they are[25] that is preferable to science and social legislation in two ways only: first, in being originary, in containing the "buds" of our thorny laws, and second, simply in knowing itself to be metaphoric, not factual. The poet is "unacknowledged" not just by societies but also by himself, since he alone can know how far he is from representing human happiness and wisdom even in poetic legislation. He is merely a better scientist than the scientist; his characteristic metaphors know more about population, for example, than do the facts of Malthus,[26] because metaphors are the tropes that, in linking things, most closely parallel the Poet's chief attribute, Love. The brief headnote to Shelley's ode is at pains to confirm the accuracy of scientific detail in the poem, not just because he believes that poetry can and should usurp the province of science, but also, as the open humanization of its "facts" implies, to concede in advance that all language is stubbornly metaphoric, and cannot supply the identity with the object (as opposed to identification with it) that the language of scientific certainty requires.

"The phenomenon alluded to at the conclusion of the third stanza" (headnote) is just the sort of science that Shelley could make the best case, in the *Defence*, for calling "poetic." It consists in a show of "sympathy" in nature, for which no explanation other than sympathy or shared consciousness is forthcoming. Since it is "well known to naturalists," it provides Shelley with an empirical approach to the animistic view of nature on which his prayer depends. This view is anticipated in the note itself: "The vegetation at the bottom of the sea . . . *sympathizes* with that of the land in the change of seasons, and is *consequently influenced* by the winds which *announce* it" (italics mine). The headnote is already part of the poem, an advance experiment in tone that lulls the reader and seems to enchant the poet into the sort of mood that may intimate a necessary "Angel of rain and lightning" announcing the human millennium. There will be more to say of Shelley's mediation between science and myth in the ode, but at present it must be borne in mind that the analytic Shelley is not wholly enchanted by animism.

The language of certainty, again, must enforce identities. Hence for Shelley to exclaim that he is "too like" the wind is also to admit that he is not enough like it, and to admit further that similitude in any form precludes the identity commanded in "Be thou me."

The "Ode to the West Wind" is neither a lament for loss of power nor is it, finally, as the "Hymn" was, a struggle to subdue the fickleness and originary priority of Power in the mind. This ode is more like a hymn than the "Hymn" was, because the poet is willing now to be the instrument of a prophecy that is not his own. "Be thou me" is a lone extravagance, a negotiation that demands the impossible in hopes of a generous settlement. What the ode questions, here most resembling its best gloss, the *Defence*, is the degree to which metaphor can harness an energy and humanize wildness. Shelley reverses the archaic quixotism of thought that marks the traditional ode in hoping to prolong a humane music of science into the encroaching priestly and tyrannical darkness that owes its reign to the "false themes" of Collins's popular superstitions. An ode in the absence of "faith"—a nemesis-word for Shelley alone among poets in the Romantic tradition—is at last truly and openly an ode, having only its own energies to invoke, chronicle, amplify, and petition. That this divestment of tradition in any form occurs just when the ode stages an unprecedented reunion with the phenomenal world and with the structure of the Greek and Hebrew hymns carries us back to an earlier theme. Wordsworth would have called this theme access of knowledge with loss of power; but for Shelley the nature of the knowledge that debilitates is more specific. He almost persuades us that *vocal* knowledge is shared between ancient poetry and the wind, but he cannot persuade even himself that power survives in the *writing* of modern poetry.

VI

There is enough mystery in the first tercet to supply a whole poem,[27] and in my view the mystery can only be lessened with reference to the sunken theme of writing. The chiastic arrangement of the simile is reinforced by a peculiar transference of attributes in the predicate from agent to reagent. On the face of the matter, it makes no sense that the ghosts are visible while the enchanter is unseen. We can save the logic of the simile by supposing that the

ghostly leaves are the leaves of a book or writing pad, and by sup-
posing further, as it is quite natural to suppose, that the enchanter
is a vocal breath.

This surmise gains strength when the terms of the opening
simile return in the fifth stanza:

> Drive my dead thoughts over the universe
> Like withered leaves to quicken a new birth!
> And, by the incantation of this verse,
>
> Scatter, as from an unextinguished hearth
> Ashes and sparks, my words among mankind!
> Be through my lips to unawakened earth
>
> The trumpet of a prophecy!

Here an incantation or enchantment is to be spoken through the
poet; he imagines himself to be speaking, but not speaking *now*.
Now, on the contrary, he is writing a petition for the recovery of
voice. The dead thoughts, "my words," are these present, written
words, to be scattered like Sibylline leaves over the ground, "sent
abroad" like the soul of Coleridge in "Dejection," leaving nothing
but Shakespeare's *moriturus* behind ("What if my leaves are falling
like its own!"). What may soon be spoken, on the other hand, is
the West Wind, passing through the poet like a god. The written
words are "angels" or harbingers of the prophecy. A poet is killed
by writing; he pours out his lifeblood over his stylus-thorn,[28] and
his self-identity is scattered abroad, in a tragic ritual, to fertilize the
coming Spring. His death, launching his legend and magnifying what
he stood for, will bring about what his imperfect and neglected
writings could not; it will generate a vocal prophecy spoken
"through" his dead lips in being heard on the lips of everyman.[29]

This is one way among several of finding plausible sense in the
last stanza, sense of the kind denied to Shelley by his detractors. It
is quite a satisfactory way, after all, since it rationalizes the general
impression the poem gives of being a consoling tragedy: the rest is
silence for Hamlet, dead finally of the poison pen he had dodged at
sea by turning it against his enemies, but Horatio will live to vindi-
cate and glorify him. We have not finished reckoning, however,
with the prefigurative first tercet, which has set these conclusions in
place. Dead leaves are dead letters, fleeing the spirit that at once

motivates writing and absents writing from its presence. The leaves are "Ghosts from an enchanter fleeing." It is not wholly clear, again on the face of the matter, why an enchanter, who is presumably a conjurer, should frighten off ghosts that would normally come when he calls them;[30] this obscurity is, in my view, the crux of the simile, and of the ode. It is a lapse that uncovers Shelley's hidden subject. The text is Intellectual Beauty, and the motive that withers and destroys the text is Power. Cast out from the field of vocal force, the poet must invoke the power of invocation, and ask the wind to "hear" his writing. When the wind chariots the wingèd seeds "to their dark wintry bed," it becomes Hermes, giver of the alphabet, trickster of Apollo, and escort of the dead to the Underworld. If Shelley's ode is a quest for the human significance of natural signs, it can be termed more precisely a hermeneutic poem, an alphabet in search of an origin.

The two requests of Shelley's petition are at odds with each other: "hear, oh, hear!" is replaced, with no assurance in the meantime that the wind has heard, by the bolder "Be thou me." The rhythmic parallelism of these requests makes it more likely that "hear, oh, hear" can become "here, oh, here." If the ode were vocal, according to wish, the sounds/hēr o hēr/would make the bravado of "Be thou me" unnecessary, but in written apostrophe "hear" is the antonym of "here." If the wind remains "there," like the Power in "Mont Blanc," then the poet must become the wind, he must go to the wind, rather than wait for it to come to him. The votum of this ode, which is entailed in the mediate status of writing, is that the poet will agree henceforth no longer to be himself. Negatively capable, he will seek so to be effaced by the natural order that his poem itself will become nature, a dead leaf that descends like a ghost and rises, like Virgil's Orpheus, as a bodiless, echoing vocative. If the poem becomes a leaf, the poet in futurity will come to be like the wind, once he has ceased striving with it in adolescent rivalry or adult desperation; he will become a passive, even inert medium, "one with" the wind as a channel is one with its current. In short, Shelley vows to become the least responsive of Aeolian lyres. His reward will be the achievement of a postscript that is also a posthumous after-song, the diminished calling of an evening ode:

> Make me thy lyre, even as the forest is:
> What if my leaves are falling like its own!
> The tumult of thy mighty harmonies

> Will take from both a deep, autumnal tone,
> Sweet though in sadness.

But the calling of prophecy cannot rest content with these metaphors, and Shelley must swerve upward to end his poem in a louder key, attempting to reverse the usual progress of an ode from afflatus to serenade. Here his difficulties begin anew. Clearly, at the start of the last stanza he has acknowledged a tonal difference, first recorded in the Romantic ode by Coleridge, between the mighty harmonies of the wind and the autumnal tone of its "subject Lute" ("The Eolian Harp," 43). Hard after this contrast would seem to be the worst possible place to say, "Be thou, Spirit Fierce,/My spirit! Be thou me, impetuous one!" The root meaning of "impetuous" is "insusceptible of petition," but that is only one aspect of the difficulty. "Me" in this place, "mi" in the musical scale, is a sweetly-sad modulator or transformer of a "fierce" and "impetuous" tone. "Me" is not even the "deep" sound it is supposed to be unless the /ē/ assonance, bridging the two words across the semantic opposition of "sweet" and "fierce," can be said either to solemnize the ego or to raise the pitch of the poet's voice to a sound of autumn that is not profound but belongs to the everyday music of Collins's bats and beetles, or of Keats's hedge crickets and swallows. This sound, to be heard also as an aural denial of depth in Wordsworth's "too deep for tears," is not a cosmic clarion but a ringing in the inner ear, the sole place or frequency where writing can be heard.

By shadowing forth the disadvantages of writing, the first tercet anticipates all the differences in provenance and sphere of being that will complicate Shelley's long apostrophe: vertical differences between nature, the expressive mind, and the power that coerces both nature and mind. There are also differences even within these spheres, differences that challenge the poet's necessary presupposition that continuity exists in space and time and is thus a medium through which his prophecy, once it is itself naturalized, can flow without interruption. These horizontal differences are previewed in the second tercet.[31] Here the leaves stand for mankind, discolored by the four imbalanced complexions of sickness and forced into fraternal conflict by the rival colorings of race[32] and rhetoric. To offset this gloomy picture, a redeeming difference appears in the conversion of the wind's toys from dead leaves to wingèd seeds, maple-gliders whose auxiliary wings aid time's wingèd chariot.[33]

Their burial causes no grief, since each is only "*like* a corpse within its grave." On the whole, differences among the lower and merely responsive orders of nature, which are equivalent to the pines and other daedal appearances in "Mont Blanc," do not seem very troublesome; all these hymnic orders, innocent as lambs or tainted at most only slightly by the way the four colors of humanity plague each other, rest in the safekeeping of some good shepherd. That Shelley will not accept an apparently benevolent order of that sort, based as it is on metaphors that carry the class system even into nature, becomes a difficulty only later in the poem.

The wind, meanwhile, in joining the traffic of the Cars that passes through all of Shelley's poetry, has changed also, causing more immediate problems. The wind has entered the realm of allegory and thus far ceased to animate the phenomenal world. Shelley could hardly wish to call his poem "Ode to Ausonius," and he must therefore control his drift toward allegory without giving up the much-needed metaleptic suasions of allegory. We return now to an earlier topic, Shelley's merger of science and mythology. "Wild Spirit, which art moving everywhere" is an exemplary solecism, like "Our Father, which art in Heaven," that reflects this merger: "which" anchors the wind as an object in nature, while "art" raises it by art toward the human and the divine. Shelley's wind must be a liminal figure, neither Ausonius-Favonius alone nor mere wind alone but a *deus faventus*, a figure that is more than natural because, contrary to appearance, it is "moving everywhere," and also because, contrary to appearance, it is self-identical, always one and the same, like Hesper-Phosphor. (One does not say "contrary to fact" here, because, of course, it is a triumph of the elegiac tradition that in these respects scientific evidence and poetic belief are in harmony.) Yet for the moment, at least, in the first stanza, Shelley will not allow the wind to be even thus cautiously transcendentalized. "Thine azure sister of the Spring" is identical with the very different, "wild" autumn wind only through the linkage of incest. She is mild and oceanic, more similar to the "azure moss and sea-flowers" on the sea floor than to her brother. When and if she comes, she will be an élan vital or force from within rather than a remote and potentially oppressive force from above. It might be easier and more profitable for the poet to invoke *her*, supposing she were available.

If we want more than mere wind, which is bound to come, we

cannot be sure about the coming of Spring. How do we get through the winter? Once we recognize Shelley's refusal to trust genealogical or eschatological comforts—even of his own invention—we must wonder whether this ode can decisively affirm any continuous, unified myth of history, however much the millennial burden of a political ode may depend on doing so. As the *Defence* makes clear, the genius of poetry must perpetually re-create its world, like the Cartesian God. One voice, therefore, will not do for two separate winds. Prophecy can never be a divination in this case, but only an intimation of the need for further intimation. Poetry looks farther ahead than science, which dissects temporality into more segments even than those given by common sense, but poetry still cannot see far enough. In his ode, Shelley soberly and perhaps even despairingly grants this failing, but we must catch him out in his concession, for he confines it exclusively to signals that are implicit in his chosen form.

The frequency of enjambment in the ode, a forward thrust of continuity, functions in opposition to the way the tercets and couplets hug themselves in separate spaces on the page, fragmenting each of the stanzas. Many of the enjambments are overstretched by the blank distance between modifiers and their nouns in an ensuing verse unit. There is a gulf of this kind between wingèd seeds and their wintry bed, between the dying year and the dirge that mourns it, and between the Atlantic's level powers and their chasms, where the division falls with special force between "powers" and "Cleave." Each of these gaps represents a distinct facet of the theme of difference: the difference between life and rebirth, thing and sign, and cause and effect, respectively. The behavior of the Atlantic disturbs us most, since it shows the wind to be a divisive oppressor and not an apocalyptic leveler of all difference. The crucial transition between the autumnal and the spring wind in the first stanza must weather the first of these dubious enjambments:

> Thine azure sister of the Spring shall blow

> Her clarion o'er the dreaming earth . . .

Here the open space is the winter itself, across which Shelley's hectoring "shall" must stretch its insistence. The "dream" in this space is the dream of locutionary power. If "blow" seems fleetingly to mean "bloom," then the leap toward Spring has been shrewdly accomplished before the ditch is dug; but primarily the passage calls for a distended voice, a connection between the natural blowing of the wind and its humanization as a trumpet. This interruption of voice halfway between unsignifying nature and significant myth marks the betrayal of voice by writing. The myth of continuity that is kept alive by voice, by the idea of vocality, gives way to the cold lacunae of graphic spacing.

In turning to the meteorology of the second and third stanzas, we can reconsider Shelley's struggle more closely with respect to the conventions of an ode. During this phase of the poem, the wind passes through a new series of oblique, fundamentally conflicting personifications. First, the wind is Dionysus (18–23), and then, in the next breath, it is a coryphaeus leading a "congregated" dirge for the death of the god, destroyed and buried by the mourning wind itself in yet a third guise, that of the Spirit that spoke through St. John on Patmos. Via Patmos, the wind continues west, from the mainland of Asia and Greece into the Italian Mediterranean and toward the Atlantic—despite being in fact what it must be as symbol if Italy is to be liberated, a western force blowing eastward from revolutionary America. These continued conflicts between myth, mythopoeia, and nature, between west and east, and between the wind's several identities as agent, reagent, and witness, all reflect Shelley's subversion of the hymnic genealogy that dictates the structure and sequence of stanzas two, three, and four: the second stanza deals with the mythological and celestial sway of the god, the third with his sublunary sway in history, and the fourth with his role in personal history.

The second and third stanzas weave an atmospheric texture around the wind, showing that it is not above and apart from the earth but the center of a vortex in which a temporal sequence of weather processes seems almost to have been spatialized. By this means Shelley supports his assertion that the wind is "blowing everywhere." In the whirl, the active and reactive elements of nature seem to interidentify, offering a solution to the class conflict between the two voices of "Mont Blanc" (ll. 76–83; see above, p. 190). But the potential identification of power and suppliant is wedged apart in each stanza by the obtrusion of a panorama between the two halves—apostrophe and petition—of a simple conative utterance: "O Thou, hear, oh, hear." The list of attributes, in other words, that is proper to hymns and odes, distances the poet from the wind he humanizes by interposing itself as a phenomenology of natural science. To be sure, the "humanization of science" that we have recognized as a Shelleyan ideal is meant to abridge or even to rationalize this distance; but no metalepsis can leap the distance between "thou" and "stream" at the beginning of the second stanza (although "whose" improves appearances there); and at the end of this stanza, the distance is just as great, if not decidedly greater, between "solid atmosphere" and "oh, hear!" Shelley's powerful mythopoeic bridges collapse under intolerable strain.

Just as Keats imagines the nightingale as a continuous and omnipresent being ("The voice I hear this passing night was heard/In ancient days by emperor and clown"), so Shelley imagines that the wind can enforce a continuity between the natural imperialism of the past[34] and the natural republicanism of the future:

> Thou who didst waken from his summer dreams
> The blue Mediterranean, where he lay,
> Lulled by the coil of his crystàlline streams,
>
> Beside a pumice isle in Baiae's bay,
> And saw in sleep old palaces and towers . . .[35]

In the present, however, there is only the fruitless burden of autobiography, an oppression by the very temporality (now chopped into "hours") that had been meant to ensure the flow from past to future: "A heavy weight of hours has chained and bowed/One too like thee: tameless, and swift, and proud." This is an autobiographical moment that is as inexplicable in the text as it stands as were Wordsworth's timely utterance and Coleridge's dark dream. We can only infer that the man Shelley was "too like" the wind when he was a rebel, and that he is now oppressed in exile by his wild reputation at home. The influence of Byronic autobiography is also important, but for the reading of Shelley's text the best models, because they are the most general, are those of Prometheus and Satan, proud republicans "too like" the tyrants they challenged. Probably the saving turn toward submission in the fifth stanza is brought about by the poet's perception of error in "too like thee," the error of having fought force with force and substituted the elitist pride of a rebel chieftain for inherited aristocracy. Just so, Prometheus perceives that he is "too like" Jupiter, and unbinds himself by uttering forgiveness, by finding in himself a new "autumnal tone,/Sweet though in sadness."

Shelley's poetic rebellion had been staged not least against Wordsworth, whose *early* as well as recent poems Shelley had been criticizing ever since his partial disillusionment of 1815 on the grounds, perhaps, that "recantations" like that of Coleridge in "France" are apt merely to declare a hitherto latent attitude. Hence in the "Hymn" and "Mont Blanc" Shelley aims his criticism of Wordsworth not against the offending *Excursion* but against earlier poems that were not overtly offensive. It proves dangerous to do so, however. The lack of real change between the early and late Wordsworth is precisely the lack that Shelley recurrently finds in himself—perhaps in consequence of having found it in Wordsworth and Coleridge. In the "Hymn," Shelley had suggested that "natural piety" was not a narrowing of Wordsworth's vision but the sole basis of his vision from the outset, only to fall himself into a coda that accepts diminishment as a condition of being. Once again in his "Ode," Shelley in the end accepts Wordsworth's sober coloring, and founds the last gasp of his own prophetic voice in hopes derived merely from phenomenal nature: "O wind,/If Winter comes, can Spring be far behind?" gathers transcendent force only from its enraptured context. Just as plainly in Shelley's conclusion, however, we hear the self-mockery of small talk about the weather, as at the beginning and end of Coleridge's "Dejection."

An important principle of dialectical materialism, one which is the basis of any Marxist critique of liberalism, is that revolution comes only from a reactionary climate. This assertion discovers millennial significance in a material or climatological ground, and thus questionably transforms analysis into prophecy. The analytic Shelley ends his prophetic ode with this same difficulty: his mythological premise had been Liberal or evolutionary, based on the imagined continuity of a wind that closes out the autumn of an old order and survives metamorphosed in a new order as a vernal and pacific "azure sister." But a darkness has intervened, or rather a sinister whiteness that is signaled by the blank spaces in the text of revolution, each of them a difficult crossing in winter. Power must remain "inaccessible," then, as in the snows of Mont Blanc, silently heaped by "conflicting winds." That poem had discovered that the radical subject and motive of any millennial predicate is Death, the handwriting on the barriers of perception. So here, Shelley is no more able to cross the blank misgiving of winter than Wordsworth was. Even the material ground itself, as Shelley's theme of difference reveals, is unstable. Hume on causation is scarcely required to make us mistrust our homilies about the weather. Old moons, new moons, the course of the seasons, all depend on our own survival; on the sublimation of Power, the death instinct, as Intellectual Beauty, the life instinct. The most antinomian of all odists, Shelley puts even the diminished calling of a weatherman in autumn as a self-searching question that fears itself and loves all humankind. As Coleridge, again, had wondered: Can darkness free darkness into the light?

This was also the self-questioning of Milton's Nativity Ode, which had to overcome its Luciferian calling in order to pioneer the hymnic theme of creature-love in the English ode. So too Wordsworth found nothing but blankness in his more daring surmises, and turned back to the fold of created things. For Milton, it will be recalled, the existence of inspiration was unquestioned, and the anxiety of his ode had rather to do with the danger of inspiration, its discovery of dark places. Perhaps Shelley's troubled movement across his "dark wintry bed" toward Spring is finally called back to the evolutionary framework of natural processes for a similar reason. Perhaps he *did* believe that his words would mulchify and rise prophetically from darkness, and perhaps he then wondered what monstrous births might rise with his voice. The "Ode to the West Wind" is, once more, a political poem. Like "France: An Ode," but more mildly and subtly, it retracts a position that it had never, perhaps, wholeheartedly taken.[36] The poet flees almost with relief from his own enchantment, as though his ashes and sparks, like Dryden's Power of Music, might "fire another Troy."

9

Voice in the Leaves
Three Odes of Keats

Enter none
Who strive therefore: on the sudden it is won.
—*Endymion* IV. 531-32

Keats would have been startled to find his 1819 odes treated as the high point of a tradition.[1] Although in April he recognized that "Psyche" was his most carefully written poem to date,[2] and although he must have thought that the other odes of that year were equal in merit to "Psyche," he rarely if ever wavered in his belief that lyric writing is an exercize of the left hand, a vacation from the labor of writing long poems. Lest we think his preference odd, though, we should bear in mind that it is scarcely easier for the critic today than it would have been for Keats himself to generalize about the unique value of his odes, if only because in most outward respects, from the standpoint of Keats's own time as much as ours, there is nothing new about them.

Like Shelley's odes, Keats's are far more traditional in their structure of argument than those of either Wordsworth or Coleridge. Conventional machinery is never suppressed in Keats; invocation, elaboration of attributes, genealogy, even petition and vow, all are always more or less clearly present. In fact, the use of these devices in Keats resembles Greek and Roman models more closely than in nearly any ode we have previously discussed. Keats's objects of address are equally traditional: he links "Psyche" to the numina addressed by the hymns of antiquity;[3] "Nightingale" and "Autumn" can be traced to the Greek idyllia; "Grecian Urn" to the poems addressed to things in the Greek Anthology; "Melancholy" and "Indolence" to the allegorization of Renaissance psychology that found its way into ode-like poems from the appearance of Burton's *Anatomy* onward.

In his use of verse forms, Keats was somewhat more innovative than in format or topic. He was certainly the first poet to evolve an ode stanza from experimentation with the sonnet, and after "Psyche" he became the first major writer of non-Horatian odes consistently to decline the Pindaric license of stanzaic variation. I think it unlikely that Keats originally meant the first stanza of "Psyche" to be a sonnet, since he could hardly have imagined the four-line proem to be suited for a sonnet induction; but it remains true that Keats connected the sonnet and the ode more closely than was customary.[4] A passage that assesses the two forms together in the 1816 verse letter to Clarke shows Keats shrewdly ascribing to the sonnet the tonal parabola that the best sonnets and odes do have in common:

> Who read for me the sonnet swelling loudly
> Up to its climax and then dying proudly?
> Who found for me the grandeur of the ode,
> Growing, like Atlas, stronger from its load?[5]

The ode for Keats was an extended sonnet or sonnet sequence, with each stanza, as in Gray's "Progress of Poesy," tending to imitate the tonal curve of the poem as a whole.

But this formal innovation, even insofar as it is really innovative, can hardly account for the excellence of Keats's odes. It remains to discover how Keats, whose cautious bow to tradition in most respects bespeaks the late stages of a brilliant apprenticeship still in progress, achieved an unrivaled success with an apprentice experiment. He himself was in no position to gauge or perhaps even fully to suspect his success, partly because his ambition was invested in Haydon-esque visions of epic monumentality,[6] and partly also because his recently dawning conviction that poetry should have a clear philo-sophical basis must have caused him to mistrust more than hitherto the sort of lyric that comes as naturally as the leaves to a tree (see *Letters* I. 238-39).[7] Owing to this latter conviction, however, his lyrics themselves became more philosophical in 1819,[8] and this ten-dency may help to explain the solidity, if not the brilliance, of the odes. Written in the summer of 1819, the enigmatic allegory of *Lamia* marks a transition from the Keats who favored the chameleon poet to the new Keats who sincerely preferred "the human friend philosopher" (*Letters* II. 139). The odes, spanning the composition of *Lamia* but placed after that poem in the 1820 collection, are all less equivocal experiments in reconciling the amoral caprice of fancy with the morally founded humanism that is always implied whenever Keats speaks of "philosophy" and the "philosopher."[9]

Like Coleridge in "Dejection," Keats seeks out a common ground for imagination and sympathy. In the terms of a later metaphysics, each ode seeks to discover how the flight toward being can avoid disconnection with being-in-the-world.[10] Until "Autumn," which poses —or at least poises—an answer to this question, each ode in turn voices a frustration at the threshold, honestly retreating from any tempting oxymoron of imaginative sympathy. In contrast with the tempered evenness of paragraphed blank verse, which "Tintern Abbey" had shown to be best suited for the merger of demarcations, the ode stanza stages and even features the candid failure of dialectic that Keats's threshold frustrations call for.

Keats's odes are a deliberate critique of lyric positivity. He submits all bias to the sublations of dialectic; and it is in the technique he devises for this purpose that his clearest apparent difference from his predecessors may be found. Every phrase in Keats's odes seems to stage its own disruption. In previous odes, the overt "counterturns" and "stands" come forward from their otherwise smoothly discursive surroundings. They are signaled by sighs, alases, lengthy qualifiers. Coleridge's struggle with the exorcism formula in "Hence viper thoughts . . . , I turn from you, and listen to the wind," is a case in point. Perhaps the most skillful engineer of lyric peripety before Keats is the underrated Akenside, but Akenside's art was made easier by the topical wandering that derived its sanction from Horace's longer odes. It had always been more difficult to redirect the headlong rhetoric called for in the sublime ode. Keats was the first to allow the momentum of his discourse typically to exhaust itself, after which the argument changes direction simply in falling out of orbit, only to rise again from the ashes of its falling. In this way Keats disarms the irony of prefiguration by giving full scope at every moment of composition to the antithetical sense of words:[11] afflatus sinks of its own weight and sadness rises from its poignancy, effecting a countermovement that almost rivals the surface argument in firmness of structure. What Keats says of experience may be applied to his poetry: "circumstances are like clouds continually gathering and bursting— While we are laughing the seed of some trouble is put into the wide arable land of events" (*Letters* II. 79).

Most odes before Keats have a steady negative pull that alternately releases and retards the sublimation of flight:

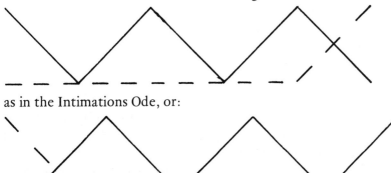

as in the Intimations Ode, or:

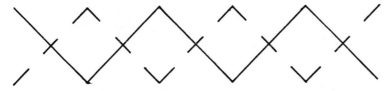

as in "Dejection." By contrast, the antithetical pattern in Keats crosses discourse dynamically at every moment of his odes, sustaining a *beau désordre* through the very intensification of dialectic:

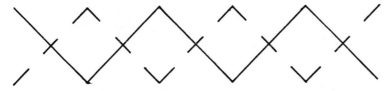

It seems to me that most Keats criticism discovers this much about what is unique in his odes, but no more. What is not usually perceived is that many aspects of the odes are *not* confined within the shaping of dialectic, that beyond the artfulness of his constant reversals Keats is drawn toward constant repetition. I shall direct much of my attention to the unshaping of Keats's odes by repetition.

It should be said again, though, here at the outset, that Keats at his best is a circumspect, analytic poet who knows that syntheses and balances will occur and depart as words rise and fall. He gives discourse freedom to become a dialogue between viewpoints that are both consciously his own; thus for him the occasion of an ode is not a birth that represses death, as in Wordsworth, nor a marriage that represses the creative ground of solitude, as in Coleridge, but a transitional moment that looks back in looking forward. His odes are not secretly ambivalent but candidly two-faced, or even many-faced. It is this multivalency that Keats himself thought of as "richness," or as an expenditure of wealth that loads every rift with ore (see *Letters*

II. 323). Few commentators have taken note of the word "rift" in this Keatsian touchstone. It is the word of one who knows the hollow center of metaphor and predication. Keats's verbal hedonism, like that of the early Stevens, is presciently designed to fill in the abysses of signification that the vocative cast of an ode may not succeed in crossing alone.

The unstructuring of Keats's odes, then, is not chiefly effected by the return of a daemon but by an o'erbrimming like that of bees in autumn. The loaded poem seems to have no brim or limits, and gives itself to an endless seepage of revery that permeates both writer and reader until neither thinks that interpretation will ever cease. Even the "Ode to Psyche," which is in some ways rather programmatic, still finally resists clear paraphrase. I suppose it must come in the form of a warning that my reading of "Psyche" and of the other odes is designed to record that resistance and to leave a residue of significance as disordered as it is in the odes themselves. It will be possible to show more fully than at present, however, that what is left over and most undesigning in Keats's odes is perhaps the most persuasive representation of consciousness as the sensation of being that the English lyric can offer.

II

> The Genius of Poetry must work out its own salvation in a man: it cannot be matured by law & precept, but by sensation and watchfulness in itself.
>
> —*Letters* I. 374

With its invocation, petition, myth, genealogy, and vow, the "Ode to Psyche" is one of the purest imitations in English of the ritual hymn. But like Shelley's "Hymn to Intellectual Beauty," Keats's ode is in part a wittily sustained joke at its own expense, and remains, therefore, very much an ode. But is it not merely a comic irreverence that makes it an ode. "Psyche" is written to show that hymnody is impossible in the Enlightenment.[12] Its vow supplants "antique vows" sung to the "fond believing lyre," and it stresses the antinomian solitude of being an ode, especially in the pointed solecism of "Let *me* be thy choir." In filling his poem with hymnic conventions, Keats stresses the distance between the antique function of the poet-priest and the Alexandrian imitation of that function to which the modern poet is perforce confined. Keats closely follows the Nativity Ode in "Psyche" because for him even more than for Milton, as he assumes, "The oracles are dumm." Keats begins, though, by echoing "Lycidas" rather than the Nativity Ode because it is closer to his purpose to create and enshrine a radically new *genius* than it is to welcome an old god in a new form. He needs his Psyche, as Milton needed his homeward-looking angel, in order to reanimate a disenchanted pleasance. All of these aims, here to be understood as a preliminary framework of allusion, belong to the enthusiastic argument of the poem and not to its witty self-abuse.

Because both Miltonic poems feature acts of substitution, both encounter the difficulty that faces the "Ode to Psyche." There is a difference, an intransitivity, between perception and re-creation, between the surprised faint of the visionary moment and the deliberate architecture of the devoted poet who needs "remembrance dear" to reconstruct his vision liturgically. We may first consider what he saw, turning later to what he builds and its tenuous relation to his vision.

What he reports having seen is the bisexual and at least partly daylit scene of creation that chaster poets, notably Collins, had tried to represent euphemistically. Whereas Collins had wished to veil the erotic basis of creation, Keats's wish, like that of Coleridge in "Dejection," is just the opposite, and just as inevitably doomed. It should be recalled again that the *nature* of an origin, whether sexual or asexual, is never the most crucial source of anxiety for a presentational poet; what troubles him most is that he cannot participate directly in the originary intuition that his compulsively contrary discourse must always defer. The more than Pindarically disconnected transitions from grove to grove in "Psyche" will reflect this frustration. Consciousness can never depict itself to itself; its figural equivalent always becomes an other insofar as it is figural, and its representation as an interior locale makes the figure indistinguishable from the ground and therefore unidentifiable as a human subject.

Keats's first forest scene is happily erotic, then, but it is still only a painterly idyll, viewed from the outside, and cannot survive in the poem as a model for any creative act in which the poet himself could participate. His rememoration of Psyche's "inspiring bower" (Collins) as a shrine will differ sharply from what he has first seen,

most obviously in having changed, as if inadvertently, into a scene
that is all too virginal; a scene that is, precisely, a "chamber of Maiden-
Thought" (*Letters* I. 281), kept apart from the fertility of nature.
The daemonic presence that the ode had hoped to enfold in a shrine
is now elsewhere, and the casement opened at the last minute, the
ode's stubborn refusal of closure, awaits what cannot happen within
a poem, the end of the poet's "enforcèd chastity." Over all the
forests of "Psyche," with their couchant lovers and suddenly vacated
clearings, the moon of *A Midsummer Night's Dream* presides. The
poet as priest must beware the threatened fate of Hermia,

> For aye to be in shady cloister mewed,
> To live a barren sister all [his] life.
> Chanting faint hymns to the cold fruitless moon.
>
> [I. i. 71–73]

But it is the warm moon, Titania's moon that looks with a wat'ry
eye, for which the poet must wait in the end if his stars without a
name are ever to receive a name from "the poet's pen":

> Why, then you may leave a casement of the great chamber window, where
> we play, open, and the moon may shine in at the casement. [III. i. 51–56]

Psyche may be compared with Bottom's dream; he awoke and found
it vanished.

These echoes carry us ahead of our reading, and we had best
return to Keats's Miltonic preliminaries. The opening allusion to
"Lycidas" is ironic: for Keats to imply that his own "sweet enforce-
ment and remembrance dear" is different from Milton's "bitter
constraint, and sad occasion dear" will prove to have been a pre-
tense. The relevance of the Nativity Ode is more complex. Like
Milton's first four stanzas, Keats's first four lines are a proem; he
too will banish obsolete oracles in favor of his own, and "prevent"
other singers with his "humble ode" to a new deity:

> O Goddess! Hear these tuneless numbers, wrung
>   By sweet enforcement and remembrance dear,
> And pardon that thy secrets should be sung
>   Even into thine own soft-conchèd ear.

This too is a pretense of a rather startling kind. The poet almost
seems to have ravished his muse,[13] like Drayton's Pyreneus, to have
burdened her with a secret that he now pours into her ear again. The

conch of Psyche's ear and the bedded grass she lies on are linked by
the visual pun of "couched" at line 9. The poet is like Porphyro at
the ear of Madeline, or like Satan at the ear of Eve; and like Por-
phyro and Satan, as we shall see in a moment, the poet is an inter-
loper in the scene. This shadow of a desired event is present through
allusion in the proem, but the main burden of these lines is of course
very different. The traditional vocative question of whether the
goddess can or will "hear" is answered pessimistically by these lines
themselves; the goddess will hear only if she is merely the poet's
own "creature," sung to as one hums tunelessly to oneself, unheeded
by any but the interior paramour.

These two readings of the proem, the former optative, the
latter concessive—and neither in the least hymnic—intersect at the
word "Even": a) forgive me for broadcasting your intimacy with me
even if only you are listening, since in receiving the libation of my
voice you know yourself to be less chaste than Collins thought you
were; or, b) *even* especially by myself I must be pardoned for cele-
brating, like Wordsworth, the beauty of my own mind. In either case,
Keats resembles Satan: he is an interloper supplanting Eve's proper
consort or else he is a solipsist whose mind is its own place. Here
concealed, concealed mainly in coming prematurely, is Keats's peti-
tion: to be pardoned for interrupting the course of evening toward
the "aurorean" renewal of a tryst that was similarly postponed in
Collins's "Ode to Evening."

In other words, Keats's figuration of Cupid and Psyche, like that
of the lovers frozen on the Grecian Urn, is carried out in defiance of
time. If the poet "dreamt today," he has reversed time by projecting
the witness of a primal scene backward from present desire, while
if he "really" saw what he reports, he can only suppose that his
presence at the edge of the scene was an unwanted interruption. His
poem, in either case, is certainly an interruption, because this first
scene is the sort that cannot be recorded without having been inter-
rupted and frozen as a snapshot. A still-life, anticipating his later
"wide quietness," is indeed what the poet both sees and composes.
The "brooklet, scarce espied" that runs through this scene is an
emblem of the moment's in-betweenness, its poise between tempor-
ality and the timeless landscape with figures that might appear on an
urn. The figures themselves form a circle of interlocked arms and
wings that excludes the onlooker. It is the poet as voyeur who has

put the pair to sleep, "disjoinèd" them in the guise of thoughtless Morpheus, securing his witness from the outraged rejoinder of mutability.

Read in this way, the first two stanzas become a negative allegory that points forward to the conflict between Eros and the soul in the fane of the imagination. If we define Keats's Psyche tentatively as the simple consciousness of being (though as yet there is no evidence for doing so), then it is clear that Cupid and Psyche run in separate channels, often in conflicting channels. For the visionary faculty to picture them together, then, it must necessarily freeze them in a tableau. But the imagination cannot resist entering its projections: vision is invasion, and the poet tells the soul what he has seen because in fact he vies with Cupid for her favors. The soul is skittish; as mere consciousness, not self-consciousness, she does not wish to know herself or her motives, and withdraws in a pique from all future scenes in which she is invited to appear. The poet knows in advance what will happen; the wish to interfere with an inexpressible fullness is highly familiar to him, *it is the compulsion to write a poem,* and so he begins his ode by asking the pardon of the simple consciousness of Being. We shall return to this allegory, but for the moment, as a gloss, we may compare Faust's jealous interruption of Paris and Helen, the two wraiths his own visionary powers have summoned.

The stanza concludes with the main positive assertion of the poem, its staged discovery:

> The winged boy I knew;
> But who wast thou, O happy, happy dove?
> His Psyche true!

There is a play here on the turtledove and the Holy Spirit, and "happy," as always in Keats, means unself-conscious—fortuitously happy; Psyche is butterfly, bird, and blithe spirit. Keats's assertion (surely the parody of an assertion, for these lines could have been written by Peter Quince on "truest Thisby") is simply that desire, which one has always known, may be harmonized with one's newly discovered peace of mind. This first attempt to reconcile psychic flight with being-in-the-world may have been influenced by the canzoni of Dante, especially the one that Keats would have found quoted in Cary's second *Purgatorio*: "Love, that discourses in my thoughts . . ." For Keats, poetry in this vein would have intensified and clarified the circumstantially confused allegory of Apuleius and the summary of Lemprière. But Keats would have felt compelled to ground the pure abstractions of the canzoni in the natural world. Thus he imagines a scene on the threshold between allegory and nature and then anaesthetizes its figures so that the whole tableau will stay in place. But the imposition of stasis on the scene excludes the imposing self, and for Keats to enter his discovery more forcefully he will need to overturn the inspiring bower and rebuild it in the mind's eye.

The revery of the first two stanzas, like an allegorical painting, cannot be lived in. Landscape grows habitable, comes to seem like a climate of being, only when its foreground figurations merge with the ground. Not just Psyche, but, later, "The moss-lain Dryads shall be lull'd to sleep." Necessarily they must sleep, since trees and their nymphs cannot appear in the same glimpse of animation any more than Cupid and Psyche can be imagined, dynamo and virgin, as a concerted force in nature. From the moment when Keats renews his apostrophe to Psyche at the start of the third stanza, she ceases to be present, having become again what she was in the proem, an ear in the shape of a bower, a figure no longer but a shrine commemorating the former presence of a figure.

In shape, the whole poem is the shrine, couched and soft-conched.[14] It is a shell, rounded as the mind, or the "whisp'ring roof" of the first stanza, a shell that is meant to house the soul, but also a wall that turns back the thrust of voice. The shape of the ode bars the doubtful questions at its borders. The preliminary question of whether the poet's voice can ravish his own soul, and the final question of whether Love will enter and discourse in the soul, are one and the same question, which goes unanswered. This question is the point of repetition in the "Ode to Psyche," writ large in the negative rondure of the poem.

But if the framework of Keats's ode attempts to couch an elusive object of curiosity, within the poem there are still three separate bowers that must be placed in a single frame of reference if they are all to house the same figures.[15] In passing from the scene in the forest to the forest of his mind, Keats must find a way of making Psyche a transitional figure; his failure to do so reveals, in my view, the deepest interest of the poem. In order to understand this failure, we must force ourselves to address the prosaic issue of what Psyche represents. At the beginning of the third stanza, she is a leftover, the sole figure who survives from the days when there was a god in every tree. Psyche herself can only be glimpsed in revery, but when she is visible her image is bright and intense. The rest of the pantheon is not said to be wholly invisible, but only "faded." We have just seen Cupid couched with Keats's latest vision. There is also a goddess still faintly perceptible in the moon, but she is known only by her adjacency to the moon's "sapphire-region'd" mineral substance. The old epithalamic Vesper can still be named, but now at most he has a weakly phallic or perhaps even charnel-house identity that just barely rises above the mineral in the chain of being. All these presences have grown nearly inanimate, and vanished from their obsolete and commonplace temples in conventional poetry. Psyche is the "loveliest vision far" in the ironic sense that she is nearly the *only* vision available to the modern poet, but also in another sense that somewhat redeems this one: if the old pantheon, a hierarchy of primitive projections, has now faded, what survives and shines brightly for the first time (being only recently "born" to perception for this reason) is the site of projection itself, the consciousness that had made Olympus possible. In this, the genealogical moment of Keats's ode, the latest born appears as the first born, turning loss to advantage as Collins turns belatedness to advantage against Milton in "Poetical Character," and launching the "Ode to Psyche" on its way toward the monopoly of the poetic field to which it aspires in common with all the major odes in its tradition.

The negative litany in the third stanza gathers confidence from the poet's sense of discovery: naïveté, the alleged "happiness" of antiquity, was simply ignorance, and now, at this moment, the true poet is born from the womb of his ordinary humanity in coming first to celebrate what the Enlightenment had made visible but not yet enshrined,[16] the germinative psyche itself. Psyche is *not* "imagination," again, but a sensation of being that is newly discovered as an object of knowledge. In this passage Keats follows Milton's rhetoric of exorcism in the Nativity Ode, and in so doing he departs from his own usual image of a light-flooded and erotically happy Greece, mixing that image with a gothicist impression of primitive Christian worship in order to leave his own supplicancy in sole possession of the enlightened present:

> Nor virgin-choir to make delicious moan
> Upon the midnight hours;
> No voice, no lute, no pipe, no incense sweet
> From chain-swung censer teeming;
> No shrine, no grove, no oracle, no heat
> Of pale-mouth'd prophet dreaming.

With Psyche, Keats at this point implies, things will be different; worship from now on will simply consist in cultivating one's awareness of selfhood.

However, Keats's ode continues to imitate traditional hymns, and so retains the archaic assumption that worship must take place at a shrine. Keats refuses to force his poem to an Enlightened conclusion, but chooses instead to repeat the archaic past, with all its errors, almost verbatim. The reason is not far to seek: morally speaking, in view of his responsibility for living in the world, the poet cannot rest satisfied with the worship of his sole self, but needs the image of a sentient double, of the self as other, even if bowing to that need entails repeating all the old postures of worship. This leads the poem out of its afflatus and into its most troublesome insight: experience, the vale of soul-making (*Letters* II. 101–12), should protect the individual against solipsism, and yet the purpose of soul-making, the achievement of the soul's identity, actually isolates the poet, drives him inward toward the psyche (now enshrined as self-identity) to a greater extent even than was usual in bygone days of celibate but imperfectly sublimated priesthood.

Suddenly those days seem preferable to the present after all. At least formerly nature seemed responsive to the midnight moan of its priests, however onanistic the office of the priests themselves may have remained. Keats now applies the Wordsworthian myth of childhood to the childhood of history, making nostalgia inevitable for the time "When holy were the haunted forest boughs,/Holy the air, the water, and the fire." Hence the primitive priest "Still is nature's priest." In the present, if a poet is to decide for the priesthood, he will need to rely exclusively on subjective evidence—"by my own eyes inspir'd"—to be sure that he is not whistling in the dark the selfsame invocation that had formerly harmonized with the priests' fond belief in a responsive universe. The nearly exact adaptation of the gentle satire in the third stanza to the poet's own role

may then be seen to explain the structural irony of the poem: after
the fading of Olympus, an ode can prolong the happy pieties of
hymnody only by imitating the posture of a hymn as closely as
possible; yet it remains, in its solitude, only an ode. There are, of
course, compensations. An ode is at least freed from the tyrannical
superstitions of hymnic cultures; hence, the "chain-swung censer"
of the old *vates* becomes the "swingèd censer" of the new poet,
still suspended from belief but only from the personal belief that
confirms itself in being celebrated. It is also an advantage, perhaps,
that the poet is no longer a "virgin-choir," since he has witnessed
and proclaimed the sexual basis of imaginative sympathy. Now the
new prophet's heat is also "thy heat," an excitement he purportedly
shares, like Numa, with his goddess. The trouble is, of course, that
if Psyche is the poet's own soul, his excitement is no different from
that of the archaic priests.

The climactic last stanza begins, then, in an extremely complex
mood, alienated on the one hand from any possible local inspiration
and therefore withdrawn from the processual nature of the outer
world, but on the other hand elated at the prospect of freedom from
superstition and at the thought of having come to trust one's own
eyes. The "Ode to Psyche" analyzes the long-standing need of an
ode to invent what it celebrates, and in so doing takes itself for an
origin more overtly than any previous ode: consciousness begins
where the ode begins. Hitherto unnoted and unenshrined, from now
on Psyche, institutionalized by the poet's decision for a priestly
calling, will be the sole foundation of poetic discourse. And yet the
foundation of her shrine results in her disappearance. The last stanza
shows that one cannot bring about the merger of *genius* with place
except by reducing the former to the latter. What further troubles
the novitiate is that through this reduction even the place itself is
made insubstantial: branchèd thoughts replace pines, stars are un-
identifiable, and all within is confessedly feigned by Fancy, whose
"breeding" in the absence of nature is a mockery of the erotic
scene in the first stanza.

Psyche's shrine is a "vale of soul-making" where self-presence
and self-identification are mutually exclusive. The "virtuous philos-
opher" or "Man of Power" (*Letters* I. 387, 184) gains an identity
but loses immediacy even to himself; this is what it means, in Keats's

letter to America, to acquire a Psyche. The "chameleon poet" or
"Man of Genius" (ibid.) is not in fact capable of choosing a role,
certainly not the role of priest. The Man of Genius appears in the
"Ode to Psyche" as one who can envision most because he controls
least: "I wander'd in a forest thoughtlessly." For Keats, the true
lyric poet has no soul, but only an erotic power of outer-ance. In
contrast with this ideal, the speaker of "Psyche" is constrained by
a role and thus far impotent. The vicarious pleasure of the first
stanza arises, as we have seen, from the speaker's effort to put him-
self in the place of Cupid, but that effort will never succeed.

The beginning and the end of the poem, again, utter the wish
that cannot be fulfilled:

> O Goddess! Hear these tuneless numbers, wrung
>> By sweet enforcement and remembrance dear,
> And pardon that thy secrets should be sung
>> Even into thine own soft-conched ear.
> ·
> And there shall be for thee all soft delight
>> That shadowy thought can win,
> A bright torch, and a casement ope at night,
>> To let the warm Love in!

Were this ode to have traced a full and faultless circle, holding its
figures in place, the vocative poet in retrospect would have *been*
Cupid,[17] and begotten a numinous identity on Psyche as it were by
stealth, simply because, as in Apuleius, that fastidious figure would
not have recognized him for what he was, namely, an interloper. As
it is, though, Psyche flees from institutionalization; she disappears
through the openings of her shrine, leaving the poet as soulless and
passive as he was in his first trance. Divorced from Power, he is left
cradling an empty space and waiting for the return of the erotic,
which is the genius of his true and only being, but which is not an
identity. The soul finally cannot be signified—it *is* the empty space—
because it is unsignifying; Psyche is the simple quiddity of things
known for what they are. She has no wings, no figure at all, and to
interrupt the erotic embrace that represents her inseparability from
things as they are, to "transport" or transcendentalize her, is to
annihilate her nature. Thus the "Ode to Psyche" invokes her pres-
ence and evokes her absence.

III

Much is lost in interpretation if we refuse to admit that Keats's odes are, in part, allegorical. His unparalleled richness of modulation must not mislead us into assuming that the odes lack schematic outlines. They certainly do have schemes, which function openly to suggest "a disjunction between the way in which the world appears in reality and the way it appears in language."[18] In fact it is in the interplay between schematism and the "fullness" of sense that the special quality of these odes may be found. Every phrase in Keats has a purpose, and is bright with it (see *Letters* II. 80), but that purpose is purposeful as well as purposive. If we set forth in advance the critical allegory that the fullness of the odes is supplied by the Man of Genius while their allegorical outline is supplied by the Man of Power, we may come to see that the theme of the odes (itself a nuanced allegory) in mirrored in a conflict of purpose that governs their composition. Hence, no matter what we choose to emphasize in the odes, we are never far from the question, What is the purpose of poetry? Should poetry offer the comfort of a program or the blandishment of a nearly imperceptible design?

Slightly skewed presuppositions about Keats keep many readers from deciding, or seeing the need to decide, what Psyche represents allegorically. She is hastily equated, as often as not, with Imagination; but far more plausibly she represents Genius, the subjective terrain over which imagination plays. Imagination itself is allegorized in the odes as Power, as the form-seeking or shrine-building passion of the speaker. Imagination is an interloper, a figure of interruption. For this reason Keats's poems are not ultimately self-reflexive; that is, they do not *finally* aim to imitate or repeat their topic in form,[19] although they do pass through that objective. The rondure of "Psyche" is created ostensibly to contain what the poem invokes, but instead, as we have seen, that very circularity is what coerces the escape of Being. In still other words, Keats's odes do not represent their representation, but attempt to carry out the more traditional function of presenting a confronted alterity. Confusion arises on this point in Keats criticism because Keats's Other is within, a Genius interrupted, jealously stalked, and driven away by Power. Power is what wills the odes into shape, "writes" them in that limited sense, and thus it is always in conflict with their representation of the ideally powerless mind. What Keats allegorizes, then, are situations that reveal the crudity of allegory and hence the crudity of the poem—of poetry—itself. And yet, on the other hand, some scheme seems necessary. Each ode expresses the poet's reluctant disillusionment with the ideal of *poésie pure*, and each ode remains, therefore, what Keats in his letters called an "abstract image." Form invokes its opposite, the sprawl of indolence.[20] If this latter is what Psyche is, it goes without saying that she wants nothing to do with imagination, with the almost grotesquely "working brain."[21] The "Ode on Indolence" is the weakest of the 1819 odes mainly because it is most doctrinaire about this incompatibility.

I would not be taken to have asserted that Keats disliked or condescended to the shaped "identity" that is the achievement of Power. In everyday life, his sincerest admiration was reserved for this quality, which he believed to be the opposite of his own poetical character. Indeed, as I have said, in 1819 Keats came more and more to disapprove of indolence even as the ground of poetic inspiration. His climactic encounter with Moneta in *The Fall of Hyperion* is a struggle against the drowsy numbness that suffuses the Nightingale Ode, but the narrative serves only to prove, once more, that one gains the stair by succumbing to numbness, as in "Psyche," "thoughtlessly":

> I strove hard to escape
> The numbness; strove to gain the lowest step.
> Slow, heavy, deadly was my pace: the cold
> Grew stifling, suffocating, at the heart;
> And when I clasp'd my hands I felt them not.
> One minute before death, my iced foot touch'd
> The lowest stair; and as it touch'd, life seem'd
> To pour in at the toes:

[I. 127–34]

Like Coleridge's "Dejection," Keats's odes vainly attempt to deny that the dull ache of inertia is the sole source of inspiration. Thus they evince a sporadic disrespect for what they invoke, which is the mark of their self-defense as poems, and constitutes an *ethical* defense of the poet's vocation. Both Coleridge and Keats resist a full acknowledgment of the passive and depressive basis of inspiration, wishing rather to view creativity as a triumph of the will over depression, and both therefore deliberately inflate the value of an active and joyful force called imagination[22]—called the Secondary Imagination by Coleridge, since his Primary Imagination is in fact as indolent as may be.[23] The imagination as an object of praise in Coleridge's celebratory poetry is not present within the allegory of Keats's odes (except where an interloper is figurally present) because it is imperiled more than in Coleridge by Keats's more consciously skeptical psychology. Keats saves the imagination from scandal by refusing to assign it the role it would inevitably assume in an ode, once admitted, the role of arch-imago.

Wordsworth had treated the problematic nature of imagination more candidly than either Coleridge or Keats; he never denied the crucial function of wise or unwise passiveness in creativity. In his prose, he speaks of imagination as a power chiefly in deference to Coleridge, but in his poetry he knows it to be the genius, possibly the evil genius, of passiveness: an "unfathered vapour from the abyss." That the "shaping spirit of imagination" is one of the more factitious notions of Romantic humanism, and that Romantic poetry persists in knowing better, in knowing that writing is the unshaping power whose origins and directives precede the intervention of Coleridge's "conscious will"—all these tensions of poetic conscience are played out, in Keats's odes, through what amounts almost to an agony of self-scrutiny. Keats's daring as a writer of odes consisted in invoking rather than repressing forces that in many ways are shadows of "easeful death," then mounting a critique of those forces in behalf of vocational dignity, and finally conceding the superiority of genius to power at the very moment when the vision of genius has fled, fled in each case from the inadequate "cheat" of imagination. After "Psyche," Keats's next coy genius is the Nightingale, who ceases to be herself when she herself becomes, briefly, the imagination.

IV

Fare thee well, nymph. Ere he do leave this grove,
Thou shalt fly him, and he shall seek thy love.
—*A Midsummer Night's Dream*, II. i. 245–46

Lapped in silence therefore wilt thou lie beneath the ground while the Nymphs' pleasure it is that the frog shall sing for ever. Yet envy them I cannot, for no sweet song sings he.
—Pseudo-Moschus, "Lament for Bion"

In the "Ode to a Nightingale," the poet begins in Coleridge's state of dejection, but unlike Coleridge, who wants to join a circle, Keats will want to insist that being cast out, being a hapless petitioner amid the alien corn, is a necessary condition of vocative poetry. This insistence will become a defense in its own right, an *assertion* of exile on which the dignity of poetry can be founded. But an ode always betrays its argument; whereas Coleridge's ode could not represent the merger with the other that his argument proclaimed as a saving grace, Keats's ode constitutes just such a merger despite itself, and cannot express the alienation from "happiness" that he takes to be the basis of poetic desire. The deepest and most disruptive anxiety of this great ode is a moral one, vocational indeed, but no longer connected with the fear of vocative failure. In this respect the Nightingale Ode is much like the Nativity Ode: that a calling may be achieved is taken for granted in both poems, and this concern is replaced by the question of whether the calling is worthwhile—whether it is perhaps only a black magic, or whether, in Keats, poetry can really offer any value or solace.

Even if poetry is not born for death—and this is never denied—it may offer cold comfort at best for the very reason that it *is* immortal. Poetry is not itself dead only because it is a composed echo of death, a "high requiem," and it may fail in solace because its articulate power is a ruse that absents us as surely as death does from the hum of being-in-the-world, from "The murmurous haunt of flies on summer eves." But Being is necessarily haunted; without the looming contrast of nothingness, Being would be nothing. The Nightingale Ode differs most from "Psyche" in its sombre exploration, along these lines, of Stevens's Keatsian adage that "Death is the mother of beauty." Like "Psyche," this ode invokes the sensation of being, but it goes on to ground that sensation in nonbeing. Thus if in some measure the invocation to Psyche is an invocation to life, the call to the nightingale is, as the sixth stanza confesses, a voicing of death:

> for many a time
> I have been half in love with easeful Death,
> Call'd him soft names in many a mused rhyme,
> To take into the air my quiet breath;

This stanza would appear to contrast death with the immortality of the nightingale, but the sense of contrast between these states will not survive the next stanza. Briefly here, during the afflatus of his

his ode, Keats has tried to allegorize the nightingale as imagination, as the immortal bird in man. But this moment will pass, leaving the immortal song "buried deep" beneath the more resonant concerns that still arise from indolence rather than imagination.

There is discovery in this ode, and a gradual filiation of its theme, but there are no turning points until well beyond the passages in the first few stanzas where readers have usually found them. I shall attempt to show in detail that the apparently contrastive states of the poem, like those of "Dejection," are all radically the same, the state of what Coleridge would have called, with far more prejudice, death-in-life.[24] Dialectic does not begin until the poem begins, in its genealogical moment ("Thou wast not born for death"), to make claims for itself as an origin. The actual counterturn comes when the momentum of self-projection has carried the poet into the pure fiction of romance, a morally useless region called "faery lands for-lorn"—lands lost to the human ear and forsaken like the outmoded deities of "Psyche." "Forlorn" is offered as a word that is specially freighted with significance, a word so strong in meaning that it can be expected to effect a reversal. And then, at the stanza break, this word, conditioning all later words in coming before them and yet at the same time the echo of a word already spoken, reduces words from signs to sounds. It is not an empty sound, for it has the tone of a ringing bell, but it loses signifying force in standing revealed as a *mere* word: "Forlorn! the very word is like a bell/To toll me back from thee"—from the nightingale as the shaping spirit of imagination —"to my sole self," to the dejection of one who cannot in con-science quite admit the grace of his forlornness, the psychic grace that is the truer guise, as we shall see, of the nightingale.[25]

In the first stanza the poet reviews the symptoms of dejection, aligning himself with the speaker of Coleridge's ode and distancing himself, in his numbness, from the portrait of the nightingale that he borrows from another poem by Coleridge:

> A melancholy bird? Oh! idle thought!
> In nature there is nothing melancholy.
> But some night-wandering man whose heart was pierced
> With the remembrance of a grievous wrong,
> Or slow distemper, or neglected love
> (And so, poor wretch! filled all things with himself,
> And made all gentle sounds tell back the tale

Of his own sorrow) he, and such as he,
First named these notes a melancholy strain.

["The Nightingale," 14–22]

In moving between these texts of Coleridge, Keats can choose be-
tween the pathetic fallacy indulged (in a vocative ode) and the
pathetic fallacy repudiated (in a sotto voce Conversation Poem).
Keats will try both approaches, depending on whether he wishes to
indicate a distance to be overcome or a discovered affinity. His
nightingale at first is a "happy" bird, like Coleridge's, but then at last
sings a "plaintive anthem," like Milton's "'Most musical, most melan-
choly' bird." Keats's eventual turning against both texts of Coleridge
consists in showing, partly against his own apparent wishes, that the
melancholy of being is the only condition that is *not* projected from
the "shaping spirit of imagination"—which fills all things with itself.[26]

Coleridge's nightingale, which is in fact no less anthropomorphic
than Milton's, hopes before evening is over to "disburthen his full
soul/Of all its music" (47–48). This moment of fullness and the
need for release that goes along with it are passed through both by
the poet and by his alleged opposite, the bird, in the first stanza of
Keats's ode, setting in motion an unceasing correspondence between
them. What bird and poet have in common, what merges them pre-
figuratively, is their feeling of repletion; the poet's surplus happiness
passes out through the nightingale, which sings richly of overripeness,
"of summer in full-throated ease." Once this affinity is cemented in
place, Keats's apparent contrast between self and alter ego amounts
only to a limited difference, the difference between the ease of re-
lease and the pain of singing with a sore throat. It is "as though," in
order to salute good health through the voice of the nightingale, the
poet has taken sedatives for a cough and drugged the fever and fret
of ill health into a state of heavy indolence, a fullness that is to sleep
as full-throated ease is to poetry. The threshold where the poet
positions himself, without ever leaving it thereafter, is the state of
narcotic revery—"Do I wake or sleep?"—that begot the first vision
in "Psyche." Perhaps for this reason wine is to be drunk from an
apothecary's "beaker" in the next stanza.

Hence from the beginning, more than his contrastive design will
allow him to confess, the poet himself approaches the benumbed
"happiness" that the nightingale possesses by nature. Secretly, they

are near allied. Just as in "Psyche" Keats offhandedly says, "The
winged boy I knew," as if nodding to an old acquaintance, so here
the nightingale is friendly enough with the poet to be interrupted
without fear of offense; she is neither invoked, formally apostro-
phized, nor even mentioned by name; she is simply conversed with.[27]
"In such a state," as Morris Dickstein says, "talk is therapy" (*Keats
and His Poetry*, p. 205). Not just the fifth line but the four preceding
lines are addressed familiarly to the nightingale; either both songs are
being sung at once or, in some sense yet to be revealed, they are the
same song. As in "Psyche," Keats almost openly addresses himself,
thereby skirting the knowledge that invocation proves the absence
of the thing invoked. It is only at the fifth line, when he designates
the nightingale as just what we must suppose her not to be, a listener,
that the imputed distance between poet and bird begins to seem
actual, enforcing to some degree the desired contrast between sore-
throated pain and full-throated ease:

> 'Tis not through envy of thy happy lot,
>> But being too happy in thine happiness,—
>>> That thou, light-winged Dryad of the trees,
>>>> In some melodious plot
>> Of beechen green, and shadows numberless,
>>> Singest of summer in full-throated ease.

Something rings hollow about the first two lines of this passage,
which I can only account for by seeming to play Monsieur Dupin's
celebrated game of Odd and Even: the poet *wants* us to suspect him,
wants the implausible non-sense of the second line to imply that he
really is envious, and is therefore clearly separated from the happi-
ness of the bird. To some extent we do suspect this, but we must
not forget that the hallucinatory atmosphere of the poem makes
feverish joy a much more probable mood. Even now, only the gram-
mar that separates I and Thou keeps open the distance between poet
and bird, who still have much in common.

Both poet and bird continue to shadow their physical ground as
ghostly presences. In "Psyche," in order to reveal the figure of a tree,
the "moss-lain Dryads" in the foreground had to be lulled to sleep
and thus, being motionless, kept out of sight; but now Keats achieves
a transparency of expression that makes the "light-winged Dryad"
almost, but not quite, invisible. She is winged transparently, like the

"viewless wings of poesy" and like the poet who leaves the world unseen. Barely distinguishable from her habitat, itself "some" indefinite place that is hard to locate, the nightingale is still one with the chameleon poet. Her "melodious plot"[28] is a camouflage, a plot against the sort of individuation that stands forth to be admired and refuses to blend into the scenery. Because her singing is not vocative but participatory, a sign, both in content and as an event, of the inevitability of natural process, the nightingale is a prophet by example, bearing witness to summer in "mid-May," as does the poet.[29]

She can prophesy because she never soars to prophetic heights. Neither the nightingale nor the poet ever levitates in this ode, but each always either sinks or flies sideways from grove to grove, to be "buried deep" at last, completely absorbed in a natural backdrop. The illusion that the poet's perceptions are caroming between contrasted worlds is fostered by our stock responses to the formulae of flight. Since talk of wings and flight has intervened, we miss the essential repetition of "Here, where men sit and hear each other groan" and "But here there is no light"; here, that is, in the place one flies to without ever leaving the "shadows numberless" of the leaves.

I would repeat in going forward that the source of complexity in the Nightingale Ode is its declaration of failure, its staged will to fail, which overshadows, perhaps partly represses, Keats's repeated and self-sufficient proofs of presence to the hum of existence, which is audible in the very syllables that lament his alienation. Strangely for an ode, it is the sound of words that is undervalued until the repetition of "forlorn"; we are persuaded before then that only the nightingale sings pure music, springtime music, moreover, which does not resemble a tolling bell. Or does it? In his rather pompously naturalized account of the nightingale's song, Coleridge mentions, among other noises, "one low piping sound more sweet than all" (61), the sound, perhaps, of the word "forlorn." Possibly, then, the nightingale even *sounds* like the poet. The alienated anti-hero who supplies the argument of Keats's ode and who manipulates its counterturns tries to conceal a truer self, nightingale-like and repetitious as a daemon, psychopomp of descent.

In outline, the second stanza fully repeats the first. Now the apothecary's beaker merges with the figure of Bacchus, "With beaded bubbles winking at the brim,/And purple-stainèd mouth," and accordingly the scene is much jollier. But the underlying pattern of narcosis, descent to the underworld, growing warmer (this time by journeying south rather than toward summer), and merging finally with a darkening greenness is exactly repeated from the first stanza.[30] This pattern is repeated obsessively as an impossible wish, again to feign privation, as though it were not a rather simple accomplishment to drink a bottle of imported wine. The implied contrast is between unself-conscious poetry—rondeaux, troubadours' songs[31]—and the rigorous distancing of an ode, between the ease of the poet's petition and the unlikelihood of its fulfillment. That the contrast is a forced one appears from the conclusion of the stanza, where the imagined draught carries the poet not to Provence but back to his own starting point in the first stanza, to the present glade of revery that is always the sole habitat of the poem. The way in which contrast is undermined by repetition appears yet more clearly if one pursues this conclusion beyond the stanza break (italics mine):

> That I might drink, and *leave* the world unseen,
>   And with thee fade away into the forest dim:
>
> Fade far away, dissolve, and quite forget
>   What thou among the *leaves* hast never known.

The generations of death "leave" the world, making it all a forest dim, a threshold "here" where a poet listens to a nightingale that is always just beyond the overgrowth. Either suffering is not elsewhere but "here," and scars even the nightingale's throat, or else the poet is "already with" the bird, with the figure of genius he enters in passing through the shrubbery to exchange suffering for a ghostly existence. That there is no third possibility, no saving contrast between presence and absence, is starkly exposed in passages like this one:

> I wish I could say Tom was any better. His identity presses upon me so all day that I am obliged to go out—and although I intended to give some time to study alone I am obliged to write, and plunge into abstract images to ease myself of his countenance his voice his feebleness—so that I live now in a continual fever—it must be poisonous to life although I feel well. Imagine "the hateful siege of contraries"—if I think of fame of poetry it seems a crime to me, and yet I must do so or suffer—I am sorry to give you pain—I am almost resolv'd to burn this—but I really have not self possession and magninimity enough

to manage the thing otherwise—after all it may be a nervousness proceeding from the Mercury—

[*Letters* I. 369] [32]

Every possible escape is mentioned here, but every one is spoiled by narcotic tension. The same dull pain is sympathetically shared by the patient, the male nurse, and even, with the correspondent's apologies, by the reader of the letter. This uniformity of feeling emanates from the strong identity of the patient, who is strengthened as a Man of Power by his very feebleness, and it saturates the writer, a Man of Genius who lacks "self possession." To escape power, to "go out" and seek liminal camouflages, even self-immolation, is to pass from fever to fever, and from the power of helplessness to the passivity of genius. There is no siege of contraries. Just so, stanza three of the Nightingale Ode remains in the forest dim no matter whither it may seem to fly. The palsy that "shakes a few, sad, last gray hairs" evokes the same Shakespearean leaves that Shelley recalls in "West Wind"; it is so dark "here" that leaden eyes and lustrous eyes seem shaded by the same sorrow; and love is not evergreen but "pines." At the end of every stanza except one, the seventh, the speaker stands in the same place, canopied by leaves "with" the bird.

Since Bacchus and poetry are nearly interchangeable metaphors in the second stanza, the contrast that opens the fourth stanza must be seen, yet again, as a forced one. [33] If one reads the second and fourth stanzas as a genealogy of poetry, then of course substantial changes can be noted: from anacreontic modes to the sublime poem, from mythological machinery to the transparencies of naturalization. But this ode does not really subsume the past; rather it constitutes the past as part of the present. Keats wrote two rondeaux at the beginning of 1819 and predicted that he would write more (*Letters* II. 26); and we know that unlike his older contemporaries he was not in the least averse to mythological machinery. In his ode, then, the difference in quality between inebriation and inspiration is hard to measure. If, for example, Keats banishes the pagan oracle of Bacchus in order to join the modern nightingale of Coleridge's poem, he is in for a surprise, because at the end of his flight to sobriety he will see:

> Many a nightingale perch giddily
> On blossomy twig still swinging from the breeze,

> And to that motion tune his wanton song
> Like tipsy Joy that reels his tossing head.
>
> ["The Nightingale," 83–86]

"Away! away!" has the appearance of an exorcism, like "Hence, viper thoughts": "away" from sedatives, from wine, from suffering, and toward the magic tenor of the nightingale on the vehicle of poetry. But nothing is exorcized, and nothing new achieved, since the poet, in a poignant ambiguity, is "Already with thee," already in the place where "the dull brain perplexes and retards," plodding down the cul-de-sacs of thought until it stupefies itself and faints into indolence. Only then, after no apparent progress, the time arrives for an event like that of the passage in Shelley that Keats echoes in *The Fall of Hyperion* (I. 131; quoted above): "Sudden, thy shadow fell on me;/I shrieked, and clasped my hands in ecstasy!"

Whether in suffering or ecstasy, the poet flies from death to death: from death-in-life, retarded and tending Lethe-wards, toward a place "here," where there is no light and darkness is embalmed. "Haply" and happily, this is a magic place where the moon and stars may be imagined freely as legions of romance, though if one does so it becomes impossible to see them with the physical eye. But this ode reduces romance, as odes always do, to its own framework, just as earlier it expropriated the lesser genres; and it implies, as odes always do, that it is the only poem that exists, containing all prior subjects, viewpoints, and conditions. As we have noted before, it is partly because the object of an ode's address is indivisible that it is destined to repeat itself in spite of every change in the course of its argument. Thus during the afflatus of reaching a transcendent site on the viewless wings of romance, Keats exactly repeats the earlier divination of the nightingale in a natural site, where it has sung easily of summer in May. Seeing nothing and "cover'd up in leaves," buried in the forest like the nightingale tipsy with wine,[34] the poet need only look within to "guess" the progress from spring to summer of

> Fast fading violets cover'd up in leaves;
> and mid-May's eldest child,
> The coming musk-rose, full of dewy wine,
> The murmurous haunt of flies on summer eves.[35]

This is the place that Oberon claims to know in *A Midsummer Night's Dream* (II. i. 249–58), the place where Puck will find a hapless sleeper and "make her full of hateful fantasies." But Keats in the long run is less credulous than Titania, and announces that "The fancy cannot cheat so well/As she is fam'd to do, deceiving elf." He knows that the magic place, insofar as it is a place at all, is not a vision furnished by romance but the native home of the liminal revery from which he has never departed.

All along, the Athenian forest has been evoked in Keats's ode, but now, claiming a progress accomplished, the speaker for the first time celebrates his power of evocation; first by alluding to a Shakespearean text that questions the ethics, if not the strength, of the "imagination all compact," and then, with "Darkling I listen," by alluding to one of the highest vocational claims ever made, Milton's blind invocation to Holy Light. Milton too was transported to a haunted place where he called on Urania and the tradition of the blind bards, but where he never forgot, or truly left behind, the framework of his vision in a fallen world where one can prophesy only the return of the seasons, like the nightingale. I quote the Miltonic passage at length, because it covers the whole territory of Keats's ode:

> Yet not the more
> Cease I to wander where the Muses haunt
> Clear Spring, or shady Grove, or sunny Hill,
> Smit with the love of sacred Song; but chief
> Thee *Sion* and the flow'ry Brooks beneath
> That wash thy hallow'd feet, and warbling flow,
> Nightly I visit: nor sometimes forget
> Those other two equall'd with me in Fate,
> So were I equall'd with them in renown,
> Blind *Thamyris* and blind *Maeonides*,
> And *Tiresias* and *Phineus* Prophets old.
> Then feed on thoughts, that voluntary move
> Harmonious numbers; as the wakeful Bird
> Sings darkling, and in shadiest Covert hid
> Tunes her nocturnal Note. Thus with the Year
> Seasons return, but not to me returns
> Day, or the sweet approach of Ev'n or Morn,
> Or sight of vernal bloom, or Summer's Rose . . .
>
> [*Paradise Lost* III. 26–43][36]

It will be noted that in Keats's ode this heroic singing bird replaces those of *Il Penseroso* and of Coleridge's poem alike; and that by this allusion Keats's generic monopoly reduces epic to his own vocative frame, leaving little in Milton's passage unrevised. If Keats is "already with" this bird, then his implied contrast between Milton's dark singing and his own dark listening is a most subtle one, since it is his own song he listens to.

It is this contrast, in any case, that for the first time doubles or divides the consciousness of the Keatsian speaker; now he is both voice and hearing, poet and man. As poet, he prefers his claim to immortality, but as a man he perceives that immortality, like the darkling thrush, is an absence from life, at best only a ghostly reflection of life's deepening gloom. As he is now divided, so too is the nightingale, into whose newly awarded immortality the poet projects his ambition, even though from the leafy covert he will continue to speak of a bird that is both natural and mortal. Out of a revery that is rich in mortality he rises to address his own shaping spirit, the avatar of Yeats's mechanical bird:

> Now more than ever seems it rich to die,
>   To cease upon the midnight with no pain,
>   While thou art pouring forth thy soul abroad
>   In such an ecstasy!
> Still wouldst thou sing, and I have ears in vain—
>   To thy high requiem become a sod.
>
> Thou wast not born for death, immortal Bird!
>   No hungry generations tread thee down;
>   The voice I hear this passing night was heard
>   In ancient days by emperor and clown:[37]

The hope of the mortal man is to load every rift of death with ore, to cover death with synaesthetic delights, soothing a sore throat in a last faint that joins "quiet breath" with full-throated ease. His hope, in other words, fully and immortally answered in every syllable, is to leave a record of mortality, "proudly dying" like a sonnet or an ode.

What sort of poet, then, is the transcendental nightingale, now no longer a leafy figure of the seasons? Increasingly, this bird is a poet of alien genres: first a troubadour poet diverting emperors and clowns (both jesters and peasants) with courtly love and country mirth, then the singer of a kind of *Ranz des Vaches* to an unwillingly Georgic reaper who is far more solitary than Wordsworth's (a poet, then, who makes sadness even sadder), and finally the voice of a disinspirited shrine for Psyche, there to be a bird of Romance whose casement is "ope" on emptiness and—even in fairyland—on "daunger" and death.[38] Keats's earlier allusion to the wiles of Oberon and Puck near the "pastoral eglantine" had already raised the question that is now carried to its pitch: Can a definite value be ascertained for the poetry that is properly to be called immortal—the blithe lyric and the native air kept alive in folkways, together with pastoral, comedy, romance, and epic? The logic of Keats's ode answers negatively, but this same logic also constitutes a defense of the *ode* as a genre of another kind, of the ode as palinode, as the same diminished calling of evening and of Being that we have traced in our study from Collins through Keats. For Keats, this would be the chameleonic poetry of Genius. All other poetry, all poetry with an identity bestowed by imaginative Power, carries man away from his place among the leaves, with the rich intimation of death it affords, to a groundless place, a fiction from which nothing can be intimated. (The reader will note that this is a generically determined opinion; as a theorist in the Letters, and as an ambitious poet who took nearly all the genres mentioned above more seriously than he took the ode, Keats clearly preferred fiction and Power to lyric and Genius.)

In contrast with the opening scene of the poem, this alien place, which has been prefigured by the exile of Ruth, represents what it is to be truly dejected, to be cast out from the ground of being into fable. The ending of the poem, then, is Keats's farewell to romance and return to his sole self, which is buried deep in revery. Neither quite awake nor quite asleep, on this passing night the poet continues in the same vitally deathlike trance that opened the poem, tolling death in nearly every pulse of being; while tomorrow, in "the next valley-glades" that so much resemble his present place, he will die, leaving behind the requiem he had been too high-minded to recognize as his own quiet suffering among the leaves, and leave-takings.

The reader is apt to feel now, as he no doubt also felt in response to my interpretation of "Dejection," that my relentless ellision of places and states of being exaggerates matters considerably. He is apt to feel further that there is a certain vagueness about the single "place" in which I locate this ode, no matter how variously I attempt to describe it; that it is neither subjective nor objective, neither the garden at Wentworth nor an island in the moon; that, in short, it is simply a leafy presence that has no place. This vagueness would seem to be the price I pay for having denied Keats the polarities of his representation. Probably so, for the place of the nightingale is unquestionably a threshold that has not been reached by progress and growth, that has not been "reached" at all, indeed, but is rather the twilit region where consciousness has always dwelt. It is a leaf-fringed legendary place that may be understood simply as—whatever we can know about reality.

More specifically, it is what a written lyric constitutes as reality. The surest meeting place of poet and bird is among the leaves of a volume. Coleridge's *Sibylline Leaves*, Leigh Hunt's *Foliage*—leaves were in the air in the late eighteen-teens. In the leaves of a book, the written word "forlorn" is not a sound but a signification, secondary to sound and thus descriptive of sound. It simultaneously immortalizes and buries the voice of the nightingale. We come finally, then, to the ode writer's typical struggle with the absence of voice from his written calling. The pure sound of "forlorn" is the pure music of the nightingale, primary but without the signifying power, without the power of screening and repression, that effects an identity—or what we now call an "ego." Voice, the knell of natural sound that echoes death, is the lost origin of an ode. By contrast, the writing of an ode, leafing over the voice, sublimates death as immortality: it is the ascription of imaginary power. Perhaps most in an ode that addresses a voice, like the Nightingale Ode, but to some extent in all of his odes, Keats works out a compromise between voice and writing. The threshold "stationing" of a Keatsian ode—as *tableau vivant*, as forest's brink, as the figuration of an urn—triumphantly records both the immortal sign-region and the mortal sound-region, having shown that despite the ambivalence of any possible discourse about them, they are not alternatives but differences of the same.

As an afterthought about both "Psyche" and the Nightingale Ode, I should wish it to be recalled that the leafy site of both odes has an important literary source in Spenser's description of the Garden of Adonis (*FQ* III. vi. 39–51), whence Keats borrowed his "wingèd boy" (st. 49), and whence he learned that the offspring of

Cupid and Psyche's union is Pleasure.[39] For Keats, who must always endlessly postpone this union, pleasure is "For ever warm and still to be enjoy'd." The most telling instruction he receives from Spenser's Garden is yet more ironic, and may be cited here to refamiliarize us, if need be, with the great Keatsian commonplace that all readers agree upon:

> But were it not, that *Time* their troubler is,
> All that in this delightful Gardin growes,
> Should happie be, and have immortall blis.

[St. 41]

When the garden reappears on an urn, Keats still remembers this passage: "Ah, happy happy boughs! that cannot shed/Your leaves." Happy enough; but poems are leaves only when they do fall, or so the "Ode on a Grecian Urn" will suggest.

V

In an important essay, Helen Vendler has argued that Keats's odes are best understood if we try to locate their "experiential beginnings" (*SiR* 12 [1973]: 591–606), by which she means, not necessarily that we should study his biography, but that we should look for points of special intensity in the odes themselves, around which each poem will then appear to take shape. At such points a veil seems to fall away, and the poet confronts, without further evasion, some inescapable force of existence. We should not assume, Vendler says, that the motive of a Keatsian ode appears at the beginning of the text; rather it is worked toward and then in some degree resolved or placated. In my opinion these observations perfectly account for the course of the "Ode to a Nightingale," which is indeed, as Vendler almost alone has argued,[40] a poem that concerns the awareness of death itself as an experiental beginning. Whatever the beauties of the first stanzas in "Nightingale," they are still postponements of an awareness that begins when the poet confesses his wish to die. I turn somewhat from Vendler's essay only when she maintains that the "Ode on a Grecian Urn" has a new and separate experiential beginning. "Grecian Urn" as I read it takes up and continues the subject that was uncovered in "Nightingale": the dialectical debate between death sublimated in art (immortality achieved through imaginative power) and living in the world with death (presence to Being achieved through the genius of camouflage).

This subject plays itself out in "Grecian Urn," leading however toward a strange conclusion, so wholly distinct in mode and mood from what precedes it that we have never quite decided how to read it. My own choice is to read the ode in a way that will make the ending seem plausible as a retrospective irony. This viewpoint can only be arrived at gradually, but it is well to begin by pointing out that the ending unquestionably harbors a *generic* irony. Whatever we make of its meaning, the final "point" of Keats's ode is exactly appropriate for the generic tradition to which its identity as an "Ode on" is joined. This ode is an inscription or epigram, and should be envisioned as though it were inscribed on a described object; the irony in Keats's case is that his concluding homily, which Lessing characterized for epigrams in general as an *Aufschluss* or extracted message, is the only part of the poem that we can possibly imagine *not* to be extracted; this is, to be inscribed literally on the urn. As an epigram, then, "Grecian Urn" concludes with an irony of presentation that returns us to its equally strong identity as an "ode to": if what is inscribed is abstracted or secondary, and certainly unclear, what is evoked or called forth in the body of the poem is the vivid rendering of the surface of a thing; far more than the inscription, the evocation is "realized" in the relatively strict sense of that term. More ode than epigram because it is more associative than inscriptive, "Grecian Urn" is, then, what Leo Spitzer has authoritatively called it, a *Dinggedicht*[41]—or, to render the term in English with its proper ambiguity, a "poem on a thing."

I shall not be concerned as much with the ontology of the poem, which, again, I think it shares with "Nightingale,"[42] as with a related aesthetic topic, namely, the superiority of a certain sort of lyric to the plastic arts and to other sorts of (verbal or nonverbal) "melodies." Keats's Dinggedicht is a poem that supplements a thing; at one and the same time it distances the thing and opens it outward by removing it from space and projecting it into the softer boundaries of time. In entering time, the "leaf-fring'd legend" of the urn begins to flourish and change.

The "Ode on a Grecian Urn" is a hermeneutic lyric that offers itself by way of example as a theory of interpretation. In so doing, it deforms itself, as we shall see, and becomes Keats's version of the unstructuring daemon in a presentational ode. Keats's ode is an attack on the notion that form constitutes a value in and of itself, and thus it reveals a new facet of his odes' continuous theme, the contrast between shapeless genius and shaping power. In itself the urn is a figure of power that immortalizes the dead, like the abstracted nightingale. In the Nightingale Ode, the bird had become an art object when it was transformed into an "immortal bird," and from that moment on the earlier ode, like "Grecian Urn," was about "art and life." A more subtle distinction between the two poems is needed than the one usually alleged between nature invoked and art invoked. Both poems concern art, but not the same kind of art; if the Nightingale Ode is a critique of all poetic genres but its own, "Grecian Urn" broadens the critique to include not only the alien genres but the plastic arts. It pronounces all art that is palpable, visible, or melodic to be trapped in its medium and cut off from any realm of signification beyond itself until it is supplied with the sort of hermeneutic commentary that appears in an ode.[43]

"What leaf-fring'd legend haunts about thy shape?" Like Psyche, knowledge of sources is a haunting intuition beyond shape, yet it can only arise in the vicinity of something that has a shape. If a poem is to capture any of that intuition, it should never come full circle. It should be left open, and accordingly, Keats's fourth stanza leaves the surface of the urn. Meanwhile, though, he experiments with *ecphrasis,* the doctrine of containment by form, and tries by means of dialectic to imitate the rondure of the urn. Not to prejudice the reader against the rather mechanical coldness of the ecphrastic ideal, the experiment begins with the most human metaphor for a circle that exists; the circle of art is addressed as if it were the family circle of man:

> Thou still unravish'd bride of quietness,
>> Thou foster-child of silence and slow time,
> Sylvan historian, who canst thus express
>> A flowery tale more sweetly than our rhyme:

Since these lines fully anticipate the course of dispute in the poem, they may usefully detain us. The urn is a family, perhaps a holy family: an unravished bride must have a foster child if she is to be a mother, and the paternal historian need not therefore be named as the father. Through the slippage of apposition, the urn makes these relationships less generative by becoming, in turn, each member of the family itself; that is, as a figure of art, it represents empathy, the entering of others that is not sexual. Thus the urn is a human totality that has been bred in purity. Of course, it has been necessary to deform this passage in order to read it this way, and that necessity is itself significant. An ode that celebrates totality should surely invoke figures that can enter formal relations without hindrance, yet the holistic reading of this passage is in effect an antithetical one, while the disturbances of the holistic reading belong to the drift of the overt argument. In point of fact, as every reader knows, the exact sense of these first lines is extremely evasive.

The appearance of a comma after "still" in the text published in *Annals of the Fine Arts* has satisfied many readers that "still" means "quiet," and that the bride therefore has nothing to fear. But apart from the difficulty of reading "quiet bride of quietness," clearly the presence of "slow time" in the next line suggests that the bride cannot be intact forever.[44] Because, being unravished, she can bear no fruit, she can have no contents except the quiet of death. She *is* a quiet bride of quiet, midway between a stillness before and a stillness after: she once contained the ashes that she will herself become. Hence the first line establishes the intimacy of the urn with death; that is the urn's primary condition. The second line, fostered by the first, presents its secondary condition. Both stillness and quietness, we assume, approach timelessness, and thus in the first line the urn is most intimately related to the circumference or framework of time, which is death. By contrast, the urn is related by adoption, in the second line, to time itself. Consciousness in history, cultural consciousness, acts custodially toward the artifacts it adopts as children—acts more conscientiously toward them in fact than toward its true children, the creatures of nature, including man, whom it takes for granted. The first two lines read together, then, harbor a paradox: holistic art is akin to death, it is like a life accomplished or consummated, but it has no kinship with the germinal cycle of the life it is conventionally said to affirm and justify.

The word "silence" in the second line must be supposed to differ from "still" and "quietness" in the first. If "silence and slow time" suggests a second marriage, that marriage too is a fruitless one that must adopt the urn; or if, to read the phrase as a hendiadys, silence is cognate with slow time, then it is like Wordsworth's "still sad music" and looks forward to the "ditties of no tone" in the next stanza. But none of these three terms for the absence of existential noise, whatever the differences between them may be, are intrinsic attributes of the urn itself; they are genetively but not germinally linked with the urn. The resonance of this variously conceived quiet can be heard near the urn, before and after it, but is never a part of it. The silent extremes of intuition and death precede the urn ("still"), and the silent extremes of contemplation and death come after it. In Crocean terms, which are highly relevant to the study of Keats's thought, all the modalities of silence constitute an "intuition-expression," while the work of art that is externalized, made manifest in a concrete medium, is merely a "represented expression." It begins to be apparent that the "Ode on a Grecian Urn" entertains what is perhaps the ultimate irony for an ode; it rejects the heard melodies of voice and prefers the leafage of writing. The lines "*Sylvan* historian, who canst thus express/A flowery tale more sweetly than our rhyme" reveal this preference metaphorically, even though the dialectical plan of the poem will not yet permit the assignment of preferred metaphors to preferred media. Later, the best foliage will lack the flowers of rhetoric.[45]

Since the rest of the stanza poses baffled questions of the sort that history could have answered readily enough, the urn as historian is shown to fail because it offers the past without interpretation.[46] Like the deferential listener of the Nightingale Ode, the museumgoer of this ode is guilty of an initial false modesty in pretending that the urn is wiser than he is. While it is not quite true that the urn explains nothing, it is certainly true that its way of communicating offers no instruction. Knowledge belongs rather to the inspiration that precedes expression and the interpretation that succeeds it. The surrounding of the round urn, necessarily but also deliberately kept from touching the urn's expressive surface, is the hermeneutic circle. Interpretation, the unfolding map or "legend" that helps us to read the urn, is an *un*expressive voice because it is indeterminate. It haunts shapes but itself resists being shaped into melody; it is a ditty of no tone, like "The murmurous *haunt* of flies on summer eves," that is rich in inconclusive knowledge.[47] As John Jones remarks, Keats "wants to *write* a Grecian urn."[48] But for the moment, Keats leaves an opening through which his argument can subtly develop by confining the urn's eventually victorious rival, poetry, to the trival-seeming channel of "rhyme." The pet-lamb versifying (see the "Ode on Indolence") implied by "our rhyme" is the collective enterprise of tame hymnody from which an ode always alienates itself. Here, though, "our rhyme" is left to stand for poetry in general in order to keep our critical attention trained on the urn.

The best gloss on the comparative values I have imputed to Keats's ode was soon to be written by Shelley in the *Defence of Poetry*:

For language is arbitrarily produced by the imagination, and has relation to thoughts alone; but all other materials, instruments, and conditions of art, have relations among each other, which limit and interpose between conception and expression. The former is as a mirror which reflects, the latter as a cloud which enfeebles, the light of which both are mediums of communication.

[Pp. 32–33]

It is not just the formal constraint imposed by the plastic and acoustic media, but their derivation from nature, from the world they are meant to represent, that muddles their communication: that is, they stand as an intermediate opacity between referee and referent, as a wall—in the present case a marble wall—that blocks the line of vision. For both Shelley and Keats, in the transvaluation that results from this insight, the Letter is closely associated with what is usually called the Spirit, while the material media have the dry obstinacy that is usually attributed to the Letter.[49]

The questions that Keats asks the urn not only reveal its opacity simply in being questions, but also repeat in content the antinomy between the finite and the borderless that is presented everywhere in the poem:

> What leaf-fring'd legend haunts about thy shape
> Of deities or mortals, or of both,
> In Tempe or the dales of Arcady?
> What men or gods are these?

The ensuing questions vary this theme as an antinomy between capture and the failure to capture:

> What maidens loth?
> What mad pursuit? What struggle to escape?
> What pipes and timbrels? What wild ecstasy?

Here both states, capture and escape, are ambivalently valued, even before their dialectical relation becomes the main subject of the second and third stanzas. Capture, the triumph of form, is an escape from fulfillment and an entrapment of potential. Escape, on the other hand, here imagined as the ecstasy of free-standing, is a failure to encircle or be encircled that restores the intuition of potential.

"What pipes and timbrels?" is understandably taken by a good many readers to be a silly question. It is only in the next stanza that the motive of this question appears. But even then, it still seems strange that with pottery and poetry already on his hands the poet should now take up music, joining his ode briefly to the Pythagorean-Boethian tradition that prefers "theoretical music" to "practical music," and thus sketching the outline of an ode against the Power of Music like Dryden's.[50] Music and poetry are, in fact, as in odes for music, parallel if not identical. Heard melodies are poems of imaginative Power, while ditties of no tone are odes of Genius. Not just the plastic arts and music, now, but also rhetorical poetry, poetry full of flowery tonality but lacking the finer tone, all are equally subject to Keats's critique of form. The "soft pipes," which are *not silent* pipes,[51] hum like the "murmurous haunt" of the sound of being. Keats has accusingly asked "What pipes and timbrels?" because he knows that the urn cannot know the answer. The urn represents absolute silence that is meant to be melodic, whereas the modestly hermeneutic ode "plays" to the inner ear a sound between silence and melody that is infinitely resonant; written among the leaves, it is the toneless potential of all sound.

At this point the first round of argument in behalf of the diminished or attenuated lyric, of an ode that is not like an ode, is complete; and for the next sixteen lines the poet lectures the figures on the urn in the full irony of having just proved that they cannot hear him. His ode now steers its course between the mute and undeclaring figures of silence and the passions of real life, which latter are just as unpoetic as the urn figures because they are not quieted and transmuted by the awareness of Being. The contrast in these lines is not so much between parched longing and *post coitu homo tristis* as between extremes of equally unproductive desire.

That the urn figures are meant to imply one such extreme is rarely disputed, since their "happiness" is quite obviously absurd.

The discomfort of their plight is excruciating until we register an irony that is more than an irony; in a burlesque of ecstasy, Keats is imitating the totemistic madness that makes people apostrophize pictures.[52] "Happy" six times: this is a serious joke that echoes the five "nevers" of Lear and the five maudlin "fallens" of Dryden's Timotheus. Perhaps a parody of choral repetition in cantatas and odes for music, this passage is more importantly a parody of Keats's own rather too sentimental portraits of unself-conscious beings in "Psyche" and the Nightingale Ode. The urn figures, then, cannot be envied, being insensate in themselves and acutely frustrated if we humanize them. Once their fair attitude has been interpreted, a contrast between them and "human passion" no longer seems possible:

> All breathing human passion far above,
>   That leaves a heart high-sorrowful and cloy'd,
>   A burning forehead, and a parching tongue.

More than a few passages in the Letters show that by "cloy'd" Keats is not apt to mean "satiated" but rather overburdened and finally numbed, as in "Nightingale," with excess of desire.[53] In other words, neither the urn figures *nor* human lovers can ever "kiss,/ Though winning near the goal." All the urn figures, especially the "happy melodist," have the double identity that Keats had first bestowed on the nightingale. Considered apart from the urn, as a "youth, beneath the trees," Keats's piper is no sentimental naif but a voice from the vale of soul-making. But as one who was not born for death, who "cannot leave his song," the youth has a fixed identity that does not belong to the "proud dying" of an ode.

But the song of the musician does set him apart from his speechless companions in desire, whose "parching tongue" makes them incapable of speech, like the Ancient Mariner; in a single phrase, "youth, beneath the trees," Keats marks the intermediary place of a hermeneutic ode between mute figuration and mute desire. Now advancing beyond the surface of the urn,[54] Keats in the fourth stanza demonstrates the strength of an interpretive act that has been released from its bondage to self-enclosed artifacts. For the rondure of a well-wrought urn, Keats now substitutes the moving perspective of an inquisitive eye. Once again the interpreter must ask questions, but now his questions are no longer rhetorical—no longer subservient, that is, to the rhetorical power of the urn. Now his questions are hermeneutic questions to which death alone can provide answers:[55]

> Who are these coming to the sacrifice?
>   To what green altar, O mysterious priest,
> Lead'st thou that heifer lowing at the skies,
>   And all her silken flanks with garlands drest?
> What little town by river or sea shore,
>   Or mountain-built with peaceful citadel,
>   Is emptied of this folk, this pious morn?
> And, little town, thy streets for evermore
>   Will silent be; and not a soul to tell
>   Why thou art desolate, can e'er return.

There are many mysteries in this extraordinary stanza that Keats's legions of interpreters have yet to explore; that is as it should be, for this stanza is Keats's example of the way a "ditty of no tone" should prolong our questioning in becoming a part of it, and not offer its two handles like an amphora to be grasped and emptied by exegesis.

Freed from the single viewpoint that must be taken toward a framed representation, the visionary eye in this landscape roams at will. At the beginning of the stanza the speaker stands in the countryside, watching the townsfolk come toward him, while at the end he is watching, or even within, the silent town. The whole surface of the earth has now become an urn, and the stanza is not "on" but contained within its vast boundaries. The only object that resists being seen is the sacrifical altar itself, though the interpreter can suspect that it is "green." But why green? Altars are not green, unless they appear beneath the leaves, as in "Psyche" with its forest and its inward altar, or as in the "Ode to a Nightingale," with its forest threshold where the humanized piper on the urn still stands in this poem. By leaving the urn, Keats has now more fully entered it, or re-entered it in the Pindaric "*return*" that closes the stanza. Perhaps he is influenced by Wordsworth's sudden discovery of the valley of death where the Solitary lives in *The Excursion:*

>   all at once, behold!
>   Beneath our feet, a little lowly vale,
>   A lowly vale, and yet uplifted high
>   Among the mountains; even as if the spot

Had been from eldest time by wish of theirs
So placed, to be shut out from all the world!
Urn-like it was in shape, deep as an urn.

[II. 327–33] [56]

Keats's green altar is not located because it is everywhere. It is the
sacrificial eye of the poet, landscaped by the poet-priest of "Psyche."
The sign or garland of his mystery is the leafy fringe that dresses
the sacrificial animal, an unmated "youth" without offspring whose
"lowing" is a forlorn sound. Like the mortal nightingale, the heifer
stands for all toneless melodists in a state of desire. The little town
that is emptied, finally, repeats more poignantly the figures of the
urn as a barren family of man that appeared in the first three lines
of the poem. The little town is the foster child of acculturation, a
defense against mortality that protects only itself, and "shal[l] re-
main" uninhabited.

The movement toward discovery is ended at this point of "re-
turn" to the inspirational locale of all the spring odes. Not just the
last two lines but the whole fifth stanza is a "Stand," an *Aufschluss*
abstracted to remind us that unlike the hermeneutic eye, with its
evocative openness, the urn is merely rhetorical, a "Fair attitude,"
and, accordingly, barren of knowledge. Because it has a definite
"shape," its pictured sides wall out any awareness of Being, and
if we take it too seriously it teases us out of interpretation. How-
ever noisy and "overwrought" the urn's rhetoric may become,
it remains only a "silent form," silent because formal; to repeat,
the urn is at once a "heard melody" that leaves nothing to the
imagination and a burial of intuition that discloses nothing to the
imagination. As an achieved form, the urn proposes itself as an
ecphrastic model of "Beauty," and proves the rhetorical nature of
its claim by interrupting the poet's interpretation with its own
adage. "Beauty is truth, truth beauty" is a variant on the first line
of *Endymion*. We may suppose that for many reasons—its jingle,
its prematurely palpable design—that line had become an embar-
rassment for Keats to remember, especially because he had noticed,
in the "Ode to a Nightingale," that "Beauty cannot keep her lus-
trous eyes." The last lines of the "Ode on a Grecian Urn" seem to
me to be unequivocally ironic. The urn is the optimistic poet of
Endymion, the poet who did not know as yet that death is the

mother of beauty, and who therefore proclaimed: "A thing of beauty is a joy forever."[57]

The ambiguity of the last two lines is deliberate, and cannot be resolved with certainty; but not as much depends on establishing a preferred reading as is usually thought, since both readings are equally ironic. The urn can tell us that "that" is all we need to know because it is an urn of decidedly limited insight. But we can also tell the urn that "that" is all *it* needs to know; an urn, after all, could get along with less knowledge by far than we seem prepared to give it credit for. Because it is an emblem of death, being both a jar of ashes and the "pictured urn" that pours out its imagery in Gray's "Progress," and thus empties its significance into life, the urn is the most ignorant of places,[58] inferior in ignorance only to the "green altar" of human habitation because it is not made of leaves. Thus Keats answers the question of how poetry originates that is of such crucial concern in the ode tradition, clearly repeating what Wordsworth disclosed against his will in the Intimations Ode: Death is the origin. Death begets the significance of which in itself, like an unmated family, it is quite barren. If Keats had completed his "Ode to Maia," he might well have shown, in the genealogical moment of that ode, that Hermes was his mother's father.[59] The songs of spring are born of the need for interpretation; the song of autumn is the fruit of interpretation.

10

"To Autumn" and the Sound of Being

> For we begin to learn what man is only when we analyze the point
> when man steps into the ring of being for a "set-to" . . . with things
> . . . ; for only then does man project something new, only then does
> he poetize in a primordial fashion (*ursprünglich dichtet*).
> —George Joseph Seidel, *Heidegger and the Pre-Socratics*

Keats's autumn is an "intensifying and prolonging."[1] It is a "mur-
murous haunt" that prolongs itself into the winter of a scientific age.
The saving sound in all of Keats's odes is not, again, an articulate
sound, nor is it offered as the imagination's resistance, through
romance or myth, to the facts of life. The "false themes" of romance
in Collins are much *too* false, too remote from experience, to interest
the lyric Keats; he is as disenchanted as Dryden already had been
with the orphist suasions of the power-of-music tradition; he agrees
with the Shelley of the 1816 "Hymn" about the superstitions of
received religion, not least about the enthusiastic theism of Words-
worth's Intimations Ode; and, finally, he is far too skeptical a pupil
in the metaphysics of presence and absence to entertain the epitha-
lamic hope of the Coleridgean Symbol. What vocality then remains?
Perhaps what remains for Keats is the pre-syntagmatic Sound of the
Oriental mystics, which may have exerted an influence over the doc-
trine of the creative Logos in Christianity—"his voice is as the sound
of many waters" (Rev. 14)—and over the parallel doctrine of the *Nad
Bind Upanishad*: "First the murmuring sounds resembling those of
the waves of the ocean."[2]

It was not merely as craftsman and connoisseur that Tennyson
learned from sounds in Keats like "The murmurous haunt of flies on
summer eves." Such sounds inform the ear in revelatory moments
like the one that climaxes *In Memoriam*, a moment evoked as the
mysterious fusion of writing and voice:

> I read
> Of that glad year which once had been,
> In those fall'n leaves which kept their green,
> The noble letters of the dead.
>
> And strangely on the silence broke
> The silent-speaking words . . .
>
> [St. 95]

This distillation of the elegiac moment as a scriptive rememoration of voice, which I have been describing as the aural sensation "among the leaves" that pervades the written Keatsian ode, is isolated and evoked without preamble or postlude in "To Autumn." In the third stanza, the poem passes into the sound of Being. There, melodies are unheard (the "*songs* of Spring," for example, are unheard), but the unmelodic sounds of nature are intensely heard. They are the soft pipes that play on, piping to the spirit ditties of no tone.[3]

The sacred region of the "Ode to Psyche" is mostly silent, but not entirely so. The delicious moan of priests both ancient and modern is linked faintly to the "whisp'ring roof" of a natural shrine discovered in revery. Between that whisper and the conventionally modest "tuneless numbers" of the first line of this first ode, there is an interplay that will become a saving undertone in the later odes. Even in the artificial and silent shrine of the last stanza, there is a future sound: "branchèd thoughts, new grown with pleasant pain, / Instead of pines shall murmur in the wind." The population of this shrine, still too dimly imagined to give forth sound, is chosen nevertheless to voice a later concerted murmur: "zephyrs, streams, and birds, and bees." Here Keats has not yet connected sound with the branchings of thought, although "instead of pines" may hint at the need for a shedding, for a fall of leaves to be dispersed like Sibylline prophecies. In the Nightingale Ode, the place of the leaves has become the scene of writing, but in that scene Keats still acts as though his poem were, or could be, the voice of the bird itself, a chorus of chirrups followed by a sustained melancholy note, "forlorn."[4] In "Grecian Urn," Keats reduces lyric to a fringe of leaves that haunts about a shape as an interpretation. In "Autumn," finally, *there are no leaves*: the one conventional attribute of autumn that Keats does not evoke is the falling of the leaves. The omission seems rather extraordinary; perhaps the poem *is* the leaves.

II

Charles Brown's well-known description of Keats's morning in the garden has an interest apart from the setting it provides for the Nightingale Ode. We can read it as an interpretive act on the part of Brown's memory, as an insight about Keats's instinctive way of making voice survive in his very habits of composition:

In the spring of 1819 a nightingale had built her nest near my house. Keats felt a tranquil and continual joy in her song; and one morning he took his chair from the breakfast-table to the grass-plot under a plum-tree, where he sat for two or three hours. When he came into the house, I perceived he had some scraps of paper in his hand, and these he was quietly thrusting behind the books. On inquiry, I found these scraps, four or five in number, contained his poetic feeling on the song of our nightingale. The writing was not well legible; and it was difficult to arrange the stanzas on so many scraps.[5]

They are not cast to the winds, these scraps, even though Keats apparently wants to lose them; rather they are thrust "behind the books." In "To Autumn," which is the most profoundly literary poem Keats ever wrote, we find confirmed the intuition of Longinus, that voice comes to each of us, if it comes at all, not exclusively from nature, not as "the leaves to a tree," but in good part, rather, from the interleaving of our literary inheritance: "For many men are carried away by the spirit of others as if inspired, just as it is related of the Pythian priestess when she approaches the tripod, where there is a rift in the ground which (they say) inhales divine vapour. By heavenly power thus communicated she is impregnated and straightway delivers oracles in virtue of the afflatus. Similarly from the great natures of the men of old there are borne in upon the souls of those who emulate them (as from sacred caves) what we may describe as *effluences* . . ." (*On the Sublime* XIII, trans. W. Rhys Roberts).

I shall point only to a handful of effluences in "To Autumn," passing over the countless models for Keats's syntax in the "iam . . . iam" locutions that organize the landscape, especially the seasonal landscape, in Greek and Latin lyric. I do wish to mention a few classical texts, however.[6] While I am convinced by Geoffrey Hartman's linkage of Keats's love of Chatterton and his "English must be kept up" with the description of the Sunday walk that inspired "To

Autumn," I feel that it is equally important for Keats's "ideological" purpose that he derive his native strains from the topics of antiquity, using echoes of English poetry to mediate between his own experience and the almost primordial utterances his experience must displace.[7] The "mists" of the first line, for example, are certainly from Thomson (*Autumn*, 736-37), but by way of Thomson they are from Book 6 of Lucretius (476ff.): "Again, we see vaporous mists [*nebulas*] ascending from every river and from the land itself. These exudations, wafted up from the earth like breath, mantle the sky with their pall and build up high clouds [*nubis*] by gradual coalescence" (*On the Nature of the Universe*, p. 232). This text not only guides us forward from the mists of the first stanza to the barred clouds that rosily pall the day in the third, but it also gathers the "Huge cloudy symbols of a high romance" ("When I have Fears") together with the cloud, in the "Ode on Melancholy," that "hides the green hill in an April shroud."

Another text that links the course of Autumn with the course of Spring in Keats, this time with respect to "mellow fruitfulness" rather than mist, is Virgil's invocation to Bacchus in the *Georgics*, which presides equally over the o'erbrimming of Autumn and the warm south of the Nightingale Ode:

> Great Father *Bacchus*! to my song repair;
> For clust'ring grapes are thy peculiar care:
> For thee large bunches load the bending Vine,
> And the last blessings of the Year are thine.
> To thee his Joys the jolly Autumn owes
> When the fermenting Juice the Vat o'erflows.
> Come strip with me, my God, come drench all o're
> Thy Limbs in Must of Wine, and drink at ev'ry Pore.
>   [Dryden's *Georgics* II. 5-12] [8]

In Keats's autumn, to be sure, wine is a discarded topic, and his native cider-presses, granaries, and stubble-plains contribute, as Hartman implies, to an alternative English Georgic. Fittingly, then, the number of Keatsian words and sounds in the passage just quoted would suggest that Virgil's effluence had passed through Dryden.

Just so, Homer's effluence passed through Chapman, whom Keats had studied with a wild surmise two years earlier. In Chapman's Homer Keats would have found a permanent autumn, bitterly remembered in Juvenal's "Fruit such as grew in Phaiacia's eternal autumn" (*Sat.* V. 151). It may be remembered bitterly by Keats also; it should be read, in any case, in contrast with a northern poet's necessary encounter with bracing weather:

> Without the Hall, and close upon the Gate,
> A goodly Orchard ground was situate
>
> . . . .
>
> Sweet figs, Peares, Olives, and a number more
> Most usefull Plants did there produce their store,
> Whose fruits the hardest Winter could not kill,
> Nor hotest Summer weather. There was still
> Fruite in his proper season all the yeare.
> Sweet Zephyr breath'd upon them blasts that were
> Of varied tempers: these he made to beare
> Ripe fruits, these blossoms, Peare grew after Peare,
> Apple succeeded apple, Grape the Grape,
> Fig after fig came; Time made never rape
> Of any daintie there. A spritely vine
> Spred here his roote, whose fruite a hote sun-shine
> Made ripe betimes. Here grew another, greene.
> Here some were gathering, here some pressing seene.[9]

This utopia is a pagan oracle that Keats will have banished from "To Autumn" by the third stanza, just as Milton had banished golden ages and heathen deities alike from his Nativity Ode.

In transplanting his autumn from the luxury of southern models to an adequacy of its own, Keats must supply a compensation that is missing from all these texts because they have no need of it—the compensation of sound. From Ovid's *Tristia* (III. 10. 71-76), he could learn what happens to the sunny temperament when it is banished to the chill of the north without the solace of sound: "Not here the sweet grape lying hidden in the leafy shade nor the frothing must brimming the deep vats: Fruits are denied in this region . . . . One may see naked fields, leafless, treeless—a place, alas! no fortunate man should visit!" That the supplement of sound is crucially necessary for all seasons in England is something that John Clare, one of the closest early disciples of the lyric Keats, very well knew. Before Keats, the late autumnal scene in English rural verse seems too stern:

the bare pastures Pan resigns.
Late did the farmer's fork o'erspread
With recent soil the twice-mown mead,
Tainting the bloom which Autumn knows:
He whets the rusty coulter now,
He binds his oxen to the plough,
And wide his future harvest throws.

[Akenside, *Odes* I. 12. Aldine ed., p. 239]

There is much for Keats here: a sturdy homekeeping, the "bloom" of autumn with the (rather forced) superaddition of a sowing for the future; but there is only one sound, the whetting of a scythe.

III

"Thou hast thy music too." So Keats reassures Autumn, promising in effect to supply the music, and thus vestigially retaining the formal hymnic votum of the "Ode to Psyche." In that poem, his promise of a shrine reflects an architechtonic view of lyric. Now Keats offers no formal trap for presence, but his boast is still much the same: no one has yet vocalized Autumn, just as no one had yet enshrined Psyche.[10] Both, indeed, are the same numen, and "Autumn" is Keats's fresh attempt at once to give her a home and interpret her nature. Now, though, he refuses to distinguish between these two acts, between votum and mythos, and thus he merges into one unit the differentiated structure of the traditional hymn. Epic middle, petition and vow are now continuous in a single act of evocation.

Perhaps more than any other naturalization of archaic forms, this one has influenced the post-Romantic lyric, and we tend to think of it as hastening the demise of genres like the formal ode. But pure evocation, or more precisely description framed by apostrophe, is in fact a mask of the ode itself, and we cannot be sure that it is not even more archaic than the complete ritual form. In the literary history of Western Europe, however, it seems likely that the habit of writing this sort of poem arose from the wish to imitate the suggestive beauty of surviving Greek fragments. It is assumed, for instance, that Sappho's distich on the Evening Star is a fragment, but its resonance as it stands is what influences later poets: "Hesperus, bringing [back] all things which bright dawn scattered; you bring the sheep, you bring the goat, you bring the child back to the mother."[11]

We assume that either Sappho or oblivion has suppressed a petition here: "therefore bring back my love to me." But the fragmentary state of the poem is what makes it, as Longinus implies, a rift in the decorum of the literary past that opens the sublime to later poets. Before turning finally to "Autumn," I wish to consider two examples of "pure" evocation, early and late, in order to show that the complete structure of the ritual ode is latent in them, as it is, also, in "To Autumn."

First, here is Horace's "Hymn to Mercury," quoted entire:

O Mercury, grandson eloquent of Atlas, thou that with wise insight didst mould the savage ways of men just made, by giving speech and setting up the grace-bestowing wrestling-ground, thee will I sing, messenger of mighty Jove and of the gods, and father of the curving lyre; clever, too, to hide in sportive stealth whate'er thy fancy chose. Once in thy boyhood, as Apollo strove with threatening words to fright thee, should'st thou not return the kine thy craft had stolen, he laughed to find himself bereft of quiver too. 'Twas by *thy* guidance also that Priam, laden with rich gifts, when leaving Ilium, escaped the pround Atridae, the Thessalian watch-fires, and the camp that menaced Troy. 'Tis thou dost bring the pious souls to their abodes of bliss, marshalling the shadowy throng with golden wand, welcome alike to gods and those below. [Loeb ed., I. 10]

Here the structure of the cult hymn is perfectly represented, but without an end. Why write such a poem? Why not ask Hermes for something? The answer is plain: the poem declares simply in existing that a request has been granted in advance. Horace's hymn is not the promise but the fulfillment of service to the god; it is the hermeneutic biography of a donor. Hermes is eloquent (*facundus*), and the poet who is therefore himself eloquent now shows that "facundity" is closely allied, as odes in general are apt to conclude, with the fecundity of youth. The movement from genealogy to the god's influence in the world is at the same time a topical movement through the ages of man from birth to death, proving that Hermes presides, in discourse, over the transactions of every state. Unlike the naïve, univocal Apollo, Hermes is a master of irony and an escort over thresholds. Trickster of the sun, Hermes presides over dialectic: revelation in concealment, return in abduction, night in day. Founder of the wrestling-ground, Hermes is also the muse of invocation; at home among shadows, he can wrestle gods both below and

above from absence into presence. Hermes, in short, can do every-
thing an ode can do; he transports bodies and spirits in every walk
and stage of life. Omnipresent himself, a guiding force in epic and
satyr-play, he even stages the monopolistic reduction of rival genres
that characterizes an ode.

For Horace, Hermes simply *is* the hymn. Ode writers from Col-
lins to Keats would imagine an all-pervasive hermeneutics as a haunt-
ing that evades contour and confinement; in Keats's "Ode on a
Grecian Urn," this haunting is represented as the lyric act, and in
"To Autumn" he sets the act in motion. He proceeds, like Horace,
from the "facundity" of jolly Autumn to an end point where sounds
from above and below linger in a common space. In another poem of
pure evocation, "Signs of Winter," John Clare begins beyond this
end point, in a world where no one thing or quality can be singled
out for apostrophe:

> The cat runs races with her tail. The dog
> Leaps o'er the orchard hedge and knarls the grass.
> The swine run round and grunt and play with straw,
> Snatching out hasty mouthfuls from the stack.
> Sudden upon the elm-tree tops the crow
> Unceremonious visit pays and croaks,
> Then swops away. From mossy barn the owl
> Bobs hasty out—wheels round and, scared as soon,
> As hastily retires. The ducks grow wild
> And from the muddy pond fly up and wheel
> A circle round the village and soon tired
> Plunge in the pond again. The maids in haste
> Snatch from the orchard hedge the mizled clothes
> And laughing hurry in to keep them dry.

This Parmenidean poem is about running in circles and getting no-
where. Being is unceremonious; in the course of things all bounds are
overstepped at random, and in the ensuing vertigo there is mixed fear
and giddiness. Yet the formalism of lyric, especially the formalism of
"To Autumn," is still an aspect of Clare's theme. His very mockery
of purposefulness draws an expanding circle around the geniality, the
still numinous identity, of a season: if even Winter, conventionally a
frozen, inactive time, is all business and haste, so it must be, and
more so, with the full cycle of the seasons. Clare hurries his barnyard
toward closure to keep it, like the maids hurrying inside, from the

foggy seasonal dews—from the mortal consequences of an utterly dis-
illusioned teleology. "The cat chases her tail" may stand as Clare's
figure of prolepsis; she is like the Oruboros that anticipates and
swallows each and every "sign" of progress or rhetorical blossoming.

From here, from Clare's effort to reclothe a nakedness that is at
once psychologically exposed and merely blank, we can readily turn
back to the beginning of "To Autumn." Among other qualities,
Keats's poem bequeathed to Clare the hermeneutic concept of de-
scription as a *sign*-system or symptomology that points toward an
absent, ever-elusive condition, as leaves cover a voice. This is an
optimistic poetics, however wryly disillusioned Clare's view of cycles
may have become: the signified condition is still a contingent fact,
abidingly so, and may be triangulated by figures. The question
remains, however, the same that has recurred in the ode from Jonson
onward: Can the poem *as* system, as defense, in fact endure the full
exposure of the signified condition? In Clare's poem, not just the
maids rush inside, but even the wise owl recoils from something he
has seen, and returns to a shelter, unwilling to test experience any
further.

Clare's homely poem of homekeeping offers a challenge to teleo-
logical skeptics from the Pre-Socratics to the present: May we not
find ourselves to have made progress after all if we can endure the
crossing of thresholds into the *Unheimlich*? Keats's ode raises this
question also, it seems to me, but then sets it aside; from the outset,
like all odes, "To Autumn" banishes false gods from precincts that
it never means to leave behind, and therefore remains stationary. It
seems the most perfect of odes, the least "limited," simply because
its preestablished locale is almost boundless.[12]

IV

We are in a Mist . . . . We feel the "burden of the Mystery."
—To J. H. Reynolds, 3 May 1818

The opening lines of "To Autumn," "Season of mists and mellow
fruitfulness,/Close bosom-friend of the maturing sun," invite com-
parison with the beginning of Collins's "Ode to Evening":

the bright-haired sun
Sits in yon western tent, whose cloudy skirts

> With brede ethereal wove,
> O'erhang his wavy bed.

Keats has saved the appearance of Collins's primal scene by reducing our resistance to it. Behind Keats's veiling or misting over of the scene there is very little to be jealous of. The sun is now an older gentleman who seems in any case to be an immemorial companion of the matronly autumn. True, they have their mystification to practice on us, but nothing their conspiracy hatches could surprise or alarm us.

Their old dodges are played out in a scene that mists over just one disturbing feature, which is also inherited from Collins. In all the manuscripts, and in the 1820 text, the word "eves" is spelled, if not wrong, at least very unusually.[13] (Keats was a bad speller, of course; but what is curious is that neither his original publishers nor any of his editors have cared to normalize the spelling.) Keats means "eaves." He had only to look in "Frost at Midnight," at the passage (ll. 65–74) that colored this one, to find the word in the singular spelled "eave." But that passage too, which graces the whiteness of Coleridge's frost, exerts its pull over Keats's misspelling. The landscape played over by these genial cronies, Autumn and the sun, is a little like a human body, like the figures that will appear in the next stanza, except that strangely enough it seems very old. It has a thatch of hair that is frosted, silvered over in the eve, perhaps even the midnight, of its life. It is bent and mossed over like a crooked tree, laden with the fruit of experience. As the genealogical "of" in the first line suggests, Autumn is born from this whitened, filmy-eyed figuration that is faintly perceptible amid the happy plenty of the landscape.[14]

But there is more than one "eve." Keats's apples collapse this first reading and refer us back to the other, nearly opposite implication of "eve," which reshapes the whole scene more recognizably as a paradise not unlike that of Homer's Phaiacians, but even more, of course, like Milton's paradise. Now the conspiracy must appear in a different light, and Collins's bright-haired youth resurges into the text to bend our first mother with the fruit of her errancy. Dimly present in Keats's happy first stanza, then, are two related mythologies of nature, first of nature decayed and then of nature corrupted, that mark the meeting place an ode can never afford to witness: the meeting place of death and conception. However much his own

witness of sun and season has mellowed and even freely accommo-
dated the unease at the heart of Collins's vision, Keats's syntax still
places the mists closest to his "Season," veiling it with a decent
covering to ensure the undisturbed emergence of an atmosphere
that would be, otherwise, too dangerously charged with suggestion.
Having effected this careful smoothing of the way, Keats still takes
no risks; we will find that he has absolved Autumn from any taint
our perversity of reading may find in her by slipping other figures,
like phantom Helens, into her place. If there is a culprit in the first
stanza, it is *summer*.

If the bees were Keats, their hearts would ache, they would be
"too happy," and with so much gorging they would be "high-
sorrowful and cloy'd." The sun and the season conspire to drug us
if we are like bees, to keep us from knowing who we are and what
we are in for.[15] All conspire together in a single exhalation brought
on by surfeit: the fullness tightens until it bursts at the stanza
end and prepares such emptying as there may be in the finale of the
poem. The overload of the bees, who are belike too stuffed and
clammy to utter their cosmic sound, is blamed at the last moment
on summer, even though autumn was co-conspirator just a few lines
before. The prior season, the culprit, makes its appearance at the
eleventh line, the line added by Keats to the ten-line unit he had
used for all his odes since "Psyche." In this poem he places a couplet
before his eleventh line, a redundancy of "more,/And still more"
heaped on to motivate the overflow, oozing away, and leave-taking
of each eleventh line, respectively.[16] Loss comes from a meridian
(summer, and the noontide feel of the whole first stanza), from a
distension or overvaluation of temporality ("hours by hours"),
and, finally, from a chilly height. Loss follows overstuffing, over-
stretching, and ascent, respectively. By contrast, the vocal fane of
Autumn, inviolate and secretly trans-seasonal, will emerge as a
middle way that preserves without wasting the sound of Being. The
first stanza, meanwhile, will now sufficiently appear to be the echo
of a ritual exorcism;[17] it is a farewell to the "fruit of the Phaiacians'
eternal autumn," with all its delusive notions and sensations. From
here we move closer to what Vendler calls, again, the "experiential
beginning" of the poem in the closing stanza.

I am in some measure persuaded by M. R. Ridley's contention
that the middle stanza was an afterthought,[18] because unlike most

readers I view the first stanza not so much as a fluid stage in the
"growth" of the poem as an opposed stage that the rest of the poem
counteracts. Or say rather, not to seem too wilfully bent on in-
version, that from the outset there are disagreeable figures and
presences needing to be purged from an otherwise fluent conception.
Thus, if the poem has an antiphonal structure, and vacates a fructi-
ferous or "facund" heaviness for the finer clearing of sound, the
middle stanza, answering to "the . . . way that some pictures look
warm" in the September journal-letter (*Letters* II. 167), may have
been written to mute the antithesis that I have deliberately over-
stated. Keats must not stress the need for gain in loss because he is
on the verge of showing that the harvest of autumn is more serial
than cereal, more plainsong than fugue. The sounds of autumn must
not be shown to require the replacement of old scenes by new ones,
since they will be made to represent the indivisibility of being. The
finest illusion of Keats's poem depends on its synecdochic logic, on
our keeping the impression that a single season, and indeed only
one mood among many even within that season, may represent the
essence and wholeness of being. Hence the suspension bridge of the
second stanza will serve to channel without constraining temporality.
It is pictorial, yes, but I would suggest that it is a picture of *audition*,
not yet purged of a drowsiness inherited from the first stanza. The
balance is thus precise, like that of the gleaner, because, as Ridley
suggests, the next stanza is already written.

The personifications of Autumn in the second stanza have
always been justly praised as perfect concrete universals; no merely
iconic attributes of the nymph are left unabsorbed by the human
scene. She enters each laborer in turn like an inspiration; without
abstracting them beyond their level of typicality in pictura,[19] she
distracts them from the individuality of their tasks. They seem
poised between memory and potential, between the *cigale* and the
fourmi, torpid from first fruits yet caught at the same time in the
posture of persons to whom something is about to be revealed. The
winnowed winnower is "careless," like the surprised poet in the
first stanza of "Psyche," and thus poised for a rare experience,
perhaps an intensification, as the transferred epithet "winnowed"
would suggest, of our normal awareness of reciprocity in the cycle
of nature. The next figure, a reaper, is sound asleep, but his "hook,"
unlike Akenside's coulter, is consciously forbearing. The gleaner

steadily crosses a threshold (the brook, and the enjambment that has received much happy comment[20]) that does not mark an outgoing or seeking but a return with a full basket from outlands to the fold. The orchard-keeper, finally, master of the fruit that burdened the first stanza, is already "patient" enough to hear the next stanza. His (or her) keeping watch is a revery that almost suspends time in the very alertness of remarking time's passage.[21] Warden of temporality, the orchard-keeper is like Adam unparadised, or perhaps like the farmer Cain, deeply enough scarred by time to put the question of the next stanza himself, but then more wisely to dismiss the question and simply listen so intensely that the listening becomes an offering, a far more grateful offering than his disastrous first fruits had been:

> Where are the songs of spring? Aye, where are they?
>   Think not of them, thou hast thy music too—
> While barred clouds bloom the soft-dying day,
>   And touch the stubble-plains with rosy hue;
> Then in a wailful choir the small gnats mourn
>   Among the river sallows, borne aloft
>   Or sinking as the light wind lives or dies;
> And full-grown lambs loud bleat from hilly bourn;
>   Hedge-crickets sing; and now with treble soft
>   The red-breast whistles from a garden-croft;
>   And gathering swallows twitter in the skies.

"The poetry of earth is never dead," but prolongs the synecdoche of Autumn into all the neighboring seasons, gathered together here as a distillation of sound. When we consider the wide commonalty of this sound, we are perhaps justified in calling the third stanza a hymn within an ode. These are all rather shrill, high-frequency sounds of the sort that I have noted playing antiphonally through the resonance-seeking words of the West Wind Ode and the Intimations Ode. Here Keats offers an opposite contrast between signifying and signified sounds; there is a quiet baritone in the words of the stanza, especially in the rhyme words; hence the "treble" sounds are evoked largely without verbal mimesis, as if to remind us again, as in "Grecian Urn," of the richly suggestive distance between things in themselves and their interpretation. It is the reader who recalls and gathers the sounds, and supplements the poem responsively, reconciled through his own memory to a condition that alters not only Homer's Garden of Alcinous but also Milton's paradisal "Now came *still* evening on": "Silence accompanied," writes Milton, since all the animals lay asleep, "all but the wakeful nightingale."

In all his previous odes, we may now perceive, Keats had tried to reconstruct Milton's sacred fane. Now he evokes a world that is too full of wispy, intermixed boundaries, starting and ending with the streaked and dotted sky, to seem enclosed.[22] Coleridge's barred clouds unmisted (as Lucretius explained that they would be) but still softened at the edges only disbar the listener if he is still not ready to hear the swallows. Then comes the stubble, then the swarm of gnats, not only audible but visible in the slanting light; then the row of willows and the river; then the fleecy "bourn," pointedly unlike the sublime cataracts of the Intimations Ode or the "wild-ridged mountains" of "Psyche"; then the hedges, then the dried rows of plants in the garden-croft, and finally the loose gathering of swallows, crisscrossing the light like black stars.[23] Every ragged threshold merges with the others, and each threshold gives forth a sound; without shape or harmony, the landscape and its voices hum in unison, a vocal scrawl.

V

So musst Du sein, Dir kannst Du nicht entfliehen.
So sagten schon Sibyllen, so Propheten;
Und keine Zeit und keine Macht zerstückelt
Geprägte Form, die lebend sich entwickelt.
—Goethe, "Urworte. Orphisch"

"Really, without joking, chaste weather—Dian skies," Keats wrote of the Sunday walk he "composed upon" (*Letters* II. 167). For the reader of his poem, this comes to mean that once the incestuous burden of the first stanza—and of the history of the ode—is removed from the poem, not by the force of repression but by the gentle gravity of the lengthening scene, what remains is the suspension of desire.[24] Again, this is an ode without a petition. Here alone, if ever, the English ode stands present to the voice it seeks, having forsaken the quest for genial shape and become instead the deciduous leaves of the Keatsian "man of genius." The unenclosing of the sacred ground strips Being of its antic postures and sacred veils, and makes dialectic impertinent. Keats's trebled eleventh lines

register temporality known as such even more perfectly than the
haunting Alexandrines of earlier odes. Eschatological anxiety in such
a poem is swallowed with full-throated ease in the patient acceptance
of seriality, hours by hours. In his "death-stanza,"[25] Keats prolongs
the season with an eleventh-line reprieve; he gathers and swallows
the ambitious metaphor of the harvest, leaving only a sound behind,
perhaps to link the sound of Being with an even finer tone beyond
the barred clouds. Or perhaps not; if the chaste skies as we hear them
can suspend desire, then the presence of "no tone" will be suffi-
cient. Keats hoped in any case that someday this might be so. On the
day he described his Sunday walk to Reynolds, he also wrote that
he was "scarcely content to write the best verses for the fever they
leave behind. I want to compose without this fever. I hope one day
I shall" (*Letters* II. 209). "To Autumn," I believe, was an attempt
at feverless composition.

The landscape of the last stanza resembles a ciphered scrawl on
"some scraps of paper," "not well legible," where each stroke still
joins the rest. In a far more disturbed vision, Pound in the *Pisan
Cantos* imagined some birds perched on a wire to be the page of
music they sang:

> three solemn half notes
>   their white downy chests black-rimmed
> on the middle wire.

Frozen in his infernal ode, horribly cramped in the darkness he
had invoked upon himself, Pound could not unstiffen this elegant
figure of seriality. Keats before him could close his own dialogue
with Dante by writing a more fluent script: "And gathering swallows
twitter in the skies." Keats discovered a saving chastity in the same
vacancy of the will that had formed quite another setting, a sunless
and godless sky, for the pair of figures in Dante who most interested
him. Paolo and Francesca were damned for reading a page too
closely, and now, in *contrapasso*, they figure forth the same manu-
script that had danced and swum before their eyes:

> I understood, that to this torment sad
> The carnal sinners are condemned, in whom
> Reason by lust is swayed. As in large troops
> And multitudinous, when winter reigns,
> The starlings on their wings are borne abroad
> . . . .

As cranes,
Chanting their dolorous notes, traverse the sky,
Stretched out in long array; so I beheld
Spirits, who came loud wailing. . . .

[Cary's *Hell* V. 38–49]

In all three of these passages there is a growing chill of solitude at the approach of winter. In each of them, the visible is reduced to a morrice of ciphers on a blank surface. For Pound and Dante, writing itself is an unbroken cry of desire that etches the vacancy of undisciplined beginnings and ends. For Keats, the relaxation of the will into vacancy writes surcease to desire. This knowledge is the harvest of revery in all his odes. "The book and writer both,/Were love's purveyors," euphemizes Francesca in Cary's translation, "In its leaves that day/We read no more." After the first stanza of "To Autumn," there are no more conspiracies in Keats of the kind that corrupt the fancies of Pound and Francesca in the warm south of Italy. In the north, where all the leaves are fallen and all melodious plots superseded, Keats writes "To Autumn" until, that day at least, he needs to read no more.

VI

"To Autumn," which Garrod has persuaded us to call an ode,[26] is neither the last ode in English nor is it necessarily a culmination. I have concluded with "Autumn," though, and bolstered the sense of its ending by treating it syncretistically, both because I view it in its own right as a conclusive achievement, and also because it redisciplines by slackening the disruptive pressures within the ode that have attracted much of my attention. I have meant to suggest, both first and last, that the ode is an infernal genre struggling to escape the hell of the psyche. I have viewed this hell as a scene that depicts the vocative poet's barren exclusion from a dubious origin. The scene is witnessed typically from a threshold or open gate, which the ode struggles to close in order to "curtain close" the scene from every future view. Once safely enclosed, a circle that excludes its maker, the disturbing garden can then safely be proclaimed as an absent paradise and reduplicated as the formal enclosure that excludes it, the shrine or *locus sanctus* of the ode itself. The very force of this repression vents the poet's afflatus: his flight aloft, his transcendentalization of the scene, is therefore doomed quickly to exhaust itself and return the poem to what I have ventured to evoke as its most authentic site, a rural garden-croft at evening.

The will of the ode to escape the bondage of its hell I have characterized as either antinomian or Satanic; the conversion of the represented space into a garden that is vacated by god and daemon alike I have described as the reconciliation of the ode with its imagined origin in hymnody. Indeed, the hymn itself, even in remotest antiquity, reconciles humanity to its common place by representing that place as an "epic middle," as the signature or trace, *in iste tempore*, of a departed god. The final representation of the trace in the ode is a bivalent death stroke, on the one hand a wound or disruption into the seriality of consciousness, and on the other a loss of consciousness and merger with simultaneity in the ground of being. In this moment the ode is fused with its occasion through the figure of writing. By means of this figure the *occasio* becomes an *adventus*, or fortunate fall: falling silent of the oracles, coming forth of the graphic word. Sometimes we can still hear a noise prolonged into our own silence, as Keats did when he preserved the twitter of departing birds in the scratching of an imperfectly pared quill, sharpened in haste for the occasion.

Postscript
The Ode After "Autumn"

Since Keats, the ode takes two directions. First, in an age so scientific that hymnic archaism seems almost extinct even as a fossil, the ode ceases to subvert the hymn and quietly retrieves its identity as a religious poem. This is the direction of Hopkins, of Claudel's "*Weltoden*,"[1] and Eliot's Quartets. Since the era spanned by those writers was really more aggressively "scientific" than our own, perhaps it is best represented by the least recent of them, Hopkins, whose importance in any complete history of the ode I shall try to indicate simply by considering his greatest invocation,

>   Thou mastering me
> God!

Here the distance between I and Thou is ambiguously qualified, as so often in the history of English Pindarism, by enjambment. Hopkins's proleptic struggle to be heard recalls in equal measure the Hebrew prophets, the Holy Sonnets of Donne, and Shelley's "Ode to the West Wind," to which last, of all odes, Hopkins's "Wreck of the Deutschland" is closest. Having wedged a violent tmesis between God's familiarity ("Thou") and God's awesome name, Hopkins then bridges absence by consonance. God is master, master of me, mastering me: "me" and "man" almost appear in the mastery, revealing Christ the familiar in God the absent. "Thou man-steering me." This consonance finally points toward the moral of devotion; since "mastering" is linked more closely to "me" than to "Thou" or to "God," Hopkins shows that the effort to be subdued is largely inward. Grace is at hand, but man must wrestle with himself in order to receive it. Although the "Wreck" is a public poem addressed first to an orthodox deity, it is still not quite a hymn. Its invocation reveals a personal quest, an inner struggle that marks the poem, decidedly, for an ode. A violence this intense will always be found in the modern religious ode, which is most often written, rather curiously, perhaps, by Catholics. Still severely antinomian, the voices of Hopkins, Claudel, and Eliot are, we would have to say, Jansenist voices.

The secular ode of presentation after Keats settles firmly into the evening space he furnished, but chills its weather yet further. In England, after the Keatsian echoes in the autumnal verse of Hood and Clare, and after some apprentice work of Tennyson,[2] the ode survives the century as a virtuoso oddity, as in certain hyperformal poems of Swinburne, in the Pindaric science of Patmore, and the still more recondite formalism of Bridges. In this century, the ode gathers new strength, especially in America, as an ironically approached last resort of ambivalence. Once more, as in Jonson's Cary-Morison Ode, the hope of dialectical progress is at once invested in and subverted by a studied formal irregularity. Worthy of mention are Allen Tate's fine ode, with which we began this study, and several odes of Auden, the best known of which explains why it is an ode in its title: "Which Side Am I Supposed to Be On?" In our time, the less ironic Pindaric ode is rivaled, and perhaps—since the fifties—supplanted by the Keatsian ode. Pindarism has continued to flourish, mainly in America, in the many incantatory poems from Whitman through Hart Crane and beyond. Crane was quite serious when he wrote, "I feel myself fit to become a suitable *Pindar* for the dawn of the machine age."[3] On the other hand, it is the brief Keatsian canon that influences both the early and late odes of Wallace Stevens.

Stevens's first sardonically formal ode, "O Florida, Venereal Soil," is his Ode on Melancholy:

> Donna, donna, dark,
> Stooping in indigo gown
> And cloudy constellations,
> Conceal yourself or disclose
> Fewest things to the lover—
> A hand that bears a thick-leaved fruit,
> A pungent bloom against your shade.

"To One of Fictive Music" is his Ode to Psyche; and, of course, his poems are full of jars and birds, which are not, perhaps, until the later poems, very kindly handled: "We heard the blatter of grackles and murmured, invisible priest!" ("Man on a Dump"). But in the tone of "To Autumn," Stevens never forsakes "these evasions of the nightingale" ("Autumn Refrain"), and finds in them, increasingly in his middle period, a merger of landscape and sound that imitates Keats's figures for vocal writing:

> The leaves cry. It is not a cry of divine attention
> Nor the smoke-drift of puffed-out heroes, nor human cry.
> It is the cry of leaves that do not transcend themselves.
>
> In the absence of fantasia, without meaning more
> Than they are in the final finding of the air, in the thing
> Itself, until, at last, the cry concerns no one at all.

This is quite simply the essential subject of Keats's odes. But Stevens chills Keats's most desolate sounds yet a little more. In his late poems, the Keatsian "Here there is no light" becomes absolutely univocal, and clears a ground from which no further exclusion of death is possible. It is just here that something like vision returns. Stevens sees in this place the true and only return of consciousness to the community of being where the "hymn," perhaps now for the first time, is no longer an ode. Thinking now not so much of Keats as of Chapman, Shelley, and Novalis, Stevens evokes "Forms of the Rock in a Night-Hymn" during an experiment with elastic enjambment, where the Power of "Mont Blanc" is harnessed as the human by a figure at the gate:

> the mind,
>
> The starting point of the human and the end,
> That in which space itself is contained, the gate
> To the enclosure, day, the things illumined
>
> By day, night and that which night illumines,
> Night and its midnight-minting fragrances,
> Night's hymn of the rock, as in a vivid sleep.

If after all there is still a prophetic trace in these lines, still a figure that does not leave the ground but does make the ground more vivid

than it ordinarily is, as if by dream or prophecy, that may be be-
cause the unstructuring of the ode leaves behind, as it always has,
vivid recognitions of the unkown.

Notes

Introduction

1 "Narcissus as Narcissus," *On the Limits of Poetry: Selected Essays: 1928–48* (New York: Swallow Press, 1948), p. 254.

2 "Autobiography," *Selected Prose Poems, Essays, and Letters,* trans. Bradford Booth (Baltimore: Johns Hopkins University Press, 1956), p. 34.

3 Kathleen Coburn, ed., *Inquiring Spirit: A Coleridge Reader* (New York: Minerva Press, 1968), p. 104.

4 John Block Friedman, *Orpheus in the Middle Ages* (Cambridge, Mass.: Harvard University Press, 1970), p. 88.

5 Thus Friedman reads the *Mitologiae* in *Orpheus in the Middle Ages,* p. 101.

6 *Poetry and the Physical Voice* (London: Routledge, 1962), p. 34.

7 With Virgil's treatment of the myth compare Jacques Derrida, *Of Grammatology,* trans. Gayatri C. Spivak (Baltimore: Johns Hopkins University Press, 1976), p. 69.

8 There are many important books and articles on this subject, and I shall refer to most of them eventually. Here, in chronological order, I list only the standard works that are historical in emphasis: Robert Shafer, *The English Ode to 1660: An Essay in Literary History* (Princeton: Princeton University Press, 1918); George N. Shuster, *The English Ode from Milton to Keats* (New York: Columbia University Press, 1940); Norman Maclean, "From Action to Image: Theories of the Lyric in the Eighteenth Century," in *Critics and Criticism Ancient and Modern,* ed. R. S. Crane (Chicago: University of Chicago Press, 1952); Gilbert Highet, *The Classical Tradition: Greek and Roman Influences on Western Literature* (New York: Oxford University Press, 1957), pp. 219–54; Carol Maddison, *Apollo and the Nine* (Baltimore: Johns Hopkins University Press, 1960); Kurt Schlüter, *Die Englische Ode* (Bonn: H. Bouvier u. Co. Verlag, 1964). Convenient

recent handbooks are: John Heath-Stubbs, *The Ode* (London: Oxford University Press, 1969); and J. D. Jump, *The Ode* (London: Methuen, 1974). In persuading myself that I need not reconstruct the efforts of these authors, I have taken heart from the remark of A.S.P. Woodhouse that "the history of the English Pindaric is familiar enough" ("The Poetry of Collins Reconsidered," in *From Sensibility to Romanticism*, ed. F. W. Hilles and Harold Bloom [London: Oxford University Press, 1965], p. 118).

9   Their definitions may be found in Shafer, *The English Ode*, p. 2. See also the definition offered by Shuster, *The English Ode*, p. 239.

10 For convenient summaries of the vast literature on this subject, see René Wellek and Austin Warren, *Theory of Literature*, rev. ed. (New York: Harper, 1956), pp. 226–37; and E. D. Hirsch, Jr., *Validity in Interpretation* (New Haven: Yale University Press, 1967), p. 107.

11 His schema is discussed from the present viewpoint in Maddison, *Apollo and the Nine*, p. 111; and Phillip Rollinson, "Milton's Nativity Poem and the Decorum of Genre," *MiltonS* 7 (1975): 165–88. See also Bernard Weinberg, "Scaliger versus Aristotle on Poetics," *MP* 39 (1942): 337–60.

12 "The Sublime Poem: Pictures and Powers," *YR* 58 (1968–69): 201.

13 "Apostrophe," *Diacritics* 7 (Winter 1977): 63.

14 The distinction between ode and hymn is rarely observed even in careful criticism. See, for example, Earl Wasserman's conflation of the terms in his painstaking reading of Shelley's "Hymn to Intellectual Beauty" (which I am about to discuss) in *Shelley: A Critical Reading* (Baltimore: Johns Hopkins University Press, 1971), p. 239. In support of my view of the hymn, see especially Northrop Frye, *The Anatomy of Criticism* (New York: Atheneum, 1962), p. 294. See also Schlüter, *Die Englische Ode*, p. 13n., for another clarification of the distinction I am drawing. I do not pretend that the distinction has not continually been abused (according to Shuster, *The English Ode*, p. 180, Addison's "Sacred Firmament on High" was variously called an "ode," "hymn," "psalm," and "sacred ode"), but I would still insist that the major hymnodists in particular are sensitive to the difference. See Isaac Watts, "Asking Leave to Sing," in Alexander Chalmers, *The Works of the English Poets from Chaucer to Cowper*, 23 vols. (London, 1810), 13:21 (hereafter cited by volume and page as Chalmers).

15 Cecil A. Moore, ed., *English Poets of the Eighteenth Century* (New York: Henry Holt and Co., 1935), p. 555.

16 Constantine A. Trypanis, ed., *The Penguin Book of Greek Verse* (Harmondsworth: Penguin Books, 1971), p. 283.

17 "Hölderlin's 'Nature and Art or Saturn and Jupiter,'" in *European Literary Theory and Practice*, ed. Vernon W. Gras (New York: Delta, 1973), pp. 175–76. (Staiger's words are "Oden" and "Hymnen." See the original of Gras's translation in *Meisterwerke Deutscher Sprache* [Zürich: Atlantis-Verlag, 1948], p. 34.)

18 See Barbara H. Smith, *Poetic Closure: A Study of How Poems End* (Chicago: University of Chicago Press, 1968), pp. 14–20, 122.

19 For a discussion of "the oral grounding of rhetoric," see Walter J. Ong, S.J., *The Presence of the Word* (New Haven: Yale University Press, 1967), p. 210.

20 Booth, *Selected Prose Poems,* p. 19.

21 *A Grammar of Motives* (New York: Prentice-Hall, 1945), p. 503.

22 Congreve is especially sensitive to this oddity: "Descend, celestial muse: thy son inspire/Of thee to sing" ("The Birth of the Muse," Chalmers, 10:272); "Thy aid invoking while thy power we praise" ("A Hymn to Harmony for St. Cecilia, 1701," ibid., 281). Note the plural in Congreve's "Hymn." See also the first invocation of Akenside's *The Pleasures of Imagination.*

23 The distinction is concisely apparent in Book Two of William Thompson's *Sickness,* which begins with an invocation to the genius of Spenser, and then proceeds to an "Apostrophe" (so named in the Argument) to the Duchess of Somerset (Chalmers, 15:38).

24 The still standard account of devotional predication is Eduard Norden, *Agnostos Theos: Untersuchungen zur Formengeschichte religiöser Rede* (Berlin: Teubner, 1913).

25 *A Handlist of Rhetorical Terms* (Berkeley: University of California Press, 1968), p. 60.

26 "Inhibitions, Symptoms and Anxiety," *The Standard Edition of the Complete Psychological Works of Sigmund Freud,* 24 vols., trans. James Strachey et al. (London: Hogarth Press, 1953–74), 20:120.

27 "The Experiential Beginnings of Keats's Odes," *SiR* 12 (1973): 591–606.

28 See N. K. Chadwick, *Poetry and Prophecy* (Cambridge: Cambridge University Press, 1942), p. 7. Chadwick calls inspiration by the dead "the most universal aspect of manticism" (p. 55). Civilized poetry tries to repress this origin, but throwbacks may be found. Samuel Boyse, who is in general curiously uninhibited on this point, invokes a dead woman for inspiration in a poem called "Friendship" (Chalmers, 14:532). The more widespread practice of invoking dead poets or the heroic dead is less primitive by far, since it has already constellated the dead and stripped them of their daemonic immanence.

29 Smith remarks *(Poetic Closure,* p. 141) that "a principle of closure is available only when the dialectic process can be represented as internally resolved." She notes further (p. 142) that the Romantic Period witnessed the rise of a kind of lyric in which the dialectic is deliberately left unresolved.

Chapter 1

1 Geoffrey Hartman, *Beyond Formalism: Literary Essays 1958-1970* (New Haven: Yale University Press, 1970), p. 56.

2 Jonson writes in *Timber:* "The Study of [Poesie] (if wee will trust *Aristotle)* offers to mankinde a certain Pattern of living well, and happily;

disposing us to all Civil Offices of Society" (C. H. Herford, Percy and Evelyn Simpson, eds., *Ben Jonson,* 9 vols. [Oxford: Clarendon Press, 1925–52], 8:597; hereafter cited by volume and page as Herford). As Earl Miner remarks, the "many aspects of the Cavalier conception of *vir bonus* and of *vita bona* seem all to come together in Jonson's regular pindaric ode" *The Cavalier Mode from Jonson to Cotton* [Princeton: Princeton Princeton University Press, 1971], pp. 70–71). The fullest reading of the Cary-Morison Ode is by Mary I. Oates, "Jonson's 'Ode Pindarick' and the Doctrine of Imitation," *PLL* 11 (1975): 126–48. Though I draw very different conclusions from hers, sometimes from the same starting points, I am still much indebted to this essay. Oates insists on the unity of the poem in a way that recalls Maddison's having called it "Palladian" (*Apollo and the Nine,* p. 296).

3 "Jonson and the Loathed Stage," in *A Celebration of Ben Jonson,* ed. William Blissett et al. (Toronto: University of Toronto Press, 1973), pp. 30–31. Oates ("Jonson's 'Ode Pindarick,'" p. 128) connects the poem with the second "Ode to himselfe" and to the failure of *The New Inne,* adding (pp. 132–33) that "Produce thy masse of miseries on the Stage" in the Cary-Morison Ode (55) may apostrophize the poet himself. If so, we may imagine Jonson approaching this poem as a compensatory private theatre or interior dialogue.

4 Here I will disagree strongly with Wesley Trimpi, who charges the Desmond and Cary-Morison odes with "attempted grandiloquence" (*Ben Jonson's Poems: A Study of the Plain Style* [Stanford: Stanford University Press, 1962], p. 102). An account that credits Jonson with more intelligence in his choice of forms may be found in Ralph S. Walker, "Ben Jonson's Lyric Poetry," in *Seventeenth Century English Poetry: Modern Essays in Criticism* (New York: Oxford Galaxy, 1962), p. 182.

5 The best study of the circle in Jonson is Thomas M. Greene, "Ben Jonson and the Centered Self," *SEL* 10 (1970): 325–48. "Jonson," writes Greene, "attempts . . . to complete the broken circle, or expose the ugliness of its incompletion" (p. 315). See also Anthony Mortimer, "The Feigned Commonwealth in the Poetry of Ben Jonson," *SEL* 13 (1973): 69–80.

6 The first post-antique writer to use Pindaric triads, Benedetto Lampridio (d. 1540), makes the structure parallel his turns of thought. Ronsard follows Pindar, however, in dividing his thoughts without regard to the division of his triads. Jonson may have derived his three terms from "volta," "rivolta," and "stanza" in Minturno's *L'Arte Poetica.* (Cp. Maddison, *Apollo and the Nine,* pp. 105, 149.) For surveys of Pindar's early reputation and currency in England, see Shafer, *The English Ode,* pp. 57–77; and Harvey Goldstein, "*Anglorum Pindarus:* Model and Milieu," *CL* 17 (1965): 299–310.

7 *Natural History,* Loeb ed., 9 vols., ed. H. Rackham (Cambridge: Harvard University Press, 1942), 2:529.

8 I follow Oates ("Jonson's 'Ode Pindarick,'" p. 136) in taking "cleare" as a verb, but the adjectival sense of "famous" (*clarus*) is also possible. See

Susanne Woods, "Ben Jonson's Cary-Morison Ode: Some Observations on Form and Structure," *SEL* 18 (1978): 66.

9 This swelling out of the circle is discussed by Hugh Maclean, "'A More Secret Cause': The Wit of Jonson's Poetry," in Blissett, ed., *A Celebration,* p. 157.

10 Herford remarks of this ode, "At the very beginning the bold mythic manner of Pindar beguiles him into bathos" (2:406). Jonson's bathos is not beguiled, I think, but beguiling.

11 This calculated spilling over is at variance with Trimpi's assertion *(Ben Jonson's Poems,* p. 199) that Jonson's windiness is caused by his need to fill out the formal conditions of the ode. As Herford rightly says (2:394), the appearance of the ode all over Europe was a leading symptom of a renewed "exacting classicism." Odes did not become havens for bombast for another fifty years.

12 William V. Spanos explains Jonson's play with indecorum as a juxtaposition of vulgar and classical *topoi* ("The Real Toad in the Jonsonian Garden: Resonance in the Nondramatic Poetry," *JEGP* 68 [1969]: 6). Arthur F. Marotti describes the Infant figure as an "anti-masque" from which formality can emerge ("All About Jonson's Poetry," *ELH* 39 [1972]: 226n.). On the fitness of the opening, see also Joseph H. Summers, "Donne and Jonson," in *Ben Jonson and the Cavalier Poets,* ed. Hugh Maclean (New York: Norton, 1974), p. 463.

13 Miner remarks (*Cavalier Mode,* p. 72) that there is a connection between Jonson's "All offices" and Cicero's *De Officiis,* but this sense of office also appears, as John E. Hankin has shown, in the passage from the ninety-third letter of Seneca's *Epistolae Morales,* which Jonson paraphrases repeatedly in stanzas 3-7 of this ode. See "Jonson's 'Ode on Morison' and Seneca's *Epistolae Morales,*" *MLN* 51 (1936): 518-20.

14 The Renaissance inherited the classical distinction between three sorts of epideictic topic: "goods of nature," "goods of fortune," and "goods of character." Plainly the third topic only is suited for moral poetry, and Jonson finds himself wondering whether it can definitely be distinguished from the first two. Concerning this matter, see O. B. Hardison, Jr., *The Enduring Monument: A Study of the Idea of Praise in Renaissance Literary Theory and Practice* (1962, reprint ed., Westport, Conn.: Greenwood Press, 1973), p. 30ff. Hardison calls our attention (pp. 142-43) to the distinction between fortune and virtue in the "Elegy on the Death of Lady Jane Pawlet": "serve not Formes, good Fame,/Sound thou her Vertues" (21-22).

15 I am indebted here and later to John Hollander's discussion of this and the other famous enjambment of the ode in *Vision and Resonance* (New York: Oxford University Press, 1975), pp. 141-42.

16 For the downward equivalent of this leap, see Geoffrey Hartman on the "'descendental' constellation" of stars that appear on earth as flowers, in *The Fate of Reading and Other Essays* (Chicago: University of Chicago Press, 1975), pp. 154-55.

17 An asterism is a printer's mark comprised of three stars signaling an important passage in a text. Hence, although the main figures exclude Jonson by expressing twinship, he does join the constellation in this word.

18 *The Odes of Pindar,* trans. C. M. Bowra (Harmondsworth: Penguin Books, 1969), p. 39. The gnomic style of both Pindar and Isaiah is aptly described in Cowley's preface to his Pindaric version of Isa. 34: "the old fashion of writing was like disputing in Enthymemes, where half is left out to be supplied by the hearer" (A. B. Grosart, ed., *The Complete Works in Verse and Prose of Abraham Cowley,* 2 vols. [Edinburgh: Edinburgh University Press, 1881], 2:29).

19 It could be remarked, for instance, that each Turn-Counterturn unit has as many lines as Morison's perfect life had years.

20 Oates has noted the close relation between this ode and Jonson's epitaph "on my First Sonne," written in the same year. In the context of my reading of the Cary-Morison Ode, the epitaph's great conclusion gains in meaning: "For why/Will man lament the State he should envie?/To have so soone scap'd worlds, and fleshes rage,/And, if no other miseries, yet age?/ Rest in soft peace, and, ask'd, say here doth lye/BEN IONSON his best piece of *poetrie*" (Herford, 8:41).

21 We may dismiss all of it with Prior's amusing "Simile," in which he compares a squirrel on a treadmill that keeps ringing a bell to "those merry blades,/That frisk it under Pindus' shades./In noble songs and lofty odes,/They tread on stars, and talk with gods" (H. B. Wright and M. K. Spears, eds., *The Literary Works of Matthew Prior,* 2 vols. [Oxford: Clarendon Press, 1971], 1:245).

22 Maddison, *Apollo and the Nine,* p. 296, points out the indebtedness of these strophes to the canzone.

23 The narration and plot of Eric Ambler's *Judgment on Deltchev* (1951) offers a striking parallel with the Desmond Ode. The narrator is an English dramatist who has agreed to play political reporter and send home bulletins about a postwar trial in the Balkans. He is hampered by censorship and considers sending his reports in code, but he also realizes that even if there were no censor he still could not sort out the facts. The prisoner Deltchev is assumed to be a "political prisoner"; both his apparently sound politics and his present misfortune arouse sympathy. But Deltchev, like Desmond, is walled off from view, and the narrator must wrestle with his own growing suspicion that Deltchev is not unjustly accused.

24 My allusions are, of course, to Freud, especially to "The Antithetical Meaning of Primal Words" *(Standard Edition,* 11:155–61) and to his explanation of "the compulsion to repeat" in *Beyond the Pleasure Principle (Standard Edition,* 18:56–59).

25 Scaliger's *Poemata Sacra* include two Pindarics called *excessus,* for which he apologizes by saying "there need be no moderation in holy things." (Cp. Maddison, *Apollo and the Nine,* p. 111.)

26 *The Works of Michael Drayton,* 5 vols., ed. J. W. Hebel, K. Tillotson, and B. H. Newdigate (Oxford: Shakespeare Head Press, 1961), 5:145 (hereafter

cited by volume and page as *Works*). "To the Reader," Drayton's preface to his *Odes,* explains his presuppositions: "an Ode is known to have been properly a Song modulated to the ancient harp: and neither too short-breathed, as hastening to the end; nor composed of longest verses, as unfit for the sudden turns and lofty tricks with which APOLLO used to manage it." There is perhaps no inconsistency in Drayton's association of brevity with grandiloquence. Rosalie Colie quotes Robortello to the effect that "the epideictic epigram is the miniature of an ode" *(The Resources of Kind: Genre-Theory in the Renaissance* [Berkeley: University of California Press, 1973], p. 68).

27 Drayton's implied dispraise of James has been noted by Richard F. Hardin, *Michael Drayton and the Passing of Elizabethan England* (Lawrence: University Press of Kansas, 1973), pp. 6-9.

28 Jonson praised (perhaps deliberately overpraised) the Drayton of *The Battaile of Agincourt* for his resemblance not only to Homer but to Tyrtaeus (Herford, 8:398).

29 Drayton probably had more firsthand knowledge of harp playing than Thomas Gray. His 1619 "Ode to . . . Sir Henry Goodere" expresses the hope that his ode will "become JOHN HEWES his Lyre,/Which oft at Powlsworth by the fire,/Hath made us gravely merry." Many of his works are dedicated to his friends the "Cambro-Britans," a circle of Welch antiquaries who knew such harpers as Thomas Pritchard of Glamorganshire (d. 1597). See *Works* 5:146, 230. Schlüter correctly points out *Die Englische Ode,* p. 29) that poets who follow the usage of Ronsard and the Humanists take the term "ode" to mean the imitation of any lyric form. But the antiquarian Drayton seems already to have a specific form of literal "lyric" in mind.

30 *Metamorphoses,* trans. Mary M. Innes (Harmondsworth: Penguin Books, 1976), pp. 123-24.

31 See his *Pandora: The Musique of the Beauty of his Mistress Diana* (1584). In his last two stanzas Drayton is probably answering Puttenham *(Arte of Englishe Poesie,* 1589), who makes scathing remarks about the barbaric versification of both Sootherne and Skelton.

32 See Tillotson in *Works* 5:148. D.S.J. Parsons notes that the odes added to the 1619 edition are all in the anacreontic or lighter Horatian vein ("The Odes of Drayton and Jonson," *QQ* 75 [1968]: 675-84). By 1619, Drayton appears to have given up the "lyre" altogether, and perhaps his note on Skelton is meant to distance his own earlier work from the present.

33 The word "absolute" could mean simply that the mid-Atlantic is too deep to be much affected by the wind; but I persist in finding these lines as they stand compressed to be rather mysterious.

34 Michael West, "Drayton's 'To the Virginian Voyage': From Heroic Pastoral to Mock-Heroic," *RenQ* 24 (1971): 501, has noted the antinomy of "pastoralism and heroism" in the poem. The closing address to Hakluyt (who owned stock in the Virginia Company) hopes for new *Voyages* as a result of the present venture, and also acknowledges the source of which much of

this poem is a paraphrase. See J. Q. Adams, *MLN* 33 (1918): 405–08, and Gerhard Friedrich, "The Genesis of Michael Drayton's Ode to the Virginian Voyage," *MLN* 72 (1957): 401–06.

Chapter 2

1 My text of the Nativity Ode is that of *The Poems of John Milton,* ed. John Carey and Alastair Fowler (London: Longmans, 1968).

2 On the significance of Milton's tense changes, see Lowry Nelson, Jr., "Góngora and Milton: Toward a Definition of the Baroque," *CL* 6 (1954): 57–58; and Frank S. Kastor, "Miltonic Narration: 'Christ's Nativity,'" *Anglia* 86 (1968): 347–49.

3 See Maynard Mack's introduction to his selected edition of *Milton* (New York: Prentice-Hall, 1950), pp. 5–6.

4 Again I would question the usual assumption that these terms are interchangeable. Phillip Rollinson ("Milton's Nativity Poem") has all the pertinent information at his disposal, but his argument goes steadily wrong, I think, owing to his having conflated these terms. Shuster is another who is not wanting in lore, yet he can say *(The English Ode,* p. 85) that after the Miltonic "hymns" that appear in Vaughan's *Silex Scintillans,* "Henceforth no *clear* line can be drawn between the religious ode . . . and the elaborate hymn." No clear line, perhaps, but the poet's orientation can always suggest where one might be drawn. See the remarks of H. Neville Davies on the conflict of "hymn" and "ode" in Maren-Sofie Røstvig, ed., *Fair Forms: Essays in English Literature from Spenser to Jane Austen* (Totowa, N.J.: Rowman and Littlefield, 1975), p. 111.

5 "On Literature and the Bible," *Centrum* 2 (1974): 38.

6 The Isaiah allusion is offset by another, to Rev. 1:22, "I am the bright and morning star," which was quoted in the Advent Sunday lesson that would have fallen on December 27 in 1629. See Lawrence W. Kinsley, "Mythic Dialectic in the Nativity Ode," *MiltonS* 4 (1972): 169, 174.

7 See, most notably, the commentary of Cleanth Brooks and John E. Hardy, *Poems of Mr. John Milton: The 1645 Edition with Essays in Analysis* (New York: Harcourt, 1951), p. 98; and John Carey, *Milton* (New York: Arco, 1970), p. 32.

8 Woodhouse and Douglas Bush, eds., *A Variorum Commentary on the Poems of John Milton: Volume Two: The Minor Poems* (New York: Columbia University Press, 1972), pp. 76–77. This citation has the tacit approval of Bush, even though he has written an article called "Ironic and Ambiguous Allusion in *Paradise Lost,*" *JEGP* 60 (1961): 631–40.

9 Hartman, *Beyond Formalism,* p. 125.

10 Raphael would seem to imply otherwise in *PL* 5. 575–76, but his meaning is, fittingly enough, obscure. The Logos is the higher language, to be sure, but I would suggest that it is pre-syntactic and not in any recognizable sense "articulate." The Word is "unexpressive" because it is not spoken in

sentences. I shall have occasion to return to this assertion repeatedly in this book, since I think the theme persists until Keats's "unheard" melodies, and beyond.

11 I quote from Merritt Y. Hughes, ed., *John Milton: Complete Poems and Major Prose* (New York: Odyssey Press, 1957), p. 670 (hereafter cited by page as Hughes).

12 Milton would have acknowledged Pindar as a forerunner in his handling of subject matter, however. See Reuben A. Brower, "The Theban Eagle in English Plumage," *CP* 43 (1948): 25–26, on the conflict between "harmonious noise" and "discordant noise" in *Pythian* I. Milton's divided allegiance between hymn and ode is echoed by countless later odists, e.g., Christopher Pitt (1727): "it would look indecent in one of my profession [a minister], not to spend as much time on the Psalms of David, as the hymns of Callimachus" (Chalmers, 12:373). See also Isaac Watts's Preface to his *Horae Lyricae*, which echoes Milton and anticipates Bishop Lowth in praising the structure, prosody, and invention of the Hebrew psalms.

13 Don Cameron Allen, "Milton and the Descent to Light," *JEGP* 60 (1961): 614–30, comments subtly on the relation between the soul's discovery of light in darkness and the Fortunate Fall. See *PL* 2. 15–18, for a demonic version of these paradoxes. "Satan and his squires," says Allen, "know this course well enough to pervert it" (p. 622). See also S. Viswanathan, "'In Sage and Solemn Tunes': Variants of Orphicism in Milton's Early Poetry," *NM* 76 (1975): 462.

14 See Donald Friedman, "Harmony and the Poet's Voice in Some of Milton's Early Poems," *MLQ* 30 (1969): 530.

15 See the *Variorum Commentary*, p. 84, for a summary of the difficulties that attach to this word.

16 For excellent treatments of this prolepsis, see ibid., pp. 66–67, and Rosamund Tuve, *Images and Themes in Five Poems by Milton* (Cambridge: Harvard University Press, 1967), p. 45.

17 See Carey and Fowler, *Poems,* p. 98. Rivalry, as between singers in pastoral, is itself a pleasant convention of classical culture from which the newly dedicated Milton must wean himself. Another important model for this ode is Virgil's fourth Eclogue, which not only initiates a resolve to sing *paulo maiora,* but contains a confession of rivalry with earlier singers: "me carminibus vincat nec Thracius Orpheus,/nec Linus" (55–56).

18 In the long run these factors must surely qualify the exuberance of those who speak of Milton's "complete identification" with his "high calling." See, e.g., J. H. Hanford, "Milton's Mosaic Inspiration," *UTQ* 8 (1938–39): 147; E.M.W. Tillyard, *Milton* (1930; reprint ed., London: Chatto & Windus, 1956), p. 42; and B. Rajan, "In Order Serviceable: Milton's 'On the Morning of Christ's Nativity,'" *MLR* 63 (1968): 13–22. J. B. Broadbent's phrase "anxiously arrogant art" is wholly apt, though he means something quite different by it than I would ("The Nativity Ode," in Frank Kermode, ed., *The Living Milton: Essays by Various Hands* [London: Routledge, 1960],

p. 30). My view of Milton's "prevention" is anticipated in Paul Sherwin, *Precious Bane: Collins and the Miltonic Legacy* (Austin: University of Texas Press, 1977), p. 56.

19 Prudentius's *Apotheosis* (*Prudentius*, Loeb. ed., 2 vols., trans. H. J. Thomson [Cambridge, Mass.: Harvard University Press, 1949], 1: 166) presents the Child in the sky, "outshining the train of ancient stars," owing to which "the astrologer . . . felt his blood curdle." It is here that Prudentius calls Christ "Luciferam . . . novam."

20 Tuve, with whose important and weighty essay I steadily disagree, thinks that Urania is still being addressed in the fourth stanza (*Images and Themes*, p. 43); but I cannot see why Urania would need Isaiah's coal, or how it sorts with her dignity to "run" at the behest of a mortal. See Brooks and Hardy, *Poems*, p. 95. On the suspect status of the Magi, see Jon S. Lawry, *The Shadow of Heaven: Matter and Stance in Milton's Poetry* (Ithaca: Cornell University Press, 1968), p. 32.

21 See A. S. P. Woodhouse, "Notes on Milton's Early Development," *UTQ* 13 (1943–44): 76; and Rajan, "Order Serviceable," p. 17.

22 Prudentius shows how very devilish Milton could find Apollo to be. "Fuge, callide serpens," says Christ in the act of banishing him, after which, adds Prudentius, "torquetur Apollo/nomine percussus Christi" (I: 150).

23 Don Cameron Allen has shown that in the celestial context the maze can be reduced to order (*The Harmonious Vision: Studies in Milton's Poetry* [Baltimore: Johns Hopkins University Press, 1970], p. 28). See also G. Wilson Knight, *The Burning Oracle* (London: Oxford University Press, 1939), p. 59ff.

24 T. K. Meier, who inverts the ideology of Milton's poem far less cautiously than I do, stresses its wintry "austerity" ("Milton's 'Nativity Ode': Sectarian Discord," *MLR* 65 [1970]: 7–8).

25 See Mack, *Milton*, p. 5.

26 Louis L. Martz finds this tone pervading the whole poem, in an essay that stresses the lightheartedness of the overall format of the 1645 *Poems*, and suggests that Milton viewed his ode as a modest but successful juvenile piece. Martz's ironic reading of the "Elegia Sexta," which earlier scholars had called a sign of "conversion," is most persuasive. See "The Rising Poet, 1645," in *The Lyric and Dramatic Milton*, ed. Joseph H. Summers (New York: Columbia University Press, 1965), pp. 3–34.

27 See Nelson, "Góngora and Milton," p. 59.

28 The earliest notice of the play on "stable" that I have seen is by David Daiches in his *Milton* (London: Hutchinson University Library, 1957), p. 48.

29 Northrop Frye remarks that the object of a poet in a "paean or psalm is not so much to be identified *with* his god as to be identified *as* his worshipper" (*Anatomy of Criticism*, p. 295). For an extremely elegant view of Milton's ending that conflicts with my own, see Laurence Stapleton, "Milton and the New Music," *UTQ* 23 (1953–54): 226. John Carey, a hostile reader of the ode in the school of Broadbent, remarks that the ending "celebrates not

love but restraint" (*Milton*, p. 31). Mother M. C. Pecheux has pointed out that Milton's title is not "about" the Son but about the morning itself ("The Image of the Sun in Milton's Nativity Ode," *HLQ* 38 [1973-74]: 315).

Chapter 3

1 The attempt has been made, however, by Richard D. Jordan in "The Movement of the 'Nativity Ode,'" *SAB* 38, no. 4 (1973): 34-39. See also David B. Morris, "Drama and Stasis in Milton's 'Ode on the Morning of Christ's Nativity,'" *SP* 68 (1971): 212-13.

2 Tuve stresses *pictura* (*Images and Themes*, passim) in keeping with her theme of "Incarnation," and the anti-Puritan Broadbent responds by stressing the masque (in Kermode, ed., *The Living Milton*, p. 24).

3 R. M. Myers ("Neo-Classical Criticism of the Ode for Music," *PMLA* 62 [1947]: 399-421) distinguishes four types of ode for music: "sacred odes," cantata odes, laureate odes, and odes for St. Cecilia's Day. In addition to Myers's article, I am most indebted to the following studies of poetry and music in this period: James Hutton, "Some English Poems in Praise of Music," *English Miscellany* 2 (Rome, 1951): 1-63; John Hollander, *The Untuning of the Sky: Ideas of Music in English Poetry: 1500-1700* (New York: Norton, 1970); Hollander, *Vision and Resonance*, cited earlier; and the essays by James E. Phillips and Bertrand H. Bronson that comprise *Music and Literature in England in the Seventeenth and Eighteenth Centuries*, William Andrews Clark Memorial Seminar (Los Angeles: Clark Library, 1953). Valuable essays relating more exclusively to Dryden and music are: James Kinsley, "Dryden and the *Encomium Musicae*," *RES* n.s. 4 (1953); Ernest Brennecke, Jr., "Dryden's Odes and Draghi's Music," in *Essential Articles for the Study of John Dryden*, ed. H. T. Swedenberg (Hamden, Conn.: Archon, 1966), pp. 425-65; Dean T. Mace, "Musical Humanism, the Doctrine of Rhythmus, and the Saint Cecilia's Day Odes of Dryden," *JWCI* 27 (1964): 251-92.

4 See Hollander, *Vision and Resonance*, p. 188. The odes of Ronsard, which seem wholly "literary" today (far more so than those of Drayton, for example), belong to an era when odes of any sort were still meant to be sung, and for that purpose the Pléiade developed the famous technique of *mésurer les vers à la lyre*. Concerning the breach of poetry and music in seventeenth-century England, if one were to count liturgical writers like Crashaw as writers of odes, the union of elaborate verse forms with music could indeed be said to have continued unbroken. Some index of the early Restoration climate of opinion on this subject may be found in Edmund Smith's "Ode in Praise of Music," in which he requests the Muse to carry him to Athens so that he can escape the fashion of deriding poetry set to music (Chalmers, 9:208).

5 See Chadwick, *Poetry and Prophecy*, pp. 8-11. Most modern treatises stress the fusion of words and music as prescribed by seventeenth-century theorists.

See Hutton, "Some English Poems," pp. 43–48, and Phillips, passim. Hollander (*Untuning*, p. 13) stresses the etymology of *mousike*, which implies "neither a linguistic nor a tonal art but . . . a unified entity."

6 Dryden's pro forma dedication for the music of *The Prophetesse* (1691) would seem to bely this conclusion: "sure [poetry and music] are most excellent when they are joined . . . for thus they appear, like wit and beauty in the same person" (quoted by Hollander, *Untuning*, p. 397). But the impatience of Dryden's "Preface to Albion and Albanius" (1685) seems rather more heartfelt: "it is my part to invent, and the musician's to humor the invention."

7 Pope, in his "Ode for Music on St. Cecilia's Day," recognizes this problem, and his invocation requests inspiration for the instruments rather than for himself so pointedly that the opening gulf cannot be closed, I think, by alleging that he hopes for contagion-by-metonymy. The part of the Orpheus story that Pope chooses to linger over is the failed descent for Eurydice. That the analogy of poetry and music had become emptily formal by Pope's time should be clear also from the fact that Thomas Parnell, in his *Essay on the Different Styles of Poetry*, reviews the Passions in sequence, just as they would be reviewed in an ode for music, without bothering to call attention to what he is doing. See Chalmers, 9:415.

8 See Hollander, *Untuning*, p. 40.

9 Humanist music theory insisted that instrumental music should only "underlie" singing, but, as Brennecke painstakingly shows, St. Cecilia's Day composers were not at all subservient (Swedenberg, *Essential Articles*, p. 436).

10 Boethius's influential *De Musica* stresses "the superiority of theoretical to practical music" (Hutton, "Some English Poems," p. 15). In Eastern religions there is no sense of sequence in Transcendental Harmony. The primal Sound, heard only by adepts, is originary and pre-articulate; the emergence of syntactical language from this sound marks the alienation of consciousness from its origins. (I have argued above that Milton's word "unexpressive" carries some of this doctrine.) See O. K. Nambiar, "Spirit—Psyche—Symbol—Song," in *Anagogic Qualities of Literature*, ed. Joseph P. Strelka (University Park: Pennsylvania State University Press, 1971), p. 58. In Plutarch, whose writings on oracles have been recognized as a source for Milton's Nativity Ode, the tale is told of a heavenly voice heard by Cadmus (inventor of the alphabet) "that was neither Lofty nor Soft, nor shattered into Trills and Divisions" (*Plutarch's Morals*, 3 vols., trans. "Several Hands" [London: William Taylor, 1718], 3:104). Preferred sounds then, are either uniform and undivided, or else "unheard are sweeter." As Northrop Frye says, "If we praise harmony we should not start any music going at all, for every piece of music is a disturbance of an underlying concord" ("Lexis and Melos," in *Sound and Poetry*, ed. Frye [New York: Columbia University Press, 1956], pp. xi–xii).

11 "Linguistics and Poetics," in *The Structuralists from Marx to Lévi-Strauss*, ed. R. and F. DeGeorge (New York: Anchor Books, 1972), p. 92. See also Jonathan Culler, "Apostrophe," p. 59.

12 This is one of Schlüter's terms, throughout *Die Englische Ode*, for the hymnic elaboration of attributes. It is my contention, here and elsewhere, that etiology is the business of all narrative in an ode, not just of part of it. The generic association of ode and epic is a long-standing commonplace; Rosalie Colie cites Minturno's observation that Petrarch's *Trionfi* are nearly epic (*The Resources of Kind*, p. 21). An etiology would be especially apt for an ode for music because Orpheus, as Apollonius says, is a singer of origins. (See W. K. C. Guthrie, *Orpheus and Greek Religion* [New York: Norton, 1966], pp. 14, 27.)

13 Dryden's letter to his sons on "Alexander's Feast" also contains his stated resolution not to curry favor with the "degenerate order" of the present reign (Sir Walter Scott, ed., *The Works of John Dryden*, 18 vols., rev. George Saintsbury [London: William Paterson, 1893], 18:134).

14 *Essays on Several Moral Subjects: In Two Parts* (1697; 5th ed., London: Daniel Brown, 1703), 2:24. Insofar as I shall take Dryden's ode to be a critique of "the goddess Persuasion" (Hollander, *Untuning*, p. 421), I shall be moving away from Hollander's emphasis. I would apply to the later ode what Jay A. Levine has said of the 1687 ode, namely, that "Dryden took the occasion of his St. Cecilia assignment to insist upon the divinely or-dained limitation of the very event he was celebrating" ("Dryden's Song for St. Cecilia's Day, 1687," *PQ* 44 [1965]: 49). Whether the Protestant objection to elaborate music in church (see Swift's "The Dean to Himself on St. Cecilia's Day," 1730) has any bearing on this poem depends, of course, on how seriously one is to take Dryden's conversion to Catholicism.

15 On this ode, which I regret passing over, the reader is referred to the su-perbly modulated essay by A. D. Hope, "Anne Killigrew, or the Art of Modulating," in *Dryden's Mind and Art*, ed. Bruce L. King (Edinburgh: Oliver and Boyd, 1969).

16 See, e.g., Earl Miner, *Dryden's Poetry* (Bloomington: Indiana University Press, 1967), who notes a measure of playfulness in the text, but then con-cludes that it is still "Dryden's assertion . . . of the dignity of his art" (p. 273).

17 My expansion and complication of the satire in "Alexander's Feast" may be considered comparable to Bruce L. King's approach to the heroic plays in *Dryden's Major Plays* (Edinburgh: Oliver and Boyd, 1966). He outlines his method on p. 2. My basic position and some of my citations are antic-ipated in J. D. C. Buck, "The Ascetic's Banquet: The Morality of *Alexan-der's Feast*," *TSLL* 17 (1975–76): 573–89.

18 My text throughout is from *The Poems of John Dryden*, 4 vols., ed. James L. Kinsley (Oxford: Clarendon Press, 1958).

19 Dryden asked Tonson to change the name of Laïs in the proofs to Thaïs: "those two Ladyes were Contemporaryes, wch caused that small mistake" (Scott, *Works*, 18:137).

20 Quoted by Phillips, *Music and Literature*, p. 13.

21 Michael Seidel has pointed out to me in conversation that Augustan typol-ogy would incline Dryden to identify with Virgil's Trojans. Isolationist

sentiment ran high against William's plan to march onto the Continent, and it may have been easy to think of him as a Greek marauder.

22 How much Dryden knew about these has been debated. Some readers have cited the technically incorrect "Lydian *measures*" (a measure is not a mode) by way of arguing that Dryden had no interest in the modes. But see Hollander's refutation (*Untuning*, p. 416ff.). It seems unquestionable to me that the 1697 ode is designed, perhaps at the insistence of the composer, Jeremiah Clark, as a tour of the modes. Very tentatively, I would suggest the following order: Dorian (20–45); Ionian (46–65); Mixolydian (66–92); Lydian (93–122); Phrygian (123–54).

23 The dubiety of this line has been pointed out by Miner, *Dryden's Poetry*, p. 268.

24 To argue thus may seem inconsistent with a serious exposé of the demonic in music, but the devil is said, after all, to be an ass. William King, in his "Orpheus and Eurydice," had already satirized the fiction of music's power, and set a precedent that must have been difficult to ignore altogether. See Chalmers, 9:284. In Dryden's 1795 ode to Purcell, the composer is seen, without irony, as Orpheus. (See Buck, "The Ascetic's Banquet," 574.)

25 There could be an allusion of some sort here to John Blow, the composer who set the 1684 St. Cecilia Ode.

26 "His last stanza," says Johnson (*Life of Dryden*), "has less emotion than the former; but it is not less elegant in diction." Congreve, in his generally very poor 1701 St. Cecilia Ode, handles the Christian progress-of-music theme with far more assurance than Dryden can muster: "The soft enervate lyre is drown'd/In the deep organ's more majestic sound." Congreve's organ has the divine afflatus, "perpetual breath" (Chalmers, 10:281). Dryden had been the first, however, to give Cecilia any serious attention (cp. Hollander, *Untuning*, p. 398), and we may assume that Congreve learned from his difficulty. Purcell's music for Christopher Fishburn's wretched 1683 ode solves the problem of Cecilia's perfunctory entry by shifting from minor to major. (See Brennecke, in Swedenberg, *Essential Articles*, pp. 428–29.) It is true that my remarks would lose some force in a musical setting; the last stanza *is* a "grand chorus," after all, and it is truly impressive in Handel's score. The original score, by Clark, has been lost.

27 Hollander takes the title of his book from his parallel impression that at the end of the 1687 ode a descent has taken place: "And music shall untune the sky." Another well-known poem that cheerfully records the passing of Voice out of the Spheres and into "Reason's ear" is Addison's "Spacious Firmament on High," which is admirably discussed by Father Ong, *The Presence of the Word*, p. 72.

28 This reading has risked over-solemnizing a clearly exuberant poem. The devil I keep conjuring with, however, is no brooding bogey but a Lord of Misrule. I see no serious inconsistency between my approach and Miner's assertion (*Dryden's Poetry*, p. 267) that "the poet and we share in the festive welter of life." Mark Van Doren's famous characterization of the meter and mood of the ode as an "immortal ragtime" cannot be bettered

(*The Poetry of John Dryden* [New York: Harcourt, Brace, and Howe, 1920], p. 246).

29 *The Poetical Works of Mark Akenside*, Aldine ed. (1845; reprint ed., New York: AMS Press, 1969), p. 241 (hereafter cited by page as Aldine ed.).

Chapter 4

1 In this chapter and the next, I quote from Roger Lonsdale, ed., *The Poems of Gray, Collins, and Goldsmith* (London: Longman, 1969; hereafter cited by page as *Poems*).

2 Paget Toynbee and Leonard Whibley, ed., *The Correspondence of Thomas Gray*, 3 vols. (Oxford: Clarendon Press, 1935), 3:1111n. (hereafter cited by volume and page as *Correspondence*).

3 W. S. Lewis, ed., *Horace Walpole's Correspondence*, 00 vols. (New Haven: Yale University Press, 1948), 13–14:60 (hereafter cited by volume and page as *Walpole's Correspondence*).

4 Roger Lonsdale, who also stresses the nature of solitude in the "Elegy," discovers the union of "darkness" and "me" in the "heavy final rhyme" ("The Poetry of Thomas Gray: Versions of the Self," *PBA* 59 [1973] : 107). Ian Jack calls "and to me" a "pathetic emphasis" ("Gray's Elegy Reconsidered," in *From Sensibility to Romanticism*, Hilles and Bloom, p. 159).

5 For another approach to the difference between the "Elegy" and the odes of Gray, see Bertrand H. Bronson, "The Pre-Romantic or Post-Augustan Mode," *ELH* 20 (1953): 26.

6 Gerald F. Bruns argues persuasively that Orphic thaumaturgy became relevant to poetry again in the eighteenth century when the controversy over the existence of external reality grew heated ("Poetry as Reality: The Orpheus Myth and Its Modern Counterparts," *ELH* 37 [1970] : 265).

7 *The Poets of Great Britain*, 54 vols. (London: John Bell, 1782), 51:114.

8 Norman Maclean (in Crane, *Critics and Criticism*, p. 439) maintains that "plot" disappeared when the "allegorical odes" of the eighteenth century supplanted the "fragmentary plot" of the earlier Great Ode. I feel, rather, that one should assume with Schlüter that there is *always* a pars epica. It is especially important to do so in resisting the naturalization that appears as a counter-rhetoric (or counterplot) in Romantic odes.

9 Patricia M. Spacks notes the "delicate avoidance of personal observation" in the opening lines, with their "special crowding," designed to "lead the reader's eye away from the object" ("Statement and Artifice in Thomas Gray," *SEL* 5 [1965] : 520).

10 See Arthur Johnston, "'The Purple Year' in Gray and Pope," *RES* n.s. 14 (1963): 389–93, for a defense of "purple" as a springtime color. Geoffrey Tillotson points out the link of *purpureum* with *ver* in Virgil (*Ecl.* 10. 40), but grants its irrelevance to an English spring (*Augustan Studies* [London: Athlone Press, 1961], pp. 205–06).

11 See Gray's early Latin epistle "Ad C. Favonium Zephyrinum," and the lament for West in Book 2 of the *De Principiis Cogitandi* (1742): "reducemque

iterum roseo ore salutem/Speravi, atque una tecum, dilecte Favoni!" (ll. 12–13).

12 The reader is referred to Lonsdale's thorough annotations in *Poems*, p. 46n. I cannot hold him responsible for my commonplace addition of *L'Allegro* to the list.

13 The psychology of Gray's word "distant" has often been noted. See, e.g., Ralph Cohen, "The Augustan Mode in English Poetry," *ECS* 1 (1967-68): 11; and Spacks, "Statement and Artifice," p. 528. For an excellent recent reading of the Eton College Ode, see Marshall Brown, "The Urbane Sublime," *ELH* 45 (1978): 238ff.

14 The reader is referred to an image study by Kenneth MacLean, which enthusiastically stresses the importance of the two subjects that I take to be conspicuously muted in Gray's poetry, namely, childhood and water: "The Distant Way: Imagination and Image in Gray," in Ben Jones and James Downey, eds., *Fearful Joy: Papers from the Thomas Gray Bicentennial Conference at Carleton University* (Montreal: McGill-Queen's University Press, 1974), pp. 136ff.

15 R. Dodsley, ed., *A Collection of Poems in Six Volumes* (London: J. Hughs, 1758), 5:330 (hereafter cited by volume and page as Dodsley).

16 I hope it is clear that I am here isolating an attitude from any probable context in Gray's ideology, and not insisting that he is systematically a linguistic skeptic. He dismissed Plato's *Cratylus*, for instance, as a youthful production, showing no interest in the problem of rooting language in what Socrates uneasily calls "primary roots" in that dialogue. See *Works of Thomas Gray in Prose and Verse*, 4 vols., ed. Edmund Gosse (New York: Frederic A. Stokes, 1895), 4:164. Nevertheless, Gray's dictum still requires some explanation beyond what it has been given. By taking it literally, Donald Greene, for example, finds improper grounds for his spirited abuse of Gray in "The Proper Language of Poetry: Gray, Johnson, and Others," (Jones and Downey, *Fearful Joy*, p. 94).

17 One may speculate that the problem, thought of in this way, belongs to the 1742 period, since a later MS, misdated 1743 and thereby showing that a considerable period of time had passed since the composition of the poem, omits the word "distant" from the title. (See *Poems*, p. 54.) The *De Principiis Cogitandi* may be read as Gray's effort in 1742 to convince himself that there is at least a Lockeian measure of continuity between the senses and "naturae ingens . . . imago/Immensae" (1. 52–53).

18 W. Powell Jones interprets a mass of evidence to indicate that humanitarian instincts about capturing birds had not yet grown active in Gray's time; but he misses the ominous prolepsis of the human condition in his title passage from Gray—and indeed suppresses the clearly bittersweet tone of nearly every passage he quotes ("The Captive Linnet: A Footnote on Eighteenth-Century Sentiment," *PQ* 33 [1954]: 330–40).

19 I would differ here from Lonsdale (*Poems*, p. 69), who concludes simply that "G. must have later decided that the distinction was immaterial."

20 "The Rising Poet," in Summers, *The Lyric and Dramatic Milton*, p. 27.

21 That it is already the self that is in some degree addressed in mid-century apostrophe is not everywhere agreed upon. Martin Price's having pointed out "the evocation of deep-lying powers within the poet" in poems of this period may again be mentioned ("The Sublime Poem," p. 201). A midway point toward complete subjectivity in personification can be found in the assertion of John Hughes, in his Preface to *The Works of Mr. Edmund Spenser* (1715), that the landscape of allegorical personification is "'visionary and typical'" (quoted by Patricia M. Spacks, *The Insistence of Horror: Aspects of the Supernatural in Eighteenth Century Poetry* [Cambridge: Harvard University Press, 1962], p. 134). Later, such landscapes are visionary but less typical-seeming. It is difficult to agree with Earl Wasserman's argument from the evidence of eighteenth-century theory that personification is an empiricist device (later to be replaced by the subjectivity of the "symbol") that serves to sort out classes of externally given data ("The Inherent Values of Eighteenth-Century Personification," *PMLA* 65 [1950]: 435-63).

22 See Otto Rank, *The Myth of the Birth of the Hero and Other Essays*, ed. Philip Freund (New York: Vintage Books, 1964), pp. 65-96.

23 Gray's notes, again, are not terribly suggestive, consisting in the present context of the remark that "the poet's art . . . enervates our resolution" (Gosse, *Works*, 4:267).

24 Bertrand H. Bronson's "peculiar satisfaction" in finding all four of his types of personification in Wordsworth might be dampened by pointing out that his fourth, from the "Ode to Duty," is a deliberate nod to Gray, and that his second and third, from the Intimations Ode, find Wordsworth already working by design in what he understands to be an artificial genre. See "Personification Reconsidered," in *New Light on Dr. Johnson*, ed. F. W. Hilles (New Haven: Yale University Press, 1959), pp. 189-231. My text for this poem, and for the poems discussed in chapter 6, is *Wordsworth's Poetical Works*, 5 vols., ed. Ernest DeSelincourt (Oxford: Clarendon Press, 1969), 4:83. I am disregarding the bracketed sixth stanza, which appears only in the 1807 version.

25 Geoffrey Hartman discusses this poem as an "inverted ceremonial of the self giving the self away" in *Wordsworth's Poetry 1787-1814* (New Haven: Yale University Press, 1975), pp. 280-81.

26 "In religion . . . , the purpose of the kerygma is to demythologize a common assumption and supplant it with a new myth" (Sanford Budich, "The Demythological Mode in Augustan Verse," *ELH* 37 [1970]: 393). Note that in the ode the typical moment of banishing false oracles might always be termed "kerygmatic."

27 See Lonsdale, "The Poetry of Thomas Gray," p. 120ff.

28 The reader is apt to experience *déjà vu* about the following list, which I shall compress as much as possible. See R. H. Griffith, "The Progress Pieces of the Eighteenth Century," *Texas Review* 5 (1920): 218-33; Geoffrey Hartman, "Blake and the Progress of Poetry," *Beyond Formalism*, pp. 193-205; W. J. Bate, *The Burden of the Past and the English Poet* (London:

Chatto & Windus, 1971); Harold Bloom, the sequence of five books that begins with *The Anxiety of Influence: A Theory of Poetry* (London: Oxford University Press, 1973); and Paul Sherwin, *Precious Bane*. For the period under consideration, see Akenside's typical concern that "I so late unlock thy purer springs" ("On Lyric Poetry," Aldine ed., p. 243). The Progress topos first appears clearly in Horace's *Ad Pisones*, 391–407. For a very early Progress Pindaric that I would nominate as a source for Gray's poem, see Ronsard's famous ode "A Michel de l'Hôpital."

29   Roger Martin writes well "des secrets de philologue, des figures . . . qui n'éveillent que des faibles échos" (*Essai sur Thomas Gray* [London: Humphrey Milford, 1934] , p. 448).

30   It may be, admittedly, that Gray was merely carried away by contemporary stock responses to *Pythian* I. John Ogilvie gives Gray's drowsy eagle the highest marks for sublimity in his *Poems on Several Subjects, to which is Prefix'd an Essay on the Lyric Poetry of the Ancients* (London: G. Keith, 1762), pp. xlviii–xlix.

31   This connection is a commonplace of Progress Poetry; see especially Thomson's *Progress of Liberty*. The tendency to mention both extremes of climate in picturing savage beginnings is perhaps meant to counteract the widespread belief (from Arbuthnot to Herder) that metaphor began in hot climates, and is meant thereby to protect the North from being thought unpoetical. See Christopher J. Berry, "Eighteenth-Century Approaches to the Origin of Metaphor," *NM* 74 (1973): 699–701. For Gray's indebtedness to Montesquieu on climate, see his "Alliance of Education and Government."

32   Joseph Warton's closest approach to Gray's epithet is in his "Ode to Fancy": "Thy brows with Indian feathers crowned." Warton's context is the same as Gray's, the celebration of Fancy at the antipodes.

33   In general, modern criticism has moved Gray perhaps a little too close to the nostalgia of the Romantic Period. Gray enthusiastically praises the passage in Plato's *Phaedrus* (274d–275b) about the secondariness of writing, but it is not clear to me that his attitude is nostalgic; he knows what is lost, clearly, but seems not to be perturbed. Here is the comment: "This discourse of Thamus (or Jupiter Ammon) on the uses and inconveniences of letters is excellent; he gives a lively image of a great scholar; that is, one who searches for wisdom in books alone" (*Works* 4:85).

34   On the conventionality of this figure, see Benjamin Boyce, "Sounding Shells and Little Prattlers in the Eighteenth-Century Ode," *ECS* 8 (1974–75): 245–64.

35   In itself a commonplace, this phrasing especially recalls Addison, who said that "Milton's story was translated in regions that lie out of the reach of the sun the sphere of day" (*Spectator* 267, in *The Works of Joseph Addison*, 3 vols. [New York: Harper & Bros., 1855] , 1:387).

36   I here echo the argument, presented in another context, of Thomas Weiskel, *The Romantic Sublime* (Baltimore: Johns Hopkins University Press, 1976), pp. 3–33.

37   A. D. McKillop has remarked of Gray's "Progress" that it "ends with a note

of exultation" ("The Romanticism of William Collins," *SP* 20 [1923] :13).

38 A minority of readers take an even more extreme position than mine, asserting that Gray is still overtly thinking of himself as a poet in the last line. See Lord David Cecil, "The Poetry of Thomas Gray," in *Eighteenth Century English Literature: Modern Essays in Criticism*, ed. James L. Clifford (New York: Oxford Galaxy, 1959), p. 240. My position is only that the topic of poetry lingers *malgré lui.* The position that the subject has wholly changed is maintained by Patricia M. Spacks, "'Artful Strife': Conflict in Gray's Poetry," *PMLA* (1966): 63.

39 This nearly universal view is colorfully stated by Norman Maclean, "Personification but Not Poetry," *ELH* 23 (1956): 164.

40 The deliberateness of this choice may be seen from his insistence everywhere in the unpublished prose on the importance of the "ear" in poetry. As Hollander points out (*Vision and Resonance*, p. 269), a printed English Pindaric retains none of its vocal ancestry and gives the overwhelming impression simply of being "a block of type on a page, framed in white space."

41 The tradition of Taliesin is, as Gray would have known, the nearest mantic tradition in time and place to his own. See Chadwick, *Poetry and Prophecy*, pp. 4–5. Chadwick says (p. 6) that the extant Celtic materials on the details of mantic trance are rich beyond parallel. Gray may certainly have seen them. Gray's experiments were by no means unique: Mason, Sir William Jones, James Clarence Mangan, and many others made numerous versions of Welsh and Norse "odes." The precedent for calling such poems odes may be traced as far back as the *Spectator* (see Shuster, *The English Ode*, p. 162).

42 The first volume of Dodsley's *Collection* opens with Thomas Tickell's "Prospect of Peace," based on Horace's Nereus Ode, which is designedly mock-prophetic. See also Joseph Warton, "The Revenge of America," in Dodsley's fourth volume. In the Romantic Period, the prophecy based on hindsight survives most notably in Byron's "Prophecy of Dante."

43 For a reading of "The Bard" that reaches some of my conclusions, although it is about pictures and not writing, see Jean H. Hagstrum, *The Sister Arts* (Chicago: University of Chicago Press, 1958), pp. 310–14. Gray's contemporaries noticed the unusual quantity of weaving imagery in his late odes. See the comments of Elizabeth Montagu and Goldsmith quoted by W. Powell Jones, "The Contemporary Reception of Gray's Odes," *MP* 28 (1930–31): 68, 73. By far the most interesting early comment on "The Bard" is that of its most famous illustrator, William Blake: "Weaving the winding sheet of Edward's race by means of sounds . . . is a bold and daring, and most masterly conception" (*The Poetry and Prose of William Blake*, ed. David V. Erdman [Garden City, N.Y.: Doubleday, 1965], p. 532).

44 Again, such Freudian papers as "Notes on a Case of Obsessional Neurosis" ("The Rat Man") and *Beyond the Pleasure Principle* stand behind generalizations of this sort. For a description of melancholia that tallies uncannily with what we know of Gray's personality, see Willard Gaylin in *The Meaning of Despair: Psychoanalytic Contributions to the Understanding of Depression*, ed. Gaylin (New York: Jason Aronson, 1968), p. 7.

45 See F. Doherty, "The Two Voices of Gray," *Essays in Criticism* 13, no. 3 (1963): 222-30, esp. 229.

46 The word "absence" conventionally appears in vernal poems (like Gray's sonnet on West) where the absence of a loved one sets the poet apart from the renewed fertility of nature. Though it is not a spring poem, Joseph Warton's "Ode to Fancy" nevertheless passes through this convention: "The pangs of absence, o remove,/For thou canst place me near my love." Akenside, "On the Winter Solstice," has a related locution grounded in anticipation: "absence heightening every charm,/Invokes the slow-returning May" (Aldine ed., p. 215).

47 This poem is conveniently available in Moore, *English Poetry in the Eighteenth Century*, pp. 67-70.

48 "Reason," writes Green, "shew'd part of spleen was substance, shadow more" (Dodsley 1:118).

49 *The Poetical Works of William Collins*, ed. A. Dyce (London: William Pickering, 1827), p. 142. Bishop Warburton's speculations on hieroglyphics in *The Divine Legation of Moses* had appeared in 1742, not long before Gray and Collins wrote their major odes.

Chapter 5

1   The desire for "contentment" as presence was so fundamental to the Age of Sensibility that it was taken for granted as a universal. Thus Rowley-Chatterton could fool the age with its own coin—which was not at all current in the Middle Ages: "All hayle, Contente, thou mayd of turtle-eyne" ("On Happiness," Chalmers, 15:397).

2   Throughout the ensuing interpretation of Collins, I shall take "chastity" to be the same as virginity. The chaste in Collins are always *maids*. It is from my confinement of chastity to this narrow sense that my differences of opinion with the best recent readers of Collins arise; where they think he is prothalamic, pre-Blakean, I assume an uneasiness in his odes about sex in general, whether hallowed or unhallowed.

3   See Maclean, "From Action to Image," pp. 441-43; and Hagstrum, *The Sister Arts*, pp. 268-69.

4   For a related rationalization of the prayer structure, see John R. Crider, "Structure and Effect in Collins' Progress Poems," *SP* 60 (1963): 59.

5   Or, as Hartman puts it in this context: *do ut des* (*Beyond Formalism*), p. 288).

6   Thus even if apostrophe seems (with no imperative in view) to be simply an address, this would in fact be the case only in a narrative structure. See Erich Auerbach's distinction between apostrophe and address in "Dante's Addresses to the Reader," *RP* 7 (1953-54): 271.

7   So Collins's 1898 editor, W. C. Bronson, described the purpose of the *Odes Descriptive and Allegorical* (quoted by Lonsdale in *Poems*, p. 417).

8   *The Penguin Book of Greek Verse*, p. 161.

9   For another interesting address to a protean numen, see the "Ode to Fancy" of William Hamilton of Bangour (Chalmers, 15:626).

10 Angus Fletcher remarks that the "Thou" of Collins's odes always seems
    daemonic, in *Allegory: The Theory of a Symbolic Mode* (Ithaca: Cornell
    University Press, 1964), p. 51n. Fletcher develops his sense of the daemon
    from the root of the word, which means "to divide" (p. 42)—or, in the
    sense I have been assuming, "to disrupt."

11 Quoted by McKillop, "The Romanticism of William Collins," p. 3.

12 The orthodox in this matter, who will have their innings in the pages that
    follow, triumphantly enlist the support of Collins's first editor, John Lang-
    horne, who noticed nothing amiss in the mesode. What, though, can they
    make of Langhorne's Collins-influenced "Sonnet"? "Let not [Fancy's]
    flattery win the youthful ear;/Nor vow long faith to such a various guest,/
    False at the last, tho' now, perchance, full dear:/the casual lover with her
    charms is blest,/But woe to them her magic bands that wear!" (quoted by
    McKillop, "The Romanticism of William Collins," p. 3).

13 These are, most notably, Northrop Frye, *Fearful Symmetry: A Study of
    William Blake* (Princeton: Princeton University Press, 1958), pp. 164–67;
    Harold Bloom, *The Visionary Company: A Reading of English Romantic
    Poetry* (1961; rev. ed., Ithaca: Cornell University Press, 1971), pp. 7–15;
    Weiskel, *The Romantic Sublime*, pp. 124–34; and Sherwin, *Precious Bane*.
    An important approach to Collins that tends to sidestep this dispute is that
    of Marshall Brown, "The Urban Sublime," p. 246.

14 For Collins's significant misreading of the *Oedipus Coloneus* 1622–25, see
    Lonsdale in *Poems*, p. 421, and Weiskel, *The Romantic Sublime*, pp. 115–
    16. On Eden in the Antistrophe of "Poetical Character" as a repressed
    primal scene, see Weiskel, *The Romantic Sublime*, p. 131.

15 It seems to have been a habit of the Warton School to under-read their
    master, Spenser, as if to demonstrate the antiquity, both primitive and
    naïve, of their inheritance. (Drayton's note on Skelton, I argued above,
    serves the same purpose.) The sentiment of Thomas Warton, in "Ode IV:
    Solitude at an Inn" (Chalmers, 18:101), is best read as a hopeful grief:
    "Much would I grieve, that envious Time so soon/O'er the lov'd strain [of
    Spenser] had cast his dim disguise." Here is yet another convenient veil.

16 As Weiskel states, "[Spenser's] girdle has the talismanic ambiguity com-
    mon in allegorical imagery; it is at once emblem and cause" (*The Romantic
    Sublime*, p. 125). Later (p. 127) he cites Angus Fletcher on the relation
    between the Greek *kosmos* and the Latin *ornament*. (Cf. *Allegory*, p. 108ff.)

17 Bloom suggests "the line of the late Drayton, Milton, of Collins himself"
    (*The Visionary Company*, p. 9).

18 I allude more to the confused kinships that obtain in any pantheon than to
    later Greek mythology. But in *The Iliad*, which I have suggested Collins
    has in mind for his "main engirting all," Aphrodite (born not from foam
    but from Zeus and Dione) is still the half sister of Hephaistos. In less cir-
    cumspect treatments of Fancy, she has a "zoneless breast" after some
    initiation, such as having been kissed by bees (cf. Thomas Marriott, "Ode
    to Fancy," Dodsley, 4:287). Christopher Smart speaks of "loosing the
    Cestus" in "Fanny, blooming Fair" (Chalmers, 16:130). In "The Passions"

(l. 91), Collins's own Mirth (than whom no one could be more alien to the genius of Collins, and who is vainly and pathetically courted in "The Manners") has her "zone unbound." Both Sherwin (*Precious Bane*, p. 19) and Weiskel have stressed the possession of the Band by Spenser's Venus. So does the leading proponent of the Lov'd Enthusiast's innocence, Earl Wasserman, but he is not disturbed by the connection because of his insistence that Collins (and also the Spenser of the "Fowre Hymnes") is observing the Plotinian distinction between the Celestial and the Earthly Venus ("Collins's 'Ode on the Poetical Character,'" *ELH* 34 [1967] : 102–03).

19 *On the Nature of the Universe*, trans. R. E. Latham (Harmondsworth: Penguin Books, 1968), p. 27.

20 "Collins's 'Ode on the Poetical Character,'" p. 98. Both Wasserman and A. S. P. Woodhouse ("The Poetry of Collins Reconsidered," in *From Sensibility to Romanticism*, Hilles and Bloom, pp. 93–138) persuade us that Collins's intentions are Platonic; the question remains whether his poem is.

21 I have transferred to an earlier place in the mesode the figure whose presence Wasserman supports with a cento of biblical examples ("Collins's 'Ode on the Poetical Character,'" p. 95). In my view, his distinction between *sapientia increata* ("called with thought") and *creata* (breathed forth by "magic notes") cannot be sustained by the phrase "called with thought to *birth*."

22 Sherwin (*Precious Bane*, p. 23) writes well on the trochaic hiatus at "aloud," which ends the only seven-syllable line of the poem, and marks the breathtaking importance of the moment.

23 "The Poetry of Collins Reconsidered," p. 129n.

24 Only H. W. Garrod, during his debunking spree, has noticed that Fancy's appearance here is "ill-conceived and disconcerting" (*Collins* [Oxford: Clarendon Press, 1928], pp. 69–70). If my explanation fails to convince, then I see no choice but to agree with Garrod.

25 Sherwin (*Precious Bane*, pp. 34–35) discusses the birth of Sin at length, but does not connect it with the mesode of this ode.

26 See *The Anxiety of Influence*, pp. 14–15, 87–89.

27 "Theories of Voice in Eighteenth-Century Poetry: Thomas Gray and Christopher Smart," in Jones and Downey, *Fearful Joy*, p. 107.

28 By way of analogy, I would cite Callimachus's critical abuse of Apollonius's *Argonautica* in behalf of a canon based on lyric compression, and Theocritus's implied disapproval of the same poem, as evidenced by his having recast some of its episodes as songs in his Idyllia. In the mid-eighteenth century we are dealing, it seems to me, with a distinctly Hellenistic period in the history of English literature.

29 See *The Anxiety of Influence*, pp. 15, 124–26.

30 Collins's reversal of antistrophe and epode in his Pindaric odes has attracted much comment, as has his fondness, recorded by Warton, for the word "anagnorisis." (See the letter of Thomas Mulso to Gilbert White, quoted by Lonsdale, *Poems*, p. 414.) I cannot agree with Lonsdale (p. 418) that "C. obviously preferred to use the calmer epode as a temporary

relief of tension rather than as a final resolution," since most of Collins's epodes comprise rather frantic and treacherous narratives. My guess is that he saw the epode as being analogous with the recitative in the cantata, and that he reserved the antistrophe for last because he understood the term to denote a reversal. (For Collins as for Aristotle, peripety and anagnorisis would preferably come simultaneously.) Gilbert West's Preface to his Pindar translations (Chalmers, 13:141) provides some interesting lore from the Scholia of Hephaestion about the significance of the triadic structure, lore that Collins may have undertaken to transgress: "the *strophe*, as they say, denoted the notion of the *higher sphere*, the *antistrophe* that of the planets, the *epode* the *fixed station* and the repose of the *Earth*." A possible authorization for Collins's practice may be found in Congreve's Preface to his Pindarics, where he says that Greek choruses sang the Epode "in the middle [meaning of course the middle of the stage], neither turning to one hand nor the other" (Chalmers, 10:301).

31 It is true that sound, especially in an ode, has a higher value than sight, and more closely approximates the Mosaic calling (see Sherwin, *Precious Bane*, pp. 28-29). My point is that for the synaesthetically devious Collins, sound is always *clouded* by a screen or acoustic deadener. One could see Collins's veils, I suppose, as an anticipation of the Burkean doctrine of "obscurity" as a source of the Sublime, but I think that Collins would happily sacrifice the Sublime or any other aesthetic if he could only see and hear more clearly.

32 Milton does mention "the monumental Oak" in *Il Penseroso* (l. 135), where perhaps, from Collins's viewpoint, the figure properly belongs, since his own Milton is a disparadised contemplative.

33 Sherwin (*Precious Bane*, p. 30) notes this connection, but treats it differently.

34 Several readers have indeed compared Milton with Adam (e.g., Sherwin, *Precious Bane*, p. 27, and E. L. Brooks, "William Collins's 'Ode on the Poetical Character,'" *CE* 17 [1955-56]: 404), but have not sufficiently weighted the comparison. Sherwin cites the passage from *Paradise Lost* (11. 328-29) that could in fact show Adam to be the "one alone." Patricia M. Spacks remarks that "an Eden is unlikely to have successive inhabitants," but she too nominates Milton for the place (*The Poetry of Vision: Five Eighteenth-Century Poets* [Cambridge: Harvard University Press, 1967], pp. 70-71).

35 Also crucial in forming this tradition is the "Veni Creator Spiritus," translated in hymn measures most notably by Dryden.

36 I am indebted to the treatment of this poem by Geoffrey Hartman, *The Fate of Reading*, pp. 147-50.

37 I would suggest that Collins's alterations of "Evening" for Dodsley in 1748 were meant to draw her figure closer to that of Simplicity.

38 The "Ode to Pity" also begins as a conjuration, but then turns prudently against the device: "But wherefore need I wander wide/To old Ilissus' distant side,/Deserted stream and mute?"

39 John Pomfret's *Upon the Divine Attributes* (Chalmers, 8:325ff.) describes

this decorum as an aspect of religious orthodoxy: "Nature and art, indeed, have bounds assign'd,/And only forms to things, not being, give;/That from Omnipotence they must receive."

40 The importance of sacred regions, as Angus Fletcher points out, lies in their freedom from "contagion or contagious magic" (see *Allegory*, p. 210ff.).

41 Some scholars still express puzzlement as to why Johnson's dislike of Gray was so vehement. I certainly feel that their ideological disparity was sufficient cause. Roger Lonsdale, who reviews the evidence without taking it to be sufficient, quotes disapproving remarks about Walpole by Dr. Burney in 1798 that do clearly represent, in my view, the depth of disapproval a Tory could feel for a Whig—an effeminate creature almost by definition. See Lonsdale's "Gray and Johnson: The Biographical Problem," in Jones and Downey, *Fearful Joy*, p. 76.

42 For the conjunction of phrases from "Lycidas" and the Death of Thomson Ode, and for the context of the preceding paragraph, see Hartman, *Beyond Formalism*, p. 317.

43 This assertion, which I shall develop below and in later chapters, stands opposed to that of Ricardo Quintana, who argues that the odes of the 1747 volume, especially the first three, are about alternative poetic kinds. See "The Scheme of Collins' Odes on Several . . . Subjects," *Restoration and Eighteenth-Century Literature*, ed. Carroll Camden (Chicago: University of Chicago Press, 1963), pp. 371–80.

44 This tacit accusation has a moral dimension, as is clear from Christopher Pitt's 1721 "Ode on the Delivery of Her Royal Highness," which defends the univocity of lyric (Apollo) against the chameleonic epic (Envy).

45 The connection between these two retreats has been explained in a very fine essay by A. D. McKillop, "Collins' *Ode to Evening*—Background and Structure," *Tennessee Studies in Literature* 5 (1960): 82.

46 This is strong wording; but see Merle E. Brown, "On William Collins' 'Ode to Evening,'" *Essays in Criticism* 11, no. 2 (1961): 137; and Martin Kallich, "'Plain in Thy Neatness': Horace's Pyrrha and Collins' Evening," *ELN* 3 (1965–66): 269.

47 The MS discovered in 1967 by Claire Lamont is entitled "Ode." See Lonsdale, *Poems*, p. 499, and Lamont, *RES* 19 (1968): 137–47.

48 When Collins wrote Dr. William Hayes concerning his new ode, "The Passions," "I have chosen the ancient tragedies to be my models, and only copied the most affecting passages in them," he means, we can assume from his practice, specifically the choral pasages (H. O. White, "The Letters of William Collins," *RES* 3 [1927]: 18).

49 Sherwin writes (*Precious Bane*, p. 123): "There is in Collins a persistent dread of what is to come: the setting of the virile sun, the northering of the poetical spirit, the veiling of the sources of inspiration." Topically, this is an excellent summary; but I should imagine rather that Collins dreads being exposed to such sources more than he dreads their departure.

50 Lonsdale (*Poems*, p. 464n.) and McKillop ("Collins' *Ode to Evening*," p. 79) liberally help us to sources for ll. 9–14 about the bat and the beetle.

Setting aside Gay's *Shepherd's Week* ("Wednesday"), if the reader will consult the *Faerie Queene* 2. 12. 36, and *Macbeth* 3. 3. 40–44, he will find the bat and beetle to appear, respectively, in remarkably sinister circumstances. Spencer's Knight of Temperance (n.b.) is in a hellish fog at sea, and Macbeth promises that "a deed of dreadful note" will be done before morning. As for Milton's Gray-fly ("Lycidas," l. 28), Merritt Y. Hughes points out that even though the next line ("Batt'ning our flocks with fresh dews of night") refers to evening, the word "sultry" places the Gray-fly in a noon-scape (*John Milton: Complete Poems and Major Prose*, p. 121n.). By allusion, then, Collins's beetle is not only suspect in character but out of its element.

51 There is another connection between Collins's "Evening" and the name Pyrrha. Both in Horace, *Carm.* 1. 2, and Milton, *Paradise Lost* 11. 12, Pyrrha is the consort of Deucalion, who prayed successfully to Themis that the Flood be abated. In Milton Pyrrha is introduced as a type for Eve in her posture of repentent prayer. The relevance of these sources for Collins has been discussed well by Henry Pettit, "Collins' 'Ode to Evening' and the Critics," *SEL* 4 (1964): 66–68. See also Kallich, "'Plain in Thy Neatness,'" 265–71.

52 "The Pre-Romantic or Post-Augustan Mode," *ELH* 20 (1953): 20.

53 Northrop Frye describes a "continuous present [maintained] by various devices of repetition" in "Towards Defining an Age of Sensibility," *Fables of Identity: Studies in Poetic Mythology* (New York: Harbinger Books, 1963), p. 133. Later in this essay (p. 135), Frye speaks of the Sensibility Poets' "concentration on the primitive process of writing."

54 What I have said here of the ode, Paul de Man has said of lyric in general, in "Intentional Structure of the Romantic Nature Image," in Bloom, *Romanticism and Consciousness*, p. 137.

55 Andrew Fichter has put this very well in remarking that, beginning with the odes of Collins, "both wills, the invoking and the invoked, are united as one identity, the genius of poetry. The subject of the ode is then the ode itself" ("Ode and Elegy: Idea and Form in Tennyson's Early Poetry," *ELH* 40 [1973]: 401).

56 Hartman compares Collins in the "Ode to Fear" ("I see, I see thee near!") to the Sorcerer's Apprentice (*Beyond Formalism*, p. 326).

57 Cf. Weiskel, *The Romantic Sublime*, pp. 110–17, for a reading of the "Ode to Fear" that is based on this supposition.

Chapter 6

1 Earl Wasserman, *The Subtler Language: Critical Readings of Neoclassic and Romantic Poems* (Baltimore: Johns Hopkins University Press, 1959), p. 11. The phrase is unfortunate, perhaps, since *kosmos* and *taxis* are synonyms; but that redundancy may be useful, on the other hand, for showing the fitness of things for the outlook in question.

2 See chapter 5 of the *Categories* in *The Basic Works of Aristotle*, ed. Richard McKeon (New York: Random House, 1941), p. 9.

3 *The Prelude or Growth of a Poet's Mind*, ed. Ernest DeSelincourt and Helen
   Darbishire (Oxford: Clarendon Press, 1959), p. 525 (quoted by the editors
   from an early notebook, and closely related to *Prelude* 2. 215–21 [1805,
   1850]).

4 As Paul de Man has pointed out with respect to the Coleridgean symbol,
   which is meant to have the "structure . . . of the synecdoche," Coleridge in
   fact deprives the symbol of "the materiality that had been used to distin-
   guish it from allegory" by referring it to a transcendent totality ("The
   Rhetoric of Temporality," *Interpretation: Theory and Practice*, ed. Charles
   S. Singleton [Baltimore: Johns Hopkins University Press, 1969], pp. 176–
   77). On the symbol as synecdoche, "assuming a sort of *participation mys-
   tique*," see also Angus Fletcher, *Allegory*, p. 17. The reader will be startled
   to find the "symbol" stressed in a discussion of Wordsworth; I have in mind
   merely the totality of reference or resonance, featured in his work as much
   as in Coleridge's, that is meant to supervene "puny boundaries."

5 Frances Ferguson, who has many valuable things to say on this subject,
   quotes Crabb Robinson's remark that the 1815 classifications were "partly
   subjective, partly objective" (*Wordsworth: Language as Counter-Spirit* [New
   Haven: Yale University Press, 1977] p. 37).

6 *Marxism and Form: Twentieth-Century Dialectical Theories of Literature*
   (Princeton: Princeton University Press, 1974), p. 327.

7 My text for Wordsworth's poetry will be *Wordsworth's Poetical Works*, 5
   vols., ed. Ernest De Selincourt (Oxford: Clarendon Press, 1969; hereafter
   referred to by volume and page as *Poetical Works*).

8 What is novel is the refinement, not the topic. Memory is a Pindaric topic
   as early as Congreve's "Daughters of Memory" (1706), and the mid-eigh-
   teenth-century lyrists wrote odes to Memory nearly as a matter of course.
   The association of the lyric with the past (and with childhood) is common
   to many of the tripartite German *Gattungsunterscheidungen*, most notably
   those of Heidegger and Emil Staiger. See René Wellek, "Genre Theory, the
   Lyric, and 'Erlebnis,'" *Festschrift für Richard Alewyn* (Cologne: Böhlau-
   Verlag, 1967), p. 400. Only Käte Hamburger, in fact, with whom Wellek
   undertakes to disagree, associates the lyric with the *present* on the grounds
   that it is the transcribed experience of an "Ich-Origo" ("Die lyrische Gat-
   tung," *Die Logik der Dichtung*, 2nd ed. [Stuttgart: Ernst Klett Verlag,
   1968], p. 188). I follow Hamburger in proposing my notion of the self-
   constitution of an ode. (See also her distinction [pp. 192–93] between
   the "Gemeinde-Ich" of the hymn and the "Ich-Origo" of what I am calling
   the ode.)

9 This is not to disagree with Thomas McFarland, who says that *all* lyrics
   are evening lyrics, and that "the ultimate poetic theme is the elegiac theme.
   Great poems are monuments to our lost selves" ("Poetry and the Poem:
   The Structure of Poetic Content," *Literary Theory and Structure*, ed.
   Frank Brady et al. [New Haven: Yale University Press, 1973], p. 104).
   The past and the past self in the ode, though, are as transparent as shad-
   ows.

10   See Abrams, "Structure and Style in the Greater Romantic Lyric," in Hilles and Bloom, *From Sensibility to Romanticism*, p. 527.

11   Cleanth Brooks pioneered this reputation in *The Well-Wrought Urn* (1947; reprint ed., New York: Harvest Books, 1975), p. 125. A. Harris Fairbanks has suggested that "ambiguity is inherent in the form of the Romantic ode" ("The Form of Coleridge's Dejection Ode," *PMLA* 90 [1976] : 881).

12   This most odic of moments is what justifies Leo Spitzer in saying, "According to the pattern fixed by Pindar, an ode must be rhapsodic, since this genre in contrast to others calls for the perpetuation, by the work of art, of the poet's original fervor" (*Linguistics and Literary History* [New York: Russell & Russell, 1962] , p. 207).

13   Appropriately identified by Ferguson as "the classical *locus amoenus*" (*Wordsworth*, p. 108).

14   *The Myth of the Birth of the Hero*, pp. 65-96. Several critics have noticed the folkloric material in the fifth stanza; Jared R. Curtis has inferred from the Earth's substitute status that she is probably to be imagined as an old nurse (*Wordworth's Experiments with Tradition: The Lyric Poems of 1802* [Ithaca: Cornell University Press, 1971] , p. 131).

15   See Lionel Trilling, "Wordsworth and the Iron Time," in *Wordsworth: A Collection of Critical Essays,* ed. M. H. Abrams (Englewood Cliffs, N.J.: Prentice-Hall, 1972), on the consequences of the sexual repression effected by Wordsworth's logic of the "unitary reality." Barbara Garlitz explains the appeal of the ode as an appeal to an age-old cultural belief that conception is a divine gift ("The Immortality Ode: Its Cultural Progeny," *SEL* 6 [1966] : 648).

16   See the remarks on this anomaly by Abbie F. Potts, "The Spenserian and Miltonic Influences in the Immortality Ode and The Rainbow," *SP* (1932): 221, and Ferguson, *Wordsworth*, p. 119.

17   Lionel Trilling, *The Liberal Imagination: Essays on Literature and Society* (Garden City, N.Y.: Anchor Books, 1953), p. 127.

18   In an argument strongly opposed to my own, Florence G. Marsh takes this passage for a transcendentally affirmative point of departure: ":Wordsworth's *Ode*: Obstinate Questionings," *SiR* 5 (1965-67): 219-30. As Curtis points out (*Wordsworth's Experiments*, p. 133), the appositions in the passage were heaped on sometime between 1804 and 1807, thus only deepening its ambivalence (I would say) in underlining its importance. For troubled readings of the passage that are related to mine, see: Helen Regueiro, *The Limits of Imagination: Wordsworth, Yeats, and Stevens* (Ithaca: Cornell University Press, 1976), p. 69; Ferguson, *Wordsworth*, p. 123; Hartman, *Wordsworth's Poetry*, p. 276; G. Wilson Knight, *The Starlit Dome: Studies in the Poetry of Vision* (New York: Barnes & Noble, 1960), p. 41.

19   There are two fine articles on memory's loss of immediacy in this poem; Stuart M. Sperry, Jr., "From 'Tintern Abbey' to the 'Intimations Ode': Wordsworth and the Function of Memory," *WC* 1, no. 2 (1970): 40-49; and Kenneth R. Johnston, "Recollecting Forgetting: Forcing Paradox to the Limit in the 'Immortality Ode,'" *WC* 2, no. 2 (1971): 59-64. I am surprised,

however, to find Johnston (pp. 61–62) reading the "obstinate questionings" as a forgetting not of sensation but of immortality. Elswhere Johnston himself quotes a passage from *The Recluse* (1. 1. 781–83) that could gloss this one against his own reading ("The Idiom of Vision," *New Perspectives on Coleridge and Wordsworth*, ed. Geoffrey Hartman [New York: Columbia University Press, 1972], p. 2). Paul de Man puts the relation of memory and absence dialectically in saying, "nostalgia can only exist when the transcendental presence is forgotten" ("Intentional Structure of the Romantic Image," in Bloom, *Romanticism and Consciousness*, p. 69).

20 Cf. E. D. Hirsch, *Wordsworth and Schelling: A Typological Study of Romanticism* (New Haven: Yale University Press, 1960), p. 161.

21 Mario D'Avanzo plausibly suggests *Aeneid* 6. 739–45, in "Immortality's Winds and Fields of Sleep. A Virgilian Elysium," *WC* 3, no. 3 (1972): 169. See the conclusion of the present discussion.

22 This is pointed out by Brooks, *The Well-Wrought Urn*, p. 127.

23 Brooks was, I believe, the first to define the "glory" thus precisely. See ibid., pp. 127–28.

24 This is the suggestion of Hartman, in *The Unmediated Vision: An Interpretation of Wordsworth, Hopkins, Rilke, and Valéry* (New York: Harbinger Books, 1966), p. 41; and in *Wordsworth's Poetry*, p. 275.

25 Wordsworth's epigraph for the 1807 Intimations Ode, *paulo maiora canamus*, was also used as an epigraph in several MSS of the later ode "On the Power of Sound" (see John Hollander, "Wordsworth and the Music of Sound," in Hartman, *New Perspectives*, p. 67); the Virgilian phrase, thus conceived, would deepen the irony of the silence that pervades the present in the Intimations Ode.

26 I suspect that Wordsworth's pastoral scene owes something to a poet who shares his grounding in the Psalms, Giles Fletcher, in *Christ's Victory in Heaven*, where after Easter, with immortality now guaranteed, the lambs hear the birds "piping grief away," and begin to "dance and play" (Chalmers, 10:76). See Ferguson on "the ancient instruments provoking the lambs' dance" (*Wordsworth*, p. 110).

27 The prominence of the rainbow may suggest that it is a talisman to keep off future floods. See Kenneth R. Lincoln, "Wordsworth's Mortality Ode," *JEGP* 71 (1972): 217. On the immanence of the Flood and its Miltonic provenance in Wordsworth, see Neil Hertz, "Wordsworth and the Tears of Adam," in Abrams, *Wordsworth*, p. 122. The Flood is still more prominent in the argument of Hartman, *The Unmediated Vision*, esp. p. 30.

28 F. W. Bateson compares Wordsworth's "calm weather" to the tranquility with which, in the "Preface," emotion is recollected, in *Wordsworth: A Reinterpretation* (London: Longmans, 1965), p. 162.

29 See John Jones's fine evocation of this passage, differing from mine, in *The Egotistical Sublime: A History of Wordsworth's Imagination* (London: Chatto & Windus, 1954), p. 96; and the equally fine discussion by W. K. Wimsatt, "The Structure of the Romantic Nature Image," *The Verbal Icon: Studies in the Meaning of Poetry* (New York: Noonday Press, 1964), pp. 114–15.

30 See Ferguson on what she calls the "heuristic language" of the poem (*Wordsworth*, p. 99); and William Heath, *Wordsworth and Coleridge: A Study of Their Literary Relations in 1801-02* (Oxford: Clarendon Press, 1970), pp. 64-65.

31 On the use of meditative formats in the Romantic Period, see Reeve Parker, *Coleridge's Meditative Art* (Ithaca: Cornell University Press, 1975).

32 See the conclusion of "To the Small Celandine" (a Poem of Fancy written in the spring of 1802) quoted later in the body of my text: "I will sing, as doth behove,/Hymns in praise of what I love!"

33 In *The Starlit Dome* (p. 38), Knight has argued that since "immortality" can simply mean "death negated," Wordsworth's ode is "a vision of life victorious," which "need have nothing to say about life-after-death."

34 *Of Grammatology*, p. 26. Later in this work, Derrida understands the evil of writing for both Rousseau and Lévi-Strauss as the rupture of the self-presence of childhood innocence.

35 *The Gay Science*, trans. Walter Kaufmann (New York: Vintage Books), p. 86.

36 *The Prose Works of William Wordsworth*, 3 vols., ed. W. J. B. Owen and J. W. Smyser (Oxford: Clarendon Press, 1974), 3:63.

37 I shall have nothing to say of the pseudo-laureate odes of 1814-16 that crow over the fall of Napoleon; the reader is referred to Byron's immensely superior and more genuinely ode-like ode on the same subject.

38 For the fullest discussion of this possibility, see Thomas McFarland, "The Symbiosis of Coleridge and Wordsworth," *SiR* 11 (1972); 267-68.

39 For discussion of this passage, see Hartman, *The Unmediated Vision*, p. 41, and Hollander, "Wordsworth and the Music of Sound," p. 79.

40 As Alan Grob has pointed out, Wordsworth experimented often in the spring of 1802 with "the lyric apostrophe to nature's more familiar and common objects" ("Wordsworth's *Immortality Ode* and the Search for Identity," *ELH* 32 [1965]: 33).

41 See Hartman on this passage in *Wordsworth's Poetry*, p. 275.

42 In stressing what remains natural in "natural piety," I follow Bloom, *The Visionary Company*, p. 173.

Chapter 7

1 Many readers have preferred the "Letter," but I agree with Max F. Schultz's succinct account of its improvement as an ode, in *The Poetic Voices of Coleridge: A Study of His Desire for Spontaneity and Passion for Order* (Detroit: Wayne State University Press, 1963), p. 28. My text throughout for Coleridge's poetry is *The Poems of Samuel Taylor Coleridge*, ed. Ernest Hartley Coleridge (London: Oxford University Press, 1964).

2 To my mind, the most important and interesting sustained reading of "Dejection" to date is that of Reeve Parker in his *Coleridge's Meditative Art*. I often concur with his emphases, but nearly always disagree with his use of them, because he takes the creative process in Coleridge to be somewhat

more complicated than I do. Parker recognizes (as few are willing to do) that depression of spirits is a creative catalyst for Coleridge, and he assembles passages from the notebooks, letters, and public addresses to support his emphasis. But where Parker (see esp. p. 192) feels that dejection is mediated and disciplined by meditation, which leads in turn to imaginative arousal, I do not feel that there is an intervening discipline between dejection and expression, nor do I find evidence for it in Coleridge's ode. Textual evidence apart, one must take into account the colorful but undisciplined streaminess of mind induced by opium. The February 1801 letter to Poole that is quoted by Parker (p. 202) suggests that the tranquility in which hallucination is recollected does not really resemble meditation: "I shall look back on my long and painful Illness only as a Storehouse of wild dreams for Poems." William Empson, with his usual slight irony, has written as shrewdly on the present subject as anyone: "There is remarkably little agony in Coleridge's theory of imagination (remarkably, I mean, for so unhappy a man)" (*The Structure of Complex Words* [Ann Arbor: University of Michigan Press, 1967], p. 370).

3   The motto has, arguably, an occasional importance. See H. M. Margoliouth's evidence, from a contemporary almanac, that the moon as described in the motto may have prompted the composition of the "Letter" (*Wordsworth and Coleridge 1795–1834* [1953; reprint ed., Hamden, Conn.: Archon Books, 1966], p. 105). Harold Bloom compares Wordsworth's and Coleridge's mottoes (1815 and 1817, respectively) in *The Visionary Company*, p. 222; see also his comments on Shelley's use of "Sir Patrick Spens" (in *The Triumph of Life* and *Prometheus Unbound*) in *Poetry and Repression; Revisionism from Blake to Stevens* (New York: Oxford University Press, 1976), p. 104.

4   I mean, of course, in the case of Coleridge, "classicism" as the term was starting to be used by Goethe and the Schlegels (in contrast with their sense of "Romantic" *Sehnsucht*)—and not English "Neoclassicism."

5   Here I run counter to I. A. Richards's well-known disquisition on the moon's reflection of "earth-light," because I think the "silver rim," which reflects the sun, is the closest equivalent, in "Dejection," to Wordsworth's "glory" (see *Coleridge's Minor Poems: A Lecture at Montana State University on April 1960* [Missoula, Mont., 1960], p. 15–16).

6   The determinancy of Coleridge's opening images is discussed in detail by W. Paul Elledge, "Fountains Within: Motivation in Coleridge's 'Dejection: An Ode,'" *PLL* 7 (1971): 304–08.

7   W. J. Bate, *Coleridge* (New York: Macmillan, 1968), p. 108.

8   As Bloom puts it, "the poet-in-a-poet cannot marry, whatever the person-in-the-poet chooses to have done" (*A Map of Misreading* [New York: Oxford University Press, 1975], p. 19).

9   That this is a "commercial metaphor" has been noted by Marshall Suther, in *The Dark Night of Samuel Taylor Coleridge* (New York: Columbia University Press, 1960), p. 126. M. H. Abrams compares the becalmed opening of "Dejection" with "the Ancient Mariner becalmed at the Equator" in

Natural Supernaturalism: Tradition and Revolution in Romantic Literature (New York: Norton, 1973), p. 275.

10 For the claim that the first stanza is an instance of the unimaginative "detailed description Coleridge disliked," see J. O. Hayden, "Coleridge's 'Dejection: An Ode,'" *ES* 52 (1971): 133.

11 Most readers refuse to find the pathetic fallacy here because that would oblige them to admit that Coleridge is not as alienated in his dejection as he says he is. John Beer, however, does note the parallelism in *Coleridge the Visionary* (London: Chatto & Windus, 1959), p. 90.

12 Margoliouth reminds us that Coleridge had jaundice in his teens (*Wordsworth and Coleridge*, p. 86). Coleridge wrote Southey in December 1801: "for what is Life, gangrened, as it is with me, an in it's very vitals—domestic Tranquility?" (*Collected Letters of Samuel Taylor Coleridge*, 6 vols., ed. E. L. Griggs [Oxford: Clarendon Press, 1956], 2:427). Paul Magnuson points out, however, that these lines can also be placed in an enthusiastic context, as when Coleridge quotes them in his "Essay on Genial Criticism" (*Coleridge's Nightmare Poetry* [Charlottesville: University of Virginia Press, 1974], p. 112).

13 Leslie Brisman's essay, "Coleridge and the Ancestral Voices," *GaR* 29 (1975): 469–98, is in part about the antithesis between the "natural man" (dubbed "Porlock") and the poet in Coleridge, and I am indebted to the lively drama Brisman stages between them; he argues for their possible fusion, however, more hopefully than I can: "the relationship that is love must come to be seen not as the natural man's alternative to vision but as the essence of the visionary relationship between all sentient things" (p. 495).

14 For another reading that takes "suspends" to be a different sort of word from, say, "abolish," see Bloom, *The Visionary Company*, p. 227.

15 This borrowing is discussed in detail by McFarland, "The Symbiosis of Coleridge and Wordsworth," p. 281.

16 George Watson notes the "odd" relation between the "almost indecently private theme" of the poem and "the most public of all forms, the neoclassical Pindaric," in *Coleridge the Poet* (London: Routledge, 1966), p. 74.

17 "The Internalization of Quest-Romance," in Bloom, *Romanticism and Consciousness*, p. 9.

18 It is true, of course, that the habit of plagiary grew upon Coleridge as his real-life dejection increased. I am not suggesting, in fact, that Coleridge meant this passage to be read as a displaced confession; rather, it is a good example of inadvertent confession in the psychopathology of everyday life.

19 Brisman cites prose passages that show Coleridge's dislike of "source-study" or dry philology ("Coleridge and the Ancestral Voices," p. 470ff.). This is certainly an aspect of "abstruse research," and "metaphysics" is perhaps more so (see *Collected Letters*, 2:445); certainly Coleridge intends a distinction, in "Dejection," between poetry and studies of other kinds, but he fails, in my view, to enforce it.

20 I mean Wordsworthia*nism* in Arnold's sense, the silly ideology of Wordsworth's devotees. But then Wordsworth himself is sometimes a Wordsworthian.

21 This parallel has been noted, e.g., by Panthea R. Broughton ("The Modifying Metaphor in 'Dejection: An Ode,'" *WC* 4, no. 4 [1973]: 246), but has always been treated as a pointed contrast.

22 "If joy is creative," writes Bate, "the poem exemplifies that dejection can be equally so" (*Coleridge*, p. 109). Perhaps it is peculiar of me to link joy with the terror of sublimity, but I mean only that both are excited, even frenzied moods; and I wonder—rather more so than Bate—whether either mood finds Coleridge at his best.

23 Irene H. Chayes notes that the devil is called a lutanist and an agent of nature's wrath in Jakob Boehme's *De Signatura Rerum* ("Rhetoric as Drama; An Approach to the Romantic Ode," *PMLA* 79 [1964]: 70n.). See also *Paradise Lost* 2. 990ff. Chayes, who sees all Romantic odes as lyric dramas, has anticipated me in reading Coleridge's seventh stanza as a subsumption of other genres (p. 70). Paul Magnuson (*Coleridge's Nightmare Poetry*, p. 118) reminds us in the present context that Coleridge had climbed the Brocken, site of an annual May *Walpurgis-Nacht.*

24 The recurrence of "moans" is added in revision (the "Letter" has "drones and rakes" for the wind and "groans low" for the child) and therefore seems pointed. Here and elsewhere I follow the text of the "Letter" printed by George Whalley in *Coleridge and Sara Hutchinson and the Asra Poems* (London: Routledge, 1955), but it should be mentioned that his text is controversial. Where he has "groans," E. L. Griggs has "moans," as in "Dejection" (*Letters* 2:797).

25 *Poetical Works* 2. 517. A. Harris Fairbanks also suggests that this note may have influenced Coleridge, in "The Form of Coleridge's Dejection Ode," p. 881.

26 *The Journal of Dorothy Wordsworth*, 2 vols., ed. Ernest DeSelincourt (London: Macmillan, 1959), 1:129.

27 Many critics call "Kubla Khan" an ode, but Coleridge himself, who rather overused the term, did not.

28 William Heath has also noted "the slightly patronizing remark about 'simple spirit'" (*Wordsworth and Coleridge*, p. 163).

29 In the "Letter," Coleridge writes far more positively of "Those dear wild Eyes, that see / Even now the Heaven, *I* see" (95–96). E. L. Griggs has "mild" for Whalley's "wild," again reducing the difference between the early and late texts.

30 *Coleridge: The Clark Lectures 1951–52* (London: Rupert Hart-Davis, 1953), pp. 165–66. My interpretation of the monstrous birth is, however, very different from House's.

31 See Angus Fletcher on "the underlying fear that one will lose one's way," in "'Positive Negation': Threshold, Sequence, and Personification in Coleridge," in Hartman, *New Perspectives*, p. 147. Later Fletcher remarks, very truly, I think, that being stationed at a threshold is "absurdly wrong . . . in general" for Coleridge (p. 151).

32 Hartman precedes me in this wordplay, in *The Fate of Reading*, p. 5.

33 Angus Fletcher's remarks on the "liminal scene" correspond in some ways

with my typological outline of the ode at the beginning of the last chapter: "this archetypal liminal scene occurs at dawn or dusk . . . and at the end of a departing year or at the start of a new year" ("'Positive Negation,'" p. 138). Drawing on Fletcher, Stuart Ende has characterized the "liminal oxymoron" as the central Romantic achievement (*Keats and the Sublime* [New Haven: Yale University Press, 1976], pp. 27-29).

34 See Michael G. Cooke, "The Manipulation of Space in Coleridge's Poetry," in Hartman, *New Perspectives,* p. 167.

35 William Heath has documented Coleridge's renewed plans, in 1801-02, to emigrate, owing to ill health, and the letters in question are once more enthusiastic about the communal life (*Wordsworth and Coleridge,* p. 71).

Chapter 8

1 In discussing the importance of the sacred place in the sublime poem, Martin Price explains why so many meditative and political odes run the same course: "the movement to a new realm may also be a movement in time, either to a prophetic futurity or to a heroic and mythical past" ("The Sublime Poem," p. 200).

2 M. H. Abrams points out that unlike radicals on the Continent, English radicals "looked on contemporary politics through the perspective of biblical prophecy" ("English Romanticism: The Spirit of the Age," in Bloom, *Romanticism and Consciousness,* p. 95).

3 My text for the 1816 poems is from *The Complete Poetical Works of Percy Bysshe Shelley,* 4 vols., ed. Neville Rogers (Oxford: Clarendon Press, 1975); for the "Ode to the West Wind," my text is from *The Poems of Shelley,* ed. Thomas Hutchinson (London: Oxford University Press, 1965).

4 Earle J. Schulze's *Shelley's Theory of Poetry: A Reappraisal* (The Hague: Mouton, 1966), esp. pp. 41-101, has been taken to task by Donald Reiman for positing "a psychology of faculties" in Shelley's thought (*The English Romantic Poets: A Review of Research and Criticism,* 3rd rev. ed., ed. Frank Jordan, Jr. [New York: Modern Language Association, 1972], p. 358), but I think Schulze's instincts are wholly sound. One can only avoid facultative thinking about Shelley if one takes concepts such as "Power" and "Intellectual Beauty" to be safely objective and nondeterminate. Yet no scholar, I think, would go this far toward the empiricization of Shelley. It must hold, therefore, that insofar as such qualities are differentiable and belong within the conscious subject, they are facultative.

5 As Earl Wasserman explains in a parallel (though metaphysically very different) vocabulary: "The apparently tautological phrase 'human thought' properly distinguishes that thought from those of the One Mind" (*The Subtler Language,* p. 297). On Shelley's reversal of the priority accorded to science by Peacock, see Harry White, "Shelley's Defense of Science," *SiR* 16 (1977): 319 ff.

6 The best summary statement on this matter remains that of C. E. Pulos: "Due attention to Shelley's scepticism disposes not only of the alleged

inconsistency between his idealism and necessitarianism but also of his alleged pseudo-Platonism" (*The Deep Truth* [Lincoln: University of Nebraska Press, 1954], p. 108). To this we may add Harold Bloom's conclusion that "Shelley is the most Humean poet in the language" ("The Unpastured Sea: An Introduction to Shelley," in Bloom, *Romanticism and Consciousness*, p. 381).

7   *Wordsworth and Schelling*, p. 152.

8   We are really in the dark, to this day, as allegorical readers of Shelley. Critics disagree so fundamentally about the simple sense of his poetry that one often wonders whether x and y are reading the same poem. Thus I find James Rieger, in his witty reading of Shelley, confidently stating that the Power in "Mont Blanc" looks forward to *Jupiter*, and that there is no difference between Power and Intellectual Beauty (*The Mutiny Within: The Heresies of Percy Bysshe Shelley* [New York: George Braziller, 1967], pp. 99–100). Bloom likewise associates the Power with Blake's Urizen, though later he associates the "Power that dwells apart" with Demogorgon, as I do (*Shelley's Mythmaking* [New Haven: Yale University Press, 1959], p. 16).

9   Elizabeth Nitchie, "Shelley's 'Hymn to Intellectual Beauty,'" *PMLA* 63 (1948): 752–53, argues that "fear" means "revere." Possibly so; but that sense cannot erase an unavoidable first impression. See also Judith Chernaik, *The Lyrics of Shelley* (Cleveland: Press of Case Western Reserve University, 1972), p. 35.

10 *The Letters of Shelley*, 2 vols., ed. F. L. Jones (Oxford: Clarendon Press, 1964), 2:154.

11 Earl Wasserman, citing passages from Shelley's *Speculations on Metaphysics*, rightly concludes that Shelley took a Humean view of causation (*The Subtler Language*, pp. 229–31). Wasserman also confirms that the relation between the Power and Phenomena is dialectical (p. 233), but then proceeds to argue that the Power *causes* Phenomena (ibid.).

12 For Shelley's "monistic interpretation of the internal and the external," see ibid., p. 203.

13 For the word used in this sense, see Plato, *Timaeus* 72.

14 In a sense, as Bloom says (*Shelley's Mythmaking*, pp. 29–30), the breast is Shelley's own, since it is his own death he thinks of; but the images would not rest in *his* breast after death.

15 To assume, as Bloom does (*Shelley's Mythmaking*, p. 30), that the image appears *when* the phantom is recalled does violence, as it seems to me, to the grammar. The image is "there" but is not quite identified *until* that time.

16 Bloom, who cites Shelley's letter to Peacock calling the mountain the throne of Ahriman, the Evil Principle, anticipates my drift here in calling Mont Blanc a "white leviathan" (*Shelley's Mythmaking*, p. 17). See also Rieger, *The Mutiny Within*, p. 78ff.

17 For an "ironic" reading of "Mont Blanc," on "the relation of power and value," see Gerald McNeice, "The Poet as Ironist in 'Mont Blanc' and 'Hymn to Intellectual Beauty,'" *SiR* 14 (1975):311.

18 I print the text of this familiar song as it appeared in John Stafford Smith, ed., *Musica Antiqua: A Selection of Music*, 2 vols. (London: Preston, 1812), 1:31. It also appeared in Joseph Ritson, ed., *Ancient Songs from the Time of Henry the Third to the Revolution* (London: J. Johnson, 1790), p. lv. See Charles Frey, "Interpreting Western Wind," *ELH* 43 (1976):259-78, for a complete account of the fortunes of this poem, which appears also to have influenced Keats's "small warm rain" (*The Fall of Hyperion* 1:98).

19 I would not deny, of course, that Shelley was mainly thinking about England in the wake of Peterloo. See Richard Holmes, *Shelley: The Pursuit* (London: Weidenfield and Nicolson, 1974), p. 529, and Carl Woodring, *Politics in English Romantic Poetry* (Cambridge: Harvard University Press, 1970), p. 274.

20 *A Defense of Poetry. The Four Ages of Poetry*, ed. John E. Jordan (Indianapolis: Bobbs-Merrill, 1965), p. 71.

21 The natural basis of the birth-quickening leaves was first explained by Arthur Wormhoudt, *The Explicator* 6 (October 1947):20.

22 See Harold Bloom on Shelley's tendency to subsume all things and genres to lyric, "The Unpastured Sea," p. 376.

23 In *Shelley's Mythmaking*, p. 76, Bloom points out that the Spring West Wind is a shepherdess, and he associates her pastoral with the Christian-redemptive pattern that he finds present in the poem as a whole.

24 The combination of the sonnet and the tercet has long been recognized. For the most recent discussion, see Ben L. Collins, "The Stanzaic Pattern of Shelley's 'Ode to the West Wind,'" *K-SJ* (1970):7-8. The ode in *terza rima* was not invented by Shelley. There are two of them, for example, in *Lucasta* (1649), a collection of the amorous poems of Richard Lovelace. See also Crashaw's "Wishes to His (Supposed) Mistress," in *Delights of the Muses* (London: H. Moseley, 1646).

25 Elizabeth Sewell equates Shelley's "colouring" with rhetoric, as I do, in *The Orphic Voice: Poetry and Natural History* (New Haven: Yale University Press, 1960), p. 31. "By dint of this superiority to science," writes Heidegger, "the poet always speaks as though the essent were being expressed and invoked for the first time" (*Introduction to Metaphysics*, trans. Ralph Manheim [New Haven: Yale University Press, 1959], p. 26). Angus Fletcher says of Shelley's "legislators": "He seems to have meant that they give mankind the laws of thought, if not of expedient practicality" (*Allegory*, p. 278).

26 I mention the scientist whose "sophisms" Shelley singled out for special abuse in the Preface to *Laon and Cythna*. On science as the prophetic revelation of "the hidden present" in shamanistic chants, see Chadwick, *Poetry and Prophecy*, p. 14.

27 I may refer here to the generally useful thesis of Peter Mortenson, that each Shelleyan lyric has an introductory image that is then unpacked and projected toward an increasingly prominent "I" ("Image and Structure in Shelley's Longer Lyrics," *SiR* 4 (1965):104-09).

28 In addition to biblical precedents for the posture of the struggling prophet,

it seems to me that two separate topoi converge in Shelley's thorns: the classical image of the nightingale singing with her breast leaning against a thorn (used by Shelley at the beginning of *Epipsychidion*) and the medieval trope of the pen as a thorn, of which Curtius cites an instance from Isidore of Seville (*European Literature in the Latin Middle Ages*, p. 314). There is also an epitaphic trope in which the thorn is an engraving instrument; see Hartman, *Beyond Formalism*, p. 210. See also p. 223, for Hartman's association of death and writing in Shelley. For another excellent review of the thorn passage, see Stuart Curran, *Shelley's Annus Mirabilis: The Maturing of an Epic Vision* (San Marino, Calif.: Huntington Library, 1975), pp. 168–69.

29 For a related reading, see Bloom, *The Visionary Company*, p. 302.

30 In order to accommodate this phrasing, Bloom (*Shelley's Mythmaking*, p. 76) must read "the ghosts fleeing from their exorcizer," making the first tercet a kind of nativity ode. I take it, though, that an enchanter must be a shaman or spellbinder, not conventionally a witch doctor.

31 On the inconsistencies of "duration" in Shelley's imagery, which creates a tension between an evolutionary and an apocalyptic politics, see the excellent remarks of Woodring, *Politics*, p. 276.

32 This implication of the leaves' colors has been discussed most recently by Seymour Reiter, *A Study of Shelley's Poetry* (Albuquerque: University of New Mexico Press, 1967), p. 231.

33 Richard Holmes describes sketches of the "wingèd seeds" in Shelley's Italian notebooks, "often resembling sycamore seeds without a round central pod and a single or double fibrous wing extension" (*Shelley*, p. 397).

34 Bloom (*Shelley's Mythmaking*, p. 83) reads the third stanza as a mellowed lament for the passing of what was "once despotical."

35 The reader in quest of surprising sources for Shelley's ode should not overlook Prior's "A Letter from Italy," which ends with a westering invocation to Liberty. "Baiae" is mentioned by Prior, but for nearly all poets the source of this rich-sounding word is Horace, who uses it repeatedly.

36 Woodring shrewdly remarks that Shelley "evades the pacifist's problem of having his potentiality taken seriously in a world of force" (*Politics*, p. 276); I would add only that in some sense he also evades the *danger* of having it taken seriously.

Chapter 9

1 In this and the ensuing chapter, I shall discuss only four of the odes, omitting "Melancholy" and "Indolence." Although I assume that the first three of these four were written in the order I assign to them, my argument for the most part does not depend on the truth of that assumption. Robert Gleckner's reminder, that we do not know as much about the sequence of the poems as our readings characteristically imply, cannot be ignored ("Keats's Odes: The Problem of the Limited Canon," *SEL* 5 [1965]:577–85). My text in this and the next chapter is *The Poems of John Keats*, ed.

Jack Stillinger (Cambridge: The Belknap Press of Harvard University Press, 1978).

2 See *The Letters of John Keats 1814-1921*, 2 vols., ed Hyder E. Rollins (Cambridge: Harvard University Press, 1958), 2:105-06 hereafter cited by volume and page as *Letters*.

3 There are, moreover, hymns to the poet's own soul from the late medieval period onward. See Curtius, *European Literature in the Latin Middle Ages*, p. 233.

4 As Shuster points out (*The English Ode*, p. 205), Collins's Scottish Superstitions Ode is very nearly a sonnet sequence, but one doubts that it was designedly so. For a denial of the hypothesis (pioneered by Garrod) that Keats developed his ode stanza from experimentation with the sonnet, see Ian A. Gordon, "Keats and the English Pindaric," *REL* 8 (1967):18. For other arguments, see L. J. Zillman, *Keats and the Sonnet Tradition* (1935; reprint ed., New York: Octagon Books, 1970), and W. J. Bate, *The Stylistic Development of Keats* (1945; reprint ed., New York: Humanities Press, 1958), pp. 127-31. One must certainly agree with Miriam Allott that the stanzas of "Psyche" are *less* like sonnets than those of the other odes, but it remains true that the first eight lines would still do for an octave (see *John Keats* [Essex: Longman Group, 1976], p. 28).

5 In 1819, if not at this time, Keats would have read, in Dryden's translation of Boileau's *Art of Poetry*, that sonnets and odes resemble each other in having a "measure" to which it is difficult to adjust "reason."

6 Once in 1817, however, Keats exempted the lyric from his contempt for smallness: "Did our great Poets ever write short Pieces? I mean in the shape of Tales" (*Letters* 1:170).

7 C. M. Bowra makes this point in *Inspiration and Poetry* (Cambridge: Cambridge University Press, 1951), p. 20.

8 On this point, see W. J. Bate, *John Keats* (New York: Oxford Galaxy, 1966), p. 499.

9 It would seem necessary thus to refine the observation of Sidney Colvin (1920) that by "philosophy" Keats means "knowledge and the fruits of reading generally" (quoted by Rollins, *Letters* 1:271n.). Colvin was right, however, to insist that Keats never uses the word to refer to metaphysics.

10 This theme is ably put, in other terms, by Jack Stillinger, "Introduction," *Twentieth Century Interpretations of Keats's Odes*, ed. Stillinger (Englewood Cliffs, N.J.: Prentice-Hall, 1968), p. 2.

11 On this subject the account of H. W. Garrod has not been bettered: "the infection of his own accidents of style . . . compel the direction of the thought; the rhythm and words together determine the stanza which comes next" (*Keats* [London: Oxford University Press, 1926], p. 111).

12 See Kenneth Allott, "The Ode to Psyche," *Twentieth Century Interpretations*, p. 30.

13 This point has been made in passing by Stuart M. Sperry, *Keats the Poet* (Princeton: Princeton University Press, 1973), pp. 249-50. For an excellent account of Keats as "the intrusive (perhaps voyeuristic) poet" in this

passage, see Michael G. Cooke, *The Romantic Will* (New Haven: Yale University Press, 1976), pp. 164-65. See also Harold Bloom, *A Map of Misreading*, p. 153.

14 On "the fane, which . . . signifies the sacred structure of poetry," see Mario D'Avanzo, *Keats's Metaphors for the Poet's Imagination* (Durham, N.C.: Duke University Press, 1967), p. 209. On the relation of Psyche's ear to the structure of the poem, see Karl Kroeber, *The Artifice of Reality* (Madison: University of Wisconsin Press, 1964), p. 71.

15 Here I would invoke Morris Dickstein's candid objection that "the separate elements" of the poem "remain somewhat discrete" (*Keats and His Poetry* [Chicago: University of Chicago Press, 1967] , p. 197).

16 Keats was by no means the first to write a lyric on Psyche. See the "Psyche" of Bishop Ken, written at the turn of the eighteenth century.

17 Keats's identification with Cupid is stressed by Bate in *John Keats,* p. 491.

18 Paul de Man, "The Rhetoric of Temporality," p. 176. I am here using the term "allegory" in a more traditional and limited sense than de Man's, but his usage is still wholly relevant in opposition to a verbal richness, as in Keats, that seems to present a reified world. On the dialectic of experiential plenitude and abstracted language, see also Jameson, *Marxism and Form,* p. 316.

19 Thus the "well-wrought urn" is, in my view, only a penultimate image for Keats's poetic objective.

20 Especially good essays on indolence as a motivating factor in all the odes are Kenneth Muir, "The Meaning of the Odes," in *John Keats: A Reassessment,* ed. Muir (Liverpool: University of Liverpool Press, 1959), pp. 61, 65; and John Holloway, "The Odes of Keats," *Cambridge Journal* 5 (1952): 416-25.

21 Though I say it without prejudice, I am not overfamiliar with early pornography, but I strongly suspect the "working face" to be a standard metonymy of that genre (it would be preceded and succeeded by a "conscious Expression"). See the cliché-strewn "Nausikaa" episode of Joyce's *Ulysses:* "His hands and face were working and a tremor went over her" (New York: Modern Library, 1942, p. 359). If we tend not to discuss what the narrator of *Endymion* and the priests of "Psyche" are doing (though metaphysically it is nearly as significant a subject in the Romantic Period as incest), Byron certainly had no doubts. See *The Works of Lord Byron. Letters and Journals,* 6 vols., ed. R. E. Prothero (London: John Murray, 1901), 5:94, 109, 117.

22 Here and later I refer to "imagination" as an *active* faculty. This is not how Keats himself is apt to use the term. The following passage, for example, is highly relevant to "Psyche": "the simple Imaginative mind may have its rewards in the repe[ti]tion of its own silent Working coming continually on the spirit with a fine suddenness" (see *Letters* 1:185; cf. 1:170). The conclusion is inescapable, I think, that Keats has no consistent notion associated with the term (see *Letters* 1:293, where it denotes the lack of a moral sense!), and I feel free therefore to use it in the Coleridgean sense

simply in order to have a name for the active principle in Keats's psychology.

23 It has not been often enough stressed that Coleridge suddenly introduced his "secondary imagination" into the *Biographia* in order to save the "conscious will" from irrelevancy to the creative process. Thomas McFarland has shown, however, that such was Coleridge's purpose by tracing the new faculty to Leibniz's *vis activa* and Nicolas Tetens's *Dichtkraft* ("The Origin and Significance of Coleridge's Theory of Secondary Imagination," in Hartman, *New Perspectives,* pp. 195–246).

24 Like Coleridge, Keats ordinarily resists concluding that the ground of creativity is scarcely ecstatic: "I feel I must begin again with my poetry—for if I am not in action mind or Body I am in pain" (*Letters* 2:12). Elsewhere Keats is more candid on this point, but he still distinguishes, certainly with more plausibility, "between an easy and uneasy conscience" (ibid. 2:77). Critics who lean toward my reduction of the seeming polarities of this ode are: R. H. Fogle, "Keats's *Ode to a Nightingale*," *Twentieth Century Interpretations,* pp. 32–33; Cleanth Brooks and R. P. Warren, "The *Ode to a Nightingale,*" ibid., p. 44; and Leslie Brisman, *Romantic Origins* (Ithaca: Cornell University Press, 1978), p. 78 ff. The appearance of dialectic in the poem comes from the fact that, as Paul de Man says, "The 'I' . . . is always seen in the movement that takes it away from its own center" ("Introduction," *John Keats: Selected Poetry* [New York: Signet, 1966], p. xxiv).

25 The revery of Keats's ode recalls Lady Winchelsea's request to the Muse, in "To a Nightingale," to "Melt a sense that shall retain/Still some spirit of the brain."

26 Coleridge's revision of the nightingale's mood is anticipated by Thomson, "Ode" ("O Nightingale").

27 The earliest draft of the poem does have an invocation, to a "Small, wingèd Dryad" (q. v., Robert Gittings, *The Odes of Keats and Their Earliest Known Manuscripts* [London: Heinemann, 1970], p. 66).

28 For another discussion of this pun, see Stuart Ende, *Keats and the Sublime,* p. 132. From the viewpoint of my own reading, it may be noted that a plot is also a gravesite.

29 On 15 May 1820, Keats wrote that he was well enough to enjoy "the summer" (Letters 2:289). Confessedly, he may, on this evidence, have thought of mid-May *as* summer, but it is also possible that his expression is prospective.

30 On this repetition, see Hartman, *The Fate of Reading,* p. 167.

31 We cannot know whether Keats read any "Provencal song," but there is a curious parallel with his own ode in Bernart de Ventadorn: "The nightingale rejoices beside the blossom on the branch, and I have such great envy of him that I cannot keep from singing" (quoted by Frank Doggett, "Romanticism's Singing Bird," *SEL* 14 [1974]: 548).

32 Kenneth Muir ("The Meaning of the Odes," p. 67) says that Keats underlined "The foul fiend haunts poor Tom in the voice of the nightingale" in *King Lear.*

33 Among several classical glosses for Keats's "Bacchus and his pards," the closest is Horace, *Carm.* 3. 3: "hac te merentum, Bacchae pater, tuae/ vexere tigres, indocili iugum/collo trahentes." Fogle ("Keats's *Ode to a Nightingale*," p. 36) anticipates me in feeling that Bacchus is not left behind in the third stanza. An important precedent for the effort to excorcize Bacchus is *Paradise Lost* 7. 32–35.

34 At l. 49 in one of the Woodhouse MSS of this poem, "dewy" replaces the crossed out "sweetest"; the original choice, a poorer word, would nevertheless have strengthened the relation between this scene and the second stanza. See Jack Stillinger, *The Texts of Keats's Poems* (Cambridge: Harvard University Press, 1974), p. 244.

35 See the remarks of Stuart Ende on this passage, which he characterizes as "a mingling of presence and absence that is unmatched," in *Keats and the Sublime*, p. 136.

36 On the importance of this passage for Keats's ode, see Bloom, *The Visionary Company*, p. 410, and "Keats and the Embarrassments of Poetic Tradition," in Hilles and Bloom, *From Sensibility to Romanticism*, p. 517.

37 One rather close anticipation of Keats's death wish is to be found in an unlikely quarter, Charles Cotton's "Melancholy. Pindaric Ode" (Chalmers, 10:734): "and think it were the greatest bliss/Even at this moment to depart!" My assumption that the bird is here transcendentalized runs counter to a dialectical reading that would see the bird's ignorance of death as its immortality. See Andrew J. Kappel, "The Immortality of the Natural: Keats's 'Ode to a Nightingale,'" *ELH* 45, no. 2 (1978): 276. Allen Tate is especially clear in reading the passage from my point of view, distinguishing between the "bird, as bird" and as "symbol" (*On the Limits of Poetry*, p. 172).

38 Many readers have noted that romance is found wanting in this poem, but most conclude equivocally, with Mary Visick, that Keats "leaves a question-mark over romance" ("'Tease us out of thought': Keats's *Epistle to Reynolds* and the Odes," *K-SJ* 15 [1966]: 97). Concerning the achieved immortality of the bird, it may be noted that it is never more mortal than just beforehand, when it is "pouring forth" its soul.

39 For a reading of the "Ode to Psyche" that implicitly stresses this Spenserian passage through its source in the *Symposium,* see James H. Bunn, "Keats's *Ode to Psyche* and the Transformation of Mental Landscape," *ELH* 37 (1970): 589.

40 Ibid., pp. 593–94. See also Brooks and Warren, "The *Ode to a Nightingale*," p. 47.

41 "The 'Ode on a Grecian Urn,' or Content *vs.* Metagrammar," *Essays on English and American Literature* (Princeton: Princeton University Press, 1968), p. 84.

42 As Dickstein says, this ode "covers in its special way the same ground as the Nightingale ode" (*Keats and His Poetry,* p. 221).

43 There are several interpretations of this poem that take it to be very severe on the subject of art. For a reading that is more categorically extreme than

I would wish mine to be, see Jean-Claude Sallé, "The Pious Frauds of Art: A Reading of the 'Ode on a Grecian Urn,'" *SiR* 11 (1972): 79-93. I do not know of a reading, however, that has found a distinction within the poem between good and bad art.

44 For Keats's phrasing, cf. Horace, *Carm.* 3. 24: "Intactis opulentior/thesaurus Arabum."

45 For another intricate reading of the first four lines, very different from mine, see Charles I. Patterson, "Passion and Permanence in Keats's *Ode on a Grecian Urn," Twentieth Century Interpretations,* p. 50.

46 Cleanth Brooks was the first to point this out, in *The Well-Wrought Urn,* p. 156.

47 Albert Gérard writes well of Keats's "longing not for art but for a free reverie of any kind" ("Prometheus and the Aeolian Lyre," *YR* 33 [1944]: 495). Earl Wasserman similarly speaks (with respect to his insistent transcendentalizing of the "finer tone") of "the point where songs are refined of tone" (*The Finer Tone: Keats' Major Poems* [Baltimore: John Hopkins University Press, 1953], p. 22).

48 *John Keats's Dream of Truth* (London: Chatto & Windus, 1969), p. 220.

49 Or, as Heidegger puts it, "Equipment has a peculiar position intermediate between thing and work" (*Poetry, Language, Thought,* trans. Alfred Hofstadter [New York: Harper & Row, 1971], p. 29).

50 Gittings reminds us that Keats was reading Dryden's odes attentively in 1819 (*The Odes of Keats,* p. 14; and *John Keats: The Living Year* [Cambridge: Harvard University Press, 1954], p. 109).

51 Cleanth Brooks writes acutely on this point: "the pipes, it is suggested, are playing very softly; if we listen carefully, we can hear them; their music is just below the threshold of normal sound" (*The Well-Wrought Urn,* p. 157). Spitzer, who once wrote a treatise on "World Harmony," also stresses this point, in *Essays,* pp. 77-78.

52 On this reason for the "embarrassment" of apostrophe, see Jonathan Culler, "Apostrophe," p. 61. Culler's important essay, to which I am indebted in many ways, should be read as a supplement to the work of Norden, Auerbach, and Schlüter (q.v. supra) on the figure of apostrophe.

53 Keats could also write of happy experiences as "parching to the tongue" (*Letters* 1:344). James H. Bunn writes of "the almost indistinguishable anticipation and satiation" in the odes ("Keats's Ode to Psyche," p. 581).

54 There is much debate about whether all or part of this stanza "appears" on the urn. I am inclined to agree with a recent writer, James Shokoff, that the figures bound for the altar could appear on the urn but that the little town could not ("Soul-Making in 'Ode on a Grecian Urn,'" *K-SJ* 24 [1975]: 105-06). Since Keats modeled this stanza after a description in one of Haydon's articles on the Elgin Marbles (q.v., Gittings, *The Odes of Keats,* p. 70), he plainly does associate it with the urn's surface, but the reader must still be left free to note that an urn can only represent so much material if it is not to become a magic frieze like the shield of Achilles. Garrod (*Keats,* pp. 105-07) keenly admires this stanza for the same reason

I do; having noted that "the fourth stanza is more beautiful than any of the others—and more true," he concludes: "This pure cold art makes, in fact, a less appeal to Keats than the ode as a whole would pretend." Jones (*John Keats's Dream of Truth*, p. 224) has called the fourth stanza the "poeticizing of art-space." See also Vendler's remarks in "Experiential Beginnings," p. 601.

55 As Albert Gérard says, "the three questions . . . are the fundamental questions that can be asked about man, his origins, his destiny" ("Romance and Reality: Continuity and Growth in Keats's Art," *Twentieth Century Interpretations*, p. 71).

56 The importance of *The Excursion* for this poem has been explored by Mario L. D'Avanzo, "'Ode on a Grecian Urn' and *The Excursion*," *K-SJ* 23 (1974): 95–105, but he does not cite the passage just quoted, which I have treated in another context in "The Absent Dead: Wordsworth, Byron, and the Epitaph," *SiR* 17 (1978): 420.

57 Critics have been leery of making this connection; but see Patterson, "Passion and Permanence," p. 53.

58 I would agree with Sperry (*Keats the Poet*, p. 276) that the urn remains "a friend to man" in that it is "a source of endless . . . speculation about our own condition," arguing only that it can be such a limitless source because it discloses nothing. For an essay that in many ways overlaps with my reading, see David Simpson, "Keats's Lady, Metaphor, and the Rhetoric of Neurosis," *SiR* 15 (1976): esp. 265–69.

59 It seems likely that Keats took his conception for this poem from Chapman's translation of the Homeric "Hymn to Hermes." Hermes' first song on his newly invented lyre is to Maia.

Chapter 10

1 See David Perkins, with whose complete phrase "intensifying and prolonging of summer," I cannot wholly agree, in "Affirmation of Process in *Ode on Melancholy* and *To Autumn*," *Twentieth Century Interpretations*, p. 91.

2 I quote these passages in tandem as they are quoted by one of the reputed esoterics of this tradition, Kirpal Singh, in *Surat Shabd Yoga* (Berkeley: Images Press, 1975), p. 33. I am no esoteric myself, and suspect, in fact, that the "Celestial Sound" (which is what Singh's title means) has a physiological basis. Just such a sound is described by John Cage as being audible in an anechoic chamber; it is nothing other than the sound of the nervous system and of the blood in circulation (*Silence* [Cambridge, Mass.: M.I.T. Press, 1969], p. 51).

3 See the richly earned distinction drawn by John Hollander between the "sound of music" in the age of Dryden and the "music of sound" in the later eighteenth and nineteenth centuries (*Images of Voice: Music and Sound in Romantic Poetry* [Cambridge: W. Heffer & Son Ltd., 1970], p. 5).

4 Like Wallace Stevens, I have never heard a nightingale; but here I follow the useful ornithology of Katharine M. Wilson, *The Nightingale and the Hawk: A Psychological Study of Keats* (London: George Allen & Unwin, 1964), p. 122. Wilson complains that Coleridge's "low-piping sound" is missing from Keats, but I have suggested above that it is present in the word "forlorn."

5 Quoted in *The Keats Circle*, 2 vols., ed. Hyder E. Rollins (Cambridge: Harvard University Press), 2:65.

6 I have taken some of my texts from sources cited in a useful article by Keith Preston, "Aspects of Autumn in Roman Poetry," *CP* 13 (1918): 272-82. In the passage from Lucretius below, the reader will find "mists" not just in modern translations but, e.g., in the "Guernier" translation, *On the Nature of Things*, 2 vols. (London: Daniel Brown, 1743), 2:271. See also the older but better-known translation by Thomas Creech, *On the Nature of Things*, 2 vols. (London: G. Sawbridge, 1714), 2:669. In addition to the texts I mention here, the reader is referred to Francis Fawkes, trans., *The Idylliums of Theocritus* (London: Dryden Leach, 1767), p. 78 (*Id.* 7:165-73).

7 See Hartman's "Poem and Ideology: A Study of Keats's 'To Autumn,'" *The Fate of Reading*, pp. 124-46. I intend no dispute here; Hartman himself says of the poem (p. 134) that "in its Hesperian reach it does not give up but joins a south to itself." On Keats's increased use of English roots in "To Autumn," see also Bate, *Stylistic Development*, pp. 134, 182. For another essay on the "ideology" of the poem, see Virgil Nemoianu, "The Dialectics of Movement in Keats's 'To Autumn,'" *PMLA* 93 (1978): 205-14.

8 Hartman cites this passage in the context of Blake's "To Autumn" (*Beyond Formalism*, p. 199).

9 *Chapman's Homer*, ed. Allardyce Nicoll, 2 vols. (Princeton: Princeton University Press, 1956), 2:122 (bk. 7. 152-70).

10 Autumn, writes Hartman, is "a shaped segment of life coterminous with that templar 'region of the mind' which the other poems seek, though they may honor more insistently the dichotomy of inside and out, fane and profane" (*The Fate of Reading*, p. 127).

11 *The Penguin Book of Greek Verse*, p. 148.

12 See Hartman, *The Fate of Reading*, pp. 128, 130.

13 The *OED* allows "eves" as a variant spelling, but cites only one instance, from 1751. On the suggestiveness in general of Keats's misspellings, see Christopher Ricks, *Keats and Embarrassment* (Oxford: Clarendon Press, 1974), pp. 70-71.

14 The genealogical "of" suggests that autumn is born from this landscape in its human figuration. Hartman also notes the trace of a hymnic genealogy in the grammar of the first line (*The Fate of Reading*, p. 142).

15 See James Lott, "*To Autumn*: Poetic Consciousness and the Awareness of Process," *SiR* 9 (1970): 73.

16 On the function of these couplets, see Bate, *Stylistic Development*, p. 184; see also Bate's *John Keats*, p. 581.

17 Cf. Vendler, "Experiential Beginnings," pp. 591-92. See also Michael Cooke, *The Romantic Will*, who remarks a pattern in the poem as a whole of "diminishing sensuousness and increasing reflection" (p. 170).

18 See *Keats's Craftsmanship: A Study in Poetic Development* (1933; reprint ed., New York: Russell & Russell, 1962), p. 282.

19 See Ian Jack, *Keats and the Mirror of Art* (Oxford: Clarendon Press, 1967), pp. 236-41.

20 F. R. Leavis, *Revaluation: Tradition and Development in English Poetry* (London: Chatto & Windus, 1959), pp. 263-64, is answered by John Hollander, *Vision and Resonance*, pp. 144-45.

21 "With these 'hours by hours' we are ready for the music of time in the final stanza" (Bloom, *The Visionary Company*, p. 434).

22 On the profusion of boundaries in the last stanza, see Arnold Davenport, "A Note on 'To Autumn,'" *Keats: A Reassessment*, ed. Muir, p. 98. For the idea that Being is framed by "music" in the last stanza, see James Land Jones, *Adam's Dream: Mythic Consciousness in Keats and Yeats* (Athens: University of Georgia Press, 1975), p. 147.

23 The Babylonians, says Curtius, called stars "'the writing of the sky'" (*European Literature in the Latin Middle Ages*, p. 304).

24 It is tempting to add that in "To Autumn" Keats suspends even the desire for human welfare that had marked the Spring odes. In the letters of autumn 1819 there is a new note, a proud indifference toward or even contempt for human beings and their affairs. Though to many readers it will seem a severe dispraise of "To Autumn" to do so, we may say that in this poem Keats replaces the human climate with a climate of being in which the human merely dwells.

25 So called by John Jones, *John Keats's Dream of Truth*, p. 263.

26 Gittings, who reviews Garrod's argument, adds that Keats himself never seems to have given the poem a title (*The Odes of Keats*, p. 7).

Postscript

1 The term is Leo Spitzer's, in "The Interpretation of an Ode by Paul Claudel," *Linguistics and Literary History* (New York: Russell & Russell, 1962), pp. 193-236.

2 See Andrew Fichter, "Ode and Elegy," pp. 398-427. I have no sufficient excuse for not having extended my study to include the "Ode on the Death of the Duke of Wellington," which, together with Marvell's Cromwell Ode, I most regret having omitted.

3 *The Letters of Hart Crane*, ed. Brom Weber (Berkeley: University of California Press, 1952), p. 129.

Index